Joseph W. Lax

Introduction To Catholicism

A Complete Course

The Didache Series

The Didache

[DID-uh-kay]

The *Didache* is the first known Christian catechesis. Written in the first century, the *Didache* is the earliest known Christian writing outside of Scripture. The name of the work, *"Didache,"* is indeed appropriate for such a catechesis because it comes from the Greek word for "teaching," and indicates that this writing contains the teaching of the Apostles.

The *Didache* is a catechetical summary of Christian sacraments, practices, and morality. Though written in the first century, its teaching is timeless. The *Didache* was probably written by the disciples of the Twelve Apostles, and it presents the Apostolic Faith as taught by those closest to Jesus Christ. This series of textbooks takes the name of this early catechesis because it shares in the Church's mission of passing on that same Faith, in its rich entirety, to new generations.

Below is an excerpt from the *Didache* in which we see a clear example of its lasting message, a message that speaks to Christians of today as much as it did to the first generations of the Church. The world is different, but the struggle for holiness is the same. In the *Didache,* we are instructed to embrace virtue, to avoid sin, and to live the Beatitudes of our Lord.

My child, flee from everything that is evil and everything that is like it. Do not be wrathful, for wrath leads to murder, nor jealous nor contentious nor quarrelsome, for from all these murder ensues.

My child, do not be lustful, for lust leads to fornication, nor a filthy-talker nor a lewd-looker, for from all these adulteries ensue.

My child, do not be an interpreter of omens, since it leads to idolatry, nor an enchanter nor an astrologer nor a magical purifier, nor wish to see them, for from all these idolatry arises.

My child, do not be a liar, for lying leads to theft, nor avaricious nor conceited, for from all these thefts are produced.

My child, do not be a complainer, since it leads to blasphemy, nor self-willed nor evil-minded, for from all these blasphemies are produced.

Be meek, for the meek will inherit the earth.

Be long-suffering and merciful and guileless and peaceable and good, and revere always the words you have heard.[1]

The *Didache* is the teaching of the Apostles and, as such, it is the teaching of the Church. Accordingly, this textbook series makes extensive use of the most recent comprehensive catechesis provided to us, *The Catechism of the Catholic Church.* The *Didache* series also relies heavily on Sacred Scripture, the lives of the saints, the Fathers of the Church, and the teaching of Vatican II as witnessed by the pontificate of John Paul II.

1. Swett, Ben H. "The Didache (The Teaching)." © January 30, 1998. http://bswett.com/1998-01Didache.html

Introduction To Catholicism

A Complete Course

General Editor: Rev. James Socias

MIDWEST THEOLOGICAL FORUM
Woodridge, Illinois

Published in the United States of America by

Midwest Theological Forum
1420 Davey Road, Woodridge, IL 60517
www.theologicalforum.org

Copyright © 2003–2009 Rev. James Socias
ISBN 978-1-890177-28-7 (ISBN-10 1-890177-28-8)
Revised First Edition

Nihil obstat
Reverend Charles R. Meyer
Censor Deputatus
October 30, 2002

Imprimatur
Most Reverend Raymond E. Goedert, M.A., S.T.L., J.C.L.
Vicar General
Archdiocese of Chicago
November 15, 2002

The Nihil obstat and Imprimatur are official declarations that a book is free of doctrinal and moral error. No implication is contained therein that those who have granted the Nihil obstat and Imprimatur agree with the contents, opinions, or statements expressed.

General and Managing Editor: Rev. James Socias

Editorial Board: Rev. James Socias, Rev. Peter Armenio, Kimberly Kirk Hahn,
           Emmet Flood, Dr. Scott Hahn, Mike Aquilina

Managing Editor: Emmet Flood

Design and Production: Marlene Burrell, Jane Heineman of April Graphics, Highland Park, Illinois

Staff Photographer: Julie Koenig

Acknowledgements

Excerpts from the English translation of the *Catechism of the Catholic Church* for the United States of America copyright ©1994, United States Catholic Conference, Inc.–Libreria Editrice Vaticana. Used by permission.

Excerpts from the English translation of the *Catechism of the Catholic Church: Modifications from the Editio Typica* copyright ©1997, United States Catholic Conference, Inc.–Libreria Editrice Vaticana. Used by permission.

Scripture quotations contained herein are adapted from the Catholic Edition of the *Revised Standard Version of the Bible,* copyright ©1946, 1952, 1971, and the *New Revised Standard Version of the Bible,* copyright ©1989, by the Division of Christian Education of the National Council of the Churches of Christ in the United States of America, and are used by permission. All rights reserved.

Excerpts from the *Code of Canon Law, Latin/English Edition,* are used with permission, copyright ©1983 Canon Law Society of America, Washington, D.C.

Citations of official Church documents from Neuner, Josef, SJ, and Dupuis, Jacques, SJ, eds., *The Christian Faith: Doctrinal Documents of the Catholic Church,* 5th ed. (New York: Alba House, 1992). Used with permission.

Excerpts from *Vatican Council II: The Conciliar and Post Conciliar Documents, New Revised Edition* edited by Austin Flannery, O.P., copyright ©1992, Costello Publishing Company, Inc., Northport, NY are used by permission of the publisher, all rights reserved. No part of these excerpts may be reproduced, stored in a retrieval system, or transmitted in any form or by any means—electronic, mechanical, photocopying, recording or otherwise, without express permission of Costello Publishing Company.

Disclaimer: The editor of this book has attempted to give proper credit to all sources used in the text and illustrations. Any miscredit or lack of credit is unintended and will be corrected in the next edition.

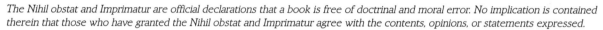

The Ad Hoc Committee to Oversee the Use of the Catechism, United States Conference of Catholic Bishops, has found this catechetical text, copyright 2003, to be in conformity with the *Catechism of the Catholic Church.*

Printed in Canada

Contents

Contents

Contents

Contents

Contents

ABBREVIATIONS USED FOR THE BOOKS OF THE BIBLE

OLD TESTAMENT

Genesis	Gen	Tobit	Tb	Hosea	Hos
Exodus	Ex	Judith	Jdt	Joel	Jl
Leviticus	Lv	Esther	Est	Amos	Am
Numbers	Nm	Job	Jb	Obadiah	Ob
Deuteronomy	Dt	Psalms	Ps(s)	Jonah	Jon
Joshua	Jos	Proverbs	Prv	Micah	Mi
Judges	Jgs	Ecclesiastes	Eccl	Nahum	Na
Ruth	Ru	Song of Songs	Sg	Habakkuk	Hab
1 Samuel	1 Sm	Wisdom	Wis	Zephaniah	Zep
2 Samuel	2 Sm	Sirach	Sir	Haggai	Hg
1 Kings	1 Kgs	Isaiah	Is	Zechariah	Zec
2 Kings	2 Kgs	Jeremiah	Jer	Malachi	Mal
1 Chronicles	1 Chr	Lamentations	Lam	1 Maccabees	1 Mc
2 Chronicles	2 Chr	Baruch	Bar	2 Maccabees	2 Mc
Ezra	Ezr	Ezekiel	Ez		
Nehemiah	Neh	Daniel	Dn		

NEW TESTAMENT

Matthew	Mt	Ephesians	Eph	Hebrews	Heb
Mark	Mk	Philippians	Phil	James	Jas
Luke	Lk	Colossians	Col	1 Peter	1 Pt
John	Jn	1 Thessalonians	1 Thes	2 Peter	2 Pt
Acts of the Apostles	Acts	2 Thessalonians	2 Thes	1 John	1 Jn
Romans	Rom	1 Timothy	1 Tm	2 John	2 Jn
1 Corinthians	1 Cor	2 Timothy	2 Tm	3 John	3 Jn
2 Corinthians	2 Cor	Titus	Ti	Jude	Jud
Galatians	Gal	Philemon	Phlm	Revelation	Rv

ABBREVIATIONS USED FOR DOCUMENTS OF THE MAGISTERIUM

AA	Apostolicam actuositatem	GS	Gaudium et spes
AAS	Acta Apostolica Sedis	HV	Humanae vitae
AG	Ad gentes	IOE	Instruction on Euthanasia
CA	Centesimus annus	LE	Laborem exercens
CCC	The Catechism of the Catholic Church	LG	Lumen gentium
CCEO	Corpus Canonum Ecclesiarum Orientalium	LH	Liturgy of the Hours
CDF	Congregation for the Doctrine of the Faith	MF	Mysterium fidei
CHCW	Charter for Health Care Workers	MM	Mater et magistra
CIC	Codex Iuris Canonici (The Code of Canon Law)	ND	Neuner-Dupuis, The Christian Faith in the Doctrinal Documents of the Catholic Church
CL	Christifidelis laici	OC	Ordo confirmationis
CPG	Solemn Profession of Faith: Credo of the People of God	OCM	Ordo celebrandi Matrimonium
		OP	Ordo paenitentiae
DD	Dies Domini	PG	J.P. Migne, ed., Patrologia Graeca (Paris, 1857- 1866)
DRF	Declaration on Religious Freedom		
DH	Dignitatis humanae	PH	Persona humanae
DIM	Decree Inter mirifici	PL	J. P. Migne, ed., Patrologia Latina (Paris, 1841-1855)
DoV	Donum vitae		
DPA	Declaration on Procured Abortion	PP	Populorum progressio
DS	Denzinger-Schönmetzer, Enchiridion Symbolorum, definitionum et declarationum de rebus fidei et morum (1965)	PT	Pacem in terris
		RH	Redemptor hominis
		RP	Reconciliatio et paenitentia
DV	Dei verbum	SC	Sacrosanctum concilium
EN	Evangeli nuntiadi	SD	Salvifici doloris
EV	Evangelium vitae	SRS	Solicitudo rei socialis
FC	Familiaris consortio	STh	Summa Theologiae
GCD	General Catechetical Directory	VS	Veritatis splendor

Introduction

Life is a journey. As part of God's plan, every person appears at a certain time, in a certain place in the history of mankind, and then leaves, at a different time and usually from a different place. Unfortunately, many people do not understand why they are here in the world and where they are going.

Introduction To Catholicism is a book that sets out the basics of why we are here and where we are going. Every baptized person has been called personally to serve God and love his neighbor. The goal of our lives is personal sanctity, and the destination is Heaven.

Jesus established his Church to map out the way for everyone, and he left his Holy Spirit to guarantee that the Church will not fail in that role.

We must become aware that it is part of God's plan that each one of us arrived at this particular time in history. Therefore, the obligation of each person is to discover through prayer and spiritual direction what role they are expected to play in God's plan of salvation. Through cooperation with the grace of God, the vocation to which each one of us is called will be made manifest.

Since every baptized person has been allotted a certain amount of time to serve Jesus in the quest for souls, that time must be spent seeking to do the will of God. This call from Jesus often goes unheard among Christians. Many Christians today are fractional Christians—they have resolved to give Jesus only a small fraction of their lives. Some are willing to give him an hour on Sunday while others pick and choose among the Commandments to decide which ones they will observe and which ones they will ignore. Because they do not understand Jesus' plan for them, they only give Jesus a fraction of their time. Jesus wants all Christians to be dedicated to doing his work all the time. Those who desire to be saints can help the fractional Christians to live as Jesus desires them to.

This book is a part of your journey on the road to sanctity. Seek to understand its message so that you will be able to complete the journey in the way Jesus desires in the time he has given you.

It is said that the human soul loves adventure, and your life will indeed present many opportunities for adventure. Remember why you are here, what the great goal is, and take as your motto, *"Sanctity will be my most important adventure."*

Chapter 1

The Call To Holiness

Our Church is the Church of Saints.

The Call To Holiness

*T*he man who approaches the Church with misgivings sees only the closed doors, the barriers, and the windows where you buy a ticket, a kind of spiritual police station.

But our Church is the Church of the saints.

To become a saint what bishop would not give his mitre, his ring, and his pectoral cross; what cardinal would not sacrifice his [red] and what pontiff his white robe, his chamberlains, his Swiss guard and all his temporal appurtenance. Who would not crave the strength to brave this marvelous adventure? For sanctity is an adventure; it is even the only adventure.

Once you have understood this, you have entered into the heart of the Catholic faith; your mortal flesh will have trembled, no longer with a fear of death, but with a superhuman hope . . .

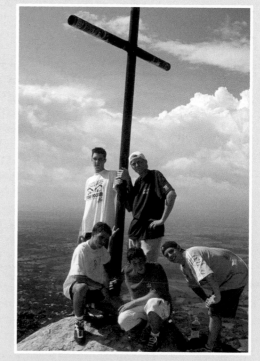

God did not create the Church to ensure the prosperity of the saints, but in order to transmit their memory . . . They lived and suffered as we do. They were tempted as we are. The man who dares not yet accept what is sacred and divine in their example will at least learn from it the lesson of heroism and honor . . .

None of us will ever know enough theology to become a priest. But we know enough to be a saint . . . Ever since God, himself, came to visit us, is there anything saints have not taken upon themselves? Is there anything which is beyond their capacity to give? – Georges Bernanos

THE CALL TO HOLINESS

All Christians in any state or walk of life are called to the fullness of the Christian life and to the perfection of charity. All are called to holiness. "You, therefore, must be perfect, as your heavenly Father is perfect" (Mt 5: 48).

> "In order to reach this perfection the faithful should use the strength dealt out to them by Christ's gift, so that...doing the will of the Father in everything, they may wholeheartedly devote themselves to the glory of God and to the service of their neighbor. Thus the holiness of the People of God will grow in fruitful abundance, as is clearly shown in the history of the Church through the lives of so many saints."[1] (CCC 2013)

The history of the Church is the history of holiness. By virtue of their prophetic mission, lay people are called to a holy witness to Christ in all circumstances, at the heart of the community. For almost two thousand years, the Church has been influencing the lives of those she has touched by passing on the example and teachings of Jesus Christ, his apostles, and the saints. During that time, many holy individuals have served Christ and spread his message to peoples and places throughout the world. Many of these people who received the message and acted upon it are officially recognized as saints.

The word saint is derived from the Latin *sanctus,* which means "holy." To become holy, to become a saint, we follow the example of Jesus' life and teachings — we must try to identify completely with Christ in both word and action.

Indeed, this imitation of Christ has led people to exciting lives. It has also helped people live their faith to the furthest limit possible. The early church, for example, saw a great number of people gladly live their new faith in Christ, then die for professing their beliefs.

Think of St. Lawrence, who was burned to death, tied to a spit like an animal. When his torturers made fun of him, he said, "You can turn me over; I'm done on this side." Remember St. Peter, who, when told he was to be crucified, requested that he be crucified upside down since he was not worthy to die in the same way that Christ had died.

The first three hundred years of the Church were certainly a time when a great many Christians were required to die for Christ. It is a fact, though, that more people were killed for Christ in the twentieth century than in any other century. During the Second World War, millions of Christians were killed by the Communists and the Nazis for witnessing to Christ.

Most followers of Christ will not be required to die for him. Christ, however, expects all of his followers to strive to become saints through living holy, if ordinary, lives.

Leading a holy life, a life of personal sanctity, is in fact our purpose on earth. Through living such a life, we hope to make it to heaven.

THE CHURCH CALLS US

From relatively early times, popes have presided over councils. These meetings were convened to settle important questions, to explain Church teachings in greater detail, or to prevent serious problems from getting out of hand.

We must try to identify completely with Christ in both word and action.

The history of the Church is the history of holiness.

The Call To Holiness

If we fail to fulfill the role Christ has planned for us, we hurt everyone else who is a member of the Mystical Body, and even worse, we fail Christ.

In 1959, Pope John XXIII called such a council at Vatican City in Rome, where the popes live. This meeting was called the Second Vatican Council (the First Vatican Council had taken place about one hundred years earlier). The main purposes of this council were to prepare the Church to deal with the changes that had occurred in the world since the First Vatican Council and to remind all Catholics that everyone is called to personal holiness.

After much discussion among the bishops at the Second Vatican Council, the Decree on the Laity (those who are not priests, nuns, or religious) was drawn up, voted upon by the bishops, and approved by the pope. This document gives us direction about the role we are to fulfill in the Church and in the world.

The Decree on the Laity talks much about the "Mystical Body of Christ," a title St. Paul gave to the Church. It indicates that through the action of Christ, each of us makes up part of Christ's Mystical Body. Just as a body has different organs that serve different purposes, likewise, each of us has a different, unique role to play in the Church. If we fail to fulfill the role Christ has planned for us, we hurt everyone else who is a member of the Mystical Body, and even worse, we fail Christ. The document states:

> The Church was founded to spread the kingdom of Christ over all the earth for the glory of God the Father to make all men partakers in redemption and salvation, and through them to establish the right relationship of the entire world to Christ. Every activity of the Mystical Body with this in view goes by the name of "apostolate"; the Church exercises it through all its members, though in various ways. In fact, the Christian vocation is, of its nature, a vocation to the apostolate as well. In the organism of a living body no member plays a purely passive part, sharing in the life of the body it shares at the same time in its activity. The same is true for the Body of Christ, the Church: "the whole Body achieves full growth in dependence on the full functioning of each part" (Eph 4:16).
>
> Between the members of this body there exists, further, such a unity and solidarity (cf. Eph 4:16) that a member who does not work at the growth of the body to the extent of his possibilities must be considered useless both to the Church and to himself.
>
> In the Church there is diversity of ministry but unity of mission. To the apostles and their successors Christ has entrusted the office of teaching, sanctifying and governing in his name and by his power. But the laity are made to share in the priestly, prophetical and kingly office of Christ; they have therefore, in the Church and in the world, their own assignment in the mission of the whole People of God.
>
> In the concrete, their apostolate is exercised when they work at the evangelization and sanctification of men; it is exercised too when they endeavor to have the Gospel spirit permeate and improve the temporal order, going about it in a way that bears clear witness to Christ and helps forward the salvation of men.[2]

To sum up, the Second Vatican Council's document on the laity says that all baptized persons in Christ's Mystical Body, the Church, are called to evangelize everyone they meet. The baptized are called to perfection of life as well as to bring all people to personal holiness by infusing the world around them with the spirit of the gospel.

We exercise this apostolate by sanctifying ourselves and encouraging others to do the same. The effect good example has on people should not be underestimated. By acting as Christ wants us to act, we show that a Christian life is possible, and how good a life it is.

The life of holiness begins with the reception of Baptism, which gives us sanctifying grace, a share in the life of God. If we are in a state of grace, God is actually present in us. "Do you not know that your body is a temple of the Holy Spirit within you, which you have from God?" (1 Cor 6:19) From our Baptism, we have the seed of sanctity, and we are to make it flower through prayer and regular reception of the sacraments.

> Grace is the help God gives us to respond to our vocation of becoming his adopted sons. It introduces us into the intimacy of the Trinitarian life. (CCC 2021)

> The divine initiative in the work of grace precedes, prepares, and elicits the free response of man. Grace responds to the deepest yearnings of human freedom, calls freedom to cooperate with it, and perfects freedom. (CCC 2022)

Through sanctifying grace, we share the life and love of the Trinity: Father, Son, and Holy Spirit. This greatest of gifts assists us to respond to the desires of the Trinity. It enables us to grow continually in wisdom and freedom to do good. Each time we choose to serve God, we become more Christ-like, and as we become more Christ-like, we have a greater effect on the world.

In the Gospels, Christ describes this transformation by comparing it to yeast. When yeast enters dough, the dough is changed; yet we do not actually see the yeast working. At first, the dough is a small lump, and then it begins to grow before our eyes. Similarly, our living witness to his presence will lead others to respond in like manner. This change is enhanced by our growth in the theological virtues of faith, hope, and charity received in Baptism, which have brought us directly into contact with Christ and his graces.

In particular, we must demonstrate our charity, which is true love of neighbor, so that the love of Christ may shine through us. We accomplish this by establishing relationships with others based on true friendship and confidence. When we become true and good friends to others, they will more easily be led to accept our suggestions regarding the direction of their lives.

This may sound like a difficult order, but we're not alone. The Holy Spirit gives special graces to assist us. By cooperating with the grace Christ has given us, we will be more effective in our apostolate. It is crucial to understand that it is not we who are making the difference, but it is through our cooperation with his grace that Christ himself will accomplish his plan.

Christ has given himself to us as the perfect model for holiness. The more our words and actions demonstrate to others that we identify with Christ's words and actions, the greater will be our success. "He who abides in me, and I in Him, he it is that bears much fruit, for apart from me you can do nothing" (Jn 15:5).

From our Baptism, we have the seed of sanctity, and we are to make it flower through prayer and regular reception of the sacraments.

We must demonstrate our charity, which is true love of neighbor, so that the love of Christ may shine through us.

In our different employments and professions, each person will follow his road to holiness within the experiences of his own life.

With hearts of:

Mercy

Humility

Kindness

Meekness

Patience

Though we are all called to imitate Christ, we are not all called to live the same type of life. Holiness unites us in the truth of God's teaching and love, yet each of us is following a personal path in his particular state of life. In our different employments and professions, each person will follow his road to holiness within the experiences of his own life. No two persons have exactly the same life experiences, so none of us should expect his or her path to be exactly like that of another.

If we are faithful to his call to us, Jesus will use our good example and prayers to motivate others to imitate our conduct.

GOD'S CALL TO US

The Lord Jesus, divine teacher and model of all perfection, preached holiness of life (of which he is the author and maker) to each and every one of his disciples without distinction: "You, therefore, must be perfect, as your heavenly Father is perfect" (Mt 5:48). For he sent the Holy Spirit to all to move them interiorly to love God with their whole heart, with their whole soul, with their whole understanding, and with their whole strength (cf. Mk 12:30), and to love one another as Christ loved them (cf. Jn 13:34; 15:12). The followers of Christ, called by God not in virtue of their works but by his design and grace, and justified in the Lord Jesus, have been made sons of God in the baptism of faith and partakers of the divine nature, and so are truly sanctified. They must therefore hold on to and perfect in their lives that sanctification which they have received from God.[3]

As we noted above, at Baptism, Jesus placed a seed of holiness within us. With it came the obligation to nurture this seed into a full-grown flower of holiness. Every baptized person including both laity and clergy has this call. We are to live as holy people, God's chosen ones, with hearts of mercy, humility, kindness, meekness, and patience.

Therefore all the faithful are invited and obliged to holiness and the perfection of their own state of life. Accordingly let all of them see that they direct their affections rightly, lest they be hindered in their pursuit of perfect love by the use of worldly things and by an adherence to riches which is contrary to the spirit of evangelical poverty, following the apostle's advice: Let those who use this world not fix their abode in it, for the form of this world is passing away.[4] (cf. 1 Cor 7:31, Greek text)

We will be recognized as Christ's followers when:

† We conform ourselves to Christ in word and deed. To make this possible, we should study the life of Christ in the Gospels and act toward others as he did. Christ was not timid. He spoke up to those who acted improperly. He did this with love for the good of all. He cared for everyone regardless of wealth or condition. We should initiate the special love Christ had for those who suffer;

† We seek the will of the Father in all things. We discover the will of the Father by praying and discussing our plans with a good confessor. Sanctity is about joining our will to God's will. The Father will guide us through the actions of the Holy Spirit, with the assistance of our spiritual director;

† We devote ourselves to God's glory. Serving God is about his glory. The good we accomplish is for his name. We will avoid bragging and claiming we are better than others or that our gifts are for our own pleasure and use. We use our gifts to serve God and our neighbor;

† We seek to serve our neighbor. God places people in our lives who are in need of our assistance. We must seek to aid those who are in need to the extent that it is prudent, and to the extent that we are able; (See CCC 826 on p. 14)

† We accept the crosses that inevitably come to us. Everyone suffers in this life. Christ gives value to our suffering when we unite it to his suffering. When we offer up our suffering for others, it has the power to save souls. (See CCC 2015, 2029 on p. 14)

At first, all this may appear to be difficult or impossible to accomplish, but it appears impossible only if we count on ourselves alone to accomplish these things. With God, all things are possible, and so we unite ourselves to Christ's grace and the guidance of the Holy Spirit. We must keep in mind that God has given us this obligation to follow Christ, and God will see that we receive the necessary gifts and graces to accomplish his will. He wants us to be saints.

> You and I belong to Christ's family, for He, Himself, has chosen us before the foundation of the world, to be saints, to be blameless in His sight, for love of Him, having predestined us to be His adoptive children through Jesus Christ, according to the purpose of His will. We have been chosen gratuitously by Our Lord. His choice of us sets a clear goal. Our goal is personal sanctity, as St. Paul insistently reminds us, "this is the will of God, your sanctification. Let us not forget, then, that we are in our master's sheepfold in order to achieve that goal.[5]

The Father will guide us through the actions of the Holy Spirit, with the assistance of our spiritual director.

THE MEANS

For those who wish to become holy, strength is acquired through the sacraments, particularly Reconciliation and the Eucharist. Since the Eucharist is the source of all the Church's gifts, it is a source of power to us as well. Each time we receive it, we are infused with the power of God's grace. Jesus' grace gives us the strength and desire to change ourselves and overcome our fears about talking to others about him.

There are similarities between success in sports and success in becoming a saint. Both require a plan, involve coaches, and have rules to be followed for success. First of all, we must find a good coach to give us spiritual direction. Spiritual direction is advice given by a priest in confession. Regular confession should be part of the plan of life we make for ourselves.

Most of us make the mistake of thinking confession is solely for the forgiveness of sins. Yes, confession is about the forgiveness of sins, but it is more than that: it helps us overcome our sinful inclinations.

Sometimes we hear people say, "I just keep committing the same sins over and over again." This is why spiritual direction is a recommended part of the Sacrament of Penance. Spiritual direction in confession begins

The Eucharist is the source of all the Church's gifts, it is a source of power to us as well.

The Call To Holiness

when we ask a priest to assist us to make a program that will enable us to overcome our sins. It is best to start by asking for assistance in conquering our most persistent sin. Once advice is given, we follow it; the next time we go to confession we discuss the results with the priest and continue with the plan.

Another helpful method of growing in faith is spiritual reading. Spiritual reading is meditating on writings that help us down the path of sanctity. The first of such writings are the Gospels, which tell us about Christ's life and actions. If we want to be more Christ-like, we must learn about him by reading the Gospels.

Over the centuries, as the litany of saints grew, the Church examined the writings of certain saints, who explained from their own lives the road to becoming a saint. The Church encouraged the faithful to read these writings, and eventually the works of many saints were collected into books, giving us insights into various paths to sanctity.

Our spiritual director normally chooses our spiritual reading after determining which books are best for us at a given point in our lives.

THE STARTING POINT OF EVANGELIZATION

Striving for holiness gives a whole new purpose to what we do. Instead of trying our best to call attention to ourselves, we work to use the talents Christ gave us to the fullest as a demonstration of our gratitude for his gifts and as a way to bring people to Christ.

We do not attempt this alone. Everyone involved in the sanctification of souls makes up one great army serving under Christ's banner. When we respond to the call to sanctification, we will be able to change the lives of those with whom we come in contact. Eventually, the society around us will begin to change as it responds to the testimony of our lives, which are filled with good works and demonstrate the reality of our belief in Jesus.

To begin this transformation, we must start with our friends. They, like us, are called to be Christians. Since personal friends can be influenced by our conduct, it is our responsibility to encourage our friends to accept a Christian way of life. It is not a matter of being "goody two-shoes," but rather of demonstrating that we believe in Christ, are happy in our belief, and want our friends to share in the same happiness.

By our conduct, we demonstrate to our friends that true happiness is not found in sin but in avoiding it. It is crucial that our friends understand that freedom is for the service of God and not for sin.

Many young persons involve themselves in serious sins involving the use of drugs, alcohol, and sex as a way of refusing to face their problems. Part of our responsibility toward them is to help them understand that sin leads to not only bad habits but bad feelings about themselves, loss of self-esteem, and loss of the trust of their parents.

Since the sacraments make grace directly and clearly available to all people, we may help those we are close to by encouraging them to return to the sacraments. One way to accomplish this is to ask them to go to Reconciliation and Sunday Eucharist with us. If at first they refuse, pray to Jesus and Mary to change their hearts, and then, ask again.

We can also demonstrate Christ's love for others by assisting in or teaching in religious education programs at the parish level. Children in grade and middle school need to see that people a few years older than they are have committed wholly to Christ and are working to spread his love. Younger students look to older students as models for life, so to the extent we model Christ for younger students, they will be inclined to follow our example.

It is a firm rule of life that you can only give to others what you have yourself, be it material goods or spiritual goods. To lead our friends to Christ, we must first be the type of friend whom they recognize as a follower of Christ.

MARTYRDOM FOR CHRIST

The word "martyr" comes from a Greek word meaning "witness." Those who died for Christ in the early Church were called witnesses or martyrs because they witnessed to their faith in Christ. Witnessing for Christ sometimes leads to suffering, as when others reject us for seeking to do good in place of the evil that envelops the world.

For those of us who refuse sins such as those involving drugs, alcohol, and sex outside of marriage, there is a price to be paid. Unlike the martyrs in the early Church, we will not be killed. Our suffering will come from our peers, who may reject us specifically because we choose to follow Christ. There will be parties and other social events where we will not be welcome, and we may be insulted and made fun of for standing by that in which we believe.

To lead our friends to Christ, we must first be the type of friend whom they recognize as a follower of Christ.

Our suffering will come from our peers, who may reject us specifically because we choose to follow Christ.

We should plan for the moment when we join the saints in God's presence, where we will share his love eternally.

The experience of rejection is not something new to the present age. Those who follow Christ in every age have suffered rejection. Christ warned us to expect this, but he spoke words of encouragement: "I am with you always, to the close of the age" (Mt 28: 20).

Ultimately, our witness will not be sterile. Though we may not know every case of whom or when, because of our example many people will choose to follow the correct path and serve Christ.

CONCLUSION

When we think of the many possibilities for success in this life, we must remember that any vocation we choose offers the possibility of becoming a true saint. As St. Paul has pointed out so well, every one of us has been called by God to play a special role in his Mystical Body, the Church. The only real failure in life is the failure to save one's soul.

Jesus has not only called us to live a life of sanctity, but he has also supplied us with all the means to accomplish it. From an eternal viewpoint, we are able to take only the actions of our lives with us when we die. When we seek sanctity, we obtain an added benefit: cooperation with God's grace empowers us to aid others to find sanctity. When we arrive in heaven, our joy will be enhanced by the presence of those for whom we were an instrument of salvation.

There are as many ways to become saints as there are people. There will be disappointments and human failings along the way, but as long as we are doing our best to serve God as he wishes, success is guaranteed. All this is made possible by participation in those graced actions of Christ called sacraments, particularly Reconciliation and the Eucharist. For our part, God expects us to choose these means he has set aside for us and to follow the direction of the Church.

We should plan for the moment when we join the saints in God's presence, where we will share his love eternally.

Chapter 1 Study Guide

SUPPLEMENTARY READING

Canonized on October 6, 2002, St. Josemaría Escrivá helped point the way to sanctity for lay men and women. Born on January 9, 1902 in the town of Barbastro, Spain, he was the second child and first son of Don Jose and Dolores Escrivá. Four girls were born to the Escrivás, but only Josemaría and Carmen, their oldest daughter, lived to adulthood. When he was young, nothing set him apart from any other boy in town. He played roll-the-hoops and cops-and-robbers with the other boys.

His parents were devout, cheerful Catholics who taught their children the importance of serving God. When he was six, Josemaría made his First Confession, which was followed by First Communion at ten.

During the Christmas season of 1917, he noticed the footprints of a discalced Carmelite priest walking barefoot in the snow. He had a sudden sense that it was Christ who had walked in the snow. It was a moment of great grace. From that time forward, he attended daily Mass and frequent Confession.

His father had indicated to him that he wished his son to study to be a lawyer, but he supported Josemaría's choice to become a priest instead. His choice to become a priest meant there would be no one to carry on the family name, so he asked God to grant his parents another son. The next year, his brother Santiago was born.

He was ordained on March 28, 1925, and spent the first part of his priesthood in a poor community where he was noted for his loving care of all. When his father died, he became the sole support of the family. To care for his mother, sister, and little brother and pay for his studies in the law, he gave Latin lessons, lectured, and taught Roman and canon law.

St. Josemaría Escrivá
(1902-1975)
Feast on June 26

What little spare time he had was spent with the poorest of the poor and the incurably ill. In return for his care, he asked those to whom he ministered to pray for the success of his priesthood.

From these poor beginnings was born his life's work, Opus Dei, which means the "Work of God." On October 2, 1928, God graced him to see that his priesthood would be devoted to helping lay men and women understand that ordinary persons could become saints. His mission was to lead all to sanctify themselves and their work for the good of the Church through a personal apostolate with others.

VOCABULARY

COUNCIL

A formal meeting of Church leaders to deliberate, clarify, study and enact decrees pertaining to the life and belief of the Church.

DECREE ON THE LAITY

Official pronouncement announcing that all the baptized are called to perfection of life and to evangelize all who they meet.

DRY MARTYR

A witness to the truth of the faith who suffers social persecution rather than death.

GRACE

The free and undeserved gift that God gives us to respond to our vocation to become his adopted children.

HOLINESS

Principally an attribute of God describing his complete separation from the sphere of the profane. Individual human beings may be holy dedicating themselves completely to God. Holiness is the perfection of charity.

LAITY

The faithful who, having been incorporated into Christ through Baptism, are made part of the people of God, the Church. They are not in Holy Orders or the consecrated life.

MARTYR

A witness to the truth of the faith, in which the martyr endures even death to be faithful to Christ. Those who die for the faith before having received Baptism are said to have received a baptism of blood, by which their sins are forgiven and they share in the joys of heaven.

SAINT

A person on earth, in purgatory, or in heaven notable for holiness and heroic virtue. The saints share in God's life, glory, and happiness. The Church may officially declare someone a saint through the process of beatification and canonization.

SANCTIFICATION

Process of being made holy. This begins with Baptism, continues throughout the life of the Christian, and is completed when a person enters heaven and becomes totally and irrevocably united with God in the beatific vision.

SPIRITUAL READING

All reading that leads us to prayer and closer union with God. First of all, the Sacred Scriptures, but also the writings and lives of popes, bishops, and saints.

STUDY QUESTIONS

1. Why does the author of the chapter's opening passage say, "Sanctity is even the only adventure"?

2. Who is called to holiness in the Church?

3. What is necessary to achieve holiness?

4. In what century were the most Christians killed for Christ?

5. Why do popes call councils?

6. Where do councils get their names?

7. How does St. Paul's title of the Church as the Mystical Body of Christ apply to us?

8. How do we exercise our apostolate?

9. How does the grace of the Trinity work in us?

10. How do we demonstrate our love for our neighbor?

11. What is the purpose of freedom?

12. Name three ways to make good use of our freedom with our friends.

13. List five actions that demonstrate to others that we are Christ's followers.

14. Who will supply the necessary gifts to accomplish our sanctification?

15. List the means to attain holiness.

16. Why do we need a spiritual director?

17. Jesus has not only called us to live a life of sanctity; he has supplied us with all the means to accomplish it. From an eternal viewpoint, we are able to take only the actions of our life with us when we die. When we seek personal sanctity, we obtain an added benefit: cooperation with God's grace empowers us to aid others to find sanctity. When we arrive in heaven, our joy will be enhanced by the presence of those for whom we were instruments of salvation. What activities are available for us to convert others?

PRACTICAL EXERCISES

1. In reference to our lives as Christians, how does the following quotation apply: "The whole body...in keeping with the proper activity of each part, derives its increase from its own internal development?" Think of the Mystical Body of Christ.

2. Write a paragraph on why someone should strive to be as holy as possible, instead of simply trying to "get by." What are some ways of striving for holiness that are open to you, as young people? (See CCC 2045 on p. 14)

3. Find a spiritual director, someone who can help you to pray every day, choose appropriate spiritual reading, and help you make important decisions about your future. To get started you may want to try a priest, sister, devout family member, teacher, or other adviser.

FROM THE CATECHISM

826 Charity is the soul of the holiness to which all are called: it "governs, shapes, and perfects all the means of sanctification" (*LG*, 42).

If the Church was a body composed of different members, it couldn't lack the noblest of all; it must have a Heart, and a Heart BURNING WITH LOVE. And I realized that this love alone was the true motive force which enabled the other members of the Church to act; if it ceased to function, the Apostles would forget to preach the gospel, the Martyrs would refuse to shed their blood. LOVE, IN FACT, IS THE VOCATION WHICH INCLUDES ALL OTHERS; IT'S A UNIVERSE OF ITS OWN, COMPRISING ALL TIME AND SPACE – IT'S ETERNAL![6]

2013 "All Christians in any state or walk of life are called to the fullness of Christian life and to the perfection of charity" (*LG*, 40 § 2). All are called to holiness: "Be perfect, as your heavenly Father is perfect" (Mt 5: 48).

In order to reach this perfection the faithful should use the strength dealt out to them by Christ's gift, so that . . . doing the will of the Father in everything, they may wholeheartedly devote themselves to the glory of God and to the service of their neighbor. Thus the holiness of the People of God will grow in fruitful abundance, as is clearly shown in the history of the Church through the lives of so many saints. (*LG*, 40 § 2)

2014 Spiritual progress tends toward ever more intimate union with Christ. This union is called "mystical" because it participates in the mystery of Christ through the sacraments — "the holy mysteries" — and, in him, in the mystery of the Holy Trinity. God calls us all to this intimate union with him, even if the special graces or extraordinary signs of this mystical life are granted only to some for the sake of manifesting the gratuitous gift given to all.

2015 The way of perfection passes by way of the Cross. There is no holiness without renunciation and spiritual battle.[7] Spiritual progress entails the ascesis and mortification that gradually lead to living in the peace and joy of the Beatitudes:

He who climbs never stops going from beginning to beginning, through beginnings that have no end. He never stops desiring what he already knows.[8]

2028 "All Christians . . . are called to the fullness of Christian life and to the perfection of charity" (*LG*, 40 § 2). "Christian perfection has but one limit, that of having none."[9]

2029 "If any man would come after me, let him deny himself and take up his cross and follow me" (Mt 16: 24).

2045 Because they are members of the Body whose Head is Christ,[10] Christians contribute to *building up the Church* by the constancy of their convictions and their moral lives. The Church increases, grows, and develops through the holiness of her faithful, until "we all attain to the unity of the faith and of the knowledge of the Son of God, to mature manhood, to the measure of the stature of the fullness of Christ."[11]

Endnotes

1. *LG*, 40 § 2.
2. *AA*, 2.
3. *LG*, 40.
4. Ibid., 42.
5. St. Josemaría Escrivá, Homily: *The Richness of Ordinary Life*, 2.
6. St. Thérèse of Lisieux, *Autobiography of a Saint*, tr. Ronald Knox (London: Harvill, 1958) 235.
7. Cf. 2 Tm 4.
8. St. Gregory of Nyssa, *Hom in Cant.* 8: PG 44, 941C.
9. St. Gregory of Nyssa, *De vita Mos.*: PG 44, 300D.
10. Cf. Eph 1: 22.
11. Eph 4: 13; cf. *LG*, 39.

Chapter 2

Prayer

Our Love Connection with God.

Chapter 2

Prayer

One Saturday, there was a line outside the confessional. One of the women in line turned to the man next to her.

"Please pray for my daughter; she just had her ninth baby."

"What's the matter?" responded the man.

"The baby was born with several defects and will die very soon. I'm so upset."

"Don't you want all your grandchildren to be saints?"

"Well, of course I do," replied the grandmother.

"Then I guess you may have to accept that God may want your grandchild to be a saint sooner than you wished."

That story points out the main difficulty for us when we pray. We always expect Jesus will answer our prayers in the way we want him to answer them. We must accept the fact that God knows the best way to answer all our prayers, even if there are times we don't understand the answer we receive, and it is difficult to accept. We must turn our prayer into our love connection with God.

A PERMANENT FRIENDSHIP

It has been said that the best time to make friends for life is high school. If high school is about anything, it is about friendship. Many adults say the best friends they have were made in high school. For us, that means we must be ready to make good friends by being willing to meet people and be the real persons we are when we do meet them.

What are some of the problems with making friends? Well, many high school students claim that true friends are difficult to find. We hear the usual complaints: "I told him special things about me and then he went and told everyone;" or, "Why are so many people backstabbers?" or, "She's nice to my face but stabs me in the back to others;" or, "Why is he so nice when we are alone, and then he pretends not to know me when his other friends are around?"

There is hope in spite of all this, for there is one true friend we can make in high school who will not tell our secrets or embarrass us or turn on us. This perfect friend is Jesus. Every moment of every day he waits to hear from each of us.

Prayer is conversation with Jesus to ask him for the good things that he desires to give us. Perfect prayer is complete submission to his will. The battle of prayer is a battle about choosing his will over our own. He truly wants us to get to know him better, and prayer is an excellent way to accomplish this. Since God blesses the human heart in prayer, we are enabled to return his blessing in prayer.

Many young people tend to complain that Jesus doesn't answer their prayers. A little questioning reveals that these same young people spend less than one minute in a day praying apart from school-directed prayer. We must remember that prayer is talking to Jesus to establish a good *continuing* relationship with him. Humanly speaking, we would all object to a friend who gave us only a minute each day of his time, yet that is often the way that we treat Jesus. Those who spend hours on the telephone with friends but give Jesus just a few moments out of their day do not see the inconsistency. Jesus is the best friend we can have.

God made everyone to love and be loved. Many try to satisfy their need for love solely through relationships with other people. Others try to put this feeling to rest through a spirituality that focuses on being at peace with oneself, denying the need for union with anything else. As Christians, however, we should recognize this restlessness for what it is, a desire to be with God.

> The desire for God is written in the human heart, because man is created by God and for God, and God never ceases to draw man to himself. Only in God will he find the truth and happiness he never stops searching for:
>
>> "The dignity of man rests above all on the fact that he is called to communion with God. This invitation to converse with God is addressed to man as soon as he comes into being. For if man exists, it is because God has created him through love, and through love continues to hold him in existence. He cannot live fully according to truth unless he freely acknowledges that love and entrusts himself to his creator."[1] (CCC 27)

Every moment of every day Jesus waits to hear from each of us.

Those who spend hours on the telephone with friends but give Jesus just a few moments out of their day do not see the inconsistency.

Jesus is the best friend we can have.

When God calls us to pray, most of us respond as Moses did: we have our excuses not to answer God's call.

GOD CALLS US TO PRAYER

We are a special creation. After God made the angels, he made us in his own image and likeness (cf. Gn 1:26). Because of our unique beginning, we have a special bond with God. Even though we sometimes turn away from God, we still sense his grace calling us to be with him. God in fact places this desire for himself in all men:

> *God calls man first.* Man may forget his Creator or hide far from his face; he may run after idols or accuse the deity of having abandoned him; yet the living and true God tirelessly calls each person to that mysterious encounter known as prayer. In prayer, the faithful God's initiative of love always comes first; our own first step is always a response. As God gradually reveals himself and reveals man to himself, prayer appears as a reciprocal call, a covenant drama. Through words and actions, this drama engages the heart. It unfolds throughout the whole history of salvation. **(CCC 2567)**

Prayer, then, in whatever form, is man's response to God's call.

We see the beginning of prayer in the Old Testament. When Adam and Eve sinned, God called out to them, and they responded. Prayer is evident in the whole history of man.

In the Bible, we see that God is always calling out to people. When man responds in prayer, he learns what God wants him to do. At this point, man often resists God's will.

Moses is an excellent example. God calls Moses to an exalted mission, but how does Moses react? He balks at God's request and offers excuses. God persists. He speaks to Moses personally. Finally, Moses agrees to do as God requests (Cf. Ex 3:1, 4:18).

When God calls us to pray, most of us respond as Moses did: we have our excuses not to answer God's call. Often, we do this because we don't want to give up our sins, or we are afraid that God will ask us to do something difficult. Still, God persists in his call to us as he did with Moses.

At first, Moses balked and offered excuses. When he responded to God's call, he became God's friend, and God gave him many blessings. As God blessed Moses, God wishes to bless us also in prayer. (See CCC 2596 on p. 29)

PRAYER IN THE NEW TESTAMENT

God knows that the only way we can find true happiness is by uniting ourselves to him and doing his will. The call to prayer, then, is a call to love, to follow his will, and to be loved by the Lord.

Jesus says, "I love you; I died for you; please love me in return. I want to be your eternal friend; I want to give you the gift of myself."

In return for his love, we pray to God to discover him and his will for us. Why does he love us so? What can we accomplish by corresponding to his love? A regular life of prayer will lead us to know God's will for us and enable us to do his will more easily.

When we pray consistently, we will discover that Jesus is always there for us, and he will help us to get through every difficult situation, whether his support comes during prayer or outside it. Praying constantly also helps us to know his will, and knowing what he wants from us allows us to be more like him. When we are more Christ-like, we will be able to bring others to Christ.

Prayer in the New Testament begins and ends with the Sign of the Cross: "In the name of the Father, and of the Son, and of the Holy Spirit." This helps remind us of the Trinitarian aspect of prayer. In Baptism, a "man becomes an adoptive son of the Father, a member of Christ and a temple of the Holy Spirit. By this very fact the person baptized is incorporated into the Church, the Body of Christ, and made a sharer in the priesthood of Christ" (CCC 1279). It may be said that a Christian prays to the Father, through the Son, with the aid of the Holy Spirit.

THE LORD'S PRAYER

St. Luke tells us that Jesus was praying one day at a certain place, when one of his disciples asked him, "Lord, teach us to pray," as John the Baptist had taught his disciples to pray (Lk 11:1).

> And he said to them, "When you pray say: Father, hallowed be thy name, thy kingdom come. Give us each day our daily bread; and forgive us our sins, for we ourselves forgive everyone who is indebted to us; and lead us not into temptation. (Lk 11: 2-4)

This prayer is called the "Our Father" or the "Lord's Prayer" because it comes from Jesus himself and sums up the whole Gospel. The Lord's Prayer teaches us that prayer is directed primarily to the Father, since it is a model for all prayer, which recognizes God as our Father and us as his children, who need his love and care. It also acknowledges that we rely upon him for everything, both food for life and food for the spirit. It clearly indicates that the Lord keeps us from temptation and reminds us that we are not to call upon him in prayer while holding our brothers unforgiven. The "Our Father" is a model to use when we kneel down to pray. (See CCC 2620 on p. 29)

PRAYER IS A RELATIONSHIP

"I pray to God, but he never answers me," is the most common complaint of people who pray. Some people think God is a type of vending machine, into which you put in a certain number of prayers and get whatever you want.

This attitude demonstrates the false belief that since we have been brought into personal contact with God, he should meet us on our own terms.

What would we do if someone who hardly ever spoke to us walked up to us and said, "You and I are going out to lunch"? Our reply would very likely be, "Hold on there; how well do I know you?"

Isn't it true that we deal with God in the same way? We want the relationship to be established on our terms. While we would object to being forced to establish a relationship with another person, we think it is all

The "Our Father" is a model to use when we kneel down to pray.

Our Father,
who art in heaven, hallowed be thy name. Thy kingdom come; thy will be done on earth as it is in heaven. Give us this day our daily bread; and forgive us our trespasses as we forgive those who trespass against us; and lead us not into temptation, but deliver us from evil. Amen.

Prayer

The key to praying is to pray as if every prayer is our last prayer.

Initially, these experiences of God occur in the family, which should be the first place of education in prayer.

right for us to attempt to force God to reply when we pray. When he doesn't respond, we decide he is not there or doesn't care. In fact, he is always there. He calls us to believe and accept that he's there even when we don't sense his presence.

When a child is learning to walk, his parents allow him to take a few steps on his own, knowing the child may fall. If he is not permitted to risk falling, though, he may never learn to walk.

Similarly, God permits our prayer to seem fruitless so we may realize our dependence. For faith is not just a feeling, it is a realization that God is there even when things aren't going our way. We have to accept the fact that it is God who controls the prayer relationship, not us.

Often we avoid praying out of fear that God will ask us for something that we don't want to give him. This can occur when we are approached about having a vocation to religious life. Perhaps a teacher or a parent suggests the possibility that God might be calling us. For some, this is a frightening thought, and their reaction is, "God wants me to be a priest or sister; I can't, I have other things I want to do with my life." Everyone has a vocation in life, and part of discovering the vocation God has chosen for us is to pray. He gives us the strength to pray to accept his will when our will does not agree with his. Remember that true happiness is found in doing what God created us to do.

Another difficulty to be faced is the fact that we have different levels of involvement in our own prayer life. Do we pray with the same intensity for everything? Isn't it a fact that we pray harder to God for some things than we do for others? Isn't it true that some days we pray with our minds on something other than our prayers? How would we react if a friend read the newspaper while we were trying to talk to him? Would we continue to pray in the same manner if we knew we would die in ten minutes? How would we pray if we knew death was moments away? The key to praying is to pray as if every prayer is our last prayer. We should begin today to pray as if we were going to meet God in a few moments—with all the love we can muster.

The best relationships are those relationships based on love. These relationships involve mutual sharing about the important things in each person's life. By beginning to share the important things in our lives with God, we will find that he will share some of his thoughts with us. Initially, these experiences of God occur in the family, which should be the first place of education in prayer.

JESUS PRAYS

Jesus comes to reveal fully the power of prayer. We begin to pray by learning how Jesus approached prayer. In every instance, Jesus prays before beginning decisive moments of his ministry. Before he starts his public life, he spends forty days in the desert in prayer. He also prays before calling the twelve apostles, he prays that Peter's faith may not be tempted; he prays at the raising of Lazarus; he prays in Gethsemane on Holy Thursday evening; and he prays while on the cross prior to his death.

Christ's call to us to pray is about *metanoia*, a change of heart. To pray successfully, we must turn our hearts toward him. Our will must be aligned with his will.

> From the *Sermon on the Mount* onwards, Jesus insists on *conversion of heart:* reconciliation with one's brother before presenting an offering on the altar, love of enemies, and prayer for persecutors, prayer to the Father in secret, not heaping up empty phrases, prayerful forgiveness from the depths of the heart, purity of heart, and seeking the Kingdom before all else.[2] This filial conversion is entirely directed to the Father. (CCC 2608)

This change of heart means we must aim to live our lives as Jesus indicates and as the Father desires. Conversion of heart is not only about changing to align ourselves with God, it is about accepting people as Jesus did with love, regardless of their faults. Christianity is different from all other beliefs because it requires us to love our enemies.

Jesus said, "Love your enemies and pray for those who persecute you" (Mt 5: 44).

This may sound difficult. Yet, as we grow in faith and cooperate with God's grace, we will be able to love even those who are our enemies. This growth in faith will help us emulate God and overcome our petty likes and dislikes. We will then be able to love others as God loves them. Faith, therefore, bears its fruit in acts of love.

This grace to love others will not come, however, unless there is effort on our part. We must be aware of our own attitudes and work to overcome those things that conflict with faith and love. Prayer, of course, is a way to recognize what we need to change about ourselves. In prayer, God will let us know what we should do.

Regular prayer on earth is a preparation for permanent conversation with God in heaven. Faith bears its fruit in acts of love. It is accomplished by abiding in the Trinity and keeping the commandments as a sign of our commitment.

> If you think you're not quite ready to pray, go to Jesus as his disciples did and say to him, "Lord, teach us how to pray." You will discover how the Holy Spirit "comes to the aid of our weakness; when we do not know what prayer to offer, to pray as we ought, the Spirit himself intercedes for us, with groans beyond all utterance," which are impossible to describe, for no words are adequate to express their depth.[3]

To assist us with our prayer, St. Luke gives us three main parables of Jesus on prayer:

† The unrelenting prayer (Cf. Lk 11: 5-13);

† The persistent widow (Cf. Lk 18: 1-8);

† The Pharisee (Cf. Lk 18: 9-14).

JESUS ANSWERS EVERY PRAYER

Yes, Jesus answers every prayer, though not always in the way we wish. This is because our prayers do not always follow his plans. When this happens, he responds by offering us the grace to accept his will.

Christianity is different from all other beliefs because it requires us to love our enemies.

This grace to love others will not come, however, unless there is effort on our part.

We are called to participate in the highest form of prayer, the Eucharist, from which all the power and goodness of the Church flow.

Unfortunately, many people refuse this grace. We, therefore, must accept that when our plans don't converge with his will, his will should take precedence for the good of our souls. (See CCC 2756 on p. 29)

There will be times when Jesus will give us what we seek. There are many examples in the Gospels of those whose prayers were heard: the cures of the leper, the Canaanite woman, the good thief, the centurion, the woman with a hemorrhage who touches his clothes, and the blind man at the pool of Siloe. His cures are in response to the faith of those who ask his assistance. When we pray, then, we should have confidence that Jesus will hear us and do what is best for us.

Our prayers will be answered when:

† We ask the Father in Jesus' Name;

† What we seek is good for our salvation;

† We pray with perseverance, humility, and confidence;

† We pray in the state of grace or to return to the state of grace.

St. Augustine wonderfully summarizes the three dimensions of Jesus' prayer: "He prays for us as our priest, prays in us as our Head, and is prayed to by us as our God. Therefore let us acknowledge our voice in him and his in us."[4] (CCC 2616)

THE CHURCH CALLS US TO PRAYER

Through her traditions, the Church calls us to prayer. First of all, on Sundays and holy days, we are called to participate in the highest form of prayer, the Eucharist, from which all the power and goodness of the Church flow. In addition, the Church calls us to morning and evening prayer, grace before and after meals, prayer in time of need, and the Liturgy of the Hours. For those who are able and wish to come closer to Christ, daily Mass is highly recommended. (See CCC 2720 on p. 29)

EXPRESSIONS OF PRAYER

The expression of individual prayer takes three forms:

† Vocal – simple conversation with God;

† Meditation – prayer of understanding;

† Contemplation – prayer of resting in God's presence.

Vocal prayer is the prayer that begins our relationship with Jesus. Through conversation, we share our joys and sorrows with him, which helps us grow in love and understanding of Jesus. We simply talk to Jesus, either aloud or in our minds, about the high and low points of each day. Jesus, our best friend, wants us to come to him and tell him of our needs and concerns. (See CCC 2721, 2722 on p. 29)

"Come to me, all who labor and are heavy laden, and I will give you rest" (Mt 11: 28).

The prayer of meditation is a higher form of prayer. It is, above all, a search in which we attempt to understand how to live a more Christian life, as well as come to a deeper understanding of why we should live this life. Meditation engages thought, imagination, emotion, and desire to consider specific concepts in relationship to Jesus such as love, grace, eternity, the Trinity, and Mary. Meditation, then, enables us to deepen and strengthen our faith in order that we might learn to follow God's will more easily and more readily. (See CCC 2724 on p. 29)

While the prayer of conversation is not planned out, but rather occurs spontaneously, the prayer of meditation requires planning and more discipline. It must be assisted by readings from the Gospels or spiritual writers to keep us on track. Meditative prayer focuses our minds to hear the voice of the Holy Spirit as we ponder God's will for us.

Contemplation has been compared to good friends or a husband and wife just being alone together in the joy of each other's presence. No words are necessary.

> Contemplative prayer seeks him "whom my soul loves."[5] It is Jesus, and in him, the Father. We seek him, because to desire him is always the beginning of love, and we seek him in that pure faith which causes us to be born of him and to live in him. In this inner prayer we can still meditate, but our attention is fixed on the Lord himself. (CCC 2709)

Contemplation is a prayer of sitting in God's presence to share love and know his love in return. It is the act of focusing one's entire heart and mind on the Lord. It is the intense prayer of a child of God who wishes to return love for love. It is a gift of God to those who have been steadfast and resolute in seeking to know God, at the deepest levels a human can understand him in this earthly life. God purifies the heart to seek only him. It unites us with the prayer of Christ to enable us to participate in the mystery of God and to accept whatever happens, good or evil, as a gift from God calling us ever closer to him.

FORMS OF PRAYER

The Holy Spirit recalls to us through the Church the things that Jesus said and did. His instruction has inspired the four basic forms of prayer. They are:

✝ Adoration – the prayer worshipping God for his greatness;

✝ Thanksgiving – the prayer of gratitude for all his gifts;

✝ Contrition – the prayer of sorrow for our sins and the sins of others;

✝ Petition – the prayer of requesting what we need for our salvation.

God deserves our adoration because of his eternal greatness. People whose lives are saved by another say, "I owe you my life." How much more do we owe to the God who wishes not only to save our lives but our souls also? He has called us into being for the sole purpose of loving us. Adoration is the prayer of honoring him who made the sun, moon, and stars. It is a prayer of worship to the only one who deserves worship.

Thanksgiving is the prayer of gratitude to him who has given us all we have and filled our lives with every good thing. It is a prayer of thanks to him who is always at our side urging us forward toward our heavenly reward. It is the prayer of the adopted child who realizes he can never repay God for all the gifts he has given.

Contemplation is a prayer of sitting in God's presence to share love and know his love in return.

Contrition is the prayer of sorrow for all the sins committed, which have shown disrespect for the love and goodness God has given to us. Think of it: one sin changed the whole history of mankind. How many sins have we committed? But does God turn away from us in return? No. He sends us his love and the grace to repent and go back to him. How great his love is for us!

Petition is the prayer of requesting the good things which God wishes to give us, and we have his assurance that we will receive only good things from him, though, as we have said, not always the good things that we ask for. "Ask, and it will be given you; seek and you will find; knock, and it will be opened to you" (Mt 7:7). Who else but God could give us such a prayer and the sure hope that it will be answered?

DIFFICULTIES IN PRAYER

Perseverance in prayer requires faith. It is an expression of our love. Some of us tend to talk to Jesus only when we want something, as if Jesus were a vending machine waiting for our requests. Others feel that prayer is just too much work and they give up easily. (See CCC 2753, 2754 on p. 30)

When we begin to pray, it is most important to have a set time for prayer. When there is no set time for prayer, we tend to put it off until later. This usually means praying less or not praying at all. Prayer should be done at the same time every day, preferably in the morning before the concerns of the day are upon us. If it is not possible to pray in a church, then a suitable location should be found, one which is quiet and free from exterior distractions such as noise or people coming and going.

If it is not possible to pray in a church, then a suitable location should be found, one which is quiet and free from exterior distractions.

Once a quiet place is found, many of the distractions that take our thoughts off prayer—outside noises, or other people wanting a piece of our time—are eliminated. The distractions we then must deal with are mental wanderings, which also remove our focus from prayer. When faced with these challenges, we should remind ourselves that nothing is more important to us than the Lord.

Another difficulty people encounter in prayer is dryness, a sense that our prayer is of no value or a waste of time. This is a difficulty that almost everyone faces at one time or another. In fact, one of the great mystics of the Church, St. John of the Cross, wrote a work called *The Dark Night*, in which he discusses the feeling of being abandoned by God. His work, however, does tell us that we must continue in faith to seek God, even when our prayers don't seem to do any good. (See CCC 2733 on p. 29)

When we have difficulties in prayer, we should rely on the Bible, the Liturgy of the Church, and the theological virtues as sources for our prayer. Tradition informs us that the Holy Spirit teaches us to pray and makes our prayer fruitful, and we must wait for his graces, which are given to us as we need and deserve them.

CONCLUSION

Eternity is the place of constant intimate prayer, an eternal conversation with the Trinity, the one God in three divine persons. Prayer in this life is the beginning of this eternal relationship and a preparation for our heavenly conversation. Jesus will help us to be aware of his love through our prayer life, but we must do our part in establishing a relationship with him. A regular prayer life will help us avoid mortal sin and reduce our tendency to commit venial sins. (See CCC 2745, 2757 on p. 30)

St. John Chrysostom said, "Nothing is equal to prayer; for what is impossible it makes possible, what is difficult, easy...For it is impossible, utterly impossible, for the man who prays eagerly and invokes God's name ceaselessly ever to sin."[6]

Those who offer their day and good works to prayer for others pray ceaselessly (Cf. 1 Thes 5:17).

SIMPLE PRAYERS

We know that if we are to grow closer to God, we must pray every day. But many people do not know how to start. For such people, many great prayers in the Catholic Church can be most helpful. If you do not know how to start praying, use one of the Church's traditional prayers.

One of these is the Rosary. For each section of this prayer, we meditate on one specific mystery from the life of Christ and his Church, while we say one Our Father, ten Hail Mary's, and one Glory Be. Generally, five of these mysteries are said at a time, and on specific days:

† The first group is the *Joyful Mysteries:* the Annunciation, the Visitation, the Nativity, the Presentation of the Infant Jesus in the Temple, and the Finding of the Child Jesus in the Temple.

† The second group is the *Luminous Mysteries:* the Baptism of Jesus, the Wedding at Cana, the Proclamation of the Kingdom, the Transfiguration, and the Institution of the Eucharist.

† The third group is the *Sorrowful Mysteries:* Jesus' Agony in the Garden, his Scourging at the Pillar, the Crowning of Thorns, the Carrying of the Cross, and the Crucifixion of Christ.

† The fourth and final group is the *Glorious Mysteries:* the Resurrection of Christ, his Ascension into Heaven, the Descent of the Holy Spirit at Pentecost, Mary's Assumption into Heaven, and her Crowning as Queen of Heaven and Earth.

Ask your teacher or priest where you can get a rosary, and have him explain the prayer more fully.

A prayer used as an offering of all our activity during the day could be said when we wake up. This is a sample:

O Jesus, through the Immaculate Heart of Mary, I offer you all my prayers, works, joys, and sufferings of this day for the intentions of your Sacred Heart, in union with the Holy Sacrifice of the Mass throughout the world, in reparation for my sins, for the intentions of our Holy Father, the pope, the intentions of all our associates, and the general intention recommended this month. Amen.

Rosary Prayers:

The Joyful,
The Luminous,
The Sorrowful,
and
The Glorious
Mysteries

Chapter 2 Study Guide

SUPPLEMENTARY READING

As a young girl, Teresa had difficulties balancing her love of God with her need for friends and fun. As a teenager, she was more interested in boys than religion. Teresa hated being sent to the convent by her father at the age of sixteen. Despite her inclinations to sin and desire for secular things, she eventually felt at home in the convent. Teresa's mind often strayed during prayer, but she persevered.

Eventually Teresa formed an order to help others overcome the temptations she had faced, the Discalced (literally "shoeless") Carmelites. Teresa taught her nuns that simple prayer was not enough, but that one must pray to God for the *ability to do good works.* She understood that a virtuous life was the fruit of a good interior life. Teresa was an ordinary woman who rose to greatness through prayer and her own efforts as a teacher and a writer.

Her most famous works are entitled *Interior Castle* and *The Way of Perfection.* Her stress on patience and the sufficiency of God's love make it easy to see why she is one of the first women to be declared a Doctor of the Church. "Be patient, let grace be the guide through the rooms of the soul's interior castle. Be brave and dare with a holy boldness." Again a poem found on her desk after her death reads: "Be not perplexed, be not afraid, everything passes, God does not change. Patience wins all things. He who has God lacks nothing; God alone suffices."

One day Teresa and some of her sisters were attempting to cross a storm-swollen stream in a small cart. Their donkey suddenly stopped,

St. Teresa of Ávila
(1515-1582)
Feast on October 15
Patroness of Headache Sufferers

the cart flipped, and Teresa ended up drenched to the skin and covered with mud. Looking into heaven, she said, "God, if this is the way you treat your friends, no wonder you have so few of them!" For St. Teresa of Ávila, God wasn't a remote distant entity but an everyday friend. St. Teresa knew that God can't be removed from the everyday occurrences of our lives. God isn't simply to be brought out on special occasions, but is to be a part of *every* aspect of our lives.

VOCABULARY

ADORATION
The acknowledgment of God as God, Creator, and Savior, the Lord and Master of everything that exists. The first commandment obliges us to adore God.

CONTEMPLATION
A form of prayer in which mind and heart focus on God's greatness and goodness in affective, loving adoration; to look on Jesus and the mysteries of his life with faith and love.

CONTRITION
Sorrow of the soul and hatred for the sin committed, together with a resolution not to sin again; necessary for the reception of the Sacrament of Penance.

DRYNESS (IN PRAYER)
Difficulty in contemplative prayer when the heart is separated from God, with no taste for thoughts, memories, and feelings, even spiritual ones.

LORD'S PRAYER
The title early Christians gave to the prayer which Jesus entrusted to his disciples and to the Church (Mt 6: 9-13). This fundamental Christian prayer is also called the Our Father, which are its first words.

MEDITATION
An exercise and a form of prayer in which we try to understand God's revelation of the truths of faith and the purpose of the Christian life, and how it should be lived, in order to adhere and respond to what the Lord is asking.

METANOIA
Greek word meaning "change of heart," "repentance," "penance." It is considered essential to the pursuit of Christian perfection.

PETITION
Form of prayer asking God to aid us or others.

PRAYER
The elevation of the mind and heart to God in praise of his glory; a petition made to God for some desired good, thanksgiving for a good received, or in intercession for others before God. Through prayer the Christian experiences a communion with God.

THANKSGIVING
Form of prayer praising God for the good he has given us.

VOCAL PRAYER
Form of prayer that is a "conversation" with God, or the angels and saints, that is formed with words of some set formula(s), i.e., Hail Mary, Glory Be, Our Father, etc.

STUDY QUESTIONS

1. Why is the Our Father called the "Lord's Prayer"?

2. What is perfect prayer?

3. Why is Jesus called the "perfect friend"?

4. Why is the desire for God written in the human heart?

5. How do we return God's love?

6. Why does God permit our prayers to appear fruitless?

7. What should we do if we feel God is calling us to religious life?

8. What is the basis of good relationships?

9. What is the key to successful prayer?

10. How did Jesus accept people?

11. What is the main difference between Christianity and non-Christian beliefs?

12. Earthly prayer is preparation for what type of prayer?

13. List the four conditions needed for our prayers to be answered.

14. What is the most important condition for beginning to pray?

15. What should be done when dryness in prayer occurs?

16. What are some modern idols that people worship?

PRACTICAL EXERCISES

1. Read the three parables on prayer from St. Luke that are mentioned earlier in the chapter. What is the message of each?

2. Look through the book of Psalms. Choose two Psalms that express your need for God's assistance, and explain why you chose them.

3. How has God loved you? Make a list of God's gifts to you.

4. Ask your spiritual director to explain the Teresian method of prayer.

FROM THE CATECHISM

2596 The Psalms constitute the masterwork of prayer in the Old Testament. They present two inseparable qualities: the personal, and the communal. They extend to all dimensions of history, recalling God's promises already fulfilled and looking for the coming of the Messiah.

2620 Jesus' filial prayer is the perfect model of prayer in the New Testament. Often done in solitude and in secret, the prayer of Jesus involves a loving adherence to the will of the Father even to the Cross and an absolute confidence in being heard.

2660 Prayer in the events of each day and each moment is one of the secrets of the kingdom revealed to "little children," to the servants of Christ, to the poor of the Beatitudes. It is right and good to pray so that the coming of the kingdom of justice and peace may influence the march of history, but it is just as important to bring the help of prayer into humble, everyday situations; all forms of prayer can be the leaven to which the Lord compares the kingdom.[7]

2720 The Church invites the faithful to regular prayer: daily prayers, the Liturgy of the Hours, Sunday Eucharist, the feasts of the liturgical year.

2721 The Christian tradition comprises three major expressions of the life of prayer: vocal prayer, meditation, and contemplative prayer. They have in common the recollection of the heart.

2722 Vocal prayer, founded on the union of the body and soul in human nature, associates the body with the interior prayer of the heart, following Christ's example of praying to his Father and teaching the Our Father to his disciples.

2723 Meditation is a prayerful quest engaging thought, imagination, emotion, and desire. Its goal is to make our own in faith the subject considered, by confronting it with the reality of our own life.

2724 Contemplative prayer is the simple expression of the mystery of prayer. It is a gaze of faith fixed on Jesus, an attentiveness to the Word of God, a silent love. It achieves real union with the prayer of Christ to the extent that it makes us share in his mystery.

2725 Prayer is both a gift of grace and a determined response on our part. It always presupposes effort. The great figures of prayer of the Old Covenant before Christ, as well as the Mother of God, the saints, and he himself, all teach us this: prayer is a battle. Against whom? Against ourselves and against the wiles of the tempter who does all he can to turn man away from prayer, away from union with God. We pray as we live, because we live as we pray. If we do not want to act habitually according to the Spirit of Christ, neither can we pray habitually in his name. The "spiritual battle" of the Christian's new life is inseparable from the battle of prayer.

2733 Another temptation, to which presumption opens the gate, is *acedia.* The spiritual writers understand this to be a form of depression due to lax ascetical practice, decreasing vigilance, carelessness of heart. "The spirit indeed is willing, but the flesh is weak" (Mt 26: 41).

2745 Prayer and *Christian life* are *inseparable,* for they concern the same love and the same renunciation, proceeding from love; the same filial and loving conformity with the Father's plan of love; the same transforming union in the Holy Spirit who conforms us more and

FROM THE CATECHISM CONTINUED

more to Christ Jesus; the same love for all men, the love with which Jesus has loved us. "Whatever you ask the Father in my name, he [will] give it to you. This I command you, to love one other" (Jn 15:16-17).

He "prays without ceasing" who unites prayer to works and good works to prayer. Only in this way can we consider as realizable the principle of praying without ceasing.[8]

2753 In the battle of prayer, we must confront erroneous conceptions of prayer, various currents of thought, and our own experience of failure. We must respond with humility, trust, and perseverance to these temptations which cast doubt on the usefulness or even the possibility of prayer.

2754 The principal difficulties in the practice of prayer are distraction and dryness. The remedy lies in faith, conversion, and vigilance of heart.

2756 Filial trust is put to the test when we feel our prayer is not always heard. The Gospel invites us to ask ourselves about the conformity of our prayer to the desire of the Spirit.

2757 "Pray constantly" (1 Thes 5:17). It is always possible to pray. It is even a vital necessity. Prayer and Christian life are inseparable.

Endnotes

1. *GS*, 19 § 1.
2. Cf. Mt 5: 23-24, 44-45; 6: 7, 14-15, 21, 25, 33.
3. *Friends of God: A Life of Prayer*, p. 219.
4. St. Augustine, *En. In Ps.* 85, 1: PL 37, 1081; cf. GILH 7.
5. Sg 1: 7; cf. 3: 1-4.
6. *De Anna* 4, 5: PG 54, 666.
7. Cf. Lk 13: 20-21.
8. Origen, *De orat.* 12: PG 11, 452C.

The Trinity

love: Father, Son, and Holy Spirit.

The Trinity

*C*ould you believe this? You are standing on a street corner when the most beautiful, wonderful person you have ever seen rushes up to you and says, "I love you. I want to be with you and share my life with you forever." Sounds far-fetched, doesn't it? Can't you just hear yourself saying, "Yeah, right"?

The fact of the matter is that this has already happened to you, and you probably have never given it much thought.

This is precisely what happened in Baptism. The Triune God, Father, Son, and Holy Spirit, rushed into you at Baptism in order to share the divine life and love with you forever. All that is asked in return is that you share your love by keeping the commandments. Does that sound too difficult?

This great, totally happy God has chosen you to be the object of his eternal love, and the only condition is that you return that love.

Will you say yes?

THE TRINITY

Our faith tells us that God is both our origin and our ultimate goal, so there is no reason to substitute anything for him or prefer anything to him. Since God is love, we should desire to be united with him as the object of his love. God, we know, loves each person completely. He loves every individual so much, in fact, that he wishes to be united to each one, so that all may share the life of the Trinity as completely as possible. Christians are monotheists, that is, they believe in one God, and yet they also profess belief in the Trinity, who is one God in three divine persons.

> The ultimate end of the whole divine economy is the entry of God's creatures into the perfect unity of the Blessed Trinity.[1] But even now we are called to be a dwelling for the Most Holy Trinity: "If a man loves me," says the Lord, "he will keep my word, and my Father will love him, and we will come to him, and make our home with him."[2] (CCC 260)

God has chosen to divinize man by sharing the life of his sanctifying grace. As long as a person is in the state of grace, the love of the Trinity is present to him and in him. Based on the moral life he leads, man chooses to demonstrate how great is his love for God.

> The mystery of the Most Holy Trinity is the central mystery of Christian faith and life. It is the mystery of God in himself. It is therefore the source of all the other mysteries of faith, the light that enlightens them. It is the most fundamental and essential teaching in the "hierarchy of the truths of faith" (GCD, 43). The whole history of salvation is identical with the history of the way and the means by which the one true God, Father, Son and Holy Spirit, reveals himself to men "and reconciles and unites with himself those who turn away from sin."[3] (CCC 234)

In the first centuries of the Church, the Church Fathers (bishops and writers who knew the apostles or those who knew them and could explain the apostles' teachings correctly) made a distinction between the theology of the Church and the economy of the Church. The theology of the Trinity refers to the life of God within the Trinity, while the economy refers to all the ways God reveals himself and communicates his life. The economy, then, is God's plan for the salvation of all people.

God is revealed in his works. We can come to understand part of the life of the Trinity by studying these works. God reveals himself in the beauty of his creation: the loveliness of flowers, clouds, stars at night, and the order of the universe. By recognizing the beauty of his creations, we see God's interior goodness.

While it is true that the goodness of God can be known from his actions, it must be recognized that his inner life, the Trinity, is a mystery of faith which can never be fully known or understood.

We know about God's inner life only because he chooses to reveal it to us. Although the Old Testament foreshadowed the revelation of the Trinity, ancient Israel remained unaware of this mystery, which was revealed explicitly by Jesus, the Messiah. Working with reason alone, we can know that God exists. Through reason alone, however, we will never be able to understand the Trinity. (See CCC 261 on p. 49)

God reveals himself in the beauty of his creation...

By recognizing the beauty... we see God's interior goodness.

The Trinity

The Trinity and the Shamrock

Legend has it that St. Patrick was responsible for ridding the Emerald Isle of snakes; but more importantly, it is said that Patrick used the shamrock as a symbol to explain the Trinity to unbelievers...

...St. Patrick would hold up a shamrock and challenge his hearers, "Is it one leaf or three?" "It is both one leaf and three," was their reply. "And so it is with God," he would conclude.

Christians pray and are baptized "in the name of the Father, the Son, and the Holy Spirit." In fact, the Trinity has been professed from the Church's beginning. As is indicated by the writings of the apostles, the Trinity was invoked in the Sacrament of Baptism and given expression in the preaching, teaching, catechesis, and prayer of the Church. The second letter of St. Paul to the Corinthians has given us the prayer, "The grace of the Lord Jesus Christ and the love of God and the fellowship of the Holy Spirit be with you all" (2 Cor 13:14). (See CCC 265 on p. 49)

To explain the Trinity, the Church took terms from Greek philosophy and raised them to a higher level of meaning.

> The Church uses (I) the term "substance" (rendered also at times by "essence" or "nature") to designate the being in its unity, (II) the term "person" or "hypostasis" to designate the Father, Son, and Holy Spirit in the real distinction among them, and (III) the term "relation" to designate the fact that their distinction lies in the relationship of each to the others. (CCC 252)

The Trinity is one God in three divine persons. The Father is God; the Son is God; and the Holy Spirit is God. There is one God, not three gods. The three persons share the oneness of God and each person is God whole and entire. Each person shares in the divine substance, yet each is distinct from the others. Each shows forth the actions proper to him. Though the work of creation is attributed to the Father, the work of our salvation is a work of the whole Trinity. God's plan is made before time and unfolds in the work of history after the fall of Adam and Eve. Each person of the Trinity performs the work of salvation according to his unique personal role.

There is no opposition in their relationships, and each is wholly in the other. (See CCC 267 on p. 49)

> "O blessed light, O Trinity and first Unity!" (*LH*, Hymn for Evening Prayer) God is eternal blessedness, undying life, unfading light. God is love: Father, Son and Holy Spirit. God freely wills to communicate the glory of his blessed life. Such is the "plan of his loving kindness," conceived by the Father before the foundation of the world, in his beloved Son: "He destined us in love to be his sons" and "to be conformed to the image of his Son," through "the spirit of sonship" (Eph 1:4-5, 9; Rom 8:15, 29). This plan is a "grace [which] was given to us in Christ Jesus before the ages began," stemming immediately from Trinitarian love.[4] It unfolds in the work of creation, the whole history of salvation after the fall, and the missions of the Son and the Spirit, which are continued in the mission of the Church.[5] (CCC 257)

Following the New Testament, the Church states that there is "one God and Father through whom all things are, and one Lord Jesus Christ, from whom all things are, and one Holy Spirit in whom all things are."[6] Thus, the whole Christian life is a communion with the entire Trinity, who give us grace without in any way being separated from each other.

> Being a work at once common and personal, the whole divine economy makes known both what is proper to the divine persons and their one divine nature. Hence the whole Christian life is a communion with each of the divine persons without in any way separating them. Everyone

who glorifies the Father does so through the Son in the Holy Spirit; everyone who follows Christ does so because the Father draws him and the Spirit moves him.[7] (CCC 259)

The whole purpose of God's plan is the entry of his creatures into the perfect unity of the most blessed Trinity. Man responds to the call of the Trinity by keeping the word God has given him. Each day should begin with a prayer to the Trinity asking it to guide us on our way to heaven.

The Trinity:

† Loves all mankind;

† Communicates its blessed life;

† Helps us to conform to the image of Jesus;

† Created everything;

† Is responsible for the works of the Son and the Holy Spirit;

† Brings the saved person into the perfect unity of the Trinity.

GOD THE FATHER

Israel often called God "Father," because he created the world. The Old Testament referred to God as Father in the books of Deuteronomy, Samuel, and the Psalms.

> By calling God "Father," the language of faith indicates two main things: that God is the first origin of everything and transcendent authority; and that he is at the same time goodness and loving care for all his children. God's parental tenderness can also be expressed by the image of motherhood,[8] which emphasizes God's immanence, the intimacy between Creator and creature. The language of faith thus draws on the human experience of parents, who are in a way the first representatives of God for man. But this experience also tells us that human parents are fallible and can disfigure the face of fatherhood and motherhood. We ought therefore to recall that God transcends the human distinction between the sexes. He is neither man nor woman: he is God. He also transcends human fatherhood and motherhood, although he is their origin and standard:[9] no one is father as God is Father. (CCC 239)

God, the Father, is the cause of all that has come into existence freely, directly, and without any assistance. His Fatherhood is eternal in his relationship to the Son, who is the Son in relation to the Father.

In the beginning of time, Jesus was present to the Father; he is called the Word in the Gospel of John and other apostolic writings. "No one knows the Son except the Father, and no one knows the Father except the Son and anyone to whom the Son chooses to reveal him" (cf. Mt 11:27). It is through Jesus' teachings that we have come to know the Father and the Spirit.

The first ecumenical council at Nicaea, in A.D. 325, declared that the Son is "consubstantial" (of the exact same nature) with the Father, and this formulation was made a part of the Nicene Creed. (See CCC 262 on p. 49)

He is neither man nor woman: he is God.

No one is father as God is Father.

Christ expresses humanly the divine ways of the Trinity.

God as the Father of all creation is a concept beyond the total understanding of man. Each person has been called into existence by the Father's creative love at a particular moment in history and is given all the graces necessary to accomplish specific tasks, in relation to his personal salvation and the salvation of others. Through prayer and spiritual direction, the Father will guide each person to his eternal life in and with the Trinity.

The Father:

† Created everything;

† Sent the Son into the world;

† Chose the Jews to be his people;

† Is consubstantial with the Son and the Spirit;

† Honors those who serve the Son;

† Speaks through Jesus;

† Is the author, with the other two persons of the Trinity, of Revelation in the Bible.

GOD THE SON

Jesus Christ is God Made Man

The chief teaching of the Catholic Church about Jesus Christ is that he is *God made man.* Jesus Christ is the second person of the Blessed Trinity. He assumed a human nature and took on flesh in order to reconcile man with God—for offenses against God can only be corrected by God. Belief in the Incarnation of the Son of God is a distinctive sign of the Christian faith.

The name Jesus means "God saves." Jesus Christ is God the Son who became man to save us. God the Son became man to make reparation for our sins to our heavenly Father; to merit for us the divine life of sanctifying grace and the right to heaven; and to be our way to heaven by his example and doctrine. Because he made reparation for our sins, our Lord Jesus Christ is the Savior and Redeemer of all men.

> "The wonderful works of God among the people of the Old Testament were but a prelude to the work of Christ the Lord in redeeming mankind and giving perfect glory to God. He accomplished this work principally by the Paschal mystery of his blessed Passion, Resurrection from the dead, and glorious Ascension, whereby 'dying he destroyed our death, rising he restored our life.' For it was from the side of Christ as he slept the sleep of death upon the cross that there came forth 'the wondrous sacrament of the whole Church.'"[10] (CCC 1067)

Divine and Human Natures in One Person

Jesus Christ has two distinct natures, human and divine. He is true God and true man. Jesus Christ is God because he is the Son of God, the second person of the Blessed Trinity: He has the same divine nature as his Father. As God, Jesus Christ has always existed. Jesus Christ is man because he is the Son of the Blessed Virgin Mary and has a body and soul like ours. As man, he began to exist from the moment of the Incarnation.

This union of two natures in one person is called the *hypostatic union,* that is, a union in the person. He became a man while remaining truly God. Through the power of the Holy Spirit, God the Son—the Second Person of the Blessed Trinity—took a human body and soul in the womb of the Blessed Virgin Mary. This mystery is called the Incarnation. It took place at the moment when the Blessed Virgin Mary agreed to become the mother of Jesus. These two natures don't split him 50% and 50%; he is 100% man and 100% God. Some people may argue that Christ cannot be 100% of two different things, but that is not true. A person can be 100% Hispanic and 100% male; one doesn't make the other impossible. Christ is wholly God and wholly man.

> The unique and altogether singular event of the Incarnation of the Son of God does not mean that Jesus Christ is part God and part man, nor does it imply that he is the result of a confused mixture of the divine and the human. He became truly man while remaining truly God. Jesus Christ is true God and true man. (CCC 464)

Christian philosophy helps us to express and understand a little the mystery of the Incarnation. This and other mysteries of our Faith are expressed with ideas of "nature" and "person." "Nature" means "what makes anything or anyone to be what it is, and to act according to what it is." It answers the questions: "What is this? What is this that is acting?"

"Person" means "what makes someone who is endowed with intelligence and free will, to be a subsistent individual—different from others of the same nature—and responsible for his own actions." It answers the questions: "Who is this? Who is this that is acting?" The early Church councils defined these truths about Christ, which Christ himself gave to his Church, and instructed believers to reject false teachings.

Jesus had both a human intellect and will and a divine intellect and will. In Christ, the human intellect and will were directed by the divine intellect and will, as in us, our intellect and will should follow God's. Christ, then, was not only incapable of sinning but also totally holy and the source of all holiness. As man, he knew God from the beginning of his humanity and exercised the divine power through his divinity.

> Because "human nature was assumed, not absorbed" (*GS,* 22 § 2), in the mysterious union of the Incarnation, the Church was led over the course of centuries to confess the full reality of Christ's human soul, with its operations of intellect and will, and of his human body. In parallel fashion, she had to recall on each occasion that Christ's human nature belongs, as his own, to the divine person of the Son of God, who assumed it. Everything that Christ is and does in this nature derives from "one of the Trinity." The Son of God therefore communicates to his humanity his own personal mode of existence in the Trinity. In his soul as in his body, Christ thus expresses humanly the divine ways of the Trinity:[11]
>
> > The Son of God...worked with human hands; he thought with a human mind. He acted with a human will, and with a human heart he loved. Born of the Virgin Mary, he has truly been made one of us, like to us in all things except sin.[12] (CCC 470)

The Trinity

"And he was transfigured before them, and his face shone like the sun, and his garments became white as light." (Mt 17:2)

"...when lo, a bright cloud overshadowed them, and a voice from the cloud said, 'This is my beloved Son, with whom I am well pleased; listen to him.'" (Mt 17:5)

And Jesus advanced in wisdom, and age, and grace with God and man.

Jesus' Early Years

As it was prophesied, Jesus was born in Bethlehem, the city of David. The feast of the birth of Jesus is Christmas Day, December 25. It is sometimes called the Feast of the Nativity, because the nativity or birth of Jesus is celebrated on this day.

After his birth, Jesus fled to Egypt with his mother and St. Joseph. They lived there until the death of King Herod and then returned to the Holy Land.

After the finding in the Temple, all we directly read from Holy Scripture are two statements: "And he went down with them, and came to Nazareth, and was subject to them...And Jesus advanced in wisdom, and age, and grace with God and men." (Lk 2:51-52) In these two sentences is contained the history of eighteen years of the life of Jesus Christ, the God-Man.

> During the greater part of his life Jesus shared the condition of the vast majority of human beings: a daily life spent without evident greatness, a life of manual labor. His religious life was that of a Jew obedient to the law of God,[13] a life in the community. From this whole period it is revealed to us that Jesus was "obedient" to his parents and that he "increased in wisdom and in stature, and in favor with God and man."[14] (CCC 531)

Lessons from Jesus' Hidden Life

As much as his words, the actions of Jesus Christ are intended to provide instruction and to serve as our example. He himself said, "I have given you an example, that as I have done to you, so you do also" (Jn 13:15). The hidden life of Jesus is for us the perfect model of humility, obedience and industriousness. He has shared the life of ordinary people.

By his hidden life, Jesus Christ teaches us to learn holiness and wisdom before we presume to teach others. By living in obscurity, he teaches us to fight against our vanity, which makes us desire to do only what seems great and important, which makes us desire to be praised and noticed.

Our Lord teaches us to subdue our pride, to live day after day without impatience or complaint, unknown to the world, and even despised, if that is the will of God. We shall then have true peace of heart. Jesus said, "Learn of me, because I am meek and humble of heart." (Mt 11:29) His meekness and humility are best shown by his long years of obscurity in Nazareth.

The hidden life of Jesus Christ is for us the perfect model of obedience: "And he was subject to them." The God of all created things, almighty and infinite, was subject to two poor and unknown human beings—Joseph and Mary of Nazareth. In all things, he obeyed them promptly, constantly, cheerfully, and with great love.

> Jesus' obedience to his mother and legal father fulfills the fourth commandment perfectly and was the temporal image of his filial obedience to his Father in heaven. The everyday obedience of Jesus to Joseph and Mary both announced and anticipated the obedience of Holy Thursday: "Not my will..." (Lk 22:42). The obedience of Christ in the daily routine of his hidden life was already inaugurating his work of restoring what the disobedience of Adam had destroyed.[15] (CCC 532)

Jesus' Public Ministry

After spending many years in obscurity and humble toil, Jesus Christ began to go about and teach publicly. Leaving his home in Nazareth, he began his public life by an act of great humility: he went to be baptized by St. John the Baptist in the river Jordan.

> The baptism of Jesus is on his part the acceptance and inauguration of his mission as God's suffering Servant. He allows himself to be numbered among sinners; he is already "the Lamb of God, who takes away the sin of the world."[16] Already he is anticipating the "baptism" of his bloody death.[17] Already he is coming to "fulfill all righteousness," that is, he is submitting himself entirely to his Father's will: out of love he consents to this baptism of death for the remission of our sins.[18] The Father's voice responds to the Son's acceptance, proclaiming his entire delight in his Son.[19] The Spirit whom Jesus possessed in fullness from his conception comes to "rest on him."[20] Jesus will be the source of the Spirit for all mankind. At his baptism "the heavens were opened" (Mt 3:16)—the heavens that Adam's sin had closed—and the waters were sanctified by the descent of Jesus and the Spirit, a prelude to the new creation. (CCC 536)

After his baptism, Jesus went into the desert. There he fasted for forty days and forty nights. He wanted to teach us to look upon baptism as a call to penance, and to prepare for all kinds of activity by mortification and prayer. After our Lord's long fast, the devil was permitted to tempt him. Jesus rebuked the devil, and angels came to minister to him.

Upon his return from his forty-day fast in the desert, Jesus called his first disciples. A few days later he performed his first miracle. He changed water into wine at a marriage feast in Cana.

During the *first stage* of his public life, Jesus drove sellers out of the Temple, saying they made it a "den of thieves;" he cured many people, such as the ruler's son, Peter's mother-in-law, the paralytic at the pool, and the daughter of Jairus.

Jesus began the *second stage* of his public life by an act of utmost significance. He chose from the many disciples who followed him "the Twelve" who became his apostles. In the Sermon on the Mount he introduced the basis of his teachings: the law of love. Jesus also performed many miracles. He cured the centurion's servant. He brought back to life the widow's son at Naim. He multiplied bread and fish. He walked on the water and bade Peter walk on it, too. He forgave Mary Magdalene and sent the apostles on their mission. He began teaching in the form of parables, connecting what he wanted to teach with common everyday things: the sower, the mustard seed, and the pearl of great price.

In his *third stage* of teaching, Jesus went to Galilee and Phoenicia. He moved on because in Judea, the envious Pharisees sought to kill him. In Phoenicia, he granted the requests of a Gentile, a Canaanite woman, who persevered in asking him to cure her daughter. In Galilee, Jesus cured a deaf and dumb man, using signs that the Church has adopted in the baptismal ceremonies. He performed the miracle of the second multiplication of the loaves. On Mount Tabor, he was transfigured in the presence of Peter, James, and John. Among other cures he did were those of the ten lepers and of the man born blind. He promised the

At his baptism, "the heavens were opened"—the heavens that Adam's sin had closed.

primacy over all to Peter, forgave the woman caught in adultery, sent out his seventy-two disciples on a mission, and instructed Mary and Martha. He told the parables of the unmerciful servant, the Good Samaritan, the lost sheep, the lost coin, the great supper, the prodigal son, the rich man and Lazarus, the Pharisee and the publican, and the laborers in the vineyard.

Jesus' Final Days

Finally, toward the end of his public life, Jesus raised Lazarus from the dead. By this time the envy of the Pharisees was so great that they were determined to put Jesus to death. Judas came as a ready tool.

In triumph, Jesus entered Jerusalem riding on a donkey with children singing and waving palms. He told the parable of the vine-dressers and the heir, to show the Pharisees that he knew of their designs against him. Finally, he ate the Last Supper with his apostles, and instituted the sacraments of Holy Orders and the Holy Eucharist.

> The Eucharist that Christ institutes at that moment will be the memorial of his sacrifice.[21] Jesus includes the apostles in his own offering and bids them perpetuate it.[22] By doing so, the Lord institutes his apostles as priests of the New Covenant: "For their sakes I sanctify myself, so that they also may be sanctified in truth."[23] (CCC 611)

Jesus' Passion, Death, and Resurrection is Our Redemption

By his passion and Resurrection, then, Jesus Christ redeemed all mankind. He offered himself to his heavenly Father, to obtain forgiveness for the sins of men, to regain for us the heavenly life we lost by sin and to merit all the graces for reaching heaven.

Briefly, Redemption means, "Christ died for our sins." His loving obedience to his Father, even to the extreme point of dying on the cross, redeemed us. The disobedience of Adam, and of all others who have listened to the devil and sinned, had offended the Father deeply, because he loves us. But Christ's act of love, dying on the cross, was more pleasing to the Father than our sins were displeasing to him.

> "For as by one man's disobedience many were made sinners, so by one man's obedience many will be made righteous" (Rom 5:19). By his obedience unto death, Jesus accomplished the substitution of the suffering Servant, who "makes himself an *offering for sin*," when "he bore the sin of many," and who "shall make many to be accounted righteous," for "he shall bear their iniquities" (Is 53:10-12). Jesus atoned for our faults and made satisfaction for our sins to the Father.[24] (CCC 615)

The *great love of God* for man is the first thing we learn from Christ's sufferings and death. The *great evil of sin* is the second thing we learn. We cannot see the harm sin does to our soul. Studying the crucifix will help us to realize the evil of sin that brought suffering and death to Jesus Christ, our Lord.

> The cross is the unique sacrifice of Christ, the "one mediator between God and men" (1 Tm 2:5). But because in his incarnate divine person he has in some way united himself to every man, "the possibility of being made partners, in a way known to God, in the paschal mystery" is

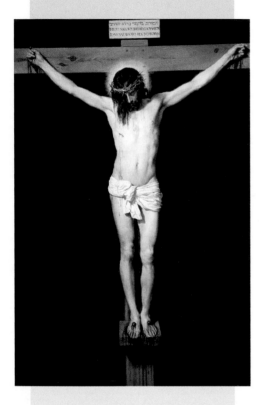

Studying the crucifix will help us realize the evil of sin.

offered to all men.[25] He calls his disciples to "take up [their] cross and follow [him]" (Mt 16: 24), for "Christ also suffered for [us], leaving [us] an example so that [we] should follow in his steps" (1 Pt 2: 21). In fact Jesus desires to associate with his redeeming sacrifice those who were to be its first beneficiaries.[26] This is achieved supremely in the case of his mother, who was associated more intimately than any other person in the mystery of his redemptive suffering.[27]

> Apart from the cross there is no other ladder by which we may get to heaven.[28] (CCC 618)

After Christ had died, one of the soldiers thrust a spear into the side of our Lord. Out of the wound a stream of blood and water gushed forth. His body and soul were separated, but his divinity remained united to both body and soul. Christ's lifeless body was taken down from the cross and buried in a tomb.

The soul of Christ "descended into hell"—that is, into the place where the souls of the just who had died before him were waiting for him. The hell into which Christ's soul descended was not the hell of the damned—it was a place or state of rest. Christ's soul went there to announce to the just the joyful news of their redemption. Meanwhile, the most holy body of Jesus Christ remained three days—but not three whole days—in the tomb: a part of Friday, the whole day of Saturday, and part of Sunday until dawn when he gloriously and triumphantly rose from the dead, never again to die. Christ reunited his soul with his body.

> Scripture calls the abode of the dead, to which the dead Christ went down, "hell"—*Sheol* in Hebrew or *Hades* in Greek—because those who are there are deprived of the vision of God.[29] Such is the case for all the dead, whether evil or righteous, while they await the Redeemer: which does not mean that their lot is identical, as Jesus shows through the parable of the poor man Lazarus who was received into "Abraham's bosom":[30] "It is precisely these holy souls, who awaited their Saviour in Abraham's bosom, whom Christ the Lord delivered when he descended into hell." (*Roman Catechism*, I, 6, 3.) Jesus did not descend into hell to deliver the damned, nor to destroy the hell of damnation, but to free the just who had gone before him.[31] (CCC 633)

Jesus said that he would rise from the dead on the third day after his death. Therefore, as he did rise from the dead, there is no doubt that he is the Son of God. The Resurrection was the greatest miracle that Christ performed, because it *proved without doubt* that he is really the Son of God. On the day of his resurrection, Jesus appeared to St. Peter, to Mary Magdalene, to the holy women, and to two disciples going to Emmaus. In the evening he appeared to the assembled apostles. In order to prove to his apostles that it was really he and not his spirit alone, Jesus asked them to touch him. He even ate with them. Later, he also appeared to more than five hundred other people (cf. 1 Cor 15: 6).

> "If Christ has not been raised, then our preaching is in vain and your faith is in vain" (1 Cor 15: 14). The Resurrection above all constitutes the confirmation of all Christ's works and teachings. All truths, even those most inaccessible to human reason, find their justification if Christ by his Resurrection has given the definitive proof of his divine authority, which he had promised. (CCC 651)

The Resurrection was the greatest miracle that Christ performed, because it proved without doubt that he is really the Son of God.

Forty days after his Resurrection, in the presence of his apostles, Christ ascended, body and soul, into heaven. In heaven, Christ prays for us as our High Priest and Mediator. He prepares a place for us at the heavenly banquet. The feast of the Ascension of Christ into heaven is celebrated on the sixth Thursday after Easter or the following Sunday, while the feast of Christ the King is celebrated on the last Sunday of the liturgical year before the Advent season.

Jesus:

† Is the second person of the Blessed Trinity, the Son;

† Is true God and true man;

† Was conceived by the Holy Spirit, born of the Virgin Mary;

† Came to show us how to be holy;

† Came to show us God's love;

† Saved us from our sins by his life, death, and resurrection;

† Came to make us partakers of divine nature;

† Is the mystery celebrated and proclaimed in the liturgy;

† Is he who sent the Paraclete.

GOD THE HOLY SPIRIT

Before his Passover, Jesus told the apostles he would send them a Paraclete (advocate). The Paraclete is the Holy Spirit, the third divine person with Jesus and the Father. The Holy Spirit was active in the Old Testament, speaking through the prophets. Now, the Spirit has been sent by the Father and Jesus to guide the Church until the end of time.

The Latin tradition of the creed confesses that the Spirit "proceeds from the Father and the Son." The Council of Florence, in 1438, explained: "The Holy Spirit is eternally from the Father and the Son, and he has his nature and subsistence at once from the Father and the Son, and he proceeds eternally from both."

As we have seen, there are parts of faith that we can come to understand through reason (such as the existence of God), and there are parts that can never be realized through reason alone (such as the existence of the Trinity). Knowledge of the faith is only possible through the Holy Spirit, which moves us to follow Christ. Even an adult's choice to be baptized arises from the action of the Spirit. In the Sacrament of Baptism, the Spirit communicates the life of grace that originates in the Father and is offered to us by Jesus in all of sacramental life. When we feel that we might be losing our faith, we should call upon the Holy Spirit to come to our assistance.

> Through his grace, the Holy Spirit is the first to awaken faith in us and to communicate to us the new life, which is to "know the Father and the one whom he has sent, Jesus Christ" (Jn 17:3). But the Spirit is the last of the persons of the Holy Trinity to be revealed. (CCC 684)

We can clearly see the Father in the Old Testament. The Son's presence is not clear, but it is hinted at. In the New Testament, the Son is revealed.

...the Spirit has been sent by the Father and Jesus to guide the Church until the end of time.

The Son then gives us a glimpse of the Holy Spirit. The Spirit now dwells among us and gives us a better understanding of who he is.

To believe in the Holy Spirit is to profess that he is God, a member of the Holy Trinity, and consubstantial with the Father and the Son. He is at work from the beginning of creation with the Father and the Son, to complete the plan of the Father for our salvation.

Through his incarnation, Jesus reveals the Spirit as a person who is given, recognized, and welcomed. The Spirit does not speak of himself but speaks through the Scriptures, which he inspired.

We know the Spirit through the Church. He:

† Is worshipped and glorified with the Father and the Son;

† Proceeds from the Father and the Son;

† Is in the Scriptures he inspired;

† Is in the Tradition handed on and witnessed to by the Fathers;

† Is in the Magisterium, the Church's teaching;

† Puts us in touch with Jesus through the words and symbols of the sacramental liturgy;

† Is in prayer, where he intercedes for us;

† Is in charisms and ministries, which build up the Church;

† Is in the signs of apostolic ministry and life;

† Is in the witness of the holy saints, through whom he shows forth his holiness and continues the work of salvation.

THE TRINITY IN HISTORY

Since her beginning, the Church recognized the Trinity: three persons in one God. In the early days of Christianity, however, some heretics in the Church taught falsely about the nature of God and the Trinity. In the Church's history, both lay people and clerics have fallen into these heresies. The fact that the doctrine of the Trinity has finally been accepted is proof that the Lord wants us to recognize him as three persons in one God—for only with the help of the Lord could this truth be recognized.

One of the main heresies against the Trinity was Arianism. Started by a priest named Arius, this false belief held that Jesus was not really God; instead, he was just a human, whom God recognized as so holy that he was given a special mission and special powers and graces. Arianism held that in essence, Christ was not a divine person from all eternity.

Many bishops in the early church worked tirelessly against this false teaching, some suffering much along the way. Three bishops in particular helped the Church defend belief in the three Divine Persons.

St. Gregory of Nyssa had to contend with Arianism in his diocese. He was so disliked by the Arians that they falsely accused him of crimes for which Gregory was imprisoned. He escaped but was deposed from his

Heretics in the Church taught falsely about the nature of God and the Trinity.

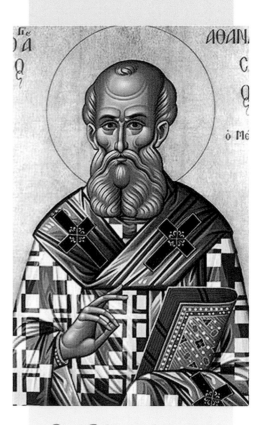

St. Athanasius was one of the most persecuted defenders of the Trinity.

Father, Son, and Holy Spirit, all three persons of the Trinity, love us beyond our understanding.

position. Later, he was restored by the Emperor Gratian, and eventually he was named Bishop of Sebaste, where he continued fighting the Arian heresy until his death.

St. Gregory Nazianzus the Younger had to fight heresy in both his own church and his own family. Gregory served as assistant Bishop of Nazianzus under his father. At that time, Arianism had taken root in Nazianzus. Even Gregory's father fell in with a heretical sect, which troubled his son greatly; however, Gregory brought his father back to the Church. Later, Gregory suffered a breakdown owing to overwork. After recovering, he wrote tirelessly against Arianism and gave famous homilies on the true nature of the Trinity. Eventually, Gregory was forced out of his office by Arians, and he died a few years later.

Undoubtedly, one of the most persecuted defenders of the Trinity was St. Athanasius of Alexandria, another bishop who fought against Arianism. In 330, the Roman emperor ordered Athanasius to allow Arian heretics to receive communion. Athanasius refused this order, even though it came from the most powerful man in the world. He then was accused of crimes he didn't commit, but he was found innocent. Next, he was accused of killing another bishop, who was actually still alive and in hiding. Over the next 26 years, Athanasius was exiled from Alexandria and reinstated again and again. He was forced to live as a hermit for six years, and his congregation was attacked. All these persecutions occurred because of his fight against Arianism.

These are just a few short stories of those who fought against one of the many heresies against the Blessed Trinity. That so many dedicated and long-suffering people rose up to defend the doctrine of the Triune God can be seen as proof in the existence of the Trinity.

Prayer

O my God, Trinity whom I adore, help me forget myself so entirely as to establish myself in you, unmovable and peaceful as if my soul were already in eternity. May nothing be able to trouble my peace or make me leave you, O my unchanging God, but may each minute bring me more deeply into your mystery. Grant my soul peace. Make it your Heaven, your beloved dwelling and place of rest. May I never abandon you there, but may I be there, whole and entire, completely vigilant in my faith, entirely adoring, and wholly given over to your creative action.
(Blessed Elizabeth of the Trinity)

CONCLUSION

Some people think that it's impossible for someone who feels completely unloved to remain alive. There are, in fact, times when some people truly believe they are unloved.

God made us for love and loves us infinitely, so that we can always know that we are loved. Father, Son, and Holy Spirit, all three persons of the Trinity, love us beyond our understanding. Their great love is discovered in regular prayer, which can enable every person to know that he is truly loved all the days of his life. Life may crush a person; friends may desert him; but the fire of God's love is always present to us to remind us that God awaits our response of love. No one is so bad, so ugly, so worthless, so forgotten, or so lost that the love of the Trinity cannot find him.

As the Bible says, "Taste and see that the Lord is good" (Ps 34:8). Resolve today to seek out the love of the Trinity in prayer and the sacraments.

God created the world to show forth and communicate his glory. By his divine plan, we have been given the opportunity to share in his truth, goodness, and beauty. By cooperating with God's plan for us, we will share in his eternal glory. Divine love is given to us to enable human love to be perfected through our relationship to the one true God: Father, Son, and Holy Spirit. (See CCC 266 on p. 49)

God made us for love and loves us infinitely.

By cooperating with God's plan for us, we will share in his eternal glory.

SUPPLEMENTARY READING

The 20th century has seen a man who was like Christ in many respects. He wasn't anything special at first, just a silly little kid. Initially, Maximilian (Max) wanted to send rockets to the moon, but a vision of Mary so touched him that he went on to become a priest and founded the Militia of the Immaculate Conception *(Militia Immaculata).* He began a Polish publication called *Knights of the Immaculata,* which soon had over 1 million subscribers. Despite tuberculosis, Fr. Max wanted to convert the entire world. He started a printing press in Japan to match the one he had started with in Poland.

Not only did Fr. Max understand the need for personal sanctity before apostolate, he understood how to use technology to spread the word and how to overcome the anti-religious movements. "Above all we must discern what is good in them and what is bad, because there is no more effective way to fight and overcome an evil trend than by recognizing the good it contains and applying it immediately to our cause."

He always taught a total consecration to Mary with a complete gift of love flowing from it: "My little children, love the Immaculata, love the Immaculata, love the Immaculata. She will make you happy. Trust her, turn yourselves over to her completely, without setting limits." He fully understood Mary's role as the Mediatrix of All Grace, with a mediation that is subordinated to Christ's. He never separated Jesus from Mary.

When the Nazis invaded Poland, it was not long before they took Fr. Max. He was sent to Auschwitz where he became prisoner 16670. One day a Nazi commandant randomly chose ten men to die. When the ninth man was selected, he began to cry for the loss of his family. Suddenly a small slight figure detached itself from the ranks and walked to the SS men. He said, "I would like to take that man's place." The commander asked: "Who are you?" "A Catholic priest," prisoner

St. Maximilian Kolbe
(1894-1941)
Feast on August 14
Patron of the Twentieth Century
and the Family

16670 replied. The commander nodded, and Franciszek Gajowniczek was spared. He later witnessed the canonization of Fr. Max.

Once in the underground cell, Fr. Max kept up the spirits of the other prisoners as they sang hymns to Mary. After more than ten days, only four of the prisoners remained alive and only Fr. Max remained conscious. Finally, the jailers injected him with carbolic acid so the bunker could be used for a new group of prisoners. Fr. Max's prayers to "be reduced to dust in the service of the Immaculata" came true as his body was thrown into the crematorium to be burned.

Fr. Max understood the need to combine a deep prayer life with an intense active life. Indeed, Fr. Max was very much like Christ in his devotion to the Blessed Mother, his dedication to prayer, his apostolic zeal, his absolute reliance on divine providence, and his willingness to sacrifice his life for another.

VOCABULARY

CATECHESIS
An education of children, young people, and adults in the faith of the Church through the teaching of Christian doctrine in an organic and systematic way to make them disciples of Jesus Christ.

CHARISM
A specific gift or grace of the Holy Spirit which directly or indirectly benefits the Church, given in order to help a person live out the Christian life, or to serve the common good in building up the Church.

CHURCH FATHERS
Church teachers and writers of the early centuries whose teachings are a witness to the Tradition of the Church.

CONSUBSTANTIAL
Belief that the three persons of the Blessed Trinity—while distinct—are of one and the same substance. The Father, Son and Holy Spirit possess exactly the same nature.

DIVINE
Of, or pertaining to, God.

ECONOMY
God's activity in creating and governing the world, particularly with regard to his plan for the salvation of the world in the person and work of Jesus Christ, a plan which is being accomplished through his Body the Church, in its life and sacraments.

INCARNATION
The fact that the Son of God assumed human nature and became man in order to accomplish our salvation in that same human nature. Jesus Christ, the Son of God, the second Person of the Trinity, is both true God and true man, not part God and part man.

INSPIRATION
The gift of the Holy Spirit which assisted a human author to write a biblical book so that it has God as its author and teaches faithfully, without error, the saving truth that God has willed to be consigned to us.

MONOTHEIST
A person believing that there is only one God, who is the Creator of the universe.

MYSTERY
A divinely revealed truth whose very possibility cannot be rationally conceived before it is revealed and, after revelation, whose inner essence cannot be fully understood by the finite mind.

NATURE
Essence of a being considered as the principle of activity. The substance of a thing as distinguished from its properties.

PARACLETE
A name for the Holy Spirit, meaning "advocate."

PERSON
An individual substance of a rational nature. Complete in itself, uncommunicable, and possessing responsibilities and rights as well as the essential elements of distinctiveness, uniqueness, intelligence, and will.

SPIRIT
That which is positively immaterial, having no dependence on matter for its existence or activities. God is uncreated pure spirit; angels are created pure spirit; human souls are created spirits. Spirits have the power to know and to love.

THEOLOGY
The study of God, based on divine revelation.

TRINITY
The mystery of one God in three Persons: Father, Son, and Holy Spirit.

STUDY QUESTIONS

1. What is the Trinity?

2. Who makes up the Trinity?

3. How long has the doctrine of the Trinity been taught?

4. Is the Father directly known in the Old Testament?

5. Can a person know God exists using reason alone?

6. Why did the Trinity create us?

7. What is important to know about the Father?

8. What is important to know about the Son?

9. What is important to know about the Holy Spirit?

10. Is Jesus Christ completely God, completely man, or both? Explain your answer.

11. Why did Jesus assume a human nature?

12. What did Jesus promise to send the apostles before his Passover? What did this turn out to be?

13. What is the first sacrament in which a person receives grace?

14. From whom does the Holy Spirit proceed?

15. What did the Holy Spirit do in the Old Testament?

16. What does the Holy Spirit do now?

17. What are five of the works of the Holy Spirit?

PRACTICAL EXERCISES

1. People have tried to explain the doctrine of the Trinity by comparison. One famous analogy is that the Trinity is like a tree: the Father is the roots, the Son is the branches, and the Holy Spirit is the fruit. Come up with your own analogy for the Trinity.

2. Although analogies can be made, the Trinity can never be fully explained or understood. Does this mean it is not true? Why or why not? What is a mystery of faith?

3. Explain why the Father is called the Father, the Son is called the Son, and the Holy Spirit is called the Holy Spirit.

4. The mystery of the Trinity is the most important truth in Christianity. Why? Think about what we are learning and how important God should be to us.

FROM THE CATECHISM

261 The mystery of the Most Holy Trinity is the central mystery of the Christian faith and of Christian life. God alone can make it known to us by revealing himself as Father, Son, and Holy Spirit.

262 The Incarnation of God's Son reveals that God is the eternal Father and that the Son is consubstantial with the Father, which means that, in the Father and with the Father, the Son is one and the same God.

263 The mission of the Holy Spirit, sent by the Father in the name of the Son (Jn 14: 26) and by the Son "from the Father" (Jn 15: 26), reveals that, with them, the Spirit is one and the same God. "With the Father and the Son he is worshipped and glorified" (Nicene Creed).

264 "The Holy Spirit proceeds from the Father as the first principle and, by the eternal gift of this to the Son, from the communion of both the Father and the Son" (St. Augustine, *De Trin.* 15, 26, 47: PL, 42: 1095).

265 By the grace of Baptism "in the name of the Father and of the Son and of the Holy Spirit," we are called to share in the life of the Blessed Trinity, here on earth in the obscurity of faith, and after death in eternal light (cf. Paul VI, *CPG*, § 9).

266 "Now this is the Catholic faith: We worship one God in the Trinity and the Trinity in unity, without either confusing the persons or dividing the substance; for the person of the Father is one, the Son's is another, the Holy Spirit's another; but the Godhead of the Father, Son and Holy Spirit is one, their glory equal, their majesty coeternal" (Athanasian Creed: DS, 75; ND, 16).

267 Inseparable in what they are, the divine persons are also inseparable in what they do. But within the single divine operation each shows forth what is proper to him in the Trinity, especially in the divine missions of the Son's Incarnation and the gift of the Holy Spirit.

Endnotes

1. Cf. Jn 17: 21-23.
2. Jn 14: 23.
3. *GCD*, 43.
4. 2 Tm 1: 9-10
5. Cf. *AG*, 2-9.
6. Cf. Council of Constantinople II: DS 421.
7. Cf. Jn 6: 44; Rom 8: 14.
8. Cf. Is 66: 13; Ps 131: 2.
9. Cf. Ps 27: 10; Eph 3: 14; Is 49: 15.
10. *SC*, 5 § 2; cf. St. Augustine, *En in Ps.* 138, 2: PL 37, 1784-1785.
11. Cf. Jn 14: 9-10.
12. *GS*, 22 § 2.
13. Cf. Gal 4: 4.
14. Lk 2: 51-52.
15. Cf. Rom 5: 19.
16. Jn 1: 29; cf. Is 53: 12.
17. Cf. Mk 10: 38; Lk 12: 50.
18. Mt 3: 15; cf. 26: 39.
19. Cf. Lk 3: 22; Is 42: 1.
20. Jn 1: 32-33; cf. Is 11: 2.
21. 1 Cor 11: 25.
22. Cf. Lk 22: 19.
23. Jn 17: 19; cf. Council of Trent: DS 1752; 1764.
24. Cf. Council of Trent (1547): DS 1529.
25. *GS*, 22 § 5; cf. § 2.
26. Cf. Mk 10: 39; Jn 21: 18-19; Col 1: 24.
27. Cf. Lk 2: 35.
28. St. Rose of Lima, cf. P. Hansen, *Vita mirabilis* (Louvain, 1668).
29. Cf. Phil 2: 10; Acts 2: 24; Rv 1: 18; Eph 4: 9; Ps 6: 6; 88: 11-13.
30. Cf. Ps 89: 49; 1 Sm 28: 19; Ez 32: 17-32; Lk 16: 22-26.
31. Cf. Council of Rome (745): DS 587; Benedict XII, *Cum dudum* (1341): DS 1011; Clement VI, *Super quibusdam* (1351): DS 1077; Council of Toledo IV (625): DS 485; Mt 27: 52-53.

The Church

The divinely authorized institution which seeks the salvation of all souls.

Chapter 4

The Church

*B*eing lost can be one of life's most unsettling experiences. When we are lost, we not only fear traveling on, but, very often, we also feel that the way back is lost as well. The less familiar the area is, the greater the confusion. It is a feeling akin to being in a fog. The denser the fog, the greater the hesitation to move in any direction.

We can experience a similar sensation in regards to truth. Doubts can and do paralyze us. The mind struggles with the questions, "What if I make the wrong choice? What will happen? How can I undo any damage that might be done?"

Jesus was well aware of the debilitating effect of doubt in our lives. To ensure that his people would always be led in the way of truth, He gave us the Church. The Holy Spirit is the support on which the rock of the papacy rests to guarantee that Jesus' Church will always teach the truth regarding the faith and morals he left us.

THE CHURCH

The Church is the group of people called by God to hear his word and go forth to evangelize the world with the spirit and words of the Gospel. It is the flock called, led, and nourished by Christ, the Good Shepherd. (See CCC 777 on p. 65)

From the beginning, the Father wanted a people that he could call his own. These people would share in his divine life. First, God chose the Jews to be this people. Later, as part of the plan of the Father, Jesus established the Church, which summons all people of good will to be called God's children.

Through the Church, God's design of communion with man is brought to fulfillment. The Church, then, is both the way the Father completes his plan and the goal of his plan.

Jesus established the Church as the instrument of salvation, for it is through the Church that God gives us sanctifying grace. The Church, then, is both the sign of God's communion with man and the way this communion is established. The Church was born from Jesus' offering of himself for our salvation—an act that was anticipated in the institution of the Eucharist and fulfilled on the Cross.

When Jesus created the Church, he established her as a hierarchy with a particular form. First, Christ chose his twelve apostles, who were led by St. Peter. Through Peter and the apostles, Jesus passed on power to continue the sacramental actions (Baptism, Eucharist, etc.) that he established while on earth. The Church is also assisted by the Holy Spirit, whom she received on Pentecost. The Holy Spirit directs the Church by the hierarchic and charismatic gifts he brings.

We must understand that the Church is something that Jesus truly created and in which God acts. Her offices of authority (pope, bishop, etc.) were established by God himself, so that with the help of God, men could lead the people the Lord has called.

Membership in the Church is indeed a calling. The Latin and Greek word for church, *ecclesia,* comes from a Greek verb meaning "to call out." The Church, then, is an assembly or calling together of people. The Septuagint, which is a Greek translation of the Old Testament made by Jewish rabbis, uses the word *ecclesia* to refer to the assembly of chosen people in the presence of God on Mt. Sinai. The young Church pictured herself as the successor of those who had stood before the Lord.

> In Christian usage, the word "church" designates the liturgical assembly,[1] but also the local community[2] or the whole universal community of believers.[3] These three meanings are inseparable. "The Church" is the People that God gathers in the whole world. She exists in local communities and is made real as a liturgical, above all a Eucharistic, assembly. She draws her life from the word and the Body of Christ and so herself becomes Christ's Body. (CCC 752)

Because of the real and active presence of God in the Church, she is not only in history but also outside it, for she resides eternally in the presence of the most Holy Trinity.

Through the Church, God's design of communion with man is brought to fulfillment.

The Church is an assembly or calling together of people.

The Church is simultaneously:

† A visible society and spiritual community;

† The earthly Church endowed with spiritual riches;

† The mystical body of Christ, a society structured with hierarchical organs.

Just as we are all on a journey toward heaven, the Church is also on a pilgrimage through time that concludes with her presence in eternity. This supernatural goal of the Church is what the visible Church works for. She is the servant of God who serves him by lighting the way for us. (See CCC 788, 799 on p. 65)

The Church serves the Lord by working to reveal Christ himself and the plan of the Father to all people. St. Paul compares Jesus' relation to the Church to that of a groom to his bride. He is the lover, and we are his beloved; all are bound together in a great communion of love. This love is a great mystery, an inner communion of all members that aims for the unity of the whole human race, a sign of the unity yet to come.

> "The Church, further, which is called 'that Jerusalem which is above' and 'our mother,' is described as the spotless spouse of the spotless lamb. It is she whom Christ 'loved and for whom he delivered himself up that he might sanctify her.' It is she whom he unites to himself by an unbreakable alliance, and whom he constantly 'nourishes and cherishes.'"[4] (CCC 757)

THE PEOPLE OF GOD

The word "catholic" means universal, and the universal Church comprises all those who love and fear God and strive to do what is right and acceptable to him.

In the strictest sense, though, the Church is composed of those who have been baptized and profess faith in Christ and obedience to the Roman Catholic Church. "Without faith it is impossible to please God" (Heb 11: 6). Faith is necessary for salvation. To be saved one must at least believe (these truths constitute the necessary instruction of a person in an emergency):

1. There is one God.

2. God rewards the good and punishes the wicked.

3. There are three divine persons in one God: the Father, the Son, and the Holy Spirit.

4. Jesus Christ is God the Son who became man and died on the cross to save us.

However, faith alone is not enough. We must practice our faith in hope and charity, study it, and attract others to it by our joy and example. This mysterious "calling out" to people binds together those who acknowledge Christ and serve him in holiness. This people:

† Is designated by God to be a chosen race, a royal priesthood, a holy nation;

† Is given new life by rebirth in water and the Spirit;

† Is a messianic people whose head is Christ;

This love is a great mystery, an inner communion of all members that aims for the unity of the whole human race, a sign of the unity yet to come.

† Has the status of children of God, who manifest a proper freedom and dignity, and in whose hearts the Spirit dwells;

† Lives by the law to love others as Christ loved all people;

† Has a mission to be "salt of the earth and light of the world";

† Is destined to be brought to perfection by God at the end of time.

ROLES OF THE PEOPLE OF GOD

The people of God share in Christ's roles of priest, prophet, and king and have responsibilities for mission and service in the Church:

The people of God share in Christ's roles of priest, prophet, and king...

† Those who are baptized are consecrated to be a spiritual house and a holy priesthood by regeneration and the anointing of the Holy Spirit.[3] In this priestly role given in Baptism, we offer our spiritual sacrifices. The priesthood of all the baptized is distinct from the ordained priesthood, which (along with spiritual sacrifices) offers the Body and Blood of Christ;

† Those who are baptized and confirmed exhibit the graces of those sacraments in their personal, family, social, and spiritual lives;

† As prophets, we are to gain the knowledge necessary to enable our lives to speak for God to others through our witness to his truth;

† We share in Christ's royal role as king through our service to those in need, particularly the poor and suffering, in whom the Church recognizes her founder. As the Catechism states:

"The sign of the cross makes kings of all those reborn in Christ, and the anointing of the Holy Spirit consecrates them as priests, so that, apart from the particular service of our ministry, all spiritual and rational Christians are recognized as members of this royal race and sharers in Christ's priestly office. What, indeed, is as royal for a soul as to govern the body in obedience to God? And what is as priestly as to dedicate a pure conscience to the Lord and to offer the spotless offerings of devotion on the altar of the heart?"[5] (CCC 786)

The sign of the cross makes kings of all those reborn in Christ...

PRECEPTS OF THE CHURCH

The Precepts of the Church summarize the core values and fundamental obligations that separate God's people from all other institutions. These cannot be replaced by good intentions, nor should they be practiced grudgingly or even superficially. The purpose of the Precepts are to foster a strong relationship with God who is *Love*. The seven Precepts that bind all baptized members of the Church are:

1. Attend Mass on all Sundays and holy days of obligation; and avoid activities that hinder the renewal of soul and body, or growth in union with the Lord.

2. Go to Confession at least once a year and receive Communion during Easter Time (traditionally from Ash Wednesday to Trinity Sunday).

3. Study the teachings of the Church in preparation for Confirmation and then use that knowledge to advance the Cause of Christ and the Mission of the Church in evangelizing the world.

The Seven Precepts of the Church are essential to being a true and solid Catholic.

4. Obey the laws of the Church concerning marriage (including teachings on birth control, abortion, divorce, etc.); provide religious training and an example of sanctity to one's children and grandchildren; use parish facilities to advance one's own religious education.

5. Contribute to the support of the Church: this is *not* just financial support, but also participating in ministry and works of charity.

6. Fast and abstain on the days appointed: the Church now says that it is acceptable to eat meat on Fridays outside of Lent *if* another pious work or practice is substituted for it.

7. Join in the missionary spirit and apostolate of the Church.

All of these are *essential* to being a true and solid Catholic. These practices form the foundation from which saints are made. It should be remembered that not only is external observance without interior fervor empty, but also that the interior life will slowly suffocate unless it expresses itself in outward observance.

Christ is the head of his Mystical Body, the Church.

THE CHURCH IS THE BODY OF CHRIST

Jesus promised to remain with his Church in the presence of the Holy Spirit, "who will tell you all things." The Holy Spirit binds together all those in the Church, which is the Mystical Body of Christ. Individual members gather around and are linked to Christ, the head of his Body, the Church.

Just as in a body, each part has a different function, so in the Mystical Body of Christ, there are many members (in fact, every Christian in the Church), who perform a variety of functions. Each member has a unique role to perform, whether as part of the ordained ministry (bishops, priests, and deacons) or the non-ordained religious and laity.

Every body has a head, and Christ is the head of his Mystical Body, the Church. He is the source of creation and redemption. Raised to the Father's glory, he is preeminent in all things, especially in the Church, through which he extends his reign over all things.

As head of the Church, Christ provides for her whole growth, endowing the Church with gifts that allow her members to assist each other in attaining holiness. The relationship between Christ and the Church is personal, manifested in the image of Christ as bridegroom and the Church as his bride. Each of us, in fact, is mystically betrothed to Jesus through the Sacrament of Baptism.

THE PAPACY

Christ instituted the Church as a collegial body with the pope at her head.

> When Christ instituted the Twelve, "he constituted [them] in the form of a college or permanent assembly, at the head of which he placed Peter, chosen from among them."[6] Just as "by the Lord's institution, St. Peter and the rest of the apostles constitute a single apostolic college, so in

like fashion the Roman Pontiff, Peter's successor, and the bishops, the successors of the apostles, are related with and united to one another."[7] (CCC 880)

The Lord made Simon alone, whom he named Peter, the "rock" of his Church. He gave him the keys of his Church and instituted him shepherd of the whole flock.[8] "The office of binding and loosing which was given to Peter was also assigned to the college of apostles united to its head."[9] This pastoral office of Peter and the other apostles belongs to the Church's very foundation and is continued by the bishops under the primacy of the Pope. (CCC 881)

To ensure that the faithful would be truthfully taught, Jesus guaranteed that St. Peter and his successors, the popes, would be free from error, i.e., infallible, in their public teachings on matters of faith and morals. Papal infallibility is made possible by the work of the Holy Spirit in the Church. Hence, the papacy preserves the truth of God that liberates Church members from error. The teaching authority of the pope and bishops is called the Magisterium, from the Latin for "teaching office."

Church teachings are free from error when:

† The pope in his office as supreme teacher makes a declaration regarding faith or morals by a definitive act;

† The pope together with the bishops exercises the Magisterium, particularly in an ecumenical council;

† The pope proposes a doctrine "for belief as divinely revealed." Such definitions "must be adhered to with the obedience of faith";

† The bishops, in communion with the pope, propose a teaching that leads to a better understanding of Revelation in a matter of faith and morals.

By looking at Church history, we recognize the validity of Christ's guarantee of freedom from error in matters of faith and morals. Since Christ founded his Church, she has taught the same truths without change. No other institution can make or demonstrate this claim.

The Holy Spirit established bishops as successors of the apostles, to be a visible foundation and source of unity to the particular churches.

Bishops have the duties of authentically teaching the faith, celebrating the Eucharist, and guiding the Church as true pastors. They are assisted by priests as co-workers and deacons who perform acts of service.

The papacy preserves the truth of God that liberates Church members from error.

THE MARKS OF THE CHURCH

The Church of Jesus Christ can be identified by four marks or attributes: unity, holiness, catholicity, and apostolicity.

The word *unity* refers to the oneness of the Church's teaching and ministry. The Church professes one Lord, one faith, one Baptism; she forms one Body, is given life by one Holy Spirit, and strives to overcome all divisions. Only in the Roman Catholic Church is this collection of truths, the one faith that Christ himself taught, still maintained. There can be no unity where there is difference of belief. Other Christian churches teach less than the complete deposit of faith given by Christ to his Church.

Unity

Holiness

Catholicity

Apostolicity

The Church is built on the lasting foundation of the apostles with Peter their head.

The *holiness* of the Church flows from Christ's death on the cross. Christ gave himself up to make the Church holy and instituted the seven sacraments to maintain and pass on his holiness through the actions of the Holy Spirit. To attain the highest level of holiness, one must be a member of Christ's Church, since the sacramental life established by Jesus is the fountain of personal holiness. Participation in the complete sacramental life established by Christ preserves the unity of the Church.

The word *catholicity* means universality. The kingdom of God proclaimed by the Church is universal; all people, without exception, are called by God and his Church. In the Old Testament, Daniel prophesied that God would set up a kingdom that shall never be destroyed. Jesus said, "This gospel of the kingdom shall be preached in the whole world for a testimony to all nations" (Mt 24:14). The Church Jesus founded subsists in, that is, lives on in, the Catholic Church. She proclaims the fullness of faith, is sent to all peoples, speaks to all people, encompasses all times in her missionary role. Since her founding, she has existed for all people of all time who accept the word of Christ.

The word *apostolicity* indicates that the Church is built on the lasting foundation of the apostles with Peter their head. Christ's Church is identified by her adherence to the teaching he gave to his apostles, whose office is continued by the pope and bishops. Because Jesus gave Peter special authority over the other apostles, members of the Church of Christ are identified by their submission to the authority of Peter's successor, the pope, the rock on which the Church is built.

THE LAST THINGS

For all this, the Church can more easily be described as the divinely authorized institution which seeks the salvation of all souls. The surest way to die a good death is to live a good Christian life. At death, the soul leaves the body and is judged immediately by God (the particular judgment); the possibility of merit, demerit, or conversion ceases. The soul will immediately go to heaven, hell, or purgatory as deserved.

> Death puts an end to human life as the time open to either accepting or rejecting the divine grace manifested in Christ.[10] The New Testament speaks of judgment primarily in its aspect of the final encounter with Christ in his second coming, but also repeatedly affirms that each will be rewarded immediately after death in accordance with his works and faith. The parable of the poor man Lazarus and the words of Christ on the cross to the good thief, as well as other New Testament texts speak of a final destiny of the soul—a destiny which can be different for some and for others.[11]

> Each man receives his eternal retribution in his immortal soul at the very moment of his death, in a particular judgment that refers his life to Christ: either entrance into the blessedness of heaven—through a purification[12] or immediately,[13]—or immediate and everlasting damnation.[14]

> At the evening of life, we shall be judged on our love.[15]
> (CCC 1021-1022)

Purgatory is a state of purification from venial sins so that souls achieve the holiness necessary to enter the joy of heaven (cf. CCC 1030-1032). These souls must suffer the inability to see God completely and be freed from attachment to creatures. These souls are in a state of grace, a part of the Communion of Saints, but have unrepented venial sins. Purgatory is not an eternal state (which would contradict the Bible), but will only last until the general judgment at the end of the world.

> All who die in God's grace and friendship, but still imperfectly purified, are indeed assured of their eternal salvation; but after death they undergo purification, so as to achieve the holiness necessary to enter the joy of heaven. (CCC 1030)

At the general judgment, God's majesty, wisdom, justice, and mercy will shine forth for all to see as Jesus Christ's final victory on earth. We will see why God sometimes allows the good to suffer and the wicked to prosper. We will also see all the good and bad effects of humans' actions. Souls will be reunited to their now immortal bodies in the resurrection. The bodies of the saints will be beautiful and luminous while the bodies of the damned will be hideous and dark. At this point Jesus will tell the good to come into the Kingdom of Heaven while sending the wicked into "the eternal fire prepared for the devil and his angels" (Mt 25: 41).

Purgatory is a state of purification.

> The Last Judgment will come when Christ returns in glory. Only the Father knows the day and the hour; only he determines the moment of its coming. Then through his Son Jesus Christ he will pronounce the final word on all history. We shall know the ultimate meaning of the whole work of creation and of the entire economy of salvation and understand the marvellous ways by which his Providence led everything towards its final end. The Last Judgment will reveal that God's justice triumphs over all the injustices committed by his creatures and that God's love is stronger than death.[16] (CCC 1040)

At the end of time, the Kingdom of God will come in its fullness. After the universal judgment, the righteous will reign for ever with Christ, glorified in body and soul. The universe itself will be renewed:

> "The Church...will receive her perfection only in the glory of heaven, when will come the time of the renewal of all things. At that time, together with the human race, the universe itself, which is so closely related to man and which attains its destiny through him, will be perfectly re-established in Christ."[17] (CCC 1042)

Hell is everlasting suffering and separation from God. The damned are never capable of repentance or making an act of love. The souls in hell died unrepentant of mortal sin or refused to the end the love and mercy of God. Jesus spoke often of hell as "fire" and "darkness" where there will be "weeping and gnashing of teeth" as condemned souls are tormented by "the worm that dies not." The souls of hell continually thirst for God while hating him.

> We cannot be united with God unless we freely choose to love him. But we cannot love God if we sin gravely against him, against our neighbor or against ourselves: "He who does not love remains in death. Anyone who hates his brother is a murderer, and you know that no murderer has eternal life abiding in him" (1 Jn 3: 14-15). Our Lord warns us that we shall be separated from him if we fail to meet the serious needs of

The Last Judgment will come when Christ returns in glory.

Only the Father knows the day and the hour; only he determines the moment of its coming.

The souls in hell died unrepentant of mortal sin or refused to the end the love and mercy of God.

the poor and the little ones who are his brethren.[18] To die in mortal sin without repenting and accepting God's merciful love means remaining separated from him for ever by our own free choice. This state of definitive self-exclusion from communion with God and the blessed is called "hell." (CCC 1033)

The teaching of the Church affirms the existence of hell and its eternity. Immediately after death the souls of those who die in a state of mortal sin descend into hell, where they suffer the punishments of hell, "eternal fire."[19] The chief punishment of hell is eternal separation from God, in whom alone man can possess the life and happiness for which he was created and for which he longs. (CCC 1035)

Heaven is the state of everlasting life in which we see God, become like him in glory, and enjoy eternal happiness. All souls in heaven are in the light of glory and have an immediate vision of God. They have made up for their sins either on earth or in purgatory. Jesus speaks of various degrees ("mansions") of happiness in his Kingdom according to the various degrees of love and friendship with God through cooperation with his grace. While these are different, each person receives *the full measure of happiness he can desire*—like jars of different sizes each filled to the brim.

This perfect life with the Most Holy Trinity—this communion of life and love with the Trinity, with the Virgin Mary, the angels and all the blessed—is called "heaven." Heaven is the ultimate end and fulfillment of the deepest human longings, the state of supreme, definitive happiness. (CCC 1024)

This mystery of blessed communion with God and all who are in Christ is beyond all understanding and description. Scripture speaks of it in images: life, light, peace, wedding feast, wine of the kingdom, the Father's house, the heavenly Jerusalem, paradise: "no eye has seen, nor ear heard, nor the heart of man conceived, what God has prepared for those who love him."[20] (CCC 1027)

CONCLUSION

Christ founded a gathering of people whom he graced to be a loving community until the end of time, sustained always by the Holy Spirit, the principal agent of the Church's mission. The community founded by Christ subsists in the Roman Catholic Church, which is Jesus' vehicle to lead all men of good will so that there may be one Church and one Shepherd. The Church herself and all her members are on a pilgrimage that will be completed in the fullness of time. This pilgrimage is aided by Scripture and oral Tradition.

To guarantee that his Church would always lead in the way of truth, Christ protected the oral Tradition and sent the Holy Spirit to guide the pope in his proclamations regarding faith and morals. The identifying marks of the Church are:

Unity, Holiness, Catholicity, and Apostolicity.

This perfect life with the Most Holy Trinity—this communion of life and love with the Trinity, with the Virgin Mary, the angels and all the blessed—is called "heaven."

SUPPLEMENTARY READING

Pope St. Leo I is one of two popes to be given the title "Great." His accomplishments as pope strengthened the Church and protected her people.

Elected pope in A.D. 440, Leo cared for the Church during a period when false teachings were everywhere. Priest argued against priest, and bishop against bishop.

The main subject of debate was the nature of Christ. The truth that Christ has two natures, one human and one divine, was being attacked on both sides: Nestorianism denied that Christ was divine, and Eutychianism denied that Christ had a human nature. Recognizing his duty as pope, Leo set out to remove these heresies from the Church.

In 451, Leo called a council in Chalcedon. This council was truly a universal meeting of the Church: at least 600 bishops attended. When a letter from Leo explaining the two natures of Christ was read aloud, the bishops cried out in assent, "Peter has spoken through Leo," affirming the pope's infallibility concerning doctrines of faith.

Leo's great works concerned more than doctrine though. During this time, Attila the Hun was ravaging Europe. When Attila entered Italy, he sacked the cities of Milan and Pavia. While the Emperor Valentinian III went to a remote fortress for his own protection and ignored his subjects, Leo himself decided to take action. Accompanied by the leaders of Rome and a few priests, Leo went to meet Attila. The Pope told him of the Church and all

St. Leo the Great
(Pope 440-461)
Feast on November 10

it had endured. He reasoned with Attila against attacking Rome, the heart of the Church. Leo argued so convincingly that Attila turned his troops around and left Italy.

For over sixteen centuries, Leo has been recognized as one of the most outstanding leaders in the history of the Church—a man who, through his own skills and the grace of God, truly earned the name Leo the Great.

VOCABULARY

APOSTOLICITY OF THE CHURCH

The Church is founded on the apostles in that: 1) she remains built on the "foundation of the apostles," 2) the Church keeps and hands on their teaching, 3) she continues to be taught, sanctified, and guided by their successors.

CATHOLICITY OF THE CHURCH

Literally "universal" in the sense of "according to the totality" or "in keeping with the whole." The Church is catholic in the dual sense that it 1) possesses the fullness of the means of salvation and 2) has been sent by Christ to the whole human race.

CHURCH

The name given the assembly of the People God has called together from the ends of the earth. In Christian usage, the word Church has three meanings: the People that God gathers in the whole world; the local church; the liturgical assembly.

DOGMA

The revealed teachings of Christ proclaimed by the fullest extent of the exercise of the authority of the Church's Magisterium. The faithful are obliged to believe the truths or dogmas contained in divine Revelation and defined by the Magisterium.

GENERAL JUDGMENT

Preceded by the resurrection of the dead, coincident with the second coming of Christ in glory at the end of time, discloses good and evil, and reveals the meaning of salvation history and the providence of God by which justice has triumphed over evil.

HIERARCHY

The apostles and their successors, the college of bishops, to whom Christ gave the authority to teach, sanctify, and rule the Church in his name.

HOLINESS

Principally an attribute of God and the Church describing complete separation from the sphere of the profane. Individual human beings may be holy dedicating themselves completely to God and the Church. Holiness is the perfection of charity.

INFALLIBILITY OF THE CHURCH

The gift of the Holy Spirit to the Church whereby the pastors of the Church, the pope and bishops in union with him, can definitively proclaim a doctrine of faith or morals for the belief of the faithful, and that proclamation is free from all error.

MAGISTERIUM

The living, teaching office of the Church, whose task it is to give as authentic interpretation of the word of God, whether in its written form (Sacred Scripture), or in the form of Tradition.

PARTICULAR JUDGMENT

The eternal retribution received by each soul at the moment of death, in accordance with that person's faith and works.

PILGRIMAGE

Journey to a sacred place undertaken as an act of religious devotion; the purpose may be to venerate a certain saint or ask some spiritual favor, beg for a physical cure or perform an act of penance, or express thanks or fulfill a promise.

POPE

Successor of St. Peter; Bishop of Rome; Supreme Pontiff of the Catholic Church. The pope exercises a primacy of authority as Vicar of Christ and shepherd of the whole Church; he receives the divine assistance promised by Christ to the Church.

VOCABULARY CONTINUED

PROPHET

One sent by God to form the people of the Old Covenant in the hope of salvation. The prophets are often authors of books of the Old Testament. John the Baptist concludes the work of the prophets of the Old Covenant.

PURGATORY

A state of final purification after death and before entrance into heaven for those who died in God's friendship, but were only imperfectly purified.

SALVATION

The forgiveness of sins and restoration of friendship with God, which can be done by God alone.

UNITY OF THE CHURCH

The gift of the Holy Spirit to the Church whereby it is undivided in itself and yet distinct from other things.

STUDY QUESTIONS

1. Define the Church.

2. How is the Church the instrument of salvation?

3. Who established the Church?

4. Who created the hierarchy of the Church?

5. What power did Jesus pass on to his apostles?

6. Who brings charismatic gifts to the Church?

7. Why is the Church both in history and outside of history?

8. What is the final destination of the pilgrim Church?

9. How does the Church serve the Lord?

10. Who, in the strictest sense, makes up the Catholic Church?

11. Who is the head of the Mystical Body of Christ?

12. Why is it good that so many people make up the Mystical Body of Christ?

13. What name did Christ give Simon when he was made the first Pope? What does this name mean? Why did Christ give Simon this name?

14. Can the pope, when acting in his office as pope and not as an individual, make a mistake on teachings of faith and morals? Why or why not?

15. All other Christian denominations were founded by men who had political or religious disagreements with the Catholic Church. How are the beginnings of these groups different from the beginning of the Catholic Church?

PRACTICAL EXERCISES

1. Suppose someone were to say to you that he was thinking of leaving the Catholic Church for another Christian group with church services that he liked more? What could you say to him to try to convince him to stay with the Catholic Church?

2. The Church is meant to be a communion, or community. List some ideas that you and your parish can do to become a closer community. Consider sharing these ideas with your spiritual director, parents, teacher, or classmates.

3. This week, try to stay after Mass to talk with others and try to plan to do something together.

FROM THE CATECHISM

777 The word "Church" means "convocation." It designates the assembly of those whom God's Word "convokes," i.e., gathers together to form the People of God, and who themselves, nourished with the Body of Christ, become the Body of Christ.

778 The Church is both the means and the goal of God's plan: prefigured in creation, prepared for in the Old Covenant, founded by the words and actions of Jesus Christ, fulfilled by his redeeming cross and his Resurrection, the Church has been manifested as the mystery of salvation by the outpouring of the Holy Spirit. She will be perfected in the glory of heaven as the assembly of all the redeemed of the earth (cf. Rv 14: 4).

779 The Church is both visible and spiritual, a hierarchical society and the Mystical Body of Christ. She is one, yet formed of two components, human and divine. That is her mystery, which only faith can accept.

780 The Church in this world is the sacrament of salvation, the sign and the instrument of the communion of God and men.

Endnotes

1. Cf. 1 Cor 11: 18; 14: 19, 28, 34, 35.

2. Cf. 1 Cor 1: 2; 16: 1.

3. Cf. 1 Cor 15: 9; Gal 1: 13; Phil 3: 6.

4. *LG,* 6; cf. Gal 4: 26;
   Rv 12: 17; 19: 7; 21: 2, 9; 22: 17;
   Eph 5: 25-26, 29.

5. St. Leo the Great, *Sermo* 4,
   1: PL 54, 149.

6. *LG,* 19; cf. Lk 6: 13; Jn 21: 15-17.

7. *LG,* 22; cf. CIC, can. 330.

8. Cf. Mt 16: 18-19; Jn 21: 15-17.

9. *LG,* 22 § 2.

10. Cf. 2 Tm 1: 9-10.

11. Cf. Lk 16: 22; 23: 43; Mt 16: 26;
    2 Cor 5: 8; Phil 1: 23; Heb 9: 27;
    12: 23.

12. Cf. Council of Lyons II (1274):
    DS 857-858; Council of Florence
    (1439): DS 1304-1306; Council
    of Trent (1563): DS 1820.

13. Cf. Benedict XII, *Benedictus
    Deus* (1336): DS 1000-1001;
    John XXII, *Ne super his* (1334):
    DS 990.

14. Cf. Benedict XII, *Benedictus
    Deus* (1336): DS 1002.

15. St. John of the Cross, *Dichos* 64.

16. Cf. Sg 8: 6.

17. *LG,* 48; cf. Acts 3: 21; Eph 1: 10;
    Col 1: 20; 2 Pt 3: 10-13.

18. Cf. Mt 25: 31-46.

19. Cf. DS 76; 409; 411; 801; 858;
    1002; 1351; 1575; Paul VI,
    CPG § 12.

20. 1 Cor 2: 9.

Chapter 5

The Blessed Virgin Mary

Hers is the only truly childlike gaze which has ever rested upon our misfortune and our shame.

The Blessed Virgin Mary

The Blessed Virgin knew no triumph and worked no miracles. Her Son did not allow her to be touched by human glory, not even to be grazed by its huge and savage wing. No one has lived, suffered, and died in greater simplicity than she, more utterly unaware of her dignity which for all that places her above the angels... Naturally she holds sin in abhorrence, but she has no experience of it — and the greatest of saints had experience of it, even the seraphic saint of Assisi. Only the Virgin looks at us with the eyes of a child; hers is the only truly childlike gaze which has ever rested upon our misfortune and our shame. If you want to pray well, you must feel it resting upon yourself...

It's a look of tender compassion, of sorrowful surprise, of some inconceivable, indefinable feeling which makes her younger than sin, younger than the race to which she belongs, and although Mother by the grace of God, Mother of the graces that flow from him, the youngest daughter of mankind.[1]

What the Catholic Church believes about Mary is based on what it believes about Christ, and what it teaches about Mary illumines in turn its faith in Christ. (CCC 487)

THE BLESSED VIRGIN MARY

God chose the Virgin Mary from all eternity to be the Mother of the Redeemer, Jesus Christ, who is God. This plan for the salvation of mankind began in the Old Testament with Adam and Eve. After Eve committed sin, she was promised a posterity who would triumph over evil. Among the precursors of Mary in the Old Testament are Hannah, the mother of Samuel, as well as Deborah, Ruth, Judith, and Esther. They exhibited qualities that Mary lived to the fullest. (See CCC 508 on p. 77)

In the Old Testament, the childless are thought to be cursed by God, for they have lost their place in history. In the case of Sarah, the wife of Abraham, God intervened by giving Sarah a male child whose birth will change the history of the world. In a similar manner with Mary, God intervened to ask a young girl who has pledged her virginity to God to say yes to accepting the Messiah as her child. Once again God intervenes to change the history of mankind. (See CCC 511 on p. 77)

HER HISTORY

According to Church tradition, Mary's parents were Joachim and Ann. She was descended through the line of David from the tribe of Judah.

Chronologically, St. Paul's letter to the Galatians was one of the first books of the New Testament to be written, and it is here that, for the first time, Mary is mentioned in the New Testament.

> But when the time had fully come, God sent forth his Son, born of woman, born under the law, to redeem those who were under the law, so that we might receive adoption as sons. (Gal. 4: 4-5).

The bulk of the information we have regarding Mary is in the Gospels of Matthew and Luke. Mary resided in Nazareth in Galilee, and it is in the Gospel of Luke that the angel Gabriel appears to her and asks her to accept being mother of the Messiah. (See CCC 973 on p. 77)

She was betrothed to St. Joseph, but according to the custom, they were not yet living as man and wife.

> The annunciation to Mary inaugurates "the fullness of time" (Gal 4: 4), the time of fulfillment of God's promises and preparations. Mary was invited to conceive him in whom the "whole fullness of deity" would dwell "bodily" (Col 2: 9). The divine response to her question, "How can this be, since I know not man" was given by the power of the Holy Spirit. "The Holy Spirit will come upon you."[2] (CCC 484)

Mary expresses her willingness to accept the role the Holy Spirit has set out for her with complete humility and submission. From the point of her acceptance of the role the Holy Spirit has chosen for her, she is joined in a mysterious manner to the work of her Son. Her "yes" to God makes up for the refusal of Eve to serve God, and from this point she is entitled to be called "the New Eve." From all eternity God had planned that the salvation of man be joined to the cooperation of Mary in accepting her role as mother of the Messiah.

> The Father of mercies willed that the Incarnation should be preceded by assent on the part of the predestined mother, so that just as a woman had a share in bringing about death, so also a woman should contribute to life.[3]

After Eve committed sin, she was promised a posterity who would triumph over evil.

Mary's "yes" to God makes up for the refusal of Eve to serve God, and from this point she is entitled to be called "the New Eve."

The Blessed Virgin Mary

Mary appeared to St. Bernadette at Lourdes and identified herself as "The Immaculate Conception."

Mary appears in the Gospels in the service of Jesus from the Incarnation to the crucifixion and finally in prayer in the upper room after the Resurrection.

Her most difficult moment occurred at Jesus' crucifixion, when she stood at the foot of the cross as an example for us of fortitude in this life in the midst of sorrow and suffering.

After the completion of her earthly life, Jesus raised Mary body and soul into his presence in Heaven to enjoy the rewards she so richly deserved. Pius XII proclaimed her Assumption into heaven as a dogma of the Church on November 1, 1950.

THE TITLES OF MARY

The Gospels refer to Mary as the Mother of Jesus. The custom of calling Mary the "Mother of God" began in the Eastern Church, and St. Ambrose was the first to use the title in the Western Church.

At first, you may ask yourself, how can Mary be called Mother of God? Well, you have a mother who is only mother in the sense she is mother of your flesh, for God supplied the spirit or soul, yet she is still your mother. In the Second Person of the Trinity, the person is Jesus who is the Son of God. Mary gave Jesus his human nature. We do not speak of motherhood in relation to nature, but a person. But Jesus is not a human person. He is a divine person with two natures, human and divine. Since the person she gave birth to is God she is rightly called the Mother of God. When she visits her cousin, Elizabeth greets her as "the Mother of my Lord." (See CCC 509 on p. 77)

Mary is also called the Immaculate Conception. When the angel Gabriel greets Mary, he greets her, "Hail, full of grace." The Church teaches that from the moment of her own conception, Mary was kept free from stain of sin by God's grace through the merits of Jesus. Two years after the Church declared Mary the *Immaculate Conception*, Mary appeared to St. Bernadette at Lourdes and identified herself by that title. Not only was she conceived free from sin but she also remained so all the days of her life.

Mary is called "Ever Virgin," and this teaching goes back to the promise of God to Isaiah 7:14, that, "a virgin shall conceive and bear a son." Her virginal conception signifies the new birth of man in the Holy Spirit.

The Bible makes reference to the "brothers and sisters of Jesus," but these are cousins. At the time the gospels were written there was no word in the Aramaic language for cousin. It was the custom to use 'brothers' to indicate either cousins or sisters and brothers. For example, St. James, whose father was Cleophas, is referred to as a brother of Jesus when in fact he was Jesus' cousin. So, the Church proclaims that Mary remained a virgin in his conception, his growth in the womb, his time of nursing, and always.

MARY, MOTHER OF THE CHURCH

Mary's role in the Church cannot be separated from that of her son for it is through her "yes" to the Father that the Church came into being. Like the Church, she embarked on a pilgrimage of faith. She joined her suffering completely to that of Jesus and consented to his suffering and death. Her support of the Church continued in her life of prayer (after his Ascension). Mary's important role in the Church was further confirmed by her Assumption into heaven.

> "Finally the Immaculate Virgin, preserved free from all stain of original sin, when the course of her earthly life was finished, was taken up body and soul into heavenly glory, and exalted by the Lord as Queen over all things, so that she might be the more fully conformed to her Son, the Lord of lords and conqueror of sin and death."[4] The Assumption of the Blessed Virgin is a singular participation in her Son's Resurrection and an anticipation of the resurrection of other Christians. (CCC 966)

The yes of Mary to the requests of the Father model the life we should lead and calls us to say "yes" to the call of the Father to live as Jesus did.

MARY EVER VIRGIN

Jesus was conceived in Mary's womb to say "yes" to the Father as the new Adam.

His virginal conception by the action of the Holy Spirit begins the new birth of God's children.

From the Church's beginning, Mary was declared ever virgin. The first mention was in the Apostles' Creed, and it was confirmed many times in councils held by the Church. The Catechism of the Catholic Church states that:

> The eyes of faith can discover in the context of the whole of Revelation the mysterious reasons why God in his saving plan wanted his Son to be born of a virgin. These reasons touch both on the person of Christ and his redemptive mission, and on the welcome Mary gave that mission on behalf of all men. (CCC 502)

Mary's perpetual virginity reflects the desire of the Spirit that Mary remain a special creation in her role as Mother of the living God. Her virginal motherhood reflects the great value of virginity, in both its bodily and spiritual manifestations in God's eyes. The call to live a life of virginity has always been honored as a reflection of Mary's virginity. Virginity frees a person to live a life dedicated totally to God. The parenthood of the few is replaced with a parenthood of the many. (See CCC 510 on p. 77)

MARY – YOUR MOTHER, TOO

As Jesus was dying on the cross, he looked at Mary and St. John and said, "Woman, behold your son!" Then he said to the disciple, "Behold your mother!" With these words, Jesus indicated that Mary was to be accepted by all as their spiritual mother, the mother of all. Since Mary is truly the Mother of God, in a real sense, she is your mother, too. Her

The Blessed Virgin Mary

Mary's virginal motherhood reflects the great value of virginity.

The call to live a life of virginity has always been honored as a reflection of Mary's virginity.

You can have a close and intimate relationship with Mary, one which can surpass all human understanding.

concern is for all the children of her Son, just as every mother has a concern for all her children regardless of the person's individual good or evil inclinations. Unlike a human mother, Mary will never lose patience with her children or reject them, no matter how wrongly they act. Her union with Jesus in holiness is so complete that she loves with a truly everlasting love.

Because of her adherence to the will of the Father, this motherhood of Mary continues until the end of time. In a completely unique way, her obedience in faith, hope, and charity enables her to cooperate in the saving work of restoring supernatural life to souls, so she is mother to us in the order of grace.

This profound truth means that you can have a close and intimate relationship with Mary, one which can surpass all human understanding. You can sense this closeness in your heart by saying the Memorare or Hail Holy Queen prayers aloud when you are alone.

Mary is always truly and totally in Jesus' presence, so you have an advocate who sees God face to face bringing your petitions to him. You are able to establish a personal relationship with Mary through prayer. One way to do this is to acquire the habit of saying the Rosary on a daily basis. It is a mini-gospel of the main events of the life of our Lord. It will not only bring you closer to Mary, but will bring a greater understanding of the major events of Jesus' life.

MARY, MODEL FOR LIFE

In today's world, many people prefer fame and fortune to service to Jesus and his Church, in stark contrast to Mary who never sought anything for herself.

Many people have noted that Mary speaks only twice in the New Testament; this reminds us that her life was one of deeds. Her life was one of service to her family where she sought to find the will of God. Her life was not easy, but Mary did the chores associated with motherhood with humility and grace. She sought neither fame nor riches but only wished to do the will of her son. Her example points to the fact that personal sanctity can be found in every life that is lived as a life of service to others. Fame and fortune may come, but all are called to fulfill their everyday duties without regard to life's merely human rewards.

ST. JOSEPH

The story of Mary would not be complete without the story of St. Joseph. The Holy Spirit chose St. Joseph to be the spouse of Mary and the foster-father of Jesus and guardian of the Holy Family. Like Mary, St. Joseph was a descendant of King David. Sacred Tradition tells us he was a carpenter.

The Father watched over Joseph with great care and led him through the presence of an angel in time of great danger. It was an angel who told Joseph it was God's plan that Mary was pregnant. When Herod wished to kill the child Jesus, an angel warned St. Joseph to flee to Egypt. He was also warned by an angel when the Holy Family returned from Egypt.

St. Joseph took Jesus to be circumcised and after a period of forty days accompanied Mary to the temple for the rite of purification as well as to fulfill the law that every first-born son was to be presented to the Lord. It was at this time that Simeon foretold that Jesus had come to bring all men to salvation, and that Mary would share Jesus' suffering.

St. Joseph is a wonderful example for us of complete trust in the will of God in every circumstance of our lives.

CONCLUSION

Because of her life and cooperation with the special graces of God, Mary is entitled to special veneration. This honor is less than the honor offered to God but is greater than that which should be offered to any other human person.

The human perfection of the Blessed Mother should motivate everyone to imitation of her. It is true that no human being can duplicate her perfection, but that should not permit us to forget that everyone can imitate her virtue to a great extent through cooperation with God's grace.

Mary still cares for us with maternal charity, so she will intercede with her Son to aid us in the quest for perfection through his manifold graces. As the good mother she is, she awaits our calls for her assistance and brings them personally to her beloved Son. (See CCC 975 on p. 77)

The human perfection of the Blessed Mother should motivate everyone to imitation of her.

She will intercede with her Son to aid us in the quest for perfection.

SUPPLEMENTARY READING

Go to Joseph!

Mount Royal dominates the city of Montreal, and is in turn dominated by the great cupola of the Oratory of St. Joseph, the massive shrine built by Blessed André Bessette, a Holy Cross lay brother who was the most well-known man in Canada in the early 1930s.

On a typical morning in those days a motley crew of the injured and the sick, poor and rich alike, would be lined up outside Brother André's small, ten-by-eighteen foot office, looking for cures from the 'miracle man of Montreal.' Brother André would welcome them for three hours in the morning and two hours in the afternoon, before spending several hours after dinner visiting the sick in their homes and hospitals. By nine o'clock, he would have already been up for four hours, having spent two hours in prayer in the chapel. The old brother prayed again for an hour before retiring to gain strength from the All-Powerful to cope with the demands of the thousands who constantly sought his miraculous cures.

"Never anything joyous, never anything amusing," he was known to comment about his work. Even so, the walls of the Oratory of St. Joseph are covered with the crutches, canes and other paraphernalia rendered unnecessary by Brother André's cures. His conversations were curt, even brusque, often consisting of nothing more than his standard advice: "Get some oil consecrated to St. Joseph and get a medal of St. Joseph. Rub the oil. Make a novena to St. Joseph. Pray to him a lot. Pray to the Good God." When the thousands would return to thank him for his miraculous intervention, he would be equally brief: "It was St. Joseph and not I who cured you. Thank St. Joseph, not me."

Brother André's life and example were a source of the increased devotion to St. Joseph

Bl. André Bessette
(1845-1937)
Feast on January 6

that has marked 20th century Catholicism. The Church has long applied the words of the Pharaoh concerning the dream translator Joseph, to the later Joseph: *Go to Joseph!* (Gn 41: 55). Brother André spoke those words to the thousands who came to Mount Royal— *Go to Joseph!*

Devotion to St. Joseph had been dormant since St. Teresa of Ávila encouraged a renewal of devotion to St. Joseph in the 16th century. Pope Pius XII instituted the feast of St. Joseph the Worker in 1955, to propose an example of a true Christian worker in response to communism. St. Joseph the Worker is celebrated on the European Labor Day (May 1st), the day the great Mayday military parades would be held during the communist period. Pope John XXIII decreed that Joseph's name be added to the Roman Canon (Eucharistic Prayer I) after that of Mary, and before all others. Pope John also commissioned a new altar of St. Joseph in St. Peter's Basilica.

Continued

SUPPLEMENTARY READING CONTINUED

Modern-day Quebec society would scoff at the concept of miracles, as does much of 20th century enlightened, rationalist opinion. But God cannot be limited to the imagination, or even to the altar. Brother André was a sign sent to a sophisticated, prosperous, forward-looking North American city that God is still at work. Now the shrine to St. Joseph draws hundreds of thousands to pray at the tomb of Brother André and to St. Joseph.

The life of Brother André echoed in some respects the life of St. Joseph, illustrating both silent ordinariness and explosions of the supernatural. Before he came to be known as a miracle worker, his life was utterly devoid of any newsworthy events. Joseph's silence bore fruit in his care for the Holy Family, as did Brother André's in the ordinary duties of a Holy Cross lay brother who first acted as a simple porter.

VOCABULARY

ANGEL
A spiritual, personal, and immortal creature, with intelligence and free will, who glorifies God without ceasing and who serves God as a messenger of his saving plan.

ANNUNCIATION
The visit of the angel Gabriel to the virgin Mary to inform her that she was to be the mother of the Savior. After giving her consent to God's word, Mary became the mother of Jesus by the power of the Holy Spirit.

ASSUMPTION
The dogma that recognizes the Blessed Virgin Mary's singular participation in her Son's Resurrection by which she was taken up body and soul into heavenly glory, when the course of her earthly life was finished.

BETROTHED
In ancient times, the beginning of the marriage process carrying the force of law.

CONSECRATED
A permanent state of life recognized by the Church, entered freely in response to the call of Christ to perfection, and characterized by the profession of the evangelical counsels of poverty, chastity, and obedience.

GABRIEL
One of the archangels, used by God many times as a messenger, in particular at the Annunciation.

IMMACULATE CONCEPTION
The dogma proclaimed in Christian Tradition and defined in 1854, that from the first moment of her conception, Mary—by the singular grace of God and by virtue of the merits of Jesus Christ—was preserved immune from Original Sin.

MESSIAH
Hebrew term meaning "anointed"; used in reference to Jesus because he accomplished perfectly the divine mission of priest, prophet, and King, signified by his anointing as Messiah, Christ.

PERPETUAL
For all time, forever.

VIRGINITY
Committed celibacy that enables people to give themselves to God alone with an undivided heart in a remarkable manner.

STUDY QUESTIONS

1. Who were Mary's parents?

Joachim and Ann

2. Where is most information about Mary found?

3. What is the name of the angel who announced to Mary the "Good News"?

4. Why is Mary called the "New Eve"?

Because she was born sinless.

5. Why is Mary called the "Immaculate Conception"?

6. Did Jesus have brothers or sisters? Aren't they mentioned in the Bible?

No.

7. What does Mary's perpetual virginity reflect?

8. How did Mary become our mother?

9. How is Mary the model for our lives?

10. What role did St. Joseph play in Jesus and Mary's lives?

PRACTICAL EXERCISES

1. Either individually or as a class, say a Rosary for your intentions—the Church, your parish, your family, school, friends, souls in purgatory, an end to abortion, peace in our world, etc.

2. Suppose you had a Protestant friend who accused you of "worshipping Mary." How would you defend asking Our Lady to intercede for us?

FROM THE CATECHISM

508 From among the descendants of Eve, God chose the Virgin Mary to be the mother of his son. "Full of grace," Mary is "the most excellent fruit of redemption" (*SC,* 103): from the first instant of her conception she was totally preserved from the stain of original sin and she remained pure from all personal sin throughout her life.

509 Mary is truly "Mother of God" since she is the mother of the eternal Son of God made man, who is God himself.

510 Mary "remained a virgin in conceiving her Son, a virgin in giving birth to him, a virgin in carrying him, a virgin in nursing him at her breast, always a virgin" (St. Augustine, Serm. 186, 1: PL, 38, 999): with her whole being she is "the handmaid of the Lord" (Lk 1:38).

511 The Virgin Mary "cooperated through free faith and obedience in human salvation" (*LG,* 56). She uttered her yes "in the name of all human nature" (St. Thomas Aquinas, *STh* III, 30, 1). By her obedience she became the new Eve, mother of the living.

973 By pronouncing her "fiat" at the Annunciation and giving her consent to the Incarnation, Mary was already collaborating with the whole work her Son was to accomplish. She is mother wherever he is Savior and head of the Mystical Body.

974 The most Blessed Virgin Mary, when the course of her earthly life was completed, was taken up body and soul into the glory of heaven, where she already shares in the glory of her Son's Resurrection, anticipating the resurrection of all members of his Body.

975 "We believe that the Holy Mother of God, the new Eve, mother of the Church, continues in heaven to exercise her maternal role on behalf of the members of Christ" (Paul VI, *CPG,* § 15).

Endnotes

1. Georges Bernanos, *Speight,* 1974, 149-50.
2. Lk 1:34-35 (Gk.).
3. *LG,* 56; cf. *LG,* 61.
4. *LG,* 59; cf. Pius XII, *Munificentissimus Deus* (1950): DS 3903; cf. Rv 19:16.

Revelation

The thoughts of God in the words of men.

Chapter 6

Revelation

*P*icture yourself sitting down at your computer. You have the idea for the greatest love story of all time. Yet, you hesitate. You have a serious question. What is the best way to guarantee your love story will be told over and over until the end of the world? After a few moments' thought, you throw away your computer. You have decided to tell your story only to men who are singers, troubadours. You are convinced that this is the best way.

This may sound like the formula for failure, but this is the way the Bible began.

God the Father inspired Moses through the Holy Spirit. He told Moses, as he had told Abraham, how he had chosen a people for himself. Then, he gave Moses the mission to continue the story and lead his people out of slavery. Moses passed on what God had told him to his followers in poetic form, and they passed it on through the generations. As the chosen people lived their way into history, they continued to tell the story of God's love and the coming Messiah. Revelation is God's love story, written especially for you.

REVELATION

If God had not chosen to reveal certain truths about himself, man would have been able to discover only a limited amount of information from nature regarding God's existence. The truths God has given to us are personified in Jesus Christ and found in the Bible and the oral Tradition. They are called divine revelation, for God has revealed to man truths about himself that could not be known unless he had chosen to reveal them. The word revelation originates from a word meaning "to unveil."

Since God has told us these truths, the Bible transmits truths necessary for salvation and is thus free from error. Likewise, there are no contradictions between the books in either Testament or between the Testaments themselves. In the language of their times, the writers of these books wrote precisely what God wanted. (See CCC 69 on p. 90)

The Holy Spirit chose certain men to pass on his truths. He "breathed" into the writers what he wished them to write, which led to the use of the term "inspired" to describe books that belong to the canon of the Bible. Both the Old and New Testaments refer to God's inspiration of the sacred authors. (See CCC 135, 136 on p. 90)

Pope John Paul II had this to say about Sacred Scripture:

> [Sacred Scripture]...is truly divine because it belongs to God truly and genuinely; God inspired it; God confirmed it; God spoke it through the sacred writers, Moses, the Prophets, the Evangelists, the Apostles, and above all, through His Son, our only Lord, in both the Old and New Testament; it is true that the intensity and depth of revelation varies, but there is not the least shadow of contradiction.[1]

Those who wonder about God's existence should read the Bible. It is the written history of God's love and care for us. It is the record of God accomplishing his wishes for mankind in spite of the failings of the very human agents he has chosen. It is a book about weak people, like ourselves, who struggle to find God's will in their daily lives. It has been called the thoughts of God in the words of men.

The Bible derives its name from a Greek word for "books," *biblia*, which itself was derived from *biblos*, meaning "the inner bark of the papyrus" and hence "paper" or "book."

Of course, the Church does not draw her certainty about God from the Holy Scriptures alone. Sacred Tradition helps us understand the truths of divine revelation. In addition it aids the Church in knowing which books belong in the Bible. Before the official canon was put together in the fourth century, the inspired books were simply handed from one generation of Christians to the next.

RELATIONSHIP BETWEEN THE MAGISTERIUM, TRADITION, AND SCRIPTURE

Sacred Tradition and Sacred Scripture make up a single deposit of the Word of God (deposit of faith), which is entrusted to the Church. The Catholic Church does not understand there to be two ways to the faith, but one—Jesus Christ. However we know from the words of St. John that:

The Holy Spirit "breathed" into the writers what he wished them to write.

The Bible is a book about weak people, like ourselves, who struggle to find God's will in their daily lives.

Only the Catholic Church has an unbroken history beginning in the time of the apostles and extending up to the present day.

The Jewish people divided the Old Testament into three parts: the Torah or law, the prophets, and the writings.

> Jesus did many other signs in the presence of the disciples, which are not written in this book; but these are written that you may believe that Jesus is the Christ, the Son of God, and that believing you may have life in his name. (Jn 20: 30-31)

(See CCC 97 on p. 90)

In fact, we know that one of the greatest writers of the New Testament was not even a follower of Christ during his life on earth. St. Paul, author of many of the epistles, learned about Jesus from his own miraculous experience on the road to Damascus and from the apostles. It could only be through the living witness of these close followers of our Lord that Paul was able to know anything at all about Jesus' life and message.

Only the Church with its living Magisterium has the authority of Jesus Christ. Only the Catholic Church has an unbroken history beginning in the time of the apostles and extending up to the present day. Jesus gave these apostles authority during his time on earth so that they may

> Go therefore and make disciples of all nations, baptizing them in the name of the Father, and of the Son, and of the Holy Spirit, teaching them to observe all that I have commanded you... (Mt 28:19-20)

The Magisterium is not the master of the Word of God, but its servant. It only teaches what was handed on originally by the one Master, Jesus Christ who was himself the "Word made flesh." It is this Master whom the Magisterium serves, and the Master has protected his Church with the seal of infallibility. This means that all the Church teaches came from Christ and that the Church has passed on all that Christ revealed *without addition or subtraction.* (See CCC 182 on p. 90)

DIVISIONS OF THE BIBLE

God chose to reveal himself to man, for he had planned from all eternity to create people with whom he could share his love and friendship. The Bible is the written record of most of his revelation. It is divided into two sections, the Old Testament, which contains forty-six books, and the New Testament, which contains twenty-seven books. (See CCC 68, 138 on p. 90)

The Old Testament is divided by Christians topically into the Pentateuch, the historical books, the prophetic books, and the wisdom books. The New Testament is divided topically into the Gospels, the Acts of the Apostles, the epistles or letters, and Revelation. The word testament is used because God made two covenants or testaments. God made the first covenant with Abraham, and Jesus gave the second testament to his Church through the apostles. (See CCC 70 on p. 90)

There is evidence, from as far back as 130 B.C., that the Jewish people divided the Old Testament into three parts: the Torah or law, the prophets, and the writings. Usually, the use of the word "law" in the writing of the prophets indicates the whole of God's teachings. After the Babylonian exile, the Pentateuch became recognized as the official sacred code, but the Jewish people never had an authority that specifically designated a canon.

The Old Testament is the pre-history of Jesus. It is the only book that foretells a coming of a personage into history. It spells out through a series of prophecies, beginning with Genesis, how the promised Messiah will be recognized. Even though the Jewish people were familiar with these messianic prophecies, they failed to recognize Jesus when he came.

THE CANON OF THE BIBLE

The term given to the correct number of books in the Bible is "canon" from the Greek word *kanon,* meaning "a reed" or "a straight rod or bar," which came to be used to indicate a correct measure. The canon is the correct measure or simply the correct number of books in the Bible. The term was first applied to the Bible in the third century. The word "canon" has also been used to indicate a list or catalogue of truths of the faith. When we refer to the correct number of books, we often use the word "canonical."

The canon began with Moses, who is traditionally thought to be the author of the Pentateuch.

Moses passed on the truths given by God in an oral fashion, and these truths were later written down. Moses required that the Pentateuch (Torah) be read aloud in the temple every seven years.

In 393 A.D., St. Augustine was present at the regional Council of Hippo, which decreed that the Old Testament as we have it is canonical. In making their determination regarding the correct number of books in the Old Testament, the bishops followed the Jewish tradition of Alexandria, Egypt, which relied on a Greek translation by seventy Jewish scholars, from whom it was given the name Septuagint. All canonical books were inspired by the Holy Spirit, who guided the Church to make the correct choice.

Those books that have always been accepted as canonical are called protocanonical. At first there were doubts about the canonicity of seven books in each of the Old and New Testaments. When these were determined to be part of the canon, they were given the title deuterocanonical. *Deutero* comes from a Greek word meaning "second." The deutero-canonical books of the Old Testament are: Tobit, Judith, Wisdom, Sirach, Baruch, and 1 and 2 Maccabees.

In the New Testament, the deuterocanonical books are Hebrews, Revelation, and the Catholic epistles: James, 2 Peter, 2 and 3 John, and Jude.

St. Augustine was present at the regional Council of Hippo, which decreed that the Old Testament as we have it is canonical.

Since the books of the New Testament were written after the Ascension, Jesus left no indication as to canonicity. It appears that all of the other apostles were dead before St. John finished his writings, so there was no opportunity to determine which books they accepted as canonical. Three reasons cited for the slow acceptance of the deuterocanonical books are:

† The faithful had been warned that some books were not authentic (apocryphal);

† Doubt as to their apostolic origin;

† They were directed to persons or local churches and were unknown to the Church at large.

The Holy Spirit has guided the Church in determining the canonicity of Scripture.

The Council of Trent, 1546
Under Pope Paul III decrees
The Canonical Scriptures

A fragment of a document from the sixth or eighth century, listing the books of the New Testament as we have them, was found by a man named Muratori in 1740. This document is called the Muratorian fragment.

Books considered non-canonical are called apocryphal. Among the books determined to be apocryphal were the Book of Enoch, the Assumption of Moses, the Gospel of Peter, the Odes of Solomon, and the Gospel of Thomas.

ORAL TRADITION

In the initial stages of their compilation, the books of both the Old and New Testaments were handed on orally. (See CCC 96 on p. 90)

The earliest writing was inscribed on clay tablets, which were baked to preserve them. At some point in their history, the Jewish people began to hand down their memories in written form. In addition to the books of the New Testament, the apostles passed on truths that were not specifically included in their writings. Because these were passed on orally, they are called the oral Tradition. Two examples of this oral Tradition are the Assumption of Mary and the prohibition against abortion. Teachings of the popes based on the teachings of Christ and the apostles are included in the oral Tradition. So, the Church bases its teaching on Scripture and the oral Traditions that have been handed down. The word tradition comes from the Latin *tradere*, which means "to hand on."

Three criteria were used to determine New Testament canonicity:

† Apostolicity – origin traceable to apostles or their associates;

† Orthodoxy – conformity to Christ's teaching and message;

† Catholicity – usage in the liturgy of the universal Church.

The Holy Spirit has guided the Church in determining the canonicity of Scripture.

> The Church has always regarded and continues to regard the Scriptures, taken together with sacred Tradition, as the supreme rule of her faith.[2]

SCRIPTURAL INTERPRETATION

Sacred Scripture is written in several different but complementary senses. Inspired by God, some authors wrote words with deeper meanings than they could have realized. As an example, we can look at the prophecy of Isaiah, "A virgin will conceive and bear a son" (Is 7:14). When we read the complete text surrounding this statement, it does not appear to make any sense. In light of the fact that the Virgin Mary conceived and bore Jesus, this prophecy takes on a special meaning: it is one of the Messianic prophecies in the Old Testament, which the Spirit caused to be written to indicate how to recognize the Messiah.

In order to interpret Scripture, the following things must be taken into consideration:

† The nature of the document;

† The character and station of the author;

† His ways of expression;

† The context in which he wrote;

† The setting in which it is read.

As we go through Scripture, we must keep in mind that it has a dual authorship, that of God and man. This dual authorship sets Scripture apart from every other written work in the history of the world. We should also remember its unity and context, which includes Tradition and the authentic interpretations of the Magisterium throughout the history of the Church.

First, we will look at two kinds of *literal* senses:

The literal sense proper is the precise sense the author intended to convey as he wrote. Moses' crossing of the Red Sea (Ex 14:15 ff.) is a good example, and actually took place.

The literal sense improper uses a figure of speech. When we say, "It rained cats and dogs," we are using a figure of speech, which is obviously not intended to be taken literally.

The writers of Scripture wrote at different times and used styles in vogue during the times in which they lived. They used various literary genres: narrative, poetry, genealogy, parable, and history.

Second, in addition to its literal meaning, Scripture also has a *plenary* meaning. This is the complete or full sense of what the Holy Spirit wants to convey. For example, in Genesis 3 God says to the serpent, "I will put enmity between you and the woman and between your seed and her seed; he (the descendant of the woman) shall bruise your head (a death dealing wound), and you shall bruise his heel (a slight wound)." The sacred writer could not have understood the plenary or complete meaning of what he wrote.

A third sense of Scripture is *typological,* in which things and people in the text have their own proper meanings but stand for other things and people at the same time. In this case, the word "type" means an image or figure that stands for something else that will come later. This typological sense is also the work of the Spirit. An outstanding type of the Old Testament is the Passover lamb, which stands for Jesus, the Lamb of the Eucharist.

The writers of Scripture wrote at different times and used styles in vogue during the times in which they lived.

PRIVATE REVELATION

There has been some confusion regarding Revelation given to the Church and private revelation. Revelation given directly to the Church by God is contained in the Scriptures and the oral Tradition and is contained in that collection of truths called the deposit of faith.

The term private revelation is applied to events of a miraculous nature when God or his mother appears to an individual or individuals to relate a message. Private revelation does not add to the deposit of faith and is different from it. It can be either an exhortation to some action or a warning and may be directed solely to the recipient, or to the whole Church.

Oral Tradition is the oral truths passed on by the Spirit and Christ.

Probably the best-known private revelation in the 20th century is the appearance of Mary to three children at Fatima, Portugal.

Probably the best-known private revelation in the 20th century is the appearance of Mary at Fatima, Portugal. Mary was seen by three children over a period of several months and warned of chastisements to be faced by the whole world if sins against purity are not reduced.

Oral Tradition is the oral truths passed on by the Spirit and Christ. Since it is oral, it is a dialogue which begins from God in the Old Testament, and is continued with the transmission of truths by Jesus to the apostles who then passed them on to others. The Spirit continues in his role to guarantee the authenticity of the truths passed on.

CONCLUSION

The Bible contains the truths the Father wished us to have. The Spirit breathed into the writers what he desired them to write for our salvation and the good of all souls. There is no other book that can compare to it in the history of mankind, for it is the thoughts of God written in the words of man.

To ensure that man would understand these truths as he wished, God gave to the Church the authority to interpret these truths and guaranteed the interpretation through his Holy Spirit.

SUPPLEMENTARY READING

Juan Diego had already been to the bishop twice to tell him of the Blessed Mother's appearance near Mexico City. However, Bishop Juan de Zumarraga was no fool, rather he was a man of practicality. If this young Juan Diego were really seeing visions demanding another church be built, he would have to prove it with a sign. On this third visit, after entering the room and bowing to the bishop, Juan Diego brought this message:

Your Excellency, I did that which you asked. I told my Mistress, the Queen of Heaven, Holy Mary, Mother of God, that you required a sign in order that you might believe what I had told you regarding the temple she enjoins you to build in the place she asks that you should erect it. And, furthermore, I said that I had given my word to bring here some sign and proof of her will, as you asked. She met your request and with graciousness accepted your condition concerning the sign you must have before her will might be accomplished.

Very early this morning she told me to come to see you again. So I asked for the sign that would make you believe and that she has said she would give me. Instantly she complied with my petition. She sent me to the top of the hill where I had previously seen her pick Castilian roses. Although I well knew that the summit of the hill is not a place where flowers grow, nevertheless I doubted nothing. And when I arrived at the top, I saw that I was in a terrestrial paradise, where every variety of exquisite flower, brilliant with dew, flourished in abundance. These I gathered and carried back to her. With her own hands she arranged them and replaced them in my robe in order that I might bring them to you. Here they are. Behold and receive them.

With that, Juan released the roses he had been guarding so zealously and watched them drop to the floor with a flourish. Relief flooded him at the delivering of the message. Yet his triumph did not end there. As his heart pounded and his eyes stared at the flowers,

St. Juan Diego
(1474-1548)
Feast on December 9

he was suddenly aware that the bishop was gazing not at the flowers, but at *him*. In fact, he had descended from his throne, dropped to his knees, and begun to pray. Concerned, Juan glanced down at himself and the tilma from which the mass of roses had just been released. On it in glorious tones was the image of the Our Lady of Guadalupe just as she had revealed herself to Juan on the heights of Mt. Tepeyac.

The tilma of Juan Diego is miraculous in at least three ways. First, the material of which the image is composed is not known to exist anywhere else in the world. Second, the colors in the image are not painted on or dyed in, but part of the fibers themselves. Third, using a microscope it has been discovered that a reflection of Juan Diego can be found in the eyes of Our Lady's image on the tilma as if it was a perfect image of her as she appeared before him.

VOCABULARY

APOCRYPHAL
Term referring to books that were rejected from the Bible because they lacked genuineness and canonicity.

BIBLE
Sacred Scripture: the books which contain the truth of God's revelation and were composed by human authors inspired by the Holy Spirit. The Bible contains both the forty-six books of the Old Testament and the twenty-seven books of the New Testament.

CANON
The Church's complete list of sacred books of the Bible.

DEPOSIT OF FAITH
The heritage of faith contained in Sacred Scripture and Tradition, handed on in the Church from the time of the apostles, from which the Magisterium draws all that it proposes for belief as being divinely revealed.

DEUTEROCANONICAL
Those books and passages of the Old and New Testaments about which there was controversy in early Christian history.

DOCTRINE
Revealed teachings of Christ which are proclaimed by the fullest extent of the exercise of the authority of the Church's Magisterium. The faithful are obliged to believe the truths or dogmas contained in Divine Revelation and defined by the Magisterium.

LITERAL SENSE IMPROPER
Method of Scriptural interpretation in which the author is inspired to use figures of speech.

LITERAL SENSE PROPER
Method of Scriptural interpretation in which the author intends precisely what he was inspired to write.

ORAL TRADITION
The living transmission of the message of the Gospel in the Church. The oral preaching of the apostles is conserved and handed on as the deposit of faith through the Church.

PHARISEE
During the time of Jesus, an avid, contentious student and/or teacher of Jewish religious law.

PRIVATE REVELATION
Revelations made in the course of history which do not add to or form part of the deposit of faith, but rather may help people live out their faith more fully. Some have been recognized by the authority of the Church.

PROPHECY
From Hebrew *hozeh* meaning "vision" or "revelation interpreted"; God's communication to his creatures of the knowledge he has, including foreknowledge of the contingent future.

PROTOCANONICAL
Those books of the Bible, especially in the Old Testament, whose inspired character has never been questioned (by any Church Father). Can be misleading because it was not the Church Fathers, but the Magisterium under the Pope that was divinely authorized.

REVELATION
God's communication of himself, by which he makes known the mystery of his divine plan. A gift of God's self-communication which is realized by deeds and words over time, and most fully by sending us his own divine Son, Jesus Christ.

SEPTUAGINT
A pre-Christian Greek translation of the Hebrew Scriptures made by Jewish scholars, and later adopted by Greek-speaking Christians.

TESTAMENT
The name given to the two major parts of the Bible; a synonym for covenant. The Old Testament recounts the history of salvation before the time of Christ (46 books), and the New Testament unfolds the saving work of Jesus and the Church (27 books).

TYPOLOGICAL SENSE
Reading of the Old Testament which discerns in God's works of the Old Covenant prefigurations of what he accomplished in the fullness of time in the person of Jesus Christ.

STUDY QUESTIONS

1. What are the two original sources of Church teaching?

2. What role did the Holy Spirit play in the writing of Sacred Scripture?

3. Where does the word "Bible" come from?

4. Who does the Magisterium get its authority from?

5. What are the two divisions of the Bible?

6. How many books are there in the Old and New Testaments?

7. How many covenants did God make?

8. When and where was the Old Testament declared canonical?

9. Who are the two authors of Scripture?

10. What is included in the oral Tradition?

11. List the three criteria used to determine the canonicity of New Testament books.

12. List the five elements of Scriptural interpretation.

13. What is contained in the Deposit of Faith?

PRACTICAL EXERCISES

1. Read the four gospel accounts of Jesus' crucifixion (Matthew 27:31-51, Mark 15:20-38, Luke 23:26-46, John 19:16-30.). Some people claim that these accounts contradict each other. What do you think?

2. Read the two accounts of creation in Genesis (Chapters 1 and 2). How do the two accounts differ? What do you think is the reason for there being two accounts of creation?

3. Besides Fatima, there are many other cases of private revelation. Ask your spiritual director if he or she believes that any of these cases might be good for you to study so as to grow in your interior life.

4. Bruno says that the story of Adam and Eve is just a fictional myth since no one was there to write a record of creation. What would you say to Bruno?

5. Justin, a Protestant, thinks that Catholics "made up" things like the Assumption of Mary and purgatory because they aren't written in the Bible. What would you say to Justin?

6. Meredith asserts that Catholics added books to the Bible that were not originally in it. Can you refute Meredith?

7. Fatima, a young girl, is excited to have learned about the apparition of Mary to three peasant children in Portugal at the town from which she gets her name. Fatima is very interested in the revelations Mary made to these children, including the revelation that Russia would spread its errors throughout the world, raising up wars and persecutions against the Church, that peace would be granted to all the world if Our Lady's requests for prayer, reparation and consecration were heard and obeyed, and the Secret, including the horrifying vision of hell where poor sinners go. She thinks the things Mary said are so important that everyone should know about them. Could the revelations be read at mass in place of one of the readings, she wonders. What would you say and why?

FROM THE CATECHISM

68 By love, God has revealed himself and given himself to man. He has thus provided the definitive, superabundant answer to the questions that man asks himself about the meaning and purpose of his life.

69 God has revealed himself to man by gradually communicating his own mystery in deeds and in words.

70 Beyond the witness to himself that God gives in created things, he manifested himself to our first parents, spoke to them and, after the fall, promised them salvation (cf. Gn 3:15) and offered them his covenant.

96 What Christ entrusted to the apostles, they in turn handed on by their preaching and writing, under the inspiration of the Holy Spirit, to all generations, until Christ returns in glory.

97 "Sacred Tradition and Sacred Scripture make up a single sacred deposit of the Word of God" (*DV*, 10), in which, as in a mirror, the pilgrim Church contemplates God, the source of all her riches.

135 "The Sacred Scriptures contain the Word of God and because they are inspired, they are truly the Word of God" (*DV*, 24).

136 God is the author of Sacred Scripture because he inspired its human authors; he acts in them and by means of them. He thus gives assurance that their writings teach without error his saving truth (cf. *DV*, 11).

138 The Church accepts and venerates as inspired the 46 books of the Old Testament and the 27 books of the New.

182 We believe all "that which is contained in the word of God, written or handed down, and which the Church proposes for belief as divinely revealed" (Paul VI, *CPG*, § 20).

Endnotes

1. Letter Patres Ecclesiae.
2. *DV*, 21.

The Old Testament

*The story of God's love for mankind
since creation began.*

Chapter 7

The Old Testament

The Old Testament is a collection of books inspired by the Holy Spirit to explain to man his origin in God, man's failure to follow God's plan and commands, God's promise of a redeemer, God's choice of a people to be his own, and the history of that people, the Jewish race, leading up to the arrival of the promised Messiah, whose coming is described in the New Testament.

The Old Testament is divided into the Pentateuch and the wisdom, the historical, and the prophetic books.

The word testament means "covenant" or "agreement," hence the title Old Testament, honoring the covenant God made with Abraham and his descendants, the Jewish people. Sometimes, the word covenant is used in place of testament.

THE OLD TESTAMENT

The first five books of the Old Testament are called the Pentateuch, which comes from a Greek word meaning "five boxes." The Jewish people called these five books the Torah and kept these writings on scrolls, which were rolled up and stored in boxes.

Moses is traditionally considered to be the author of the Pentateuch, in the sense that he passed on the information that he received from God in verbal form to the Jewish people.

The names of the five books are Genesis, Exodus, Leviticus, Numbers, and Deuteronomy. Genesis means "beginning" in Greek, and so the book of Genesis tells of the beginning of man and the origin of the world. Exodus records the deeds of Moses and the freeing of the Jewish people from slavery under the pharaoh. Leviticus tells of the formation of the priestly caste of Levi and the rules God gave for worship. Numbers describes the life of the Jewish people in the wilderness. Deuteronomy, or "second law," summarizes the early law and contains Moses' farewell to his people.

GENESIS

Genesis introduces us to the creation of the world and all that is in it, including man. It is the beginning of the family tree of man, not a scientific treatise but an account by primitive people of man's origins, and it contains historical elements. Here are some truths contained in the first eleven chapters of Genesis:

† God created everything and is eternal;

† We are made in God's image;

† Everything God created was good;

† God made the seventh day holy;

† There is only one God;

† All die because of Adam's sin;

† All are descended from Adam and Eve;

† All inherit the effects of Adam's sin;

† Man is higher than all the animals;

† Marriage is of divine origin.

God gives Adam and Eve only one commandment and warns them of the serious consequences to be faced if they disobey. "You may freely eat of every tree of the garden; but of the tree of knowledge of good and evil you shall not eat, for in the day that you eat of it, you shall die" (Gn 2:16-17).

Adam and Eve refuse to honor the one command of God and commit the first or original sin.

As a result, they lose God's grace, find their bodies at war with their spirits, and are cast out of the garden. No longer able to speak to God face-to-face, they lose physical immortality (though their souls remained immortal), and are sent to live in the world of suffering that results from their refusal to obey God.

Genesis introduces us to the creation of the world.

Adam and Eve refuse to honor the one command of God and commit the first or original sin.

Abraham

Father of a multitude.

Jacob

Grandson of Abraham named Israel by God.

Joseph

Son of Jacob becomes the most powerful man in Egypt.

The God who created them out of love does not abandon them. God promises warfare between the descendants of Adam and Eve and the devil. "I will put enmity between you and the woman and between your seed and her seed; he shall bruise your head and you shall bruise his heel" (Gn 3:15). This statement is called the proto-evangelium or first announcement of salvation by God. The Church considers this a foreshadowing of Mary's role as the new Eve, who will overcome Satan by her "yes" to God. Sin spreads to the family with the slaying of Abel by Cain and ultimately to society, as is demonstrated at the Tower of Babel. The early history of man concludes with the story of Noah and the flood.

There is a gap of indeterminate time until the appearance of Abraham commences the unfolding of God's plan of salvation. Around 1850 B.C., God calls Abram to leave his father's people, who are polytheists in Ur of the Chaldees, and go to the land of Canaan. Faith, the ability and power to believe, is always a gift from God. Abram accepts God's gift of faith. In return for Abram's acceptance of God's commands, he is given a new name, Abraham, which means "father of a multitude." Although his wife is childless and beyond the years for childbearing, God promises Abraham a son, the first of many descendants, "who will be as numerous as the stars." Furthermore, his descendants will be given the land of Canaan. Abraham and his posterity are to accept circumcision as a sign of their belief in the one God, monotheism. This personal covenant is sealed by the sacrifice of animals and will be renewed again on Mt. Sinai with Moses.

Abraham has a son whom he names Isaac, who has a son called Jacob. Like his grandfather Abraham, Jacob is given a new name by God, Israel, and the descendants of Jacob's twelve sons are called the Israelites. Genesis concludes with the story of Joseph, the son of Jacob, who is sold into slavery in Egypt, where he becomes the most powerful man after the pharaoh.

EXODUS

Exodus means "leaving" in Greek, and the name refers to the departure of the Israelites from slavery in Egypt.

Four hundred years pass between Joseph's death in Egypt, which is described at the end of the book of Genesis, and the appearance of Moses, which is described near the beginning of the book of Exodus. During this period, the descendants of Jacob grow into a large clan, but finally a pharaoh arises who "did not know Joseph" and his service to Egypt. This pharaoh commands the midwives to kill the sons of the Jewish people. Because the midwives fear God, they do not follow the pharaoh's orders, and the Jewish people increase in number. Pharaoh then commands that all Jewish male children be drowned in the Nile. Moses is placed in the Nile in a reed basket, discovered, and reared by the daughter of Pharaoh. Moses remains true to the beliefs of his fathers and in defense of a Jewish man kills an Egyptian and is forced to flee. While he is tending sheep in exile, God calls Moses to dedicate himself to freeing God's people from the Egyptians.

Like Abraham, Moses places his trust in God. He confronts pharaoh on

God's orders and, by means of ten plagues visited upon Egypt, demonstrates to pharaoh that he serves the true God.

Eventually, pharaoh relents, and the Jewish people are allowed to leave and pass through the Red Sea by the power of God. God makes a covenant with Moses that:

† Makes the Jewish people his own;

† Fulfills the covenant made with Abraham;

† Promises them the land of Canaan;

† Promises the protection of Israel;

† Gives them a law to regulate their religious and moral life;

† Tells them that Yahweh is the One God, the only god they may worship.

Like Abraham, Moses is a man of faith who follows Yahweh's commands. The one instance in which he doubts God costs him his chance to enter into the Promised Land.

Moses foreshadows Jesus as a leader of God's people, as a miracle worker, and as one who frees the Jewish people from slavery.

LEVITICUS

Leviticus begins with the second year after the departure from Egypt, but is mainly a book about worship. Jewish worship practices begin to be described in Exodus, which includes specifications about the tent of meeting, but in Leviticus, Moses develops the forms of worship in more detail. Proper worship and holiness of life are the main points of Leviticus.

To Yahweh alone are worship and sacrifice to be offered. The five forms of worship are:

† The holocaust or principal sacrifice, in which the victim is consumed by fire;

† The peace offering, in which priest and people share the sacrifice;

† The sin and trespass offering (sins are inadvertent, trespasses are on purpose);

† The bloodless sacrifice, usually an offering of grain;

† The guilt offering, to make reparation to God for failure to do or give something owed.

Priests are to be chosen only from the tribe of Levi and are expected to be holy, because God whom they serve is holy. Laws of purification are made to set the practices of the Hebrews apart from those of the pagans. The Levitical sacrifices foreshadow Jesus' perfect sacrifice on the Cross. A Day of Atonement is established, on which the Hebrews are purified externally from their sins. Rules for the treatment of the members of the community promise rewards for those who follow the law and serious punishments for those who break the law.

Man's sin requires sacrifice to be made to God in atonement. Since man himself is not capable of making complete atonement, God designates his Son, the Messiah to come, who alone has the power to make a perfect sacrifice for man's sin.

In Exodus, Moses foreshadows Jesus as a leader of God's people.

In Leviticus, Moses develops the forms of worship in more detail.

Numbers is a history of the Israelites' travels in the desert. Their story reminds us that we too are guilty of sin, despite the loving care we have received from Christ and his Church.

Deuteronomy is Moses' last statement to the people of Israel concerning Yahweh's unfailing love.

NUMBERS

Numbers picks up from the second year after the departure from Egypt. In the Hebrew language, the book is called "in the wilderness." It is a history of the Israelites' travels in the desert and is divided into three parts:

† Travels in the Sinai;

† Wandering in the wilderness;

† Travels on the plains of Moab.

God calls for a census to demonstrate that he has kept his promise to Abraham. The family of Jacob and his twelve sons has grown to 600,000 people in four hundred years, and they are divided into twelve tribes. God calls upon the Jews to be a holy people. Because they doubt God, they travel for thirty-eight years in the desert under the protection of Yahweh, who appears to them in the form of a cloud. Most of those who leave Egypt die before the entrance into Canaan. When they reach the gates of Canaan, they sin against Yahweh's law with the Moabite women.

The Israelites are often rebellious, and Yahweh even calls them hardhearted. But in reading their story, we must keep in mind that they are a primitive people, kept in slavery for a long period in Egypt, and they did not have the Church and the sacraments, which make it easier to serve God. Their story reminds us that we too are guilty of sin, despite the loving care we have received from Christ and his Church.

DEUTERONOMY

Deuteronomy means "second law" in Greek. This book gets its Greek title from its second proclamation of the law, although the Jews refer to it as "The Words." Moses realizes he is near death, promulgates the Ten Commandments, and repeats the law to remind the Israelites they are to maintain their relationship to the one God. He orders that the law be read out every seven years as a reminder to them of their obligations.

Israel is to love and adore the one true God, who has created all things. They are to follow the religious and civil laws out of love, for Yahweh has loved them freely above all other peoples. We must see the commandments as part of our heritage, which enables us to be free of sin. They are not exterior to us but must be internalized if we are to live as Jesus desires. Deuteronomy reminds us that God is constantly watching over us in our struggles, and our complete fidelity to his wishes is required.

Deuteronomy contains the beautiful prayer:

Hear, O Israel: The Lord our God is one Lord; and you shall love the Lord your God with all your heart and all your soul and with all your might. And these words I command you this day shall be upon your heart; and you shall teach them diligently to your children, and shall talk of them when you sit in your house, and when you walk by the way, and when you lie down, and when you rise. And you shall bind them as a sign upon your hand, and they shall be as frontlets between your eyes. And you shall place them upon the door posts of your house and on your gates. (Dt 6: 4-9)

We could call Deuteronomy Moses' last statement to the people of Israel concerning Yahweh's unfailing love. It is filled with affection for his people while reminding them of God's goodness and mercy, which are shown above all in the prophecies of the Messiah to come. Moses is the legislator of the old law, and Jesus is the legislator of the law to come. Some of the greatest passages regarding love of neighbor are contained in Deuteronomy. It is filled with compassion for those who suffer and defends the weak while extolling public and private morality. Its warnings regarding those who sin are for us as well as the Israelites.

The historical books are: Joshua, Judges, Ruth, 1 and 2 Samuel, 1 and 2 Kings, 1 and 2 Chronicles, Ezra, Nehemiah, Tobit, Judith, Esther, and 1 and 2 Maccabees.

The wisdom books of the Bible are: Job, Psalms, Proverbs, Ecclesiastes, Song of Songs, Wisdom, and Sirach.

The prophetic books of the Bible are Isaiah, Jeremiah, Lamentations, Baruch, Ezekiel, Daniel, Hosea, Joel, Amos, Obadiah, Jonah, Micah, Nahum, Habakkuk, Zephaniah, Haggai, Zechariah, and Malachi.

CONCLUSION

The Old Testament is the story of God's love for mankind since creation began. After the Fall of Adam and Eve in the garden, God enacts several covenants with mankind through Abraham first, and later through Moses. After the Jewish people are freed from slavery in Egypt, Moses instructs them in how God wants them to worship him (Leviticus) and what laws to follow (Deuteronomy).

The many other books in the Old Testament give us an idea of the history of the Jewish people, teach us their wisdom, and foretell the coming of a Savior. These prophecies and words of wisdom, as well as the law, will come to fulfillment in Jesus Christ.

Moses is the legislator of the old law, and Jesus is the legislator of the law to come.

Deuteronomy is filled with compassion for those who suffer.

The Fifth Day of Creation

And God said, "Let the waters bring forth swarms of living creatures, and let birds fly above the earth across the firmament of heavens." (Gn 1:20)

SUPPLEMENTARY READING

The single most decisive man in Jewish history was a complex figure: both a freedom fighter and a lawgiver, a heroic leader tortured by self-doubt, a stutterer who spoke to God, a loving shepherd and a ruthless warrior, and God's friend who was denied the right to set foot on the Promised Land. Moses was an ordinary human being called on to do extraordinary things.

His Israelite parents who sought to save him from the pharaoh's decree to kill all firstborn sons left him floating on the river in a basket. Pharaoh's daughter saved the child and raised him as a prince. As Moses grew up, he grew in his concern for the Israelite people. One day as a taskmaster mercilessly beat an Israelite slave, Moses' outrage led him to kill the master and flee Egypt. While shepherding his flock, God called to Moses from "a bush that burned but was not consumed."

In many ways, the story of Moses acts as a precursor to the story of Jesus. In pharaoh's death sentence on the firstborn of Israel, we see Herod's slaughter of the innocents that sent the Holy Family to Egypt. The crossing of the Red Sea shows our flight from sin and death through the waters of Baptism. The miracle of the manna and quail gives us a glimpse at Jesus' first multiplying the loaves and fish, and later his instituting the Eucharist.

Moses was a man known for his willingness to do what was best rather than what was easiest. In fact, the whole purpose of Moses' ministry appears to be to make clear that we as humans ultimately have two choices:

Moses
The single most decisive man
in Jewish history.

life or death, love or hate, hope or despair, compassion or cruelty. "I call heaven and earth to witness against you this day, that I have set before you life and death, blessing and curse; therefore choose life, that you and your descendants may live" (Dt 30:19). Let us remember the many struggles and conquests of Moses as we pray to God that we may choose wisely and inherit eternal life.

VOCABULARY

ATONEMENT

Reparation for an offense through a voluntary action that compensates for the injustice done.

EXODUS

God's saving intervention in history by which he liberated the Hebrew people from slavery in Egypt, made a covenant with them, and brought them into the Promised Land. The Book of Exodus, the second of the Old Testament, narrates this saving history.

HOLOCAUST

A type of Old Testament sacrifice in which the entire item of sacrifice was burned on the altar and the scent rose heavenward.

ISRAELITES

The Jewish people, chosen by God to be his people and named after Israel (Jacob), from whose twelve sons the tribes of Israel descend. God formed Israel into his priestly people in their exodus from the slavery of Egypt, when he made the Old Covenant.

LEVITICUS

Third book of the Bible; named from its contents which deal entirely with the service of God and the religious ceremonies to be performed by the members of the tribe of Levi, both priests and Levites.

OLD TESTAMENT

The forty-six books of the Bible, which record the history of salvation from creation through the old alliance or covenant with Israel, in preparation for the appearance of Christ as Savior of the world.

ORIGINAL SIN

The sin by which the first human beings disobeyed the commandment of God, choosing to follow their own will rather than God's will. As a consequence they lost the grace of original holiness, and became subject to the law of death; sin became universally present in the world. Besides the personal sin of Adam and Eve, original sin describes the fallen state of human nature which affects every person born into the world, and from which Christ, the "new Adam," came to redeem us.

PASSOVER

Also known as *Pasch*; Jewish feast commemorating the deliverance of the Jewish people from death by the blood of the lamb sprinkled on the doorposts in Egypt, which the angel of death saw and passed over. The Eucharist celebrates the new Passover.

PENTATEUCH

The first five books of the Old Testament: Genesis, Exodus, Leviticus, Numbers, and Deuteronomy.

PHARAOH

In ancient times, leader of the Egyptians; often worshipped as a god by the Egyptian people.

PROTO-EVANGELIUM

The "proto" or first Gospel: the passage in Genesis (3:15) that first mysteriously announces the promise of the Messiah and Redeemer.

YAHWEH

The personal name of the God of Israel, revealed to Moses on Mt. Sinai, meaning "I am who I am."

STUDY QUESTIONS

1. In what sense is Moses considered to be the author of the Pentateuch?

2. How is the Old Testament divided?

3. What sin did Adam and Eve commit, and what did they lose?

4. In return for his acceptance of God's commands, what was Abram given?

5. What was God's promise to Abraham? Explain.

6. What new name did God give to Jacob?

7. Who is Joseph?

8. What word refers to the departure of the Israelites from slavery into Egypt?

9. Who is Moses and what did he do?

10. What is contained in God's covenant to Moses?

11. What are the five forms of proper worship according to Moses?

12. Which sacrifices foreshadow Jesus' sacrifice on the cross?

13. What punishment did the Jewish people suffer for doubting God?

14. Why should Christians read the Old Testament with the New Testament in mind?

PRACTICAL EXERCISES

1. Read Adam and Eve's reaction to God after they sinned. Does this relate to us in our reactions to our personal sins?

2. Despite our reaction, we can take comfort in God's loving mercy. Be sure to go to confession this week to make atonement ("at one"-ment) for your sins.

3. Read the story of Joseph and his brothers. What lessons can be learned from this story?

4. Read the story of pharaoh and the ten plagues. Write a short description of pharaoh and his stubborn attitude. Is it possible for us to be as stubborn?

5. Scan the Wisdom writings (Proverbs, Sirach, etc.) for some advice you can take to heart and live out this week. Share it with your parents and spiritual director.

FROM THE CATECHISM

72 God chose Abraham and made a covenant with him and his descendants. By the covenant God formed his people and revealed his law to them through Moses. Through the prophets, he prepared them to accept the salvation destined for all humanity.

135 "The Sacred Scriptures contain the Word of God and because they are inspired they are truly the Word of God" (*DV,* 24).

136 God is the author of Sacred Scripture because he inspired its human authors; he acts in them and by means of them. He thus gives assurance that their writings teach without error his saving truth (cf. *DV,* 11).

137 Interpretation of the inspired Scripture must be attentive above all to what God wants to reveal through the sacred authors for our salvation. What comes from the Spirit is not fully "understood except by the Spirit's action" (cf. Origen, Hom. In Ex. 4, 5: PG, 12, 320).

138 The Church accepts and venerates as inspired the 46 books of the Old Testament and the 27 books of the New.

140 The unity of the two Testaments proceeds from the unity of God's plan and his Revelation. The Old Testament prepares for the New and the New Testament fulfills the Old; the two shed light on each other; both are true Word of God.

141 "The Church has always venerated the divine Scriptures as she venerated the Body of the Lord" (*DV,* 21): both nourish and govern the whole Christian life. "Your word is a lamp to my feet and a light to my path" (Ps 119:105; cf. Is 50:4).

179 Faith is a supernatural gift from God. In order to believe, man needs the interior helps of the Holy Spirit.

180 "Believing" is a human act, conscious and free, corresponding to the dignity of the human person.

182 We believe all "that which is contained in the word of God, written or handed down, and which the Church proposes for belief as divinely revealed" (Paul VI, *CPG,* § 20).

315 In the creation of the world and of man, God gave the first and universal witness to his almighty love and his wisdom, the first proclamation of the "plan of his loving goodness," which finds its goal in the new creation in Christ.

316 Though the work of creation is attributed to the Father in particular, it is equally a truth of faith that the Father, Son, and Holy Spirit together are the one indivisible principle of creation.

317 God alone created the universe freely, directly, and without any help.

319 God created the world to show forth and communicate his glory. That his creatures should share in his truth, goodness, and beauty—this is the glory for which God created them.

1977 Christ is the end of the law (cf. Rom 10:4); only he teaches and bestows the justice of God.

1980 The Old Law is the first stage of revealed law. Its moral prescriptions are summed up in the Ten Commandments.

1982 The Old Law is a preparation for the Gospel.

Chapter 8

The New Testament

*The story of the greatest sacrifice
in the history of the world.*

The New Testament

*I*t is claimed that everyone loves a love story. Whether that is true or not, the literature of most cultures certainly has a fair share of love stories. In the English-speaking world, the most famous love story is probably *Romeo and Juliet,* which reflects our culture's distorted belief that romantic love is the best kind of love. All love, if it is true, is about sacrifice.

The longest continuing love story in the history of mankind is the love of God for his children. The New Testament records the life of the Son of God, who came to earth to save all people from sin. The story of our salvation is also the story of the greatest sacrifice in the history of the world. Unlike other love stories, this one has no ending, for it will continue throughout eternity.

NEW TESTAMENT

The New Testament includes the Gospels, which tell of the words and actions of Jesus, and the writings of the apostles, which include the epistles, the Acts of the Apostles, and the Book of Revelation. The New Testament completes the revelation that began in the Old Testament. The two Testaments are not separate books; they are the complete gift of the Father to his children to enable us to understand and to live his loving plan for us.

> "The Word of God, which is the power of God for salvation to everyone who has faith, is set forth and displays its power in a most wonderful way in the writings of the New Testament"[1] which hand on the ultimate truth of God's Revelation. Their central object is Jesus Christ, God's incarnate Son: his acts, teachings, Passion and glorification, and his Church's beginnings under the Spirit's guidance.[2] (CCC 124)

THE GOSPELS

The word Gospel means "good news" or "good tidings," and the Gospels, as our principal source for the life and teaching of Jesus, bring us the good news of our salvation. They were originally transmitted through the preaching of the apostles and their followers, who were protected from error by the Holy Spirit. The Church has always held that the four Gospels are apostolic and historical and teach faithfully the truths that Jesus handed on to his apostles until his Ascension. Divine written revelation ends with the death of St. John, who was the last eyewitness to Jesus and his teachings.

> The Church has always and everywhere maintained, and continues to maintain, the apostolic origin of the four Gospels. The apostles preached, as Christ had charged them to do, and then, under the inspiration of the Holy Spirit, they and others of the apostolic age handed on to us in writing the same message they had preached, the foundation of our faith: the fourfold Gospel, according to Matthew, Mark, Luke and John.[3]

The writers of the Gospels intended to pass on faithfully what Jesus said and did, as they witnessed it or as it was told to them. In doing this, they were guided to fuller understanding by the Holy Spirit. St. Luke specifically mentions writing a narrative of the events fulfilled "among us." St. John quotes Jesus as saying, "When the Spirit of truth comes, he will guide you into all the truth" (Jn 16:13). The Gospel writers used both oral and written sources. Sts. John and Matthew wrote what they saw, while Mark and Luke recorded what Mary and the apostles told them. Each writer selected certain events and discourses of Jesus with a view toward instructing individual churches. For instance, St. Matthew sought to convince the Jewish people that Jesus was the Messiah, so he quoted words and actions of Jesus that could be tied to Old Testament prophecies. The authors reported the sayings and doings of Jesus in different orders, and did not try to copy each other.

The Gospels were originally transmitted through the preaching of the apostles and their followers.

Matthew wrote to convince his own people that Jesus was the Messiah who lived on earth.

ST. MATTHEW

According to written testimony from the second century, Matthew was the first to write a version of the Gospel. Eusebius wrote in his history that Matthew wrote the "oracles of the Lord." Matthew wrote his Gospel in Palestine and addressed it to Jewish people living in Palestine. He is thought to have written the original version in Aramaic, the language of the Jewish people at that time, between A.D. 50 and 69, several years before the destruction of the temple in Jerusalem, which occurred in A.D. 70. The version of Matthew's Gospel that the Church now possesses was written in Greek around A.D. 70, possibly after St. Mark's Gospel was written.

Matthew was an eyewitness to the words and actions of Jesus, who chose him as an apostle even though he was a tax collector and publican, an official employed by the hated Roman government. In fact, Jesus called him away from a tax table. Most Jews who collected taxes for the Romans from their own countrymen were held in low esteem, but according to Luke, Matthew had many friends in Capernaum.

As a devout Jew who revered the Hebrew Scriptures, Matthew wrote to convince his own people that Jesus was the Messiah who lived on earth, founded a Church, announced the Kingdom of God, was the Son of God, suffered, died, was buried, and rose from the dead.

He connects the messiahship of Jesus with specific Old Testament prophecies to show how Jesus fulfilled them. In Matthew's account of the Sermon on the Mount, Jesus tells us about the Father's plan for the fulfillment of the kingdom. For this reason, Matthew's Gospel is sometimes called the "Gospel of the kingdom." According to the Beatitudes, which Jesus gave us in his Sermon on the Mount, the kingdom of heaven belongs to the poor in spirit (Mt 5:3).

Jesus gave to the apostles the power to carry on his mission to save all men through the administration of the sacraments and the preaching of the good news. This includes everything that contributes to making us holy and increases our faith.

We are to be guided by the "rock" of the papacy which will direct us to all truth regarding Jesus' teachings, life, and worship for all generations to come, for he will be with the Church till the end of time.

The kingdom is found by being poor in spirit through detachment from earthly things. Possession of material resources is the means to live life while in this earthly kingdom, but we must take care not to prefer any earthly treasure to our treasure in heaven.

ST. MARK

Mark was born in Jerusalem. St. Peter took refuge in the home of Mark's mother after being miraculously freed from prison (cf. Acts 12:12).

St. Mark wrote his Gospel for Christians of gentile origin who lived in Rome. According to Papias, Mark was a disciple and interpreter of St. Peter on his travels. Mark wrote what Peter told him of all that Jesus said and did, for he was not himself a disciple of Jesus. St. Irenaeus said that

Mark delivered to the Church all St. Peter had preached. Since Mark mentioned Jesus' prediction of the destruction of the temple in Jerusalem, his Gospel is dated prior to A.D. 70.

Mark's Gospel has been called "the Gospel of miracles." Although it is the shortest Gospel, it includes almost all the miracles mentioned by the other evangelists. Mark also describes two miracles, the curing of a deaf and dumb man and the curing of a blind man by the saliva of Jesus, which are not recorded in the other three Gospels.

Mark demonstrates that Jesus could work all these miracles because he was the Son of God and had God's powers to work miracles. Despite his miracles, the scribes and Pharisees refused to accept him as the Messiah. Jesus came to heal everyone, even the Samaritans who were despised by the Jewish people of Jerusalem. Although they knew the Scriptures, the scribes and Pharisees did not see that Jesus had come to heal all men because they believed that only the Jewish nation would be saved.

Mark stresses the prayer life of Jesus, in particular Jesus going alone in private to seek the assistance of the Father in prayer. He is making the point that prayer should be a trusting conversation between a child and God, the Father, in which the child is totally accepting of what the Father indicates in response to prayer. This prayer is the prayer of a child who calls God "Abba," which means "Daddy." It is a prayer of love and familiarity with God. It is also the prayer of one who accepts, as Jesus accepted, that the Father calls us to accept out of love the sufferings that come to us, in the sure knowledge that the Father will see us through by his grace. We are called to identify our will with God's in a free and ready manner, demonstrating our love as children of God.

ST. LUKE

St. Luke was a Greek from Antioch, a disciple of St. Paul who went on Paul's second and third journeys. Luke was an educated man, a physician. When St. Paul was imprisoned in Caesarea and when he went to Rome, Luke accompanied him.

It is difficult to establish the precise date for Luke's Gospel, which he wrote in Greek, but many think it was written prior to the destruction of the temple (in A.D. 70). Luke also wrote the Acts of the Apostles.

Though he does not name them, Luke mentions eyewitnesses who told him of the events he records. Obviously, Mary would have been the person who told him of the appearance of the angel Gabriel, her own visit to Elizabeth, and the infancy narrative of Jesus.

Luke writes a chronological narrative of events, for he is pointing out the connection between the Old Testament and Jesus, the Messiah. He ties Malachi's prophecy of the Messiah's precursor directly to St. John the Baptist, its fulfillment. He even notes that John, who goes before the Lord, is also conceived before Jesus' human conception. Also, Mary's virginal conception fulfills the prophecy of Isaiah.

When the child Jesus is brought to the temple to be circumcised, the Holy Spirit indicates to Simeon that this is the promised Messiah. Luke

Luke points out the connection between the Old Testament and Jesus, the Messiah.

While on the cross, Jesus entrusted his mother to John.

records Simeon's words that Jesus is the fulfillment of Isaiah's prediction of one who "would free his people from every kind of affliction."

This Gospel is about the universal salvation of mankind that starts with the activities of Jesus in Jerusalem and spreads to the whole world. For Luke, Jesus' whole life is working toward its conclusion in Jerusalem. Here, Jesus in his role as high priest will institute the Eucharist, the sacrificial renewal of his death on the Cross, then die on the Cross to redeem all men from sin.

Luke wants us to see that the Messiah has come, and that we are called to follow in his footsteps. All who wish to follow him "must deny themselves and take up their cross daily." God's assistance is to be obtained by being virtuous, which is possible through chastity, charity, temperance, and justice. Prayer and sacrifice are required to accomplish this.

We are able to follow in Jesus' footsteps and serve God in any and every occupation.

> He waits for us every day, in the laboratory, in the operating theatre, in the army barracks, in the university chair, in the factory, in the workshop, in the fields, in the home, and in the immense panorama of work.[4]

The story of Mary and Martha (Lk 10: 41-42) clearly indicates that there is a time for work and a time for prayer, but prayer has a higher value than action, for prayer "is the better part."

ST. JOHN

St. John is thought to have been a native of Bethsaida in Galilee, on the shore of Lake Gennesaret. Zebedee and Salome were his parents, and St. James the Greater was his brother. Like his father, John was a fisherman.

When John the Baptist began to preach, St. John became his disciple. When Jesus appeared, he became Jesus' disciple. When the Baptist identified Jesus as "the Lamb of God," John was there, and he followed Jesus along the shore of the lake and talked to him for several hours. John was probably the youngest of the apostles.

John and his brother were given the name "sons of thunder," possibly for asking Jesus to destroy a Samaritan village with fire and brimstone because the inhabitants would not receive Jesus (Lk 9: 52-55). John had great fortitude and determination, which he demonstrated when he stood with Mary at the foot of the cross. He was the only apostle who remained with the Lord until his death. While on the cross, Jesus entrusted his mother to John.

St. Polycarp said John moved to Ephesus; later he was exiled by Domitian to the island of Patmos. There he wrote the Book of Revelation, but he returned to Ephesus after Diocletian's death to write his Gospel and three epistles. Though he does not refer to himself by name, the other three Gospel writers refer to him many times by name.

John, like Matthew, indicates that Jesus is the Messiah by correlating Old Testament prophecies to Jesus' life. He wrote for the Christians of Asia Minor to convince them that Jesus Christ is the Son of God made man.

He presents Christ as the eternal "Word" – co-Creator with the Father but a distinct Person from him – who has existed since before time began. In Christ, the Old Covenant is fulfilled in the New. He demonstrated his messiahship by his miracles, even working them on the Sabbath to demonstrate that he is God and Lord of the Sabbath.

John's narrative of the Lord's Passion is frequently used to show that the Church and the sacraments flow directly from Christ's death on the cross.

As a witness of Christ's death and Resurrection, John gives a very detailed account of these events to prove that the Resurrection really happened. After running with St. Peter to the empty tomb, John noted the two cloths used to cover Jesus and Peter's reaction. He describes how the Lord gave power to forgive sins to the apostles on Easter evening, and how he installed Peter as the head of the Church.

THE ACTS OF THE APOSTLES

Based on the writings of St. Jerome, Clement of Alexandria, Origen, and St. Irenaeus, as well as on information contained in the work, St. Luke is accepted as the author of the Acts of the Apostles. The style, vocabulary, and doctrinal themes of Acts are similar to those of Luke's Gospel. According to some scholars, he seems to have written it in Rome between A.D. 62 and 64, prior to the death of Paul and the persecution of Christians by the emperor Nero. Other sources indicate, however, that Acts was not written until about A.D. 75. Like Luke's Gospel, it is an orderly account of the spread of Christianity among the gentiles as Christ had predicted.

He notes that three thousand people were converted on Pentecost; they were later exiled for their Christianity. He specifically mentions the spread of Christianity to Judea, Samaria, and Galilee, and later to Cyprus and Antioch.

Acts is also a record of the Holy Spirit's work in spreading the Church. Peter preaches the messianic reality of Jesus, his fulfillment of the Old Testament prophecies, and his Resurrection from the dead. The Spirit is preached as distinct from the Father and the Son. Luke records the first Church council held in Jerusalem under the guidance of the Spirit.

THE EPISTLES

The epistles were written by St. Peter, St. Paul, St. James, St. John, and St. Jude. St. Paul is the best-known of the New Testament writers. St. Paul wrote his epistles (another word for letters) to the new Christian communities that he had founded in order to clarify doctrines or correct deviations from the truth.

St. Paul was born of Jewish parents in Tarsus of Cilicia. He was a Pharisee, trained by the great Jewish teacher, Gamaliel, and was a fierce defender of the Jewish religion. When St. Stephen was slain, St. Paul was present. At his own request, he was given papers empowering him to arrest and bring to trial Jewish people who were converting to Christianity.

Acts tells us that three thousand Jewish people were converted on Pentecost.

St. Paul experienced a radical change of heart unique in the history of the world. He went from persecutor to persecuted, from attacker to defender, from zealous believer in the revelation of Moses to promoter of the teachings of Christ almost in the blink of an eye. His identification with Christ was the source of his abundant zeal.

He made three missionary journeys to preach Jesus to the gentiles. The first was to Asia Minor from A.D. 45 to 49. After this journey, he attended the Council of Jerusalem, which determined that Christians were not required to follow the Mosaic law. Silas traveled with him from A.D. 50 to 52, on his second journey, which began in Asia Minor and concluded in Macedonia. His third journey began in Antioch between A.D. 53 and 58, and concluded in Jerusalem, where he was imprisoned by Jewish leaders. He was held captive in Caesarea for two years. In A.D. 60, he was sent under guard to Rome, where he lived under loose guard until A.D. 63.

According to the tradition, St. Paul was martyred in Rome, in A.D. 67. Because he was a Roman citizen, he could not be crucified, so he was beheaded outside the walls of Rome. The Church of St. Paul Outside the Walls was built on the spot of his burial.

The chronological order of his letters appears to be:

✝ A.D. 50-52 1 and 2 Thessalonians

✝ A.D. 53-58 1 and 2 Corinthians, Galatians and Romans

✝ A.D. 61-63 Roman captivity: Ephesians, Philippians, Colossians, and Philemon

✝ A.D. 65-67 Timothy and Titus

The Epistle to the Hebrews is authentically part of the canon of Scripture, but it is possible that it was written by a disciple of St. Paul rather than Paul. Some believe Barnabas or Silas might have written it at Paul's direction.

THE CATHOLIC EPISTLES

From the second century of the Church, the Epistles of Sts. Peter, James, John, and Jude have been called the Catholic Epistles because they were written to the whole Church, rather than to a particular community in the Church.

The Epistle of James is attributed to James, the son of Cleophas and Mary, who was the cousin or sister of Mary, mother of Jesus. Some scholars argue that this is the James called 'James the Less,' who was one of the twelve apostles. The author of the Epistle of James was bishop of Jerusalem until his death in A.D. 62, and was described as "one of the pillars of the Church" by St. Paul. His epistle is obviously written by a person who is extremely knowledgeable about the Old Testament and the teachings of Jesus. He says he is writing to "the twelve tribes of the dispersion," who were scattered around the Roman Empire.

1 and 2 Peter were apparently written before the persecution of Nero. These letters addressed to the Christians of Asia Minor call all to lead holier lives and warn against the false teachings of the Gnostics.

St. Paul experienced a radical change of heart unique in the history of the world.

1 John was written in Ephesus, near the end of the first century. John identifies himself as one who has seen, heard, and touched the Savior. It is similar to his Gospel. His second letter is addressed to the Church, and the third to Gaius, a Christian official in Asia Minor.

St. Jude, like St. James the Less, was a cousin of Jesus. He wrote between A.D. 62 and 66 to Christian converts from Judaism scattered throughout the Roman Empire. Like Peter and Paul, he warns against false teachers who subvert the faith.

BOOK OF REVELATION

St. John wrote the Book of Revelation, or the Apocalypse, around the year A.D. 95, toward the end of the reign of the Roman Emperor Domitian. It is similar in style to his Gospel.

Apocalyptic writings are a variant of prophetic literature. Prophetic literature judges human events in the light of the Covenant, while apocalyptic literature uncovers the future based on the inspiration of God.

The Apocalypse of St. John contains a series of warnings projected into the future, and it is addressed to people of all places and times until the end of the world. It warns about dangers to the Church from both the inside and the outside. The sacrificed and risen Lamb leads the struggle between the city of God and the city of man.

The Apocalypse begins with the persecutions that the early Christians suffered from the time of Nero onward, and warns of trouble to come from heresies and defections from the Church.

The early Christians wondered about the return of the Lord, and so St. John tries to demonstrate that the Church is already victorious in Christ. Nevertheless, the Church will be persecuted until at last the final victory over Satan is won. Christians will suffer, as Jesus did, but must remain faithful until death to share in his victorious return at the end times.

John uses concrete realities to convey spiritual realities beyond the grasp of men. The Book of Revelation is about the triumph of those who align themselves with Jesus Christ, in spite of the persecutions and difficulties that both the Church and the followers of Christ will face until the end of the world.

CONCLUSION

Jesus' role as Messiah included the truths he shared with his apostles and their followers. Under the guidance of the Holy Spirit, his teachings were gathered in the Bible and called the New Testament because it was a new agreement with all people whether Jew or Gentile, by the Father as foretold in the Old Testament and by Jesus in the New Testament. It is the testimony of the mighty works done by Jesus and his associates who followed the New Way that Jesus had set out for them.

The Revelation To John

"…in his right hand he held seven stars, from his mouth issued a sharp two-edged sword, and his face was like the sun shining in full strength.

When I saw him, I fell at his feet as though dead. But he laid his right hand upon me, saying, "Fear not, I am the first and the last,…" (Rv 1:16-17)

SUPPLEMENTARY READING

The New and Old Testaments hinge on one man. One man alone acts as the Precursor to the Savior Jesus Christ. One voice cries "out in the wilderness." One man prepares the way of the Lord. One man brings a message of repentance. One man was to be the dawn that announced the coming Day. One man alone is the first to point us toward the great Messiah. One man's martyrdom foretells the Passion. Yet John's was a passing voice; Christ is the eternal Word.

St. John the Baptist had a mission not unlike our own, to prepare men's hearts for Jesus. In this we may imitate John the Baptist, for his apostolate was one of bold teaching and upright behavior. These two together are the best proof to others that what we say is true. As God's forerunner to others, "He must increase while [we] must decrease." This is our life's work, to let Jesus fill us completely with his goodness, love, and joy. Thus, we may have the moral authority to say "Behold the Lamb of God."

No fear: John preached what specific individuals needed to hear in their place in the world. He spoke with common townspeople, government officials, soldiers, teachers, and even King Herod. On August 29th, the feast of his martyrdom, we hear the reading from Jeremiah: "Brace yourself for action. Stand up and tell them all I command you. Do not be dismayed at their presence…I, for my part, will make you into a fortified city, a pillar of iron, and a wall of bronze to confront the whole land: The kings of Judah, its princes, its priests and the country people will fight against you, but shall not overcome you, for I am with you to deliver you." The Lord asks us to be ready every day to fight against ignorance and evil by our witness of love without fearing the loss of human respect (the first of the devil's temptations).

St. John the Baptist
(1st c.)
Feast on June 24

John's profession of the truth about the sin of Herod's marriage to his brother's wife (Herodias) led to his imprisonment. Herodias eventually tricked Herod into killing John the Baptist by promising her daughter anything "even if it be half my kingdom." John gratefully accepted these sufferings because he understood that they were necessary for him to be united to Christ—whose own Passion was still to come. It was only through these sufferings that John could hope to enter into Jesus' Resurrection.

So also, each of us must be *willing* to suffer for Jesus—this may not mean that he will call us to suffer, but if we are unwilling then we lack true faith. When we have it, we will move mountains, and that which seems humanly impossible will become possible with God. The obstacles we overcome will make us bigger, stronger, and more prepared to love God with all our heart, all our mind, and all our strength.

VOCABULARY

APOCALYPSE
Literally "unveiling"; The Book of Revelation commonly attributed to St. John the Apostle; a prophetical work foretelling the fall of Rome and the final victory of Christ and his Church; it is subject to numerous legitimate interpretations.

APOSTLES
A term meaning one who is sent as Jesus was sent by the Father, and as he sent his chosen disciples to preach the Gospel to the whole world. Twelve chosen witnesses of his Resurrection and the foundation on which the Church is built.

ASCENSION
The entry of Jesus' humanity into divine glory in God's heavenly domain, forty days after his Resurrection.

CATHOLIC EPISTLES
Letters written to the "universal" church (James, 1 and 2 Peter, Jude, 1, 2 and 3 John as distinct from letters written to a particular region [Romans, Colossians, etc.]).

DEVOTION
Disposition of will to do promptly what concerns the worship and service of God; ultimately rooted in great love for God (charity).

EVANGELIST
One who works actively to spread and promote the Christian faith.

GOSPEL
The good news of God's mercy and love revealed in the life, death, and resurrection of Christ. It is this Gospel or good news that the Apostles, and the Church following them, are to proclaim to the entire world.

NEW TESTAMENT
The twenty-seven books of the Bible written by the sacred authors in apostolic times, which have Jesus Christ, the incarnate Son of God—his life, teachings, Passion and glorification, and the beginnings of his Church—as their central theme.

SCRIBE
Well-educated Jew who studied and explained the law; not a priest; some were members of the Sanhedrin.

STUDY QUESTIONS

1. What is the relationship between the Old Testament and the New Testament?

2. What does the Church hold regarding the four Gospels?

3. When did Divine Revelation end?

4. What was the intention of the Gospel writers?

5. What two sources did the Gospel writers use?

6. What is the difference between the writings of John and Matthew as opposed to Mark and Luke?

7. Who was Matthew writing for and in what language? *Greek*

8. Who wrote his Gospel for Christians of Gentile origin who lived in Rome?

9. What two miracles of Jesus recorded by St. Mark are not mentioned in the other three Gospels?

10. What is the focus of Luke's gospel?

11. What is one possible reason that Jesus called St. John and St. James "sons of thunder"?

12. Why does John give so much detail in describing Christ's death and resurrection?

13. Who are the epistle writers?

14. Explain why St. Paul wrote his epistles.

15. Why was St. Paul beheaded?

16. Why were the "Catholic Epistles" given such a name?

17. What does the Apocalypse of St. John contain and to whom is it addressed?

18. How does private revelation differ from Revelation?

PRACTICAL EXERCISES

1. A great piece of oral Tradition is the Stations of the Cross. Ask your teacher to let the class perform "living" stations. If this is not possible, go to your Church and experience the Stations there.

2. Look online for a medical description of Jesus' Passion. As you read (in class) the pains he suffered for us, reflect on how much Jesus must love us if he was willing to go through such agony for each one of us.

3. The truth of the Resurrection is the basis for much of Christian belief. Many people have tried to explain this truth away with various medical theories. Why is Jesus' resurrection from the dead believable?

FROM THE CATECHISM

68 By love, God has revealed himself and given himself to man. He has thus provided the definitive, superabundant answer to the questions that man asks himself about the meaning and purpose of his life.

69 God has revealed himself to man by gradually communicating his own mystery in deeds and in words.

73 God has revealed himself fully by sending his own Son, in whom he has established his covenant forever. The Son is his Father's definitive Word: so there will be no further Revelation after him.

96 What Christ entrusted to the apostles, they in turn handed on by their preaching and writing, under the inspiration of the Holy Spirit, to all generations, until Christ returns in glory.

97 "Sacred Tradition and Sacred Scripture make up a single sacred deposit of the Word of God" (*DV*, 10), in which, as in a mirror, the pilgrim Church contemplates God, the source of all her riches.

134 All Sacred Scripture is but one book, and this one book is Christ, "because all divine Scripture speaks of Christ, and all divine Scripture is fulfilled in Christ" (Hugh of St. Victor, De arca Noe 2, 8: PL, 176, 642: cf. ibid. 2, 9: PL, 176, 642-643).

139 The four Gospels occupy a central place because Christ Jesus is their center.

140 The unity of the two Testaments proceeds from the unity of God's plan and his Revelation. The Old Testament prepares for the New and the New Testament fulfills the Old; the two shed light on each other; both are true Word of God.

866 The Church is one: she acknowledges one Lord, confesses one faith, is born of one Baptism, forms only one Body, is given life by the one Spirit, for the sake of one hope (cf. Eph 4: 3-5), at whose fulfillment all divisions will be overcome.

868 The Church is catholic: she proclaims the fullness of the faith. She bears in herself and administers the totality of the means of salvation. She is sent out to all peoples. She speaks to all men. She encompasses all times. She is "missionary of her very nature" (*AG*, 2).

Endnotes

1. *DV*, 17; cf. Rom 1: 16.
2. Cf. *DV*, 20.
3. *DV*, 18.
4. St. Josemaría Escrivá, *Conversations*, p.14.

The Sacraments

Sources of life that flow from the side of Christ.

Chapter 9

The Sacraments

*I*n a manner of speaking, sacraments can be called "the complete package."

In sports, the phrase "the complete package" refers to a person who can do it all. If he is a basketball player, he can run, shoot from all locations on the floor, score, and rebound.

Sacraments are the complete package spiritually. They do it all for us. They bring us into God's love in Baptism and feed us with the Eucharist. When we soil ourselves with sin, Reconciliation removes the dirt. Confirmation gives us additional strength for life's big battles. In Holy Orders and Matrimony, we are supported by God's grace in our choice of vocation, and at the end of life, the Anointing of the Sick sees us safely home to God's presence. Sacraments really are "the complete package."

THE SACRAMENTS

While on earth, Christ instituted the sacraments to enable us to share his divine life and to assist us in reaching our heavenly home.

> The sacraments are efficacious signs of grace instituted by Christ and entrusted to the Church, by which divine life is dispensed to us. (CCC 1131)

There are seven sacraments: Baptism, Confirmation, the Eucharist, Reconciliation, the Anointing of the Sick, Holy Orders, and Matrimony. These signs are effective because Christ works through them. We see the visible actions of the minister, but it is Christ who accomplishes the sacramental action. The visible rite of each sacrament makes present the particular graces conferred by the sacrament and accomplishes much through the cooperation of those who receive it with the proper attitude. Each sacrament in its own way enables us to serve God as he intended, while supplying us with grace to help us accomplish his plan for our salvation and the salvation of others. The word sacrament is derived from the Latin word *sacramentum*, the initiation oath of soldiers into the Roman army. Thus, we may say sacraments are our initiation rites into the mysteries of the Church. St. Isidore thought the word meant something hidden or secret. Others believe it was synonymous with the Greek word *mysterion*, meaning mystery. It is used to describe something holy or sacred, which sanctifies man to accomplish a mission.

> "The purpose of the sacraments is to sanctify men, to build up the body of Christ, and finally, to give worship to God. Because they are signs, they also instruct. They not only presuppose faith, but by words and objects they also nourish, strengthen, and express it. That is why they are called 'sacraments *of faith*.'"[1] (CCC 1123)

Jesus' words and actions during his public life were saving, for they anticipated the power of his death and Resurrection on Easter. The Gospels record his institution of the Church and sacraments in his saving acts directed to men. They reveal in a particular way the special relationship between the sacraments and Christ's Incarnation, Passion, and Church. Since the source of our salvation is the Crucifixion, all the effects of the sacraments flow from this act.

> Sacraments are "powers that come forth" from the Body of Christ,[2] which is ever-living and life-giving. They are actions of the Holy Spirit at work in his Body, the Church. They are "the masterworks of God" in the new and everlasting covenant. (CCC 1116)

When we think of the Church, our first thought is usually of our participation in the sacraments. By the action of Christ, each sacrament gives a particular sacramental grace from the Holy Spirit. These graces enable their recipient to cooperate with the plan of God.

The sacraments are associated with three divine calls:

† *A call to personal holiness.*
Baptism calls each recipient to a life of personal holiness to accomplish a mission known to God, which will be worked out over a lifetime.

There are seven sacraments:

Baptism,
Confirmation,
the Eucharist,
Reconciliation,
the Anointing of
the Sick,
Holy Orders, and
Matrimony.

The words are called the "form" of the sacrament and the actions or objects are called the "matter."

† *A call to worship.*
A crucial aspect of this call is to worship God as his Church indicates, in order to acquire the graces necessary to accomplish this call.

† *A call to a correct moral attitude.*
The moral teachings of the Church instruct the baptized about the will of Christ concerning their moral choices.

Guided by the Holy Spirit, the Church recognizes the sacraments as treasures that Christ gave to his Church. They unite us to God, particularly in our union with Jesus through the Eucharist. This is a mystical union of Christ with his Body, the Church, to which we are joined in loving communion through Baptism.

SIGNS OF GOD'S POWER

The Church was instituted by Christ to confer the graces he wishes to give us, so it is proper to call the Church a sacrament. The Church is the inheritor and guarantor of our eternal life. The Church is the sacramental key that opens the door to all the other sacraments.

Christ could have chosen to apply the benefits of his life, death, and resurrection in any number of ways. Since he is the God who made us sensible creatures, he chose sensible ways and gave us a visible Church and visible sacraments. Sacramental signs are visible realities that point to what is occurring spiritually through the sacraments. A sacrament is a sign of a sacred act or thing. That is to say, the sacraments bring about what they signify from the actions of Christ. They are the only signs that cause what they signify; all other signs merely point to something else but do not cause anything. Smoke, for example, is a sign of a fire, but it is not the cause. The signs of the sacraments cause the resulting interior action.

The act of circumcision in the Old Law was a sign of the Jewish people's invisible covenant between themselves and God.

The signs of each sacrament indicate the New Covenant between God and man and direct us to the inner reality of the change in our souls through the effective action of Christ. For instance, the water of Baptism removes our sins, both original and actual sin, if present. The exterior sign of water that we see points to the interior cleansing of our souls, which we cannot see.

The ritual use of a certain thing (such as water, bread, and wine) in the liturgical action is the sign, not the thing used in itself. It is Jesus who has both given us the ritual action and designated the particular sign. Every sacramental action of the New Law is composed of sensible actions, objects, and words. The words are called the *form* of the sacrament and the actions or objects the *matter.* Together they make up the substance of the sacrament.

NECESSITY OF THE SACRAMENTS

Before Adam sinned, there was no need for the sacraments. After Adam's sin, God determined that sacraments were the best and wisest means for us to attain our salvation. God chose the sacraments because of:

- ✝ Man's nature – Divine wisdom gives sensible signs to appeal to the human nature of man.
- ✝ Man's sinfulness – They apply a spiritual remedy for sin through sensible signs.
- ✝ Man's inclinations – They apply sensible sanctified signs to enable man to avoid superstitious practices.

The action of Christ operates to accomplish what the sacrament signifies independently of the personal holiness of the minister. God's power acts through the agency of man. For us believers, sacraments are a necessary component of our salvation; they indicate that this sacred thing sanctifies man here and now.

Sacraments also have social value, for they enable us to live in community with charity toward all while binding every member of the community to one another to the extent that each cooperates with them.

Sacraments also set us aside as worshippers of the true God. They call us to manifest the truth of God's commands by our acceptance and response to his call to be witnesses to others.

GOD'S GRACE

Each sacrament confers graces upon us, for the sacramental action confers grace of itself, as long as the recipient places no obstacles in the way.

The first grace we receive is sanctifying grace, which is conferred by every sacrament. While God has given us human life through our parents, he also gives us a share in his own divine life through the sacraments. This divine life is so different that St. Paul refers to it as "a new creation."

This sanctifying grace is a supernatural reality, which enables us to share in God's life, to become temples of the Trinity, adopted sons and friends of God, and heirs to heaven, able to perform acts that will merit us eternal life in heaven. It gives us a share in God's own divine life. This is a great mystery, over which we should pray for understanding.

In no sense do we deserve this freely given gift of God. Without his grace, we would live a purely natural level of life, bound to earth with no direct connection to God. When we are baptized, we are connected directly to God. Since his life is above and beyond ours, we say that we share in his supernatural life, a life above and beyond that lived by man in his simply human existence. This share in God's life enables us to accomplish things beyond the capacity of natural human beings. For almost two thousand years, the Church has witnessed to the accomplishments of saints who lived and died for Christ.

The lives of saints are heroic, for they serve Christ by bringing his love and life to every place in the world, regardless of conditions or hardships.

When God created Adam and Eve, he made a covenant with them that made them his friends and gave them the power to choose, free of any inclination to sin. Because they chose to disobey him, they lost this friendship and the ability to make choices free from inclination to sin.

Sacraments also have social value, for they enable us to live in community with charity toward all.

For almost two thousand years, the Church has witnessed to the accomplishments of saints who lived and died for Christ.

Actual grace is supernatural help from God to do good and avoid evil for the purpose of saving our souls.

Three of the sacraments imprint a perpetual character or mark on the soul, which distinguishes the followers of Christ from others.

From their first disobedience, we have inherited original sin and its consequence, our inclination to actual sin.

Few people in this world wish to do evil or to be evil people. All of us often do evil when we wish we wouldn't. We have all shared the experience of St. Paul, who said, "I do not do the good I want, but the evil I do not want is what I do" (Rom 7:19).

Through the actual graces we receive from Jesus' life, death, and Resurrection, we are enabled to fight the temptation to sin. God has given us both the gift of new life in him and the gift of actual grace to enable us to live this new life. Actual grace is supernatural help from God to do good and avoid evil for the purpose of saving our souls.

Actual grace is given to us every time God wishes us to do a good work or we are tempted to sin. This freely given grace does not force us to choose good over evil; rather, it enables us to see what God wishes us to do, so that we may make the right moral choice. It has been compared to a gentle breeze, which blows away the fog on a dark night to enable a person to see the safe way to go.

When temptations occur, some say, "I don't want to be a goody two-shoes." This attitude denies our serious responsibility to choose between sinning and returning God's freely given love to us through cooperation with his grace. Every temptation presents an opportunity to demonstrate our love for God. We succeed in the service of God only by opening our actions to God's grace.

SACRAMENTAL CHARACTERS

Three of the sacraments imprint a perpetual character or mark on the soul, which distinguishes the followers of Christ from others. This indelible mark is imprinted on the soul in the sacraments of Baptism, Confirmation, and Holy Orders, which can each be received only once. When we arrive in heaven, we will be able to distinguish those who received these permanent signs from those who did not.

This character or sign:

† Configures us to Christ;

† Distinguishes us perpetually from those who do not have the sign;

† Disposes us to cooperate with grace.

MINISTERS OF THE SACRAMENTS

Christ in his human nature is both the principal minister of God in the institution of the sacraments and the principal minister of the sacraments. He employs secondary, visible ministers in their accomplishment, for he wishes to associate men with the fulfillment of his work. Baptism and Matrimony do not require an ordained man to administer them, but all the other sacraments do. To confer a Christian sacrament, the minister must intend the sacramental result while using the correct form and proper matter.

Since the minister acts in the name of Christ and Christ's Church, he must not be in mortal sin, for he is doing the sacred work of God. But if the minister is in the state of mortal sin the sacrament is still valid, but the minister commits a sin.

Baptism and Reconciliation do not require their recipients to be free from mortal sin, but the other five sacraments do.

NEW CREATURES IN CHRIST

Unfortunately, many people have recourse to the sacraments only when they are culturally expected, such as Baptism for an infant, or absolutely necessary, such as Reconciliation for someone in a state of mortal sin. To accept this situation is to accept a life lived to the minimum. Sacraments are much more than this.

Sacraments enable us to be Christ to others. Regular reception of the sacraments graces us to become more like Christ in word and action.

Often we hear someone say, "I don't like that person's personality." Personality is the word used to describe our social traits, yet our social traits are reflections of the condition of our souls. Regular reception of the sacraments graces us to become more like Christ inwardly. As we become more holy inwardly, there is an outward manifestation of our interior goodness, which affects our personality.

In recent history, Mother Teresa of India is an excellent example of this sacramental personalism. She gave up her life as a teacher to minister to the poorest of the poor. To all outward appearances, nothing distinguished her from any other woman. Yet, she was one of the best-known people in the entire world. People were attracted to her because she had become Christ-like through a life dedicated to living the sacraments and responding to the initiative of grace.

Jesus' call to us in the sacraments is a call to become new creations, who reflect the image of Christ in our being.

Sacraments enable us to be Christ to others.

As we become more holy inwardly, there is an outward manifestation of our interior goodness.

People were attracted to Mother Teresa because she had become Christ-like through a life dedicated to living the sacraments and responding to the initiative of grace.

SUPPLEMENTARY READING

The first priest to be killed in the Nazi concentration camps, Otto Neururer, was hung upside down until he died on May 30, 1940, at Buchenwald, having previously endured hideous torture there and in Dachau.

Otto Neururer was born on the feast of the Annunciation in 1882, the last of twelve children in a peasant Austrian family. His upbringing and early priesthood were unremarkable, and while he was a zealous young priest especially committed to the Church's social doctrine, no one would have figured the somewhat timid Otto for a hero. Yet when the Nazis took over Austria in 1938 and began a bloody persecution of the Church, Otto, by then a parish priest in Götzens, a town near Innsbruck, was not intimidated.

He advised a young woman in his parish not to marry a certain German who was already divorced and leading a notorious life. The spurned suitor, as it were, became enraged and urged his friend, the local Nazi governor, to take action. Otto was arrested on the peculiar charge of "slander to the detriment of German marriage"—ironic since he had defended the sanctity of Christian marriage in advising against what would have been an adulterous relationship in the eyes of God. He was sent to Dachau, and subsequently to Buchenwald where the proximate cause of his death was his commitment to another sacrament.

A fellow prisoner had requested to be baptized. Otto suspected a trap, but acceded to the request out of a sense of priestly duty. Two days later as a consequence, he was taken to the "bunker" of extreme punishment where he died.

"Otto Neururer lived a priestly life, always simple, discrete, ordinary, but characterized

Bl. Otto Neururer
(1882-1940)

by an extraordinary fidelity to his priestly work," wrote Reinhold Stecher, the bishop of Innsbruck on the occasion of Otto's beatification on November 24, 1996. His words were poignant, for the new blessed had prepared Bishop Stecher for First Communion as a child, and much later, they were both imprisoned together as priests.

The sacraments are at the heart of the Christian faith, and are of infinite value. Sacraments take what is ordinary—bread, wine, oil, water, gestures, words—and, by the institution of Christ, transform them into avenues of grace. In the death camps Otto used God's grace to transform what was ordinary—toil, torture, hunger, disease, filth, and hatred—into something glorious: a place of redemption and the antechamber of heaven.

VOCABULARY

ACTUAL GRACE
Free and undeserved gift from God that helps us to conform our lives to his will.

ACTUAL SIN
Any thought, word, deed, or omission contrary to God's eternal law. It is a human act that presumes 1) knowledge of wrong-doing, 2) awareness of malice in one's conduct and 3) consent of the will. A genuine offense against God.

CELEBRANT
Bishop, priest, or deacon who presides at a liturgical function.

CONCUPISCENCE
Human appetites or desires which remain disordered due to the temporal consequences of original sin, which remain even after Baptism, and which produce an inclination to sin.

FORM
The words and signs that accompany a sacrament.

MATTER
That part of the sacrament with which or to which something is done in order to confer grace, e.g., water in Baptism, bread and wine in the Eucharist, chrism in Confirmation.

PERSONALITY
That quality or assemblage of qualities which makes a person what he is, as distinct from other persons.

SACRAMENT
An efficacious sign of grace, instituted by Christ and entrusted to the Church, by which divine life is dispensed to us through the work of the Holy Spirit. The sacraments are seven in number.

SACRAMENTAL CHARACTER
Indelible mark imprinted on the soul at Baptism, Confirmation, and/or Holy Orders that gives the person a greater share in the priesthood of Christ.

SACRAMENTS OF HEALING
Sacraments used to restore our bodies and souls in Christ's work of healing and salvation: Penance and Anointing of the Sick.

SACRAMENTS OF INITIATION
Lay the foundation of every Christian life in a way similar to natural life: born anew in Baptism, strengthened in Confirmation, given food of eternal life in the Eucharist.

SACRAMENTS AT SERVICE OF COMMUNION
Sacraments directed toward the salvation of others, conferring a particular mission in the Church and serving to build up the People of God.

SANCTIFYING GRACE
The grace which heals our human nature wounded by sin by giving us a share in the divine life of the Trinity. It is a habitual, supernatural gift which continues the work of sanctifying us — of making us perfect, holy, and Christ-like.

STUDY QUESTIONS

1. List the seven sacraments.

2. Who is the chief minister of the sacraments?

3. List and explain the three divine calls of the sacraments.

4. What institution is the inheritor and guarantor of our eternal life?

5. Why do we say that sacramental signs cause what they signify?

6. What was the sign of God's covenant in the Old Testament?

7. Why do we say that sacraments have a social value?

8. What are the effects of sanctifying grace received in Baptism?

9. From whom did we receive original sin?

10. List three effects of sacramental signs.

PRACTICAL EXERCISES

1. A Lutheran friend tells you that in her church they only have three sacraments (Baptism, Eucharist, and Confirmation). Where can you look in the Bible to help show her that Jesus instituted four other Sacraments? You may also want to use other writings from the early Church Fathers (try *The Writings of the Early Fathers* by William Jurgens).

2. You have another friend who attends non-denominational Christian services. He says all he wants is a personal relationship with Jesus. He claims that Jesus is the only Mediator between God and men, and that he doesn't need a priest to be close to Jesus. How can you use the Bible to help your friend see that Jesus intended us to be helped by others, beginning with his apostles? How can you help your friend see that Jesus gave us the gifts of the Sacraments so that we could have a personal relationship with him?

3. Our God never says "Enough!" If we only need God's sanctifying grace to get into heaven, why does he also give us actual grace in the sacraments?

FROM THE CATECHISM

1111 Christ's work in the liturgy is sacramental: because his mystery of salvation is made present there by the power of his Holy Spirit; because his Body, which is the Church, is like a sacrament (sign and instrument) in which the Holy Spirit dispenses the mystery of salvation; and because through her liturgical actions the pilgrim Church already participates, as by a foretaste, in the heavenly liturgy.

1131 The sacraments are efficacious signs of grace, instituted by Christ and entrusted to the Church, by which divine life is dispensed to us. The visible rites by which the sacraments are celebrated signify and make present the graces proper to each sacrament. They bear fruit in those who receive them with the required dispositions.

1133 The Holy Spirit prepares the faithful for the sacraments by the Word of God and the faith which welcomes that word in well-disposed hearts. Thus the sacraments strengthen faith and express it.

1134 The fruit of sacramental life is both personal and ecclesial. For every one of the faithful on the one hand, this fruit is life for God in Christ Jesus; for the Church, on the other, it is an increase in charity and in her mission of witness.

1275 Christian initiation is accomplished by three sacraments together: Baptism which is the beginning of new life; Confirmation which is its strengthening; and the Eucharist which nourishes the disciple with Christ's Body and Blood for his transformation in Christ.

1276 "Go therefore and make disciples of all nations, baptizing them in the name of the Father and of the Son and of the Holy Spirit, teaching them to observe all that I have commanded you" (Mt 28:19-20).

1277 Baptism is birth into the new life in Christ. In accordance with the Lord's will, it is necessary for salvation, as is the Church herself, which we enter by Baptism.

1315 "Now when the apostles at Jerusalem heard that Samaria had received the word of God, they sent to them Peter and John, who came down and prayed for them that they might receive the Holy Spirit; for it had not yet fallen on any of them, but they had only been baptized in the name of the Lord Jesus. Then they laid their hands on them and they received the Holy Spirit" (Acts 8:14-17).

1316 Confirmation perfects Baptismal grace; it is the sacrament which gives the Holy Spirit in order to root us more deeply in the divine filiation, incorporate us more firmly into Christ, strengthen our bond with the Church, associate us more closely with her mission, and help us bear witness to the Christian faith in words accompanied by deeds.

1317 Confirmation, like Baptism, imprints a spiritual mark or indelible character on the Christian's soul; for this reason one can receive this sacrament only once in one's life.

1406 Jesus said: "I am the living bread that came down from heaven; if any one eats of this bread, he will live for ever; … he who eats my flesh and drinks my blood has eternal life and … abides in me, and I in him" (Jn 6:51, 54, 56).

1408 The Eucharistic celebration always includes: the proclamation of the Word of God; thanksgiving to God the Father for all his benefits, above all the gift of his Son; the consecration of bread and wine; and participation in the liturgical banquet by receiving the Lord's body and blood. These elements constitute one single act of worship.

1409 The Eucharist is the memorial of Christ's Passover, that is, of the work of salvation accomplished by the life, death, and resurrection of Christ, a work made present by the liturgical action.

1485 "On the evening of that day, the first day of the week," Jesus showed himself to his apostles. "He breathed on them, and said to them: 'Receive the Holy Spirit. If you

FROM THE CATECHISM CONTINUED

forgive the sins of any, they are forgiven; if you retain the sins of any, they are retained'" (Jn 20: 19, 22-23).

1486 The forgiveness of sins committed after Baptism is conferred by a particular sacrament called the sacrament of conversion, confession, penance, or reconciliation.

1487 The sinner wounds God's honor and love, his own human dignity as a man called to be a son of God, and the spiritual well-being of the Church, of which each Christian ought to be a living stone.

1490 The movement of return to God, called conversion and repentance, entails sorrow for and abhorrence of sins committed, and the firm purpose of sinning no more in the future. Conversion touches the past and the future and is nourished by hope in God's mercy.

1526 "Is any among you sick? Let him call for the presbyters of the Church, and let them pray over him, anointing him with oil in the name of the Lord; and the prayer of faith will save the sick man, and the Lord will raise him up; and if he has committed sins, he will be forgiven" (Jas 5: 14-15).

1527 The sacrament of Anointing of the Sick has as its purpose the conferral of a special grace on the Christian experiencing the difficulties inherent in the condition of grave illness or old age.

1590 St Paul said to his disciple Timothy: "I remind you to rekindle the gift of God that is within you through the laying on of my hands" (2 Tm 1: 6), and "If any one aspires to the office of bishop, he desires a noble task" (1 Tm 3: 1). To Titus he said: "This is why I left you in Crete, that you amend what was defective, and appoint presbyters in every town, as I directed you" (Ti 1: 5).

1591 The whole Church is priestly people. Through Baptism all the faithful share in the priesthood of Christ. This participation is called the "common priesthood of the faithful." Based on this common priesthood and ordered to its service, there exists another participation in the mission of Christ: the ministry conferred by the sacrament of Holy Orders, where the task is to serve in the name and in the person of Christ the Head in the midst of the community.

1597 The sacrament of Holy Orders is conferred by the laying on of hands followed by a solemn prayer of consecration asking God to grant the ordinand the graces of the Holy Spirit required for his ministry. Ordination imprints an indelible sacramental character.

1659 St. Paul said: "Husbands, love your wives, as Christ loved the Church….This is a great mystery, and I mean in reference to Christ and the Church" (Eph 5: 25, 32).

1661 The sacrament of Matrimony signifies the union of Christ and the Church. It gives spouses the grace to love each other with the love with which Christ has loved his Church; the grace of the sacrament thus perfects the human love of the spouses, strengthens their indissoluble unity, and sanctifies them on the way to eternal life (cf. Council of Trent: DS, 1799).

1677 Sacramentals are sacred signs instituted by the Church. They prepare men to receive the fruit of the sacraments and sanctify different circumstances of life.

Endnotes

1. *SC*, 59.
2. Cf. Lk 5: 17; 6: 19; 8: 46.

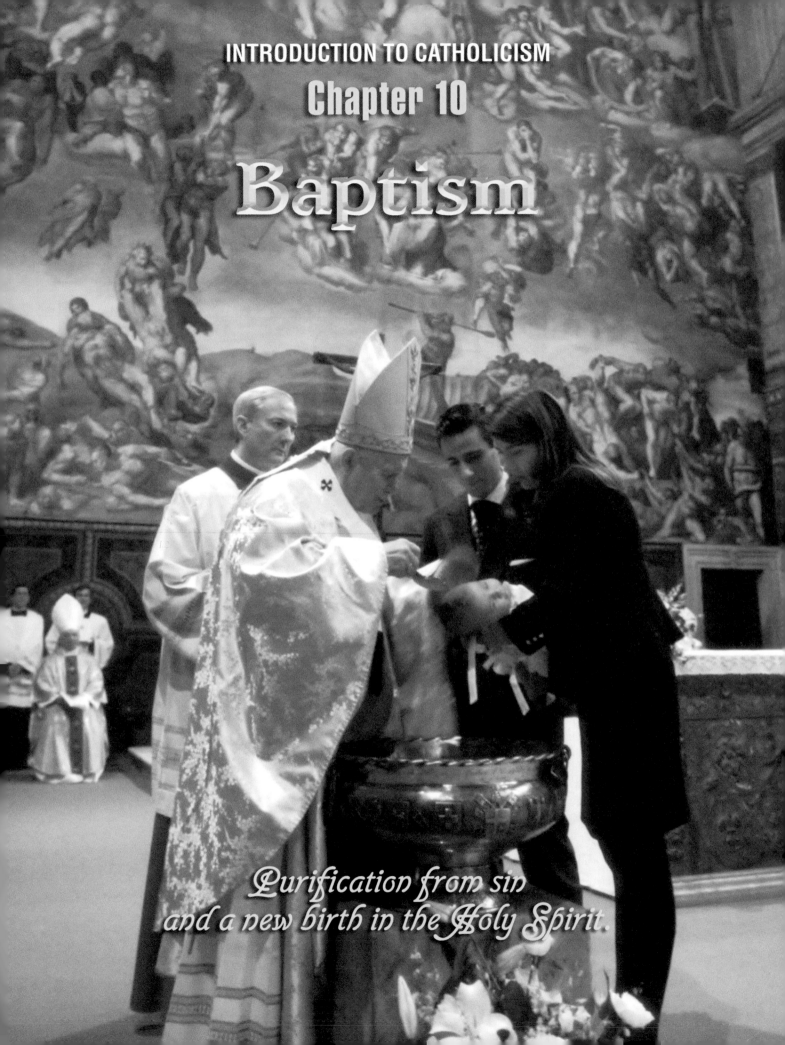

Baptism

*Purification from sin
and a new birth in the Holy Spirit.*

Chapter 10

Baptism

*A*nd behold, an Ethiopian, a eunuch, a minister of Candace the queen of the Ethiopians and in charge of all her treasure, had come to Jerusalem to worship and was returning; seated in his chariot, he was reading the prophet Isaiah. And the Spirit said to Philip, "Go up and join this chariot." So Philip ran to him and heard him reading Isaiah the prophet and asked, "Do you understand what you are reading?" And he said, "How can I, unless someone guides me?" And he invited Philip to come up and sit with him. Now the passage of the scripture which he was reading was this: "As a sheep led to the slaughter / or a lamb before its shearer is dumb, / so he opens not his mouth. / In his humiliation, justice was denied him. / Who can describe his generation? / For his life is taken up from the earth."

And the eunuch said to Philip, "About whom, pray, does the prophet say this, about himself or about some one else?" Then Philip opened his mouth, and beginning with this scripture, he told him the good news of Jesus. And as they went along the road, they came to some water, and the eunuch said, "See, here is water! What is to prevent my being baptized?" And he commanded the chariot to stop, and they both went down into the water, Philip and the eunuch, and he baptized him. And when they came up out of the water, the Spirit of the Lord caught up Philip; and the eunuch saw him no more, and went on his way rejoicing. (Acts 8: 27-39)

BAPTISM

Now the eleven disciples went to Galilee to the mountain to which Jesus had directed them. And when they saw him, they worshipped him, but some doubted. And Jesus came and said to them, "All authority in heaven and on earth has been given to me. Go, therefore, and make disciples of all nations, baptizing them in the name of the Father, and of the Son, and of the Holy Spirit, teaching them to observe all that I have commanded you; and lo, I am with you always, to the close of the age." (Mt 28:16-20)

Baptism is the Sacrament of Initiation that joins a person to Christ's Church. When a person is baptized, water is poured over that person while the words prescribed by Jesus are said: "I baptize you in the name of the Father, and of the Son, and of the Holy Spirit." By this sacrament, the baptized person is cleansed of all sin and receives sanctifying grace, the grace needed to enter heaven.

> Holy Baptism is the basis of the whole Christian life, the gateway to life in the Spirit *(vitae spiritualis ianua)*,[1] and the door that gives access to the other sacraments. Through Baptism we are freed from sin and reborn as sons of God; we become members of Christ, are incorporated into the Church and made sharers in her mission: "Baptism is the sacrament of regeneration through water and in the word."[2] (CCC 1213)

Water has long held an important role in the history of salvation, as the Church reminds us in the liturgy of the Easter vigil. During that liturgy, the first reading from the book of Genesis describes how, at the dawn of creation, the Spirit breathes on the waters and makes them a wellspring of holiness. Other stories from the Old Testament, including Noah's preservation during the great flood, the Israelites' escape from enslavement by crossing the Red Sea, and the Jewish people's entrance into the promised land by crossing the Jordan River, also signify the place of water in the plans of the Father. The importance of water in man's salvation is made even clearer in the New Testament, which tells how Jesus sought the baptism of John at the Jordan River.

The Church has celebrated Baptism from her first beginning, on the day of Pentecost.

> All the Old Covenant prefigurations find their fulfillment in Christ Jesus. He begins his public life after having himself baptized by St. John the Baptist in the Jordan.[3] After his resurrection Christ gives this mission to his apostles: "Go therefore and make disciples of all nations, baptizing them in the name of the Father, and of the Son, and of the Holy Spirit, teaching them to observe all that I have commanded you."[4] (CCC 1223)

Following this command, the Church has celebrated Baptism from her first beginning, on the day of Pentecost. If a person has faith in Jesus Christ, then he is baptized. Faith in Christ requires acceptance of the teachings of his apostles.

The sacrament of Baptism wondrously transforms a person's soul:

> Do you not know that all we who have been baptized into Christ Jesus have been baptized into his death? We were buried therefore with him by Baptism into death, so that as Christ was raised from the dead by the glory of the Father, we too might walk in newness of life.

Baptism

Gift

Grace

Baptism

Anointing

Enlightenment

Clothing

Bath

Seal

For if we have been united with him in a death like his, we shall certainly be united with him in a resurrection like his. We know that our old self was crucified with him so that the sinful body might be destroyed, and we might no longer be enslaved to sin. For he who has died is freed from sin. But if we have died with Christ, we believe that we shall also live with him. For we know that Christ being raised from the dead will never die again; death no longer has dominion over him. The death he died he died to sin, once for all, but the life he lives he lives to God. So you also must consider yourselves dead to sin and alive to God in Christ Jesus. (Rom 6: 3-11)

Baptism, then, makes possible the holiest and most wonderful existence for any creature: life with God.

"Baptism is God's most beautiful and magnificent gift....We call it gift, grace, anointing, enlightenment, garment of immortality, bath of rebirth, seal, and most precious gift. It is called *gift* because it is conferred on those who bring nothing of their own; *grace* since it is given even to the guilty; *Baptism* because sin is buried in the water; *anointing* for it is priestly and royal as are those who are anointed; *enlightenment* because it radiates light; *clothing* since it veils our shame; *bath* because it washes; and *seal* as it is our guard and the sign of God's Lordship."[5] (CCC 1216)

EFFECTS OF THE SACRAMENT

Original sin is the name given to the sin freely committed by our first parents, Adam and Eve. As a result of this first sin, the gates of heaven were closed to mankind. Baptism removes both original sin and any actual sins committed. In like manner, the baptized person receives many gifts from this Sacrament of Initiation:

† Removal of original sin and of actual sin, if present;

† Imprinting of an indelible sign that consecrates the person for Christian worship;

† Entry into Christ's Mystical Body, the Church;

† Sanctifying grace, which is a share in God's own life;

† Adoption by God as his child;

† Becoming a temple of the Holy Spirit, capable of worshipping God as He desires;

† Actual grace, which is assistance from God to resist sin;

† The theological virtues of faith, hope and charity;

† The moral virtues of prudence, justice, temperance, and fortitude, which help to perfect the theological virtues;

† Entry into Paradise after a life lived in Christ.

GRACE OF BAPTISM

The two principal effects of Baptism are purification from sin and new birth in the Holy Spirit. The grace of Baptism forgives all sins, both original and personal, and remits all punishment for sin.

Nevertheless, consequences of sin remain. Even after Baptism, human beings must endure suffering, illness, and death. Frailties inherent in human nature remain, such as weakness of character and inclination to sin, which is called concupiscence. These human weaknesses, however, are far outweighed by the blessings that Baptism brings:

> The Most Holy Trinity gives the baptized sanctifying grace, the grace of *justification:*
> – enabling them to believe in God, to hope in him, and to love him through the theological virtues;
> – giving them the power to live and act under the prompting of the Holy Spirit through the gifts of the Holy Spirit;
> – allowing them to grow in goodness through the moral virtues.
> Thus the whole organism of the Christian's supernatural life has its roots in Baptism. (CCC 1266)

In addition to sanctifying grace, actual grace is received in Baptism. Each time God calls us to some good or we are tempted to sin, God supplies the necessary actual graces to accomplish the good or resist the temptation.

The brotherhood of Christ that is brought about by Baptism presents us with the opportunity to be Christ for everyone around us. How will people see Christ unless we become Christ for them? Putting on or being Christ means that we must pray, act, and speak in every situation as Christ would.

If we truly desire to cooperate with Christ's grace, we should be set on fire with his love so that others will recognize it in our lives.

CELEBRATION OF THE RITE OF BAPTISM

The rite of Baptism requires the use of water and recitation of the Trinitarian formula; these two elements must be present for a valid Baptism in every situation, even in an emergency. The one who baptizes must also have the intent to baptize.

In non-emergencies, the rite of Baptism is much more elaborate and symbolic. This longer rite should be followed, among other reasons, to remind the faithful of the importance of the Sacrament.

The celebrant (usually a priest or deacon) begins the rite by making a sign of the cross on the forehead of the candidate for Baptism, indicating that the person will soon belong to Christ. Passages from the Bible are read to explain how Baptism makes possible the entry into the life of faith. The celebrant says an exorcism over the candidate to signify liberation from sin, and he anoints the candidate with oil. Then the candidate (or his sponsors, in the case of an infant) recites the baptismal promises, which comprise the renunciation of Satan and profession of faith.

Baptism is administered by immersing the candidate in water or by pouring water over his head three times, while saying, "I baptize you in the name of the Father, and of the Son, and of the Holy Spirit." Either way is proper, as both customs are traceable to the early Church. Only pure water should be used for Baptism.

The newly baptized person is anointed with sacred chrism, blessed by the bishop, to indicate the anointing of the Spirit, and given a white

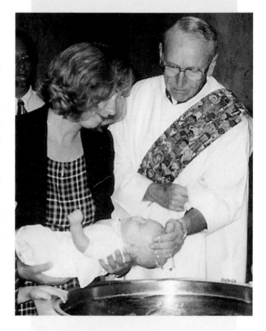

The brotherhood of Christ that is brought about by Baptism presents us with the opportunity to be Christ for everyone around us.

Following the example of the apostles, the Church makes Baptism available to anyone who believes and requests the sacrament.

garment to indicate that he has risen with Christ. A candle is lit from the Easter candle to remind the faithful that the baptized are to be the light of the world.

WHO CAN RECEIVE BAPTISM?

Both adults and infants have been baptized since the early days of the Church.

> The practice of infant Baptism is an immemorial tradition of the Church. There is explicit testimony to this practice from the second century on, and it is quite possible that, from the beginning of the apostolic preaching, when whole "households" received baptism, infants may also have been baptized.[6] (CCC 1252)

In the case of infants, the Church recognizes their need of the priceless gift of Baptism, as well as the responsibility of parents, as nurturers of the life that God has entrusted to them, to have their children baptized. Baptism should be administered as soon as possible after birth, usually within one month, for it is a grace of God freely given.

Some who criticize the practice of infant baptism say that older persons should be allowed to choose whether or not to be baptized, but this idea ignores the very nature of parenthood. Out of both duty and love, parents do what is best for their children. Parents make choices regarding food, clothing, and medical care for their offspring. The same love and duty motivate parents to have their children baptized, for they understand that Baptism is best for their children's souls.

With respect to adults, the Church of today follows the practice of Baptism found in the New Testament. On the day of Pentecost, the apostles offered Baptism to anyone who believed Jesus was the Messiah. Following the example of the apostles, the Church makes Baptism available to anyone who believes and requests the sacrament.

Under normal circumstances, adults who wish to be baptized must undergo a period of preparation before receiving the sacrament. This preparation, which is called the catechumenate, is aimed at bringing the conversion and faith of the candidate to maturity.

The catechumenate is a response to God's action, performed in union with the whole church community. The catechumenate includes an introduction into the life of faith, the liturgy, and the love of the people of God through these successive rites of initiation. By accepting a catechumen, the local church manifests Christ's love as reflected in his community. The whole church community, in fact, bears some responsibility for the development and safeguarding of the grace given at Baptism.

Baptism requires either two sponsors or one sponsor and one Christian witness. A sponsor promises to ensure that the newly baptized lives the faith in the case of the parents' death or failure to nurture the faith. A sponsor must

† Be a baptized Catholic;

† Have received the Sacraments of Initiation;

† Be over fifteen years of age;

† Live the faith seriously.

The role of sponsor is a serious obligation. Sponsors are required to care spiritually for the person they sponsor, through both prayer and encouragement. Should the parents fail to live up to their responsibilities, sponsors are expected to do all that is possible and prudent to protect the faith of the child.

A Christian witness is a baptized non-Catholic Christian who attests to the occurrence of Baptism. He is not expected to ensure the faith of the newly baptized.

In the Latin Church, the ordinary minister of Baptism is a bishop, priest, or deacon. In the case of necessity, though, anyone may baptize, even a non-baptized person, provided that he intends to accomplish what the Church intends and pours the water while saying the Trinitarian formula.

Since it leaves a permanent mark on the soul of the recipient, Baptism can be administered only once. No one should be baptized against his will.

By its very nature, infant Baptism requires a post-baptismal catechumenate. Not only is there a need for instruction after Baptism, but also for the necessary flowering of baptismal grace in personal growth.

TYPES OF BAPTISM

For those who have had the Gospel preached to them and have had the possibility of asking for it, Baptism by water is necessary for salvation.

In addition to Baptism by water, the Church recognizes that Baptism of desire and of blood allow their recipient to be saved and enter heaven. Baptism of blood occurs when a person who has not been baptized with water suffers death for the sake of his faith in Jesus. This person is baptized by and for his death, a martyrdom suffered for and with Christ (Mt 10:32, 39; Lk 9:24), which configures him to the death of Christ. Baptism of blood was common in the early Church, when many were killed for Christ before they were baptized with water.

Baptism of desire refers to the salvation of those who believe in a supreme being and strive to serve him as best they are able.

> "Since Christ died for all, and since all men are in fact called to one and the same destiny, which is divine, we must hold that the Holy Spirit offers to all the possibility of being made partakers, in a way known to God, of the Paschal mystery."[7] Every man who is ignorant of the Gospel of Christ and of his Church, but seeks the truth and does the will of God in accordance with his understanding of it, can be saved. It may be supposed that such persons would have *desired Baptism explicitly* if they had known its necessity. (CCC 1260)

In the case of children who have died before being baptized, the Church invites us to trust in God's mercy and pray for their salvation.

> With respect to children who have died without Baptism, the liturgy of the Church invites us to trust in God's mercy and to pray for their salvation. (CCC 1283)

Baptism by water.

Baptism of desire.

Baptism of blood.

When a person is baptized, he is made a member of the Church.

Baptism

Baptism carries both blessings and responsibilities.

We no longer belong to ourselves but to Christ and to his Church, which we must work to build up.

INCORPORATION INTO THE CHURCH

Baptism is the first of the Sacraments of Initiation. When a person is baptized, he is made a member of the Church established by Christ and led by the apostles and their successors. This membership, then, joins all the people of God in the Mystical Body of Christ: "For by one Spirit we were all baptized into one body" (1 Cor 12:13).

By Baptism, we are called to be living stones in a spiritual house. We share in the priesthood of Christ and in his priestly, prophetic, and royal mission. This role is both a great blessing and a great responsibility. We no longer belong to ourselves but to Christ and to his Church, which we must work to build up. We are therefore called to submit ourselves to Christ and to the commands of his Church. We must hold leaders of the Church in respect and affection.

> Baptism is birth into the new life in Christ. In accordance with the Lord's will, it is necessary for salvation, as is the Church herself, which we enter by Baptism. (CCC 1277)

CONCLUSION

God has called us into existence to share his love, and he desires that we be the source of his love to others. He has chosen to give us himself in the sacraments, the first of which is Baptism, which grants us the grace needed to enter heaven and makes us members of Christ's Church. Baptism carries both blessings and responsibilities. Since all have not been baptized, we must realize that we are called personally to be part of a great mystery, the mystery of God's plan of salvation for all men.

Although Baptism is a gift beyond our understanding, we are obligated to use the graces we have received through Baptism to live a life that reflects our belief in the living God. In the Sacrament of Baptism, all are given the grace to love him and to accomplish what he expects. This Sacrament marks a permanent change in who we are and what we can accomplish. We must accept this gift and treasure it for the whole of our life.

Examination of Conscience Regarding Baptism:

† Do I make a continuing effort to keep my baptismal promises?

† Do I try to live as a true child of God?

† Do I avoid persons and things that could harm my faith?

† Do I have a plan to strengthen my relationship with Jesus?

† Do I pray to the Holy Spirit to enlighten my mind?

Chapter 10 Study Guide

SUPPLEMENTARY READING

Before his Ascension into heaven, Christ commanded his followers to "make disciples of all nations, baptizing them in the name of the Father, and of the Son, and of the Holy Spirit, teaching them to observe all that I have commanded" (Mt 28:19-20). Few Christians have followed these instructions with more passion than St. Francis Xavier.

St. Francis is perhaps the greatest missionary in the Church after St. Paul, who, more than anyone else, brought Christianity from Israel to the lands along the Mediterranean Sea. Like Paul, Francis did not always follow the path to sainthood.

Born into a noble family in what is now Spain, Francis showed a strong mind even as a young boy. When his older brothers took up military careers, Francis was sent to Paris to study. While living there, he befriended Ignatius of Loyola, who was forming what would become the Society of Jesus. Ignatius was in Paris to complete his education, since extensive learning was essential for the members of the order he wished to establish.

Ignatius recognized the brilliance of Francis. The two enjoyed each other's company, but Francis initially found Ignatius's life of poverty and self-denial unattractive, for Francis' mind was on worldly things. Infatuated with his own intelligence, Francis wanted recognition and praise for his genius.

Eventually Francis experienced a change of heart, prompted by Ignatius's repeated question, "For what will it profit a man, if he gains the whole world and forfeits his life?" (Mt 16:26) Francis renounced his desire for praise and reputation, studied for the priesthood, and traveled to Italy, where, with the pope's permission, he was ordained a priest. Francis worked in Rome for a short time until, chosen to replace another future Jesuit who had fallen ill, he went as a missionary to the East Indies.

With great perseverance, Francis instructed those who had fallen away from the faith and

St. Francis Xavier
(1506-1552)
Feast on December 3

baptized new converts. In his own letters, he wrote of baptizing so many people that he could barely move his arms, weary from having poured out so much holy water. On one island, he baptized a woman who was enduring a painful childbirth, and she delivered her child quickly, without further pain. This miracle helped to convert most of the village.

In these new lands, language barriers might have hindered Francis from converting and baptizing, but he received the gift of tongues, so that he was able to speak and understand languages he had never learned.

Francis Xavier performed many other miracles during his missionary work. Once he raised a man from the dead, and so converted an entire village. Another time, when his ship was on the verge of sinking, Francis' prayers brought the ship safely to shore.

In the final ten years of his life, Francis Xavier left his homeland and family, traveled thousands of miles, baptized tens of thousands of people, and risked violent death, all so that he could bring people from faraway lands into the Catholic Church.

VOCABULARY

BAPTISM

The first of the seven sacraments, and the door which gives access to the other sacraments; first and chief sacrament of forgiveness of sins because it unites us with Christ. A believer receives the remission of both personal and original sin.

BAPTISM OF BLOOD

Those who suffer death for the sake of the faith without having received Baptism are baptized by their death for and with Christ; brings about the fruits of Baptism without being a sacrament.

BAPTISM OF DESIRE

For those who believe in a supreme being and strive to serve as best they are able, who die before their Baptism, their explicit desire to receive it, together with repentance for their sins, and charity, assures them the salvation that they were not able to receive through the sacrament.

CATECHUMEN

A person preparing to receive the sacrament of Baptism.

CATECHUMENATE

The formation of persons in preparation for their Christian Initiation; aims at bringing their conversion and their faith to maturity within the ecclesial community.

COMMUNION OF SAINTS

The unity in Christ of all the redeemed, those on earth and those who have died; it has also been interpreted to refer to unity in the holy things *(communio sanctorum)*, especially the unity of faith and charity through the Eucharist.

ENLIGHTENMENT

Another name for the Sacrament of Baptism because in Baptism, those who receive this catechetical instruction are enlightened in their understanding; the person baptized has been "enlightened," he becomes a "son of light," and he becomes "light."

EXORCISM

The public and authoritative act of the Church to protect or liberate a person or object from the power of the devil (e.g., demonic possession) in the name of Christ.

RENUNCIATION

To give up something to which a person has a claim. Everyone must renounce sin and those creatures that are proximate occasions to sin. This includes the renunciation of Satan at Baptism.

RITE

Diverse liturgical traditions in which the one catholic and apostolic faith has come to be expressed and celebrated in various cultures and lands. Rite and ritual are sometimes interchanged, as in the sacramental rite or the sacramental ritual.

SEAL

Permanent mark given to the soul at the Sacraments of Baptism, Confirmation, and Holy Orders, designating one as a follower of Christ.

SPONSOR

Most often a person who presents a child at Baptism (or anyone at Confirmation) and professes faith in the child's name; this person acts as a proxy if anything happens to the parents; an official representative of the community of faith.

TRINITARIAN FORMULA

The form used in the Sacrament of Baptism: "I baptize you in the name of the Father, and of the Son, and of the Holy Spirit."

STUDY QUESTIONS

1. Give three effects of Baptism.

2. What must be done and said for a sacramental Baptism to take place?

3. Who commanded that the Church baptize?

4. Does Baptism remove original sin? Actual sin? The tendency to sin?

5. Which is more powerful: man's weaknesses, which remain even after Baptism, or the graces of Baptism?

6. Can an adult be baptized?

7. What are a sponsor's responsibilities?

8. Who baptizes under normal circumstances?

9. Who can baptize in an emergency?

10. What are the three types of Baptism? Explain each.

11. Can someone who has not received sacramental Baptism get into heaven?

12. Can someone who has not received any sort of Baptism get into heaven?

13. How does Baptism join people to one another? What is this union called?

PRACTICAL EXERCISES

1. Write a news story about the day you were baptized. Be sure to include who baptized you, the name of the church where you were baptized, the names of your godparents, and some recollections of those who were present.

2. Adults who want to enter the Church must learn about the faith by attending the Rite of Christian Initiation for Adults. These adults will then be brought into full communion with the Church during the Easter Vigil. Talk to your parents, pastor, or spiritual director about becoming an RCIA sponsor either this year or in the future, especially if you know someone who wants to be Catholic but isn't sure how to take the first step.

3. Can a person who has tried to live a good life by following his conscience and searching for the truth get into heaven without receiving sacramental Baptism? Explain your answer.

4. Is it good for parents to have their children baptized as infants, before the children can make the decision on their own? Why or why not? Use the Bible to defend your answer.

FROM THE CATECHISM

1276 "Go therefore and make disciples of all nations, baptizing them in the name of the Father, and of the Son, and of the Holy Spirit, teaching them to observe all that I have commanded you" (Mt 28:19-20).

1277 Baptism is birth into the new life in Christ. In accordance with the Lord's will, it is necessary for salvation, as is the Church herself, which we enter by Baptism.

1278 The essential rite of Baptism consists in immersing the candidate in water or pouring water on his head, while pronouncing the invocation of the Most Holy Trinity: the Father, the Son, and the Holy Spirit.

1279 The fruit of Baptism, or baptismal grace, is a rich reality that includes forgiveness of original sin and all personal sins, birth into the new life by which man becomes an adoptive son of the Father, a member of Christ and a temple of the Holy Spirit. By this very fact the person baptized is incorporated into the Church, the Body of Christ, and made a sharer in the priesthood of Christ.

1280 Baptism imprints on the soul an indelible spiritual sign, the character, which consecrates the baptized person for Christian worship. Because of the character Baptism cannot be repeated (cf. DS, 1609 and DS, 1624).

1281 Those who die for the faith, those who are catechumens, and all those who, without knowing of the Church but acting under the inspiration of grace, seek God sincerely and strive to fulfill his will, can be saved even if they have not been baptized (cf. *LG*, 16).

1282 Since the earliest times, Baptism has been administered to children, for it is a grace and a gift of God that does not presuppose any human merit; children are baptized in the faith of the Church. Entry into Christian life gives access to true freedom.

1283 With respect to children who have died without Baptism, the liturgy of the Church invites us to trust in God's mercy and to pray for their salvation.

1284 In case of necessity, any person can baptize provided that he have the intention of doing that which the Church does and provided that he pours water on the candidate's head while saying: "I baptize you in the name of the Father, and of the Son, and of the Holy Spirit.

Endnotes

1. Cf. Council of Florence: DS 1314: *vitae spiritualis ianua.*
2. *Roman Catechism,* II, 2, 5; cf. Council of Florence: DS 1314; CIC, Can. 204 § 1; 849; CCEO, can. 675 § 1.
3. Cf. Mt 3:13.
4. Mt 28:19-20; cf. Mk 16:15-16.
5. St. Gregory of Nazianzus, *Oratio* 40, 3-4: PG 36, 361C.
6. Cf. Acts 16:15, 33; 18:8; 1 Cor 1:16; CDF, instruction, *Pastoralis actio*: AAS 72 (1980) 1137-1156.
7. *GS*, 22 § 5; cf. *LG*, 16; *AG*, 7.

Confirmation

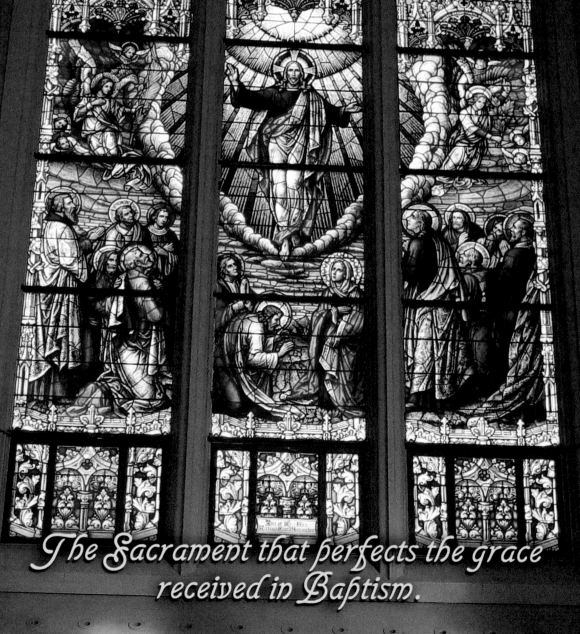

The Sacrament that perfects the grace received in Baptism.

Confirmation

*Y*ou've heard it before. During the teen years you'll be faced with many challenges and choices about what type of life to lead, what type of friends to have, what to believe. It sounds routine by now.

But just because you've heard it often doesn't make it any less true. You will be, and probably are now, facing a lot of choices. One of the choices you'll make is how seriously you live your faith. Most people your age who have been going to Mass their entire lives want to stand up for what they've been taught. Sometimes, though, the courage to live and defend your faith is hard to muster. That is where Confirmation comes in.

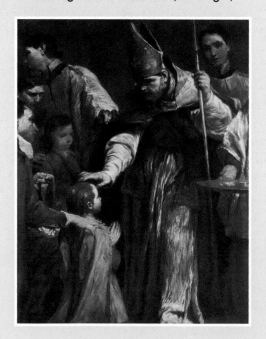

Confirmation is the sacrament that gives people courage: courage to do what they know is right, even when others mock their beliefs; courage to defend the truth, even when people deny that such a thing as truth exists; courage to profess their faith in Jesus, even when no one else around them believes.

CONFIRMATION

When the day of Pentecost had come they were all together in one place. And suddenly a sound came from heaven like the rush of a mighty wind, and it filled all the house where they were sitting. And there appeared to them tongues as of fire, distributed and resting on each one of them. And they were all filled with the Holy Spirit and began to speak in other tongues, as the Spirit gave them utterance. (Acts 2:1-4)

Now when the apostles at Jerusalem heard that Samaria had received the word of God, they sent to them Peter and John, who came down and prayed for them that they might receive the Holy Spirit; for it had not yet fallen on any of them, but they had only been baptized in the name of the Lord Jesus. Then they laid their hands on them and they received the Holy Spirit. (Acts 8:14-17)

Before Pentecost, the members of the early Church were, for the most part, a frightened people who gathered secretly to worship behind closed doors. At Pentecost, the Holy Spirit came upon the Church, each member receiving gifts that strengthened both the individual and the Church as a whole. The apostles and all who received the Holy Spirit became brave individuals, unafraid to stand up for the new faith. When converts were won over by these brave people, they followed Baptism with a laying-on of hands that would confer these same gifts of the Holy Spirit upon their new brothers and sisters. The laying-on of hands continues to this day as the Sacrament of Confirmation.

Confirmation is the Sacrament of Initiation that passes on the grace of Pentecost by the laying-on of hands, the anointing of oil, and the saying of the words, "Be sealed with the gift of the Holy Spirit." It perfects the grace of Baptism through the action of the Holy Spirit. With the graces of this sacrament, we are able to spread and defend the teachings of Christ and the Church.

Before the Second Vatican Council, Confirmation included a light slap on the cheek to remind the recipient that the service of Christ is difficult and calls for soldierliness. This slap has disappeared, for the most part, from the celebration of Confirmation. This is a time, though, when we need to understand ourselves as soldiers of Christ. The Church is under a greater attack now than at possibly any time in her history. Newspapers and television often transmit stories attacking the Church for daring to defend the teachings of Jesus Christ regarding abortion, contraception, divorce, and homosexuality. However, many Catholics, afraid to speak up in defense of the Church, stay on the sidelines, forgetting that Confirmation gives them the spiritual strength to speak up for Christ.

In the Old Testament the prophets announced that the Spirit of the Lord would rest on the hoped-for Messiah for his saving mission.[1] The descent of the Holy Spirit on Jesus at his baptism by John was the sign that this was he who was to come, the Messiah, the Son of God.[2] He was conceived of the Holy Spirit; his whole life and his whole mission are carried out in total communion with the Holy Spirit whom the Father gives him "without measure" (Jn 3:34).

This fullness of the Spirit was not to remain uniquely the Messiah's, but was to be communicated to the *whole messianic people*.[3] On several

This is a time when we need to understand ourselves as soldiers of Christ.

Many Catholics, afraid to speak up in defense of the Church, stay on the sidelines, forgetting that Confirmation gives them the spiritual strength to speak up for Christ.

Confirmation

In Confirmation, we are given increased love and increased strength to serve the Church, in order that we may be enabled to bring not only ourselves but also others to God.

occasions Christ promised this outpouring of the Spirit,[4] a promise which he fulfilled first on Easter Sunday and then more strikingly at Pentecost.[5] (CCC 1286-1287)

The word *Christian* means "anointed." In Baptism, the Trinity came to us to share life and love. In Confirmation, we are given increased love and increased strength to serve the Church, in order that we may be enabled to bring not only ourselves but also others to God. The Letter to the Hebrews mentions the connection between Baptism and Confirmation among the first elements of Christian instruction.

To signify the gift of the Spirit, the Church anoints the confirmed with chrism, a sacred oil. The prophet Isaiah indicates that anointing with oil is a sign of abundance and joy. The use of oil indicates the connection between Baptism and Confirmation as a "double sacrament," in the words of St. Cyprian. The pre-baptismal anointing with the oil of catechumens signifies cleansing and strengthening. By Confirmation, Christians, that is, those who are anointed, share more completely in the mission of Jesus Christ and the fullness of the Holy Spirit with which he is filled, so that their lives may give off the "aroma of Christ" (2 Cor 2:15).

CELEBRATION OF THE RITE

The sacred oil of chrism that is used in Confirmation is consecrated during the Chrism Mass on Holy Thursday. In most cases, Confirmation is celebrated separately from Baptism, so the liturgy of Confirmation begins with the confirmands (those who are to be confirmed) renewing their baptismal promises and making a profession of faith. This symbolizes that Confirmation follows and is linked to Baptism. It also serves as a reminder of the commitment made to Christ in Baptism. In a case of adult Baptism, Confirmation and the reception of First Eucharist follow immediately after Baptism, all in one ceremony.

After the profession of faith, the bishop extends his hands over the confirmands to signify the gift of the Holy Spirit and recites the following prayer:

> All-powerful God, Father of our Lord Jesus Christ, by water and the Spirit you freed your sons and daughters from sin and gave them new life. Send your Holy Spirit upon them to be their helper and guide. Give them the spirit of wisdom and understanding, the spirit of right judgment and courage, the spirit of knowledge and reverence. Fill them with the spirit of wonder and awe in your presence. We ask this through Christ our Lord.[6]

The essential rite of the sacrament (that which must be done for the sacrament to be validly given and received) follows with the anointing with chrism on the forehead and the laying-on of hands, accompanied by the words, "Be sealed with the gift of the Holy Spirit." The sign of peace concludes the rite, indicating that the confirmand is in communion with the church, the members of the faithful, and the bishop.

The ordinary minister of the sacrament of Confirmation is the bishop. Though the faculty may be given to a priest, ideally one's bishop should administer this sacrament as a sign of the union between the individual members of the faithful and their particular bishop.

In the Eastern Church, Confirmation is administered immediately after Baptism and is followed by reception of the Eucharist. The joint celebration of these sacraments in this order reminds us of the unity of Christian initiation.

WHO CAN RECEIVE CONFIRMATION?

Every baptized person who has not received this sacrament can and should be confirmed, for Baptism, Confirmation, and the Eucharist form a unity of sacraments that bring us into the Church. If someone has not received all three sacraments, the initiation of that person into the church remains incomplete. In the Latin rite, the recipient of Confirmation must normally be at least the age of reason, but the precise age of reception is left to the discretion of the local bishop. However, every Christian in danger of death who has not received Confirmation (including infants) should receive this sacrament.

REQUIREMENTS FOR RECEPTION:

Under normal circumstances, candidates for Confirmation, like the other sacraments, must meet certain conditions, Confirmands must:

† Be in the state of grace;

† Have reached the age of reason;

† Make a profession of faith;

† State their intention to receive the sacrament;

† Accept their obligation to profess Christ in both the Church and the world.

It has become the custom lately to administer Confirmation at the end of grammar school or the beginning of high school to indicate that the confirmand is expected to act as a mature Christian. This means that the recipient is capable of spiritual maturity and acting as Christ wishes even in difficult situations with the aid of grace. The time before Confirmation should be filled with intense prayer to prepare the recipient to receive the strength of the Holy Spirit with docility and a sense of mission.

> Preparation for Confirmation should aim at leading the Christian toward a more intimate union with Christ and a more lively familiarity with the Holy Spirit—his actions, his gifts, and his biddings—in order to be more capable of assuming the apostolic responsibilities of Christian life. To this end catechesis for Confirmation should strive to awaken a sense of belonging to the Church of Jesus Christ, the universal Church as well as the parish community. The latter bears special responsibility for the preparation of the confirmands.[7] (CCC 1309)

Candidates for this sacrament should seek the help of a sponsor, someone to whom they can talk openly about their shared faith. To emphasize the unity of Baptism and Confirmation, it is appropriate for one of the baptismal godparents to fulfill this role. It is a good practice to take the

Baptism, Confirmation, and the Eucharist form a unity of sacraments that bring us into the Church.

"Be sealed with the gift of the Holy Spirit."

Confirmation

St. Helena

Mother of Constantine the Great, Christian Emperor of the Roman Empire 312-337. In 326, at the age of 80, St. Helena unearthed the True Cross of the Crucifixion, the nails used to pierce the body of our Saviour and the headboard (Titular). She built a church on the spot where the cross was found.

St. Helena greatly influenced the wider spread of Christianity. The poor and destitute were special objects of her charity.

name of a saint you admire upon Confirmation. This saint will serve as a constant role model of service to Christ and his Church. Having a specific saint as your patron also guarantees the prayers of that holy person.

EFFECTS OF CONFIRMATION

Like Baptism, Confirmation imprints a permanent mark on the soul. Because of this permanence, Confirmation is received only once.

Simply stated, Confirmation is the full outpouring of the Holy Spirit, as was granted to the disciples at Pentecost. From this Sacrament of Initiation:

† Baptismal grace is increased and deepened;

† An indelible mark is imprinted on the soul (like Baptism);

† The confirmed person is rooted more deeply as a child of the Father;

† The confirmed person is united more closely to Christ;

† The gifts of the Holy Spirit (wisdom, understanding, counsel, fortitude, knowledge, piety, and fear of the Lord) increase;

† The confirmed person's bond with the Church is perfected;

† Special graces are given to the confirmed person to enable him to spread and defend the faith by word and deed as a true witness to Christ;

† The confirmed person is enabled to confess Christ boldly and never be ashamed of the Cross.

All of the graces of Confirmation prepare us as Christians to practice what is known as the apostolate, the work of evangelizing those around us for Christ. Confirmation helps us do this apostolate by presenting the truths of the Church, thereby bringing people closer to faith.

We are called to do apostolate with both our fellow Catholics and those whom we meet outside the faith. The best preparation for this work is a regular prayer life and a serious intention to become fully knowledgeable regarding the history and teachings of the Church.

MINISTER OF THE SACRAMENT

The original minister of the Sacrament of Confirmation was the bishop, the head of the local church. In his role as shepherd of the local church, he administered the Sacraments of Initiation: Baptism, Confirmation, and the Eucharist. As the Church grew in number, though, it became nearly impossible for the bishop to administer all of these sacraments to everyone who requested them. A change was made, therefore, which separated Confirmation from the other Sacraments of Initiation. Baptism and the Eucharist were administered by priests, while Confirmation remained the work of the bishop. Most dioceses in the United States continue to celebrate Confirmation separately from the other Sacraments of Christian Initiation. It is usually celebrated after Baptism, although the precise age for Confirmation varies.

The usual minister of this sacrament, then, remains the local bishop or his auxiliary. Today, this indicates that the bishops, as successors to the apostles, unite the confirmands more closely to the Church, to her apostolic origins, and to her mission of bearing witness to Christ.

For grave reasons, however, the bishop may cede the authority to confirm to a priest, and if someone is in danger of death, a priest may immediately confirm any Christian. Also, when an adult converts to Catholicism, a priest can administer the Sacrament of Confirmation.

CONCLUSION

The essential effect of Confirmation is to perfect the grace received in Baptism, strengthening the already existing bond that the baptized has with the Church through the power of the Holy Spirit. It graces the confirmed to witness to Christ by word and life. The phrase *divine filiation* is the key to understanding the mission of a person confirmed in Christ. As sons and daughters of God, the confirmed are called upon to act in every situation as Christ himself would act. This requires that they use the strength of Confirmation in all cases where they are tempted to deny their beliefs, either in word or deed.

Doing what God wants us to do may sometimes lead to loss of friends or good times. Acting contrary to how Jesus wishes us to act, however, makes it more difficult to do the correct thing in more serious situations, when our own spiritual well-being or that of someone we love is in jeopardy. It is possible to do as the Spirit wishes if we cooperate with his grace.

As sons and daughters of God, the confirmed are called upon to act in every situation as Christ himself would act.

The Pope Speaks

The Church which Christ founded by His blood, He strengthened on the day of Pentecost by a special power, given from Heaven....[S]itting now at the right hand of the Father, He wished to make known and proclaim His Spouse [the Church] through the visible coming of the Holy Spirit with the sound of a mighty wind and tongues of fire. For just as He Himself when he began to preach was made known by His Eternal Father through the Holy Spirit descending and remaining upon Him in the form of a dove, so likewise, as the Apostles were about to enter upon their ministry of preaching, Christ our Lord sent the Holy Spirit down from Heaven, to touch them with tongues of fire and to point out, as by the finger of God, the supernatural mission and office of the Church.[8] — Pope Pius XII

SUPPLEMENTARY READING

Imagine for a moment that you're in a dimly lit chapel. Candles light the altar as you are engulfed by soft voices praying the rosary. You promise to focus completely on the prayers. You lift up your heart and… fall asleep. It's just another day in the life of St. Thérèse of Lisieux, better known as the "Little Flower." More than any other saint, Thérèse understood and explained the mystery of divine filiation, of living as a child of God. She loved Mary, but didn't enjoy the Rosary. She was a mystic, but hated retreats. St. Thérèse never got upset about falling asleep because she was confident that God, like a good parent, loved his children even when they were sleeping.

Commenting on the mystery of her vocation Thérèse writes, "Jesus does not call those who are worthy, but those he wants to call." This call began as a call to Carmel, a cloistered convent cut off from all of civilization. This call led to her being named the patroness of missionaries by Pius XI. Why would the Church choose as its patroness of missions one who had never physically done a mission? The answer quite simply is that the essence of missions is not persuading, or using a technique, or blasting radio and TV ads. Evangelization is the *transmission of life*, not of words. Words are certainly useful, but "The preachers of the Gospel could well tire themselves out, toil and lay down their lives to lead pagans to the Catholic religion; they might be ever so industrious, ever so diligent and use every means known to man; but none of this would be to any avail, everything would be in vain, if God, with his grace, were not to touch hearts, then the toil of missionaries would be in vain" (Pius XI, *Rerum Ecclesiae*).

Thérèse knew that she must be a child of God, that her only chance at holiness was to trust in God for all things. In the last pages of her

St. Thérèse of Lisieux
(1873-1897)
Feast on October 1

autobiographical *Story of a Soul*, she writes, "In the eve of my life, I will come before you with nothing in my hands because I do not ask you to count the things I've done." Thérèse's holiness flew in the face of the dominant Pelagian heresy of her (and our) time — that it is better and safer to rely on ourselves than to receive God's grace. She truly lived Jesus' words: "Without me you can do nothing."

Instead, Thérèse let God act through her. Whenever God inspired her to a certain kind act, Thérèse shouted "yes!" unreservedly, faithfully, and happily. She didn't try to "earn grace" by her sacrifices and exterior acts, but rather saw each trial as a gift from God so that she may be more closely united to her Savior Jesus Christ. In all things, St. Thérèse acted as a child of God, and in all things she was rewarded as a child of God.

VOCABULARY

ANOINTING
Symbol of the Holy Spirit, whose anointing of Jesus as Messiah fulfilled the prophecies of the Old Testament. Christ (in Hebrew, Messiah) means "Anointed One." Anointing is the sacramental sign of Confirmation, Anointing of the Sick, and Holy Orders.

APOSTOLATE
The activity of the Christian which fulfills the apostolic nature of the whole Church by working to extend the reign of Christ to the entire world.

CHRISM
Perfumed oil, consecrated by the bishop, which signifies the gift of the Holy Spirit; used for consecration in the Sacraments of Baptism, Confirmation, and Holy Orders.

CONFIRMAND
Person preparing to receive the Sacrament of Confirmation.

CONFIRMATION
One of the Sacraments of Initiation; completes the grace of Baptism by a special outpouring of the gifts of the Holy Spirit, which seal or confirm the baptized in union with Christ and equip them for worship and apostolic life in the Church.

COURAGE
One of the four cardinal moral virtues which ensures firmness in difficulties and constancy in doing the good; also one of the seven gifts of the Holy Spirit.

DIVINE FILIATION
One's acceptance by God as a child of God, a consoling mystery bringing one a spirit of sincerity and trust while filling us with love and wonder; see the parable of the Prodigal Son (Lk 15:11-32).

PENTECOST
The fiftieth day at the end of the seven weeks following Passover (or Easter). At the first Pentecost, the Holy Spirit was manifested, given and communicated to the Church, fulfilling the paschal mystery of Christ.

TEMPTATION
An attraction, either from outside oneself or from within, to act contrary to right reason and the commandments of God. Jesus himself during his life on earth was tempted, put to the test, to manifest the opposition between himself and the devil.

STUDY QUESTIONS

1. Describe the change in the members of the early Church which occurred after they received the fullness of the grace of the Holy Spirit.

2. How are these graces received today?

3. Confirmation perfects the grace of what other sacrament? Through the action of which divine person?

4. What does Confirmation give us the strength to do?

5. What are the other two sacraments to which the Sacrament of Confirmation is linked? Why are they joined together?

6. What words are said during the laying-on of hands in the rite of Confirmation?

7. Why is the bishop the ordinary minister of Confirmation?

PRACTICAL EXERCISES

1. Many people disagree with certain things that the Church teaches are sinful. List three of these and explain what is wrong with them. Also, come up with realistic situations in which the strength we receive in the Sacrament of Confirmation would be needed to defend the Church's teachings.

2. One of the most beautiful aspects of Confirmation is a deepening of one's roots in the divine filiation, which makes one cry, "Abba, Father!" How are we God's children?

3. Because of her writings on being a child of God, St. Thérèse of Lisieux was made a Doctor of the Church even though she died at the age of 24. Ask your spiritual director, pastor, or teacher to recommend a good book on St. Thérèse of Lisieux and divine filiation.

FROM THE CATECHISM

1315 "Now when the apostles at Jerusalem heard that Samaria had received the word of God, they sent to them Peter and John, who came down and prayed for them that they might receive the Holy Spirit; for it had not yet fallen on any of them, but they had only been baptized in the name of the Lord Jesus. Then they laid their hands on them and they received the Holy Spirit" (Acts 8: 14-17).

1316 Confirmation perfects Baptismal grace; it is the sacrament which gives the Holy Spirit in order to root us more deeply in the divine filiation, incorporate us more firmly into Christ, strengthen our bond with the Church, associate us more closely with her mission, and help us bear witness to the Christian faith in words accompanied by deeds.

1317 Confirmation, like Baptism, imprints a spiritual mark or indelible character on the Christian's soul; for this reason one can receive this sacrament only once in one's life.

1318 In the East this sacrament is administered immediately after Baptism and is followed by participation in the Eucharist; this tradition highlights the unity of the three sacraments of Christian initiation. In the Latin Church this sacrament is administered when the age of reason has been reached, and its celebration is ordinarily reserved to the bishop, thus signifying that this sacrament strengthens the ecclesial bond.

1319 A candidate for Confirmation who has attained the age of reason must profess the faith, be in the state of grace, have the intention of receiving the sacrament, and be prepared to assume the role of disciple and witness to Christ, both within the ecclesial community and in temporal affairs.

1320 The essential rite of Confirmation is anointing the forehead of the baptized with sacred chrism (in the East other sense-organs as well), together with the laying on of the minister's hand and the words: *"Accipe signaculum doni Spiritus Sancti"* (Be sealed with the Gift of the Holy Spirit.) in the Roman Rite, or: *"Signaculum doni Spiritus Sancti"* (the seal of the gift of the Holy Spirit) in the Byzantine rite.

1321 When Confirmation is celebrated separately from Baptism, its connection with Baptism is expressed, among other ways, by the renewal of baptismal promises. The celebration of Confirmation during the Eucharist helps underline the unity of the sacraments of Christian initiation.

Endnotes

1. Cf. Is 11: 2; 61: 1; Lk 4: 16-22.
2. Cf. Mt 3: 13-17; Jn 1: 33-34.
3. Cf. Ez 36: 25-27; Jl 3: 1-2.
4. Cf. Lk 12: 12; Jn 3: 5-8; 7: 37-39; 16: 7-15; Acts 1: 8.
5. Cf. Jn 20: 22; Acts 2: 1-4.
6. *OC*, 25.
7. Cf. *OC* Introduction 3.
8. Pope Pius XII, *The Pope Speaks,* edited by Michael Chinigo, New York, Pantheon, 1957.

The Eucharist

"Do this in memory of me."

Chapter 12

The Eucharist

*I*magine this television commercial:

"Success Breakfast Food is seeking teenagers, ages twelve to seventeen, to try a new product, Breakfast of Professionals. Breakfast of Professionals is a newly-developed food product based on a mixture of whole grain foods with enhanced vitamins. You are guaranteed to make it in the pro career of your choice when you start each day with a bowl of Breakfast of Professionals. Preliminary studies indicate that athletes using our new product will be able to perform at the highest level in their chosen sport."

Would every young person be interested? The answer seems obvious. Well, that will never happen on the human level, but on the supernatural level it's a reality. Reception of the Eucharist increases the power of Jesus' love in us every time we receive it. Christ not only wants us to be as much like him as possible, but he makes it a reality because the grace of regular reception of the Eucharist will enable us to identify with Christ so that we act toward others as he did.

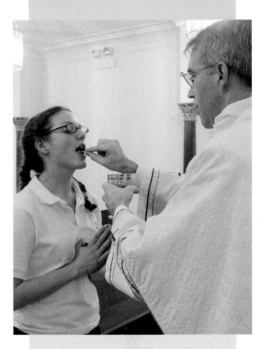

THE EUCHARIST

Jesus is truly, really, and substantially here on the earth. Through the actions of the Holy Spirit, he is found under the appearance of bread and wine in the Eucharist—the body and blood, soul and divinity of Christ. It is the sacrifice of Christ in our own time.

It is highly fitting that Christ should have wanted to remain present to his Church in this unique way. Since Christ was about to take his departure from his own in his visible form, he wanted to give us his sacramental presence; since he was about to offer himself on the cross to save us, he wanted us to have the memorial of the love with which he loved us "to the end" (Jn 13:1), even to the giving of his life. In his Eucharistic presence he remains mysteriously in our midst as the one who loved us and gave himself up for us,[1] and he remains under signs that express and communicate this love:

"The Church and the world have a great need for Eucharistic worship. Jesus awaits us in this sacrament of love. Let us not refuse the time to go to meet him in adoration, in contemplation full of faith, and open to making amends for the serious offenses and crimes of the world. Let our adoration never cease."[2] (CCC 1380)

Since the Eucharist truly is Christ, it is the source and summit of Christian life. Every action of the Church that is motivated by grace, whether of sacrament or ministry, is tied to this sacrifice.

The writers of the first three Gospels, as well as St. Paul, recorded Christ's institution of this great miracle at the Last Supper.

Jesus chose the time of Passover to fulfill what he had announced at Capernaum: giving his disciples his Body and his Blood:

"Then came the day of Unleavened Bread, on which the passover lamb had to be sacrificed. So Jesus sent Peter and John, saying, 'Go and prepare the passover meal for us, that we may eat it....' They went...and prepared the passover. And when the hour came, he sat at table, and the apostles with him. And he said to them, 'I have earnestly desired to eat this passover with you before I suffer; for I tell you I shall not eat it again until it is fulfilled in the kingdom of God.'...And he took bread, and when he had given thanks he broke it and gave it to them, saying, 'This is my body which is given for you. Do this in remembrance of me.' And likewise the cup after supper, saying, 'This cup which is poured out for you is the New Covenant in my blood.'"[3] (CCC 1339)

All this occurred on the Jewish holiday of Passover, the night before Jesus was crucified. By doing this, he established the Eucharist as an offering to the Father for all men. The fact that the Last Supper occurred during Passover gives the old Passover its definitive meaning. The old meal for Passover included unleavened bread and a lamb sacrificed to God so his wrath would *pass over* those at the meal. The Passover meal established by Christ is unleavened bread, which Christ, who is called the Lamb of God, turns into his body. Christ instituted this new Passover at the Last Supper as a pledge of his love, as a way of remaining with us forever, as a memorial of his death and Resurrection, and to make us sharers in his Passover, through which man is spared from God's wrath. Because the sacrifice of Christ allows men to be saved, it is at the center of Catholicism.

The Eucharist is the source and summit of Christian life.

Because the sacrifice of Christ allows men to be saved, the Eucharist is at the center of Catholicism.

The Eucharist

The Eucharist is the heart and the summit of the Church's life, for in it Christ associates his Church and all her members with his sacrifice of praise and thanksgiving offered once for all on the cross to his Father; by this sacrifice he pours out the graces of salvation on his Body which is the Church. (CCC 1407)

The doors to God's kingdom, in fact, are opened through Jesus' Passion, death, and Resurrection. Since the Eucharist is one and the same with Jesus' sacrifice on the Cross, it stands as the greatest proof of God's love, for when we receive the Eucharist, Christ actually becomes one with us. It is our duty to return this great love by truly becoming imitators of Christ in thought, word, and deed.

As a Sacrament of Initiation, the Eucharist is a true and substantial reality. It is a memorial, a reminder, of Christ's Passover and sacrifice on the Cross, which completed his work of salvation. But more than just a memorial, the actual sacrifice of Christ is presented to us in the Liturgy of the Eucharist.

Like all sacraments, the Eucharist is a gift from God made possible by the power of the Holy Spirit. We must therefore accept that the Eucharist is:

† A gift of thanksgiving and praise to the Father;

† Identical to Jesus' death on the Cross;

† The sacrificial memorial of Christ and his body;

† Christ made present by the power of his Word and of the Holy Spirit;

† A true sacrifice;

† A revelation of these truths to us by Jesus;

† Offered for the living and the dead to obtain spiritual and material benefits.

(See CCC 1414 on p. 168)

It is obvious from this list that the Eucharist is many things and points to several truths. For this reason, it has many names:

† The word *Eucharist* comes from the Greek *eucharistein*, meaning "to give thanks," which reminds us of the Jewish custom of recalling the blessings of God's works of creation, sanctification, and redemption at every meal.

† It is called the Lord's Supper because of its connection to the Last Supper. This name is also an anticipation of the wedding feast of the Lamb in the heavenly Jerusalem.

† The Eucharistic celebration, the Mass, is called the breaking of the bread because it is part of the Last Supper rite, and because it was when Jesus broke bread that the disciples recognized him after the Resurrection.

† The Eucharist is also called a memorial because it reminds us of the Lord's Passion and Resurrection.

† Eucharistic assembly refers to the fact that the Eucharist is celebrated in the midst of the assembly of the faithful.

† Finally, the Eucharist is called the Holy Sacrifice since it completes and surpasses all sacrifices of the Old Testament.

Like all sacraments, the Eucharist is a gift from God made possible by the power of the Holy Spirit.

All of the Old Testament sacrifices, in fact, foreshadow the sacrifice of Christ, but particularly the sacrifice of the priest Melchizedech, who offered bread and wine to God. For bread and wine are key to the Eucharistic celebration.

> At the heart of the Eucharistic celebration are the bread and wine that, by the words of Christ and the invocation of the Holy Spirit, become Christ's Body and Blood. Faithful to the Lord's command the Church continues to do, in his memory and until his glorious return, what he did on the eve of his Passion: "He took bread...." "He took the cup filled with wine...." The signs of bread and wine become, in a way surpassing understanding, the Body and Blood of Christ; they continue also to signify the goodness of creation. (CCC 1333)

THE MYSTERY OF TRANSUBSTANTIATION

> The essential signs of the Eucharistic sacrament are wheat bread and grape wine, on which the blessing of the Holy Spirit is invoked and the priest pronounces the words of consecration spoken by Jesus during the Last Supper: "This is my body which will be given up for you....This is the cup of my blood...." (CCC 1412)

In the sixth chapter of the Gospel of St. John, Jesus refers to himself as the "bread come down from heaven" (Jn 6: 41). This statement should be taken literally. When the priest says the words of consecration over the bread and wine, by the power of the Holy Spirit acting through Jesus the substance of the bread and wine is changed into the Body and Blood of Christ. It is Christ himself, living, glorious, truly and really present, body and blood, soul and divinity.

This transformation is an act of God. After the words of consecration, there is no longer any bread or wine present. Every single bit of bread and every last drop of wine have been completely changed. Though the appearances of bread and wine remain so that we will be able to receive them during Communion, they have both truly become Christ.

Catholics hold that when the bread and wine are consecrated they become completely the body and blood of Jesus Christ, with no trace of bread and wine remaining except in mere appearance. This is the doctrine of transubstantiation, which includes the following articles:

† The whole Christ is present under each and every part of the Eucharist;

† The whole Christ is present if the parts are divided;

† The whole Christ is present as a substance;

† The presence of Christ is sacramental;

† The presence of Christ endures as long as what remains appears to be bread and wine, recognizable as such, and uncorrupted.

Even outside the Mass, Christ remains in our presence in this visible form. He remains as a proof of his love and a reminder that he gave himself up for us, and also as proof that he wishes to share himself with us as often as possible. Christ's desire for so intimate a union with us requires that we love Christ in the Eucharist in return.

After the words of consecration, there is no longer any bread or wine present.

Because it is Christ himself, the Eucharist is the holiest thing in the world.

It is clear from the writing of St. Paul in his first letter to the Corinthians that Christ is actually present in the Eucharist under the appearance of bread and wine. What else could he be talking about when he says that whoever "eats the bread or drinks the cup of the Lord in an unworthy manner will be guilty of profaning the body and blood of the Lord" (1 Cor 11: 27)?

Indeed, there have been many Eucharistic miracles in which the Body and Blood of the Lord changed in appearance, no longer keeping the form of bread and wine but looking like flesh and blood. In the town of Ostia, in Italy, a consecrated host actually bled. The altar cloth with dried blood can be seen there today.

All this should make us realize how close the Lord is to us. Jesus himself is in the tabernacle at your Church.

> "Jesus, knowing that the hour of his death was come, desired to leave us, before he died, the greatest pledge of his affection that he could give us; and this was the gift of the Most Holy Sacrament: He loved them to the end; which St. Chrysostom explains, 'He loved them with extreme love.' He loved men with the greatest love with which he could love them, by giving them his whole self. But at what time did Jesus institute this great Sacrament, in which he has left us himself? On the night preceding his death: The same night in which he was betrayed (writes the Apostle), He took bread; and giving thanks, broke and said, Take ye and eat; this is my Body. At that very time that men were preparing to put him to death, he gave them this last proof of his love."[4]

REQUIREMENTS FOR RECEPTION

Because it is Christ himself, the Eucharist is the holiest thing in the world. Therefore we must be very careful to treat the Eucharist with the utmost respect when we receive it. This means that to receive this Sacrament of Initiation, the recipient must:

† Be a baptized Catholic;

† Have attained the age of reason (usually seven years);

† Have received first Reconciliation prior to first reception of the Eucharist;

† Must fast from all food and drink except water or medicine for one hour prior to reception;

† Have no mortal sin present on his soul.

Before receiving it for the first time, a person must also understand what the Eucharist really is. Those making their first communion should receive some instruction in that regard.

It is a most serious sin of sacrilege to receive the Eucharist in the state of mortal sin. The Eucharist is called a sacrament of the living to indicate that the grace of God must be alive in us in order to receive it.

St. Paul warns us about receiving the Eucharist when we should not: "Whoever eats this bread or drinks this cup of the Lord unworthily will be guilty of the body and blood of the Lord… for he who eats and drinks unworthily, without distinguishing the body, eats and drinks judgment unto himself" (1 Cor 11: 27-29).

The requirement to fast for one hour prior to reception of the Eucharist is the Church's gentle reminder that the Eucharist is the Lord himself, rather than just another food. It reminds us to prepare ourselves to receive this great gift with all possible due respect.

The share each person has in the Eucharist in this life foreshadows his share in the eternal banquet that awaits all who follow Christ. For this reason, all should strive to receive the Eucharist with great reverence and devotion and as often as is possible. At a minimum, every Catholic is required to receive the Eucharist once yearly. The more Christ is permitted to pour his life into our lives, the more we will enjoy his love in heaven.

FRUITS OF REGULAR RECEPTION

The extreme respect individuals should have for the Eucharist and their sense of unworthiness used to be expressed poorly, with people shying away from receiving this sacrament on a frequent basis. However, in recent years people have come to a greater understanding of Eucharistic communion, and are now encouraged to receive it often, even daily if they are properly disposed and if it is possible. The person who receives this sacrament is blessed with many graces. Among these graces, the Eucharist:

† Stabilizes and increases the intimate union with Christ;

† Reinforces the unity of the Church as the Mystical Body of Christ;

† Removes venial sins;

† Preserves from grave sins;

† Diminishes sinful love of self;

† Strengthens against temptation;

† Decreases purgatorial debt;

† Reduces the drives of concupiscence.

Whenever we receive the Eucharist while in a state of grace, our intimate union with Christ is strengthened. This union preserves, increases, renews, and nourishes the life of grace received at Baptism. This strengthening is the foremost grace of the Eucharist.

Receiving the Eucharist also unites all the faithful more closely to each other while incorporating us more deeply into the Church. Since receiving the Eucharist fulfills the call to become one body in Christ, the Church highly recommends that the faithful receive the Eucharist whenever they participate at Mass, and *requires* that Catholics receive the Eucharist at least once a year during the period from Ash Wednesday to Trinity Sunday.

The mystery of the Eucharist is one that faith enables us to accept on the word of God, who is all-powerful. It is beyond proof. Since the Eucharist is food for the spirit, it should be received as often as is possible to strengthen the spirit, particularly when the moment of death appears to be imminent.

The Church highly recommends that the faithful receive the Eucharist whenever they participate at Mass.

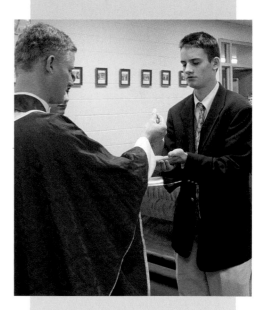

Whenever we receive the Eucharist while in a state of grace, our intimate union with Christ is strengthened.

During Mass, it is good to remind ourselves that in a few minutes, we will be receiving Christ, the God of all, in the Eucharist.

THE MINISTER OF THE EUCHARIST

Christ, the eternal High Priest, presides over the Mass, acting through the priest to offer the Eucharistic sacrifice to make up for the sin of man.

Thus St. John Chrysostom declares:

> It is not man that causes the things offered to become the Body and Blood of Christ, but he who was crucified for us, Christ himself. The priest, in the role of Christ, pronounces these words, but their power and grace are God's. This is my body, he says. This word transforms the things offered.[5] (CCC 1375)

Through the sacrament of Holy Orders, only validly ordained bishops and priests, acting in the person of Christ, have been given this power to say the Mass and transform the bread and wine to the body and blood of Christ. This is not to say that everyone else at a Mass is simply an observer. All people present also have a role to play, including readers, those who distribute communion, and the whole people of God, who participate through their prayers. Lay people usually offer the gifts to indicate that our hearts are united in praise, thanksgiving, and atonement for our sins.

The ordinary distributor of the Eucharist is the bishop, priest, or deacon. The Church permits the use of extraordinary ministers of the Eucharist, but extraordinary ministers of the Eucharist may distribute Holy Communion at Eucharistic celebrations only when there are no ordained ministers present or when those ordained ministers present at a liturgical celebration are truly unable to distribute Holy Communion. They may exercise this function at Eucharistic celebrations when there are particularly large numbers of the faithful present, which would excessively prolong the Mass because of an insufficient number of ordained ministers to distribute Holy Communion. Those chosen as extraordinary ministers are to be instructed in the Eucharist and their roles, and these ministers are not to receive the Eucharist at the same time as the celebrant as if they are concelebrants with the priest.

PARTICIPATION IN THE MASS

Our participation in the Eucharistic celebration—the Mass—should be total, a participation of body and soul. When we enter church, we should genuflect, greet Jesus personally, and then look over the readings prior to Mass. These readings are chosen because they relate to the Mass of the day and to each other. Since the readings at Mass offer an opportunity to hear God speak to us personally, looking them over should lead to a better understanding of what God wants for us. It will also help us to stay focused during Mass. People who are genuinely involved with something never complain about being bored with it.

During Mass, it is good to remind ourselves that in a few minutes, we will be receiving Christ, the God of all, in the Eucharist. Even if we were to pray over this for all our lives, we could hardly begin to understand his love. The Lord loves us so much that he wishes to be truly, really, and substantially joined to us. If we understand that the Eucharist is the summit of Christian life, it should be clear that frequent reception of the Eucharist, even daily when possible, will bring us closer to the risen Christ.

THE EUCHARISTIC LITURGY

> It was above all on "the first day of the week," Sunday, the day of Jesus' resurrection, that the Christians met "to break bread" (Acts 20: 7). From that time down to our own day the celebration of the Eucharist has been continued so that today we encounter it everywhere in the Church with the same fundamental structure. It remains the center of the Church's life. (CCC 1343)

Evidence for the basic outlines of the Eucharist goes back to the writings of St. Justin Martyr in the year 155, with two basic divisions of the Eucharistic celebration. These divisions remain to this day:

Liturgy of the Word:

† Gathering – All stand and sing as the celebrant and readers process into church;

† Penitential rite – All ask God and our neighbor for forgiveness for sins committed and requirements omitted;

† First reading – usually from Old Testament;

† Responsorial psalm – reflecting on the first reading;

† Second reading – from New Testament, usually from one of Paul's letters;

† Third reading – always from one of the Gospels;

† Homily – a commentary on the readings;

† Creed – a concise statement of Catholic beliefs;

† General Intercessions – a series of prayers for the good of the whole Church.

Liturgy of the Eucharist:

† Presentation of the bread and wine and the offerings of the faithful;

† The offering made in Christ's name of the bread and wine for and with the whole Church;

† Consecratory prayer changing the bread and wine into the body and blood of Christ;

† Reception of the Eucharist by the priest and the people;

† Prayers of conclusion.

It is during this liturgy, beginning at the moment the words of consecration are spoken, that Christ is made present. After the words:

> "Take this all of you and eat it, this is My Body, which will be given up for you . . .

> "Take this all of you and drink from it. This is the cup of My Blood, the blood of the new and everlasting covenant. It will be shed for you and for all so that sins may be forgiven. Do this in memory of me."

Readings at Mass offer an opportunity to hear God speak to us personally.

The altar represents both the table of the Lord at the Last Supper and the Cross upon which Christ was sacrificed.

Jesus Christ is truly, really, and substantially there—a presence in the truest sense, as present as the person sitting next to you in Mass. Belief in this transubstantiation of the body and blood of Jesus is demonstrated in the liturgy when people kneel during the consecration and genuflect or bow when approaching the altar, indicating their adoration of the Lord.

What is accomplished by the Eucharistic liturgy is truly amazing. Through the death and Resurrection of Jesus the whole of creation loved by God is presented as a gift to the Father. For as everything was tainted by the Fall, so everything in creation has been redeemed by Christ's Sacrifice. The Eucharist both makes present and re-presents (presents again) this sacrifice of Jesus. The gift of the Eucharist, then, empowers the Church to offer to God this sacrifice for the good of all he has made. The Eucharist also demonstrates all that God has accomplished through creation, redemption, and sanctification.

> In the sense of Sacred Scripture the *memorial* is not merely the recollection of past events but the proclamation of the mighty works wrought by God for men.[6] In the liturgical celebration of these events, they become in a certain way present and real. This is how Israel understands its liberation from Egypt: every time Passover is celebrated, the Exodus events are made present to the memory of believers so that they may conform their lives to them. (CCC 1363)

As a gift from God, the Mass directly benefits every believer. The sacrifice of the Mass is offered for all people, from the pope to the laity. The Eucharist is also offered for the faithful departed who have not yet entered heaven.

As often as the sacrifice of the Cross is celebrated on the altar, the work of our salvation is carried out. This is because the sacrifice of the Eucharist and the sacrifice of Christ on the Cross are one single sacrifice. The Eucharistic sacrifice, itself, fulfills the four Old Testament requirements for a sacrifice:

† It is offered by a priest;

† The victim is an unblemished male;

† It is offered in remission for sin;

† It is destroyed in some manner.

Since the Eucharist is meant for our good, Christ told us to make use of it.

> We carry out this command of the Lord by celebrating the *memorial of his sacrifice.* In so doing, *we offer to the Father* what he has himself given us: the gifts of his creation, bread and wine which, by the power of the Holy Spirit and by the words of Christ, have become the body and blood of Christ. Christ is thus really and mysteriously made *present.* (CCC 1357)

Because the Mass is the primary way to bring about holiness in the people of God, it is full of symbolism. The altar represents both the table of the Lord at the Last Supper and the Cross upon which Christ was sacrificed. The altar of Christ is the image of the body of Christ, and the liturgy expresses the unity of the sacrifice with communion with Jesus.

Each time we attend the Liturgy of the Eucharist, Christ invites us to share in his Body and Blood so that we may have divine life in us.

Outside the liturgy, the reserved hosts are handled with utmost care in the tabernacle, in solemn veneration, and in carrying them in procession. The tabernacle should be located in a particularly worthy place in church and should be constructed to indicate the emphasis on and the truth of the real presence.

SPIRITUAL COMMUNION

When we are not able to attend Mass daily, we can still receive the Lord spiritually in our hearts through the practice of spiritual communions. This is a form of prayer in which we ask Jesus to make himself present in our souls in a spiritual manner. Jesus told St. Catherine of Siena that regular reception of the Eucharist is golden, and the practice of spiritual communion is silver. Spiritual communion may be received as often as we say the prayer. It is a good habit, for it helps to keep God present to us throughout the day.

A spiritual communion can be made in the following words:

> My Lord, I wish to receive you with the purity, humility, and devotion with which your most holy Mother received you, with the spirit and fervor of the saints.

EUCHARISTIC DEVOTIONS OUTSIDE OF MASS

Outside of the Liturgy of the Eucharist, the Church recommends two devotions to Jesus present on the altar.

The first of these is Benediction. The word benediction comes from a Latin phrase meaning "to bless." Benediction is a para-liturgical service accompanied with appropriate music and prayers in which the Eucharist is placed on the altar to be adored. At the conclusion, the priest or deacon conducting the service blesses all present with the Eucharist.

The second of these devotions is adoration, in which the Eucharist is placed in a monstrance that allows people to see the Eucharist while still protecting it. During Eucharistic adoration, the faithful may remain in the presence of the Eucharist for long periods, in deep prayer and meditation on this miracle of God.

CONCLUSION

There is no greater love on the earth than the love of God for his creatures. Christ shares his love with us by joining himself to us in the Eucharist. Though it is beyond our poor power to understand his desire to be one with us, we would be foolish not to take advantage of this reality.

Before Christ ascended into heaven he promised to be with us until the end of time. Christ has kept this promise to us by remaining present in the Eucharist. At the instant the words of consecration are spoken, he

Christ shares his love with us by joining himself to us in the Eucharist.

Before Christ ascended into heaven he promised to be with us until the end of time.

> *The reception of the Eucharist is a participation in the life of the Trinity that foreshadows the complete and eternal participation in heaven.*

becomes truly present in flesh and blood. The reception of the Eucharist is a participation in the life of the Trinity that foreshadows the complete and eternal participation in heaven.

EXAMINATION FOR THE EUCHARIST

† Do I receive the Eucharist only when I am in the state of grace?

† Do I prepare myself through prayer for Jesus' arrival in the Eucharist?

† Do I spend at least ten minutes in thanksgiving after reception?

† Do I take advantage of every opportunity to receive the Eucharist?

† Do I encourage others to partake of the Eucharist often?

† Do I act respectfully while in the presence of the Eucharist?

SUPPLEMENTARY READING

When the great bell of St. Peter's began tolling on August 19th, 1914, it summoned the faithful of Rome to pray for Pope Pius X, unexpectedly on his deathbed. The great bell could also have been tolling for the "long nineteenth century," the period from the French Revolution of 1789 to the outbreak of the First World War in the summer of 1914. The "long nineteenth century" was a nightmare for the Church in Europe. Pius X opened the twentieth facing a crisis in France. When the French government secularized the schools, subjected religious orders to state control, and created state-controlled "cultural associations" to seize Church properties, Pius responded with condemnations. This reduced the Church in France to material poverty, but secured its independence from the state. Pius also acted forcefully to end the "imperial veto" that allowed the Holy Roman Emperor to preemptively veto any candidate that the conclave might choose as pope.

These and other moves set the stage for the Church in the twentieth century as she would be able to speak with greater freedom—and greater moral authority—unencumbered by state support and entanglement with the high politics of the European powers. In a century in which the state was to become the major enemy of human life and liberty, the Church was able to speak ever more prophetically against the powers and principalities of the twentieth century.

Pius' internal governance of the Church could be severe, and never more so than in his condemnation of "Modernism" as the "synthesis of all heresies." Modernism was an intellectual movement that generally measured Church teaching against the standard of

St. Pius X
(1835-1914)
Feast on August 21

modern philosophy, science and historical criticism, resulting in an undermining of traditional doctrine. Pius imposed an "anti-modernist" oath on all clergy. The action was effective in stamping out Modernism in the Catholic Church.

Of course, Pius' most important reform was in the norms for the reception of Holy Communion. For quite some time even devout Catholics received Holy Communion infrequently, motivated by an improper sense of unworthiness. Pius encouraged frequent, even daily, reception of Holy Communion, and he lowered the age of First Communion as well. No other decree in the history of the Church resulted in such an increase in reception of the sacraments throughout

Continued

SUPPLEMENTARY READING CONTINUED

the whole Church. Whatever else Pius may have done as pope, nothing unleashed the floodgates of grace in the Church as much as the practice of frequent Holy Communion. All of this century's saints nourished their souls on the Holy Eucharist — a grace made available to them by the pastoral wisdom of Pius X.

Pius X was canonized in 1954 — the first pope to be canonized since Pius V (d. 1572) — because of his personal holiness. A saint was needed at the end of the "long nineteenth century" to prepare the Church for the horrors of the twentieth, already underway as the bell tolled in St. Peter's that day in 1914.

VOCABULARY

ADORATION
The acknowledgment of God as God, Creator and Savior, the Lord and Master of everything that exists through worship and prayer.

BENEDICTION
A prayer invoking God's power and care upon some person, place, thing, or undertaking. The prayer of benediction acknowledges God as the source of all blessing.

COMMUNION
Holy Communion, the reception of the Body and Blood of Christ in the Eucharist; more generally, our fellowship and union with Jesus and other baptized Christians in the Church, which has its source and summit in the celebration of the Eucharist.

CONSECRATION
The dedication of a thing or person to divine service by a prayer or blessing.

EUCHARIST
The ritual, sacramental action of thanksgiving to God which constitutes the principal Christian liturgical celebration of and communion in the paschal mystery of Christ; traditionally known as the Holy Sacrifice of the Mass.

SACRAMENTAL PRESENCE
The real, true, and substantial existence of both Christ's divinity and humanity in the Holy Eucharist, under the appearance of mere bread and wine.

SPIRITUAL COMMUNION
Conscious burning desire to receive Holy Communion when unable to do so physically.

TABERNACLE
The receptacle in the church in which the consecrated Eucharist is reserved for Communion for the sick and dying.

TRANSUBSTANTIATION
The scholastic term used to designate the unique change of the entire substance of the Eucharistic bread and wine into the Body and Blood of Christ.

STUDY QUESTIONS

1. Who established the Eucharist and why?

2. Why is the Eucharist called the source and summit of Christian life?

3. Where in the Bible can we find the institution of the Eucharist?

4. At what Jewish holiday was the Eucharist established? Explain the symbolism of the Eucharist being established at that time.

5. Is the Eucharist the same sacrifice as Jesus' sacrifice on the Cross? *Yes*

6. Whose sacrifice in the Old Testament in particular foreshadows the Eucharist? Why this sacrifice?

7. What are the essential signs of the Eucharist?

8. Who has the power, with Christ acting through him, to consecrate the bread and wine?

9. After Mass, does any leftover Eucharist go back to being just bread or wine? *No*

10. Under normal circumstances, can a non-Catholic receive Communion? *No*

11. Does someone have to be in a state of grace to receive Communion? *yes*

12. How long do you have to fast before receiving Communion? *1 hour*

13. What is the foremost grace we receive from the Eucharist?

14. Can anyone prove that the Eucharist is Jesus' Body and Blood?

15. To whom is the Eucharist offered as a gift?

16. Who is empowered to offer the gift of the sacrifice of the Eucharist?

17. What are three ways we can show love for Jesus in the Eucharist outside of Mass?

PRACTICAL EXERCISES

1. List four things that we can do to prepare for receiving the Eucharist. Do *at least* one of them this Sunday.

2. Why do you think it is a sin to receive the Eucharist without "discerning" it as the body and blood of Christ? Does this have anything to do with respect and love for Jesus?

3. Other Christian communities have ceremonies that seem like Eucharistic Communion but are not. Why are they not? Who has to consecrate the bread and wine for Jesus to actually be present?

4. Eucharistic miracles exist throughout the world. Go online and see what Eucharistic miracles you can find outside of Ostia. How do these miracles help establish Jesus' true presence in the Eucharist?

FROM THE CATECHISM

1406 Jesus said: "I am the living bread that came down from heaven; if any one eats of this bread, he will live for ever;…he who eats my flesh and drinks my blood has eternal life and…abides in me, and I in him" (Jn 6:51, 54, 56).

1407 The Eucharist is the heart and the summit of the Church's life, for in it Christ associates his Church and all her members with his sacrifice of praise and thanksgiving offered once for all on the Cross to his Father; by this sacrifice he pours out the graces of salvation on his Body which is the Church.

1408 The Eucharistic celebration always includes: the proclamation of the Word of God; thanksgiving to God the Father for all his benefits, above all the gift of his Son; the consecration of bread and wine; and participation in the liturgical banquet by receiving the Lord's body and blood. These elements constitute one single act of worship.

1409 The Eucharist is the memorial of Christ's Passover, that is, of the work of salvation accomplished by the life, death, and resurrection of Christ, a work made present by the liturgical action.

1410 It is Christ himself, the eternal high priest of the New Covenant who, acting through the ministry of the priests, offers the Eucharistic sacrifice. And it is the same Christ, really present under the species of bread and wine, who is the offering of the Eucharistic sacrifice.

1411 Only validly ordained priests can preside at the Eucharist and consecrate the bread and the wine so that they become the Body and Blood of the Lord.

1412 The essential signs of the Eucharistic sacrament are wheat bread and grape wine, on which the blessing of the Holy Spirit is invoked and the priest pronounces the words of consecration spoken by Jesus during the Last Supper: "This is my body which will be given up for you….This is the cup of my blood…."

1413 By the consecration the transubstantiation of the bread and wine into the Body and Blood of Christ is brought about. Under the consecrated species of bread and wine Christ himself, living and glorious, is present in a true, real, and substantial manner: his Body and his Blood, with his soul and his divinity (cf. Council of Trent: DS, 1640; 1651).

1414 As sacrifice, the Eucharist is also offered in reparation for the sins of the living and the dead and to obtain spiritual or temporal benefits from God.

1415 Anyone who desires to receive Christ in Eucharistic communion must be in the state of grace. Anyone aware of having sinned mortally must not receive communion without having received absolution in the sacrament of penance.

FROM THE CATECHISM CONTINUED

1416 Communion with the Body and Blood of Christ increases the communicant's union with the Lord, forgives his venial sins, and preserves him from grave sins. Since receiving this sacrament strengthens the bonds of charity between the communicant and Christ, it also reinforces the unity of the Church as the Mystical Body of Christ.

1417 The Church warmly recommends that the faithful receive Holy Communion when they participate in the celebration of the Eucharist; she obliges them to do so at least once a year.

1418 Because Christ himself is present in the sacrament of the altar, he is to be honored with the worship of adoration. "To visit the Blessed Sacrament is…a proof of gratitude, an expression of love, and a duty of adoration toward Christ our Lord" (Paul VI, *MF,* 66).

1419 Having passed from this world to the Father, Christ gives us in the Eucharist the pledge of glory with him. Participation in the Holy Sacrifice identifies us with his Heart, sustains our strength along the pilgrimage of this life, makes us long for eternal life, and unites us even now to the Church in heaven, the Blessed Virgin Mary, and all the saints.

Endnotes

1. Cf. Gal 2:20.
2. John Paul II, *Dominicae cenae,* 3.
3. Lk 22:7-20; cf. Mt 26:17-29; Mk 14:12-25; 1 Cor 11:23-26.
4. St. Alphonsus di Liguori, *Octave of Corpus Christi,* Meditation IV.
5. St. John Chrysostom, *prod. Jud.* 1:6: PG 49, 380.
6. Cf. Ex 13:3.

Chapter 13

Penance

An opportunity to turn back to God.

Chapter 13

Penance

*M*any people associate the Catholic Church with guilt. The Church, they feel, makes unreasonable demands on how people should act. When a person fails to live up to these demands, they say, the Church makes them admit to a priest how they have sinned, causing humiliation and shame.

But this is not the case at all. Every person has a sense of right and wrong. The guilty feelings we get come not from some person or group outside ourselves scolding us, calling us sinners. Rather, the guilty feelings come from inside ourselves because we know, in our hearts, that we have done wrong, that we have offended the Lord – for our consciences tell us so.

By offering us the Sacrament of Penance, God works through his Church to offer us healing and a way to clear our consciences. Through this sacrament, we are given an opportunity to turn back to God.

Yes, before going to Confession, we feel guilty. This is because we *are* guilty. Ask any good Catholic whom you trust, though, and they will tell you this: When we leave the confessional, if we have been completely honest with the priest, we have a feeling that is much more powerful than the feeling of guilt. It is a sense of indescribable relief and a feeling of truly being loved. We know that all is right. We have returned to the Lord.

PENANCE

> On the evening of that day, the first day of the week, the doors being shut where the disciples were, for fear of the Jews, Jesus came and stood among them and said to them, "Peace be with you." And when he had said this, he breathed on them, and said to them, "Receive the Holy spirit. If you forgive the sins of any they are forgiven; if you retain the sins of any, they are retained." (Jn 20:19, 22-23)

> "Those who approach the sacrament of Penance obtain pardon from God's mercy for the offense committed against him, and are, at the same time, reconciled with the Church which they have wounded by their sins and which by charity, by example, and by prayer labors for their conversion."[1] (CCC 1422)

Penance is a Sacrament of Healing in which Jesus Christ himself, through the actions of a priest, forgives the sins committed after Baptism. It is the way God restores his bond with us after we have broken it by committing mortal sin or damaged it by committing venial sin. Jesus has decided that his healing of human beings is continued by the Holy Spirit acting through the Church in the Sacrament of Penance, which reconciles us to God and the Church community.

What great love Jesus has for us! No matter how often we sin or how seriously we sin, he loves us so much that he will forgive our sins when we seek him out in the Sacrament of Reconciliation. Compare his love with human love. How many friendships fail because one person refuses to apologize for offending the other or refuses to accept the other's apology? Jesus' friendship is not like human friendship, nor is his love like human love. It is never-ending, and it purifies us.

> ...though your sins are like scarlet, they shall be as white as snow; though they are red like crimson, they shall become like wool. (Is 1:18)

There are many different names for the Sacrament of Penance:

✝ It is called the Sacrament of Conversion because it makes Jesus' call to conversion present in sacramental form;

✝ It is called the Sacrament of Penance for its consecrating effect upon the sinner's personal and ecclesial steps of conversion, penance, and satisfaction;

✝ It is called the Sacrament of Confession because it involves the personal disclosure of sins to a priest as an essential part of the sacrament;

✝ It is called the Sacrament of Forgiveness because God forgives sins through the priest's action, which imparts pardon and peace;

✝ It is called the Sacrament of Reconciliation for its gift of the life of God, who reconciles the sinner to himself.

Though Baptism made us new and free from the blemish of sin, it has not destroyed our weakness in relation to sin nor the inclination to sin, which is called concupiscence. God recognizes this, and he gives us the Sacrament of Penance as a *spiritual healing*, a way to remove sin when we fall into it. We must struggle to be holy—for this is how we get to heaven. By conversion, we become more holy, and as Baptism is

Jesus' friendship is not like human friendship, nor is his love like human love.

It is never-ending, and it purifies us.

the first conversion, Reconciliation is the opportunity for many more conversions. For as often as we sin, Jesus wants us to repent and return to him once again.

THE PRODIGAL SON

The parable of the prodigal son helps us to have a better understanding of this sacrament. It begins with the son collecting what he would inherit from his father while his father lived and striking out on his own in a foreign country. The collecting of the inheritance indicates a subtle break with God's rules and refers to our acceptance of some sins as not important. Those people turning away from God's grace begin their journey with a choice to overlook certain venial sins. When this happens, they have decided to do their own will and reject God's will. The choice to overlook the seriousness of any sin, no matter how slight, leads inevitably to the acceptance of mortal sins of the same type.

The prodigal son in the story is said to be in a foreign country because he has strayed far from God. His choice to commit serious sin has made him foreign to God and to repentance.

The son finds himself completely destitute, with neither friends, nor food, nor money, all because he is alienated from his father. God often permits man to sink deeper into sin like this, forcing man to face up to his dismal condition. Some people only return to God when they are faced with tragedy caused by repeated serious sin in their lives. An example would be a person who regularly abuses alcohol: One night he drives while drunk and kills an innocent person. The shock of having killed another person forces him to come to terms with the sin of getting drunk.

Finally, when the prodigal son finds himself wanting to eat the slop given to pigs, he realizes how low he has fallen. This realization is an awakening to the fact that without God's grace, the soul is starved to death.

Without God's grace, the soul is starved to death.

The father in the story represents God, who watches and waits for our return. When the son finally comes home and admits his sins, begging for mercy, the father throws a great banquet for the return of his beloved son. The patient love of the father represents God's grace sent to motivate us to return home to the loving God who is calling us. The father in the story sees his returning son coming from a long way off, so he must have been looking from the high point on his property. In like manner, the Father watches over sinners and awaits their return.

RITE OF RECONCILIATION

Christ entrusted the ministry of reconciliation to the Church. The forgiveness of sins through the ministry of the Church, Christ decided, was the ordinary way for people to return to God's grace. This power has been passed down by the Church to bishops and priests through the Sacrament of Holy Orders.

The ordinary means of reconciliation with God in instances of mortal sin is an individual and total confession followed by absolution from the priest.

Confession must be made out of a sincere desire to live the faith. In preparation to receive Reconciliation, an examination of conscience is made to recall the sins committed since the last Confession. The best approach is to have a copy of the commandments and the precepts of the Church. This list will help you make a good examination. After the examination of conscience, an act of contrition or sorrow for sins is made, as well as a resolution to try to avoid sin in the future and to avoid occasions of sin, that is, people, places, or things that may lead to sin.

The penitent then enters the confessional and makes his Confession. We are required to tell every mortal sin we are aware of for the Confession to be valid. If you forget a mortal sin, don't worry—the Confession is still valid. You must, however, tell the sin to the priest during your next Confession. Before penance and absolution are given, the penitent should state aloud an Act of Contrition in the presence of the priest.

A penance will then be given to atone for the sins committed. The penance should be said or done as soon as the rite is concluded. The final step in the Sacrament of Confession is the rite of absolution, said by the priest.

> The formula of absolution used in the Latin Church expresses the essential elements of this sacrament: the Father of mercies is the source of all forgiveness. He effects the reconciliation of sinners through the Passover of his Son and the gift of his Spirit, through the prayer and ministry of the Church:
>
> > God, the Father of mercies,
> > through the death and the resurrection of his Son
> > has reconciled the world to himself
> > and sent the Holy Spirit among us
> > for the forgiveness of sins;
> > through the ministry of the Church
> > may God give you pardon and peace,
> > and I absolve you from your sins
> > in the name of the Father, and of the Son, and of the Holy Spirit.[2]
> > (CCC 1449)

Simply stated, the six points to make a good confession are:

† An examination of conscience;

† Sorrow for sin;

† A resolve to avoid sin in the future;

† Confession of sins; for mortal sins, according to their species and number;

† Making an Act of Contrition;

† Doing the assigned penance.

The priest assigns a penance to repair the harm of sin and to point the way to habits that will prevent sin henceforth.

For Confession to be fully worthwhile, the penitent must be contrite for his sins and do the assigned penance. There are two types of contrition for sins: "perfect" and "imperfect." When someone is sorry for his or her sins because of a love for God above all else, it is called perfect contrition, which obtains forgiveness for mortal sins if it is coupled with

Confession must be made out of a sincere desire to live the faith.

For Confession to be fully worthwhile, the penitent must be contrite for his sins and do the assigned penance.

True love of Jesus should lead us to confess as soon as possible after any mortal sin.

Monthly confession can be compared to the practice of athletes who review games in order to see their past mistakes.

the resolution to go to Confession as soon as possible. When sorrow arises from hatred for the ugliness of sin, fear of hell, or fear of other penalties, it is called imperfect contrition.

To be reconciled with God and the Church, you must confess your sins whenever you are in mortal sin and at least once yearly. True love of Jesus should lead us to confess as soon as possible after any mortal sin. Just as apologizing when you wrong a friend makes it easy to restore that friendship, so confessing all sins keeps you close to Jesus.

Every sin harms and weakens us by inclining us to sin again. Sins also harm our relationship with our neighbor and the whole Church community. We must struggle for interior penance, a radical reorientation of our lives toward Jesus, who will give us a new heart.

In addition to this interior struggle, justice requires that we undo the external harm we have caused by sinning. For instance, a person who has stolen must return the stolen goods, or a person who has lied and caused serious harm must go to the person to whom the statement was made and tell them it was false. Often the priest will assign a penance that makes reparation for one of the sins confessed to him.

Though it is not required that venial sins be confessed, the Church recommends monthly confession. This practice makes it easier for us to recognize our venial sins and work so that they do not become habits. Monthly confession can be compared to the practice of athletes who review games in order to see their past mistakes so they can avoid them in the future.

The only ordinary means of absolution for grave sins is complete Confession directly to a duly authorized priest, who will absolve us from sins in the name of the Church.

EFFECTS OF THE SACRAMENT

Reconciliation with God is the whole purpose of this sacrament of healing. Confession of sins:

† Forgives sins, thereby restoring sanctifying grace when it is lost by mortal sin;

† Remits eternal punishment caused by mortal sin;

† Imparts actual graces to avoid sin in the future;

† Reconciles the penitent person with the Church;

† Remits part of purgatorial punishment;

† Gives peace of conscience and spiritual consolation.

In the encyclical *Mystical Body,* Pope Pius XII enumerated some benefits of frequent confession of sins:

† Genuine self-knowledge is increased;

† Bad habits are corrected;

† The conscience is purified;

† Christian humility grows;

† The will is strengthened;

† Lukewarmness and spiritual neglect are resisted;

† Self-control is increased.

> "Whoever confesses his sins…is already working with God. God indicts your sins; if you also indict them, you are joined with God. Man and sinner are, so to speak, two realities: when you hear 'man'—this is what God has made; when you hear 'sinner'—this is what man himself has made. Destroy what you have made, so that God may save what he has made….When you begin to abhor what you have made, it is then that your good works are beginning, since you are accusing yourself of your evil works. The beginning of good works is the confession of evil works. You do the truth and come to the light."[3] (CCC 1458)

A necessary part of sorrow for sin is satisfaction: making up for the sins committed. We should strive to make up for sins in our everyday life, going beyond the penance we are given in Confession. We can make this type of satisfaction by:

† Mass attendance and personal prayer;

† Giving alms to the poor;

† Fasting and sacrifice of time and pleasures.

We can also make satisfaction for our sins through self-denial, such as eating a little less than we want, sacrificing our own time for others, doing works of mercy, and accepting the little crosses that come each day when there are disagreements with friends or when things don't go well.

FORMATION OF CONSCIENCE

Conscience is the informed judgment of the morality of an act being considered, being performed, or already completed. When we prepare for Confession, the conscience acts as the diary of our bad moral choices. It reminds us of what we have done wrong.

All people are born with a conscience in which God has placed an elementary knowledge of good and evil. It is a gift from God that helps us avoid sin and recognize when we need to change our ways. Since it is a gift, we should work to develop it properly.

As a child grows, his conscience is informed first by his parents as to the morality of specific acts. When he begins grammar school, he learns additional information about what is right and wrong. Later still, we learn the rules that help us make decisions about concrete situations. Correct formation of conscience is based on the teaching of the Catholic Church. Right conscience tries to inform itself from the Bible, the teachings of the Church, and human reason.

KINDS OF SIN

"Sin came into the world through one man" (Rom 5:12). The sin of Adam is called the *original sin,* for it was the first sin. Every person is born with a flaw in his nature resulting from this sin. It is inherited from our parents at the moment of conception.

Conscience is a gift from God that helps us avoid sin and recognize when we need to change our ways.

Penance

Venial sin harms the spiritual relationship between God and man, but mortal sin completely breaks the spiritual relationship between God and man.

The good works of Christ and the saints can be applied to other people so that they don't have to suffer in purgatory.

Different from original sin but resulting from it is actual sin, which is sin committed personally. Catholic moral tradition has divided actual sin into two categories according to gravity: mortal and venial. Venial sin harms the spiritual relationship between God and man, but mortal sin completely breaks the spiritual relationship between God and man.

When you commit a mortal sin, you cut yourself off entirely from the life of Christ and have deliberately chosen to give up your place in heaven. Moral theology lists three conditions for mortal sin:

† Grave or serious matter – The act must be serious as defined by the Church;

† Full knowledge – You must be aware this act will separate you from God;

† Complete consent – You know it is grave and choose to do it anyway.

If all three conditions are not met, the sin is not mortal.

The fact that venial sin does not completely sever our relationship with God does not mean it can be dismissed as unimportant. Venial sins lead to mortal sins. Many criminals don't start out robbing banks or committing murder; they start with petty theft and vandalism.

An act in which someone breaks a law of God or the Church intentionally by *doing* a forbidden act is called a sin of commission—for it involves an act being committed. *Refusing* to do an act that is required (e.g., Sunday Mass attendance) is called a sin of omission: for a required act is omitted. It should be noted that personal sin can harm others beside the sinner. Our acts influence others, so we could lead another person into sin simply because they are aware of our sins. It can also be taken up by others and affect the structure of society. For example, one employer's refusal to pay just wages can lead others to imitate this sinful act. Some may even refuse to pay a just wage because of an employee's race, ethnic origin, or religion.

INDULGENCES

Sin has a double consequence. Mortal sin deprives us of communion with God and takes away the promise of eternal life we received in Baptism.

All sin is the result of an inordinate attachment to creatures, which must be purified here or in purgatory after death. This purification is called temporal punishment and is required before man can enter heaven.

We can be released from this punishment, however, by earning an indulgence. An indulgence is the remission granted by the Church of the temporal punishment from sins that have already been forgiven. It does this by applying the infinite satisfaction that has, quite literally, been stored up in Christ's Church through the acts of the Virgin Mary, the saints, and Christ himself. In short, the good works of Christ and the saints can be applied to other people so that they do not have to suffer in purgatory.

The treasury of these goods includes the satisfaction gained by the life, death and Resurrection of Jesus (which by itself is infinite), the prayers and good works of the Virgin Mary, and the prayers and good works of all the saints. This is made possible by the link of charity between those who have attained heaven, those suffering in purgatory, and the faithful on earth still on their pilgrimage.

Indulgences are *partial* when they remove part of the temporal punishment due to sin or *plenary* when they remove all. We can earn indulgences for ourselves and for those who have died and are in purgatory. We cannot earn an indulgence for a person who is still alive.

Indulgences may be gained by formal acts of worship combined with good works. They usually involve making sacramental Confession, receiving Holy Communion, and praying for the intentions of the pope.

SPIRITUAL DIRECTION

In simple terms, spiritual direction may be defined as spiritual advice given regularly to direct one's life toward God. This advice must be given by someone qualified to give it, e.g., a priest or qualified lay person.

Some people object that they don't need outside help in their lives. We can see, however, that most people who truly excel at something have personal coaches for their specialty: athletes, musicians, etc. A spiritual director is a coach who guides us to follow the correct road to heaven.

Spiritual direction must be sought regularly if it is to be beneficial. At the least, we should seek advice from a priest in Confession once a month. Time should be set aside to discuss any progress since the last Confession, problems that may have arisen, and what goals should be set for the month ahead. We should follow this advice and go over the results in the next Confession.

Man has been given Reconciliation to assist him to be totally what Jesus wishes him to be.

Spiritual direction must be sought regularly if it is to be beneficial.

When a person realizes he has offended God, the ugliness of his sins seems overwhelming.

Man must concentrate on the desire to return to God, rather than being afraid because of sins.

CONCLUSION

Jesus calls man to everlasting love in the Sacrament of Baptism. Man's sin divides his soul. One part wishes to serve Jesus, while another part wishes to serve the sinful self. It is as if man is at war with himself; part of him has become foreign to what Jesus wishes. Man has been given Reconciliation to assist him to be totally what Jesus wishes him to be.

When a person realizes he has offended God, the ugliness of his sins seems overwhelming. Like Adam and Eve in the garden, he wants to hide from Jesus as they hid from the Father. What must be kept in mind, though, is that what is most important to Jesus is his love. He desires to increase his love and return man to his friendship. It is his grace that has brought all to the sacrament where his mercy is dispensed, so man must concentrate on the desire to return to God, rather than being afraid because of sins. Jesus reaches out to embrace man like the father of the prodigal son: he has been watching for and looks forward to the sinner's arrival. All must learn to rush to his arms. If you have mortal sins on your conscience, tell them first. Christ smothers all penitent souls with the loving kisses of his grace. Be not afraid.

EXAMINATION FOR RECONCILIATION

✝ Do I confess my sins at least once a month?

✝ Do I confess all mortal sins as to kind and number (what they were and how many times they were committed)?

✝ Do I follow the advice given in Confession?

✝ Do I request and follow the advice from my spiritual director?

✝ Do I make regular acts of reparation for my sins?

✝ Do I make reparation for the sins of others?

Chapter 13 Study Guide

SUPPLEMENTARY READING

In Confession, though we tell our sins to the priest, we are really telling them to Jesus the Lord. What the priest hears in the confessional he can never reveal—for what goes on in Confession is between the person making the Confession and the Lord. We have only to look at St. John Nepomucene to see that this is true.

St. John Nepomucene was a priest in Prague, which is in the modern-day Czech Republic. A gifted preacher, St. John was chosen by King Wenzel as the preacher for the royal court. The queen also recognized the wisdom and goodness of John, and she chose him as her confessor.

One day, King Wenzel called John in for a private meeting. When they were alone, the King asked John what his wife had confessed. John was shocked and explained to the King what he already knew: under no circumstances could the priest reveal anything he has heard in Confession, no matter who asked for the information.

The king tried to persuade John to break the rules, just for this case. He even hinted that John might receive the office of bishop if he cooperated. John still refused. This of course brought down the anger of the king upon the upright priest. John was thrown into prison and tortured, but he did not reveal a word of what the queen had told him.

King Wenzel was persuaded to release John, but the saint knew his trials were not yet over. He went to pray for the strength to endure what was coming.

Once again the king called John in, demanding to know what the queen confessed. If John refused, he was told, he would be drowned. John had prepared for a martyr's death, and refused the king's demand. The king had his men tie John up and throw him off a bridge into the Moldau River.

St. John Nepomucene
(1345-1393)
Feast on May 16

As soon as John drowned, five lights appeared where he had been thrown in the river. The king saw these lights from his palace and fled the city, fearing the people would riot over the saint's death. John's body was found by fishermen a few days later, and that summer, a horrible drought came upon Prague, practically drying up the river in which John drowned.

Centuries later, when the Church was investigating the life of John Nepomucene to see whether he was worthy to be named a saint, his tomb was opened. His body was nothing but bones and dust, except for one thing. His tongue, which he had kept pure by refusing to reveal the secrets of the confessional, was whole and incorrupt. It had not decayed at all. To this day it remains that way—a sign of God's role in the Sacrament of Confession.

VOCABULARY

CONSCIENCE

The interior voice of a human being, within whose heart the inner law of God is inscribed. It moves a person at the appropriate moment to do good and to avoid evil.

EXAMINATION OF CONSCIENCE

Prayerful self-reflection on our words and deeds in the light of the Gospel to determine how we may have sinned against God. The reception of the Sacrament of Penance ought to be prepared for by such an examination of conscience.

IMPERFECT CONTRITION

Sorrow of the soul and detestation for the sin committed, together with the resolution not to sin again that is born of the consideration of sin's ugliness or the fear of eternal damnation and the other penalties threatening the sinner.

INDULGENCE

The remission before God of the temporal punishment due to sin whose guilt has already been forgiven.

MORTAL SIN

Destroys charity in the heart of man by a grave violation of God's law; it turns man away from God, who is his ultimate end and his beatitude, by preferring an inferior good to him.

PARTIAL INDULGENCE

An indulgence that removes part of the temporal punishment due to sin.

PENANCE

Interior: a conversion of heart toward God and away from sin, which implies the intention to change one's life because of hope in divine mercy. *Exterior:* fasting, prayer, and almsgiving.

PERFECT CONTRITION

Sorrow of the soul and detestation for the sin committed, together with the resolution not to sin again that arises from a love by which God is loved above all else.

PLENARY INDULGENCE

An indulgence that removes all of the temporal punishment due to sin.

SATISFACTION

An act whereby the sinner makes amends for sin, especially in reparation to God for offenses against him.

SIN OF COMMISSION

A willful act, such as theft, that is contrary to a negative precept, such as *do not steal.*

SIN OF OMISSION

Willful neglect or positive refusal to perform some good action, such as attending Mass, that one's conscience urges one to do.

SPIRITUAL DIRECTION

Assisting persons to understand themselves and, with divine grace, to grow in the practice of Christian virtue. While a person is often helpful, the Holy Spirit is the true Spiritual Director.

TEMPORAL PUNISHMENT

Purification of the unhealthy attachment to creatures either during our earthly life through prayer and conversion which comes from fervent charity, or after death in purgatory, as a consequence of sin.

VENIAL SIN

Sin which diminishes and wounds the divine life in the soul; the failure to observe necessary moderation, in lesser matters of the moral law, or in grave matters acting without full knowledge or complete consent of the will.

STUDY QUESTIONS

1. What are the main effects of the Sacrament of Penance?

2. List and explain the different titles of the Sacrament of Penance.

3. Who is actually forgiving us in the confessional? *God*

4. How is Christ's love different from human love?

5. Explain how the parable of the prodigal son is like the journey of a sinner from sin to repentance.

6. To whom did Christ entrust the Sacrament of Reconciliation? Who has the authority to forgive sins now and how did they get it?

7. What sins are you required to tell the priest? Why should you tell more than those?

8. What are the six elements of a good confession?

9. When are you required to go to confession?

10. How does sin harm us?

11. What are the benefits of frequent confession?

12. What is satisfaction for sin?

13. Are people born with a conscience? Can it be developed?

14. How did sin come into the world?

15. How can our sins hurt others?

16. What are the two consequences of mortal sin?

17. Why do people need a spiritual director? What is the purpose of spiritual direction?

PRACTICAL EXERCISES

1. Suppose a Catholic friend tells you that God will forgive your mortal sins even if you don't go to Confession. Is this ever true? Why should you go to Confession? (Think about who created the sacrament.)

2. In *The Screwtape Letters*, C. S. Lewis writes from the perspective of the demon Screwtape teaching his nephew how to lead a human into sin. This tempter demon has the *opposite* role of a guardian angel. Imagine you are Uncle Screwtape. Write a letter to your nephew describing how you would tempt your classmates, your parents, or yourself.

3. Are the following behaviors sins? If so, what kind of sins are they? Venial or mortal, sins of commission or sins of omission?

4. Tim was helping his teacher count the money his class raised during a fundraiser. There was a lot of money, and he knew he could get away with taking some. Did he sin by thinking about stealing the money?

5. Carl learned in religion class that getting drunk was a sin, and he understands that it is sinful and why it is sinful, yet on the weekend, he went over to his friend's house and had too much of his friend's father's beer.

6. Max understands that he has a serious obligation to go to Mass on Sunday, yet he skipped Mass the weekend his parents were out of town. Tom has never been told how important it is to go to Mass, and he skipped one weekend also. What, if anything, is Max guilty of? What, if anything, is Tom guilty of?

7. Chris goes to Confession, but he intentionally does not mention one mortal sin that he doesn't want to talk about. Is the Confession valid?

FROM THE CATECHISM

1485 "On the evening of that day, the first day of the week," Jesus showed himself to his apostles. "He breathed on them, and said to them: 'Receive the Holy Spirit. If you forgive the sins of any, they are forgiven; if you retain the sins of any, they are retained'" (Jn 20:19, 22-23).

1486 The forgiveness of sins committed after Baptism is conferred by a particular sacrament called the sacrament of conversion, confession, penance, or reconciliation.

1487 The sinner wounds God's honor and love, his own human dignity as a man called to be a son of God, and the spiritual well-being of the Church, of which each Christian ought to be a living stone.

1488 To the eyes of faith no evil is graver than sin and nothing has worse consequences for sinners themselves, for the Church, and for the whole world.

1489 To return to communion with God after having lost it through sin is a process born of the grace of God who is rich in mercy and solicitous for the salvation of men. One must ask for this precious gift for oneself and for others.

1490 The movement of return to God, called conversion and repentance, entails sorrow for and abhorrence of sins committed, and the firm purpose of sinning no more in the future. Conversion touches the past and the future and is nourished by hope in God's mercy.

1491 The sacrament of Penance is a whole consisting in three actions of the penitent and the priest's absolution. The penitent's acts are repentance, confession or disclosure of sins to the priest, and the intention to make reparation and do works of reparation.

1492 Repentance (also called contrition) must be inspired by motives that arise from faith. If repentance arises from love of charity for God, it is called "perfect" contrition; if it is founded on other motives, it is called "imperfect."

1493 One who desires to obtain reconciliation with God and with the Church, must confess to a priest all the unconfessed grave sins he remembers after having carefully examined his conscience. The confession of venial faults, without being necessary in itself, is nevertheless strongly recommended by the Church.

1494 The confessor proposes the performance of certain acts of "satisfaction" or "penance" to be performed by the penitent in order to repair the harm caused by sin and to re-establish habits befitting a disciple of Christ.

1495 Only priests who have received the faculty of absolving from the authority of the Church can forgive sins in the name of Christ.

1496 The spiritual effects of the sacrament of Penance are: –reconciliation with God by which the penitent recovers grace; –reconciliation with the Church; –remission of the eternal punishment incurred by mortal sins; –remission, at least in part, of temporal punishments resulting from sin; –peace and serenity of conscience, and spiritual consolation; –an increase of spiritual strength for the Christian battle.

1497 Individual and integral confession of grave sins followed by absolution remains the only ordinary means of reconciliation with God and with the Church.

1498 Through indulgences the faithful can obtain the remission of temporal punishment resulting from sin for themselves and also for the souls in Purgatory.

Endnotes

1. *LG*, 11 § 2.
2. *OP*, 46: formula of absolution.
3. St. Augustine, *In Jo. ev.* 12, 13: PL 35, 1491.

Anointing of the Sick

To see us safely through the doorway into the next life.

Chapter 14

Anointing of the Sick

*M*illions of dollars are spent each year by those seeking cures for various diseases. In spite of all the money spent, it is rare for cures to be found. Those who have been sick for a long time are often heard to remark, "When you have your health, you have everything."

Large amounts of money are currently being spent to overcome the effects of aging. Some people long to be able to live forever. Some people have even had themselves placed in a frozen state until a time when they expect to be called back to life.

The only life worth living permanently is life with Christ. For those facing death, he has left the perfect cure: the Sacrament of Anointing of the Sick. This sacrament has the power to forgive all our temporal punishment due to sin, and in some instances will cure the body as well.

ANOINTING OF THE SICK

Is any among you sick? Let him call for the elders of the church, and let them pray over him, anointing him with oil in the name of the Lord; and the prayer of faith will save the sick man, and the Lord will raise him up; and if he has committed sins, he will be forgiven. Therefore confess your sins to one another, and pray for one another, that you may be healed. (Jas 5:14-16)

Anointing of the Sick is a Sacrament of Healing that gives health of soul and sometimes body by prayer and anointing with oil. Its purpose is to confer special grace on Christians who are suffering from grave illness or the exhaustion of old age.

In simple terms, Anointing of the Sick helps to heal the ill person physically, or it gives grace that allows him to accept God's will and die a good death.

"By the sacred anointing of the sick and the prayer of the priests the whole Church commends those who are ill to the suffering and glorified Lord, that he may raise them up and save them. And indeed she exhorts them to contribute to the good of the People of God by freely uniting themselves to the Passion and death of Christ."[1] (CCC 1499)

The Jewish people of the Old Testament understood illness as linked to sin and found that conversion led to healing. We can see this pattern in Christ the healer, whose presence indicates that God has visited his people to heal them of their sins and illnesses, both of body and of soul.

Often Jesus asks the sick to believe.[2] He makes use of signs to heal: spittle and the laying of hands,[3] mud and washing.[4] The sick try to touch him, "for power came forth from him and healed them all."[5] And so in the sacraments Christ continues to "touch" us in order to heal us. (CCC 1504)

Illness, suffering, and death are the problems of life that people usually find most difficult to accept. It is important, though, that people learn how to deal with their suffering. Illness can either harm a man's soul by causing him to become self-centered, focusing on his own suffering and nothing else, or else lead him to greater maturity in accepting what he does not totally understand.

We can arrive at this maturity when we understand both the cause of suffering and Christ's role as a healer. Man's fallen nature is physically vulnerable to suffering. Christ announced that the kingdom of God had arrived, bringing victory over sin and death. This victory first benefits those who offer up their suffering in this life as part of their work on the way to heaven.

The Bible records many instances of Jesus curing people. Two examples are Mark's description of the cure of St. Peter's mother-in-law and Luke's description of the cure of a man suffering from dropsy:

Now Simon's mother-in-law lay sick with a fever, and immediately they told him of her. And he came and took her by the hand and lifted her up, and the fever left her; and she served them. (Mk 1:30-31)

One sabbath when he went to dine at the house of a ruler who belonged to the Pharisees, they were watching him. And behold, there was a man

Its purpose is to confer special grace on Christians who are suffering from grave illness or the exhaustion of old age.

The Bible records many instances of Jesus curing people.

"So they went out and preached that men should repent. And they cast out many demons, and anointed with oil many that were sick and healed them."

before him who had dropsy. And Jesus spoke to the lawyers and Pharisees, saying, "Is it lawful to heal on the sabbath, or not?" But they were silent. Then he took him and healed him, and let him go. And he said to them, "Which of you, having an ass or an ox that has fallen into a well, will not immediately pull him out on a sabbath day?" And they could not reply to this. (Lk 14:1-6)

Christ healed people both to demonstrate that he was the Messiah and out of compassion for those who were suffering. All Christians are called to have this compassion, and we are to live it out by caring for the sick and suffering as much as possible.

> Christ's compassion toward the sick and his many healings of every kind of infirmity are a resplendent sign that "God has visited his people"[6] and that the Kingdom of God is close at hand. Jesus has the power not only to heal, but also to forgive sins;[7] he has come to heal the whole man, soul and body; he is the physician the sick have need of.[8] His compassion toward all who suffer goes so far that he identifies himself with them: "I was sick and you visited me" (Mt 25:36). His preferential love for the sick has not ceased through the centuries to draw the very special attention of Christians toward all those who suffer in body and soul. It is the source of tireless efforts to comfort them. (CCC 1503)

These healing acts performed by Christ show us that the Kingdom of God has come upon us, and that this kingdom brings a more radical healing than merely physical cures: it brings healing and victory over sin and death through Christ's own death on the cross. Christ's suffering and death tell us that suffering, if understood properly, can make us like him and unite us to his redemptive acts.

> Christ invites his disciples to follow him by taking up their cross in their turn.[9] By following him they acquire a new outlook on illness and the sick. Jesus associates them with his own life of poverty and service. He makes them share in his ministry of compassion and healing: "So they went out and preached that men should repent. And they cast out many demons, and anointed with oil many that were sick and healed them."[10] (CCC 1506)

CELEBRATION OF THE SACRAMENT

The Church has received the charge from the Lord to heal the sick and strives to accomplish it through Anointing of the Sick.

> This sacred anointing of the sick was instituted by Christ our Lord as a true and proper sacrament of the New Testament. It is alluded to indeed by Mark, but is recommended to the faithful and is promulgated by James the apostle and brother of the Lord.[11]

This sacrament, like the others, is celebrated with its own liturgy. Its celebration is not a private act but involves the Church as a whole.

> Like all the sacraments the Anointing of the Sick is a liturgical and communal celebration,[12] whether it takes place in the family home, a hospital or church, for a single sick person or a whole group of sick persons. (CCC 1517)

Anointing of the Sick is administered by a priest or bishop. The principal elements are the laying-on of hands, prayer said over the person requesting the special grace, and the anointing of the forehead and hands with olive oil (called the oil of the sick) which has been blessed by a bishop. In an emergency, any vegetable oil may be used when blessed by a priest. If the hands of the person cannot be touched, the forehead is anointed or, in case of grave necessity, any part of the body may be touched.

The prayer for Anointing of the Sick is:

> Through this holy anointing, by his most loving mercy, may the Lord assist you by the grace of the Holy Spirit so that freed from your sins, he may save you and raise you up.

Ideally, Anointing of the Sick is to be celebrated along with the Sacrament of Penance and reception of the Eucharist. The first sacrament to be received should be Confession, in which those in mortal sin seek reconciliation with God. Next comes the Anointing, which is followed by the Eucharist, received as *viaticum* (from the Latin for "traveling provisions"). The faithful should receive the Eucharist as preparation for the moment of passing over from this life to the next—for it is the seed of eternal life and has the power of the Resurrection.

We should keep in mind, however, that this sacrament is not only for those who are just moments from death. It is fitting to receive this sacrament just prior to a serious operation and as soon as there is danger of death from sickness or old age. Anointing of the Sick may be repeated if during a person's illness the condition becomes more serious.

This sacrament may never be delayed when a person is clearly in danger of death. While some may find it difficult to accept, those clearly in danger of death should be told of their condition to enable them to make their final peace with God.

EFFECTS OF THE SACRAMENT

Like all the sacraments, Anointing of the Sick imparts special graces on those who receive it. The graces of the Anointing of the Sick are:

- ✝ Union of the sick person to the Passion of Christ for his own good and the good of the Church;
- ✝ Strength, peace, and courage to endure in a Christian manner the sufferings of illness or old age;
- ✝ Forgiveness of sins and of penalty for sin if the person is sorry for his sins and unable to receive the Sacrament of Penance;
- ✝ Restoration of sanctifying grace if sorrow for mortal sin is present;
- ✝ Restoration of health if it is good for the salvation of the person's soul;
- ✝ Preparation for passage to eternal life;
- ✝ Reduction or removal of all temporal punishment due to sin when the ill person is properly disposed.

Those who are facing death need the grace of God to ensure that they accept the death that God has permitted them to suffer. The Sacrament of Anointing gives the peace and power necessary to resist the devil as they face passage from this world to the next.

The principal elements are the laying-on of hands, prayer said over the person requesting the special grace, and the anointing of the forehead and hands with olive oil (called the oil of the sick) which has been blessed by a bishop.

Original sin is in all of us. No one, then, is free to complain that suffering is unwarranted.

RECIPIENTS OF THE SACRAMENT

There is no need to wait till a person is in danger of death to call the priest for Anointing. The question of when to anoint can be answered by asking the following questions:

† Is this a life-threatening or grave disease?

† Is the person about to undergo surgery for a serious illness?

† Is the person of advanced age?

† Has a fatal illness become more serious?

This sacrament may be received with each new serious illness or when a particular illness worsens. The recipient must be at least the age of reason, for to sin one must be this age, and only a person who is capable of sinning has need of the sacrament.

The sacrament may be given conditionally to those who are unconscious or to those in a coma as long as they have been baptized and were aware of the penalty for dying without sorrow. Dead people may also be anointed conditionally for a limited time after they have been pronounced clinically dead, for those who appear to have already died are not always dead.

THE ACCEPTANCE OF SUFFERING

No one denies that sickness and suffering are evils in themselves. These evils, the Church teaches, are caused by original sin. Original sin has given all people a fallen nature that includes a weakened physical state. We must accept that original sin is not just something that Adam did for which we are suffering, but that original sin is in all of us. No one, then, is free to complain that suffering is unwarranted. We should accept the fact that each and every one of us, as individuals, have a fallen nature and suffer as a result.

This suffering, though, should not be pointless. We can turn our pain into something positive by uniting it to the pain of Jesus, thereby making it salvific. Jesus' suffering has this saving power because he chose to offer his pain for the good of human beings. His pain and death were suffered in penance for our sins. In the same way, we can unite our pain with Jesus' suffering, giving a new meaning to suffering in this life. Those who join their anguish to Jesus' suffering on the cross can fill up what Christ left open in his suffering for the good of his body, the Church.

Christ invites all of us to take up this cross—for doing so will give us a new outlook on illness and the sick. By accepting suffering for the well-being of others, we imitate the loving Jesus, who accepted suffering for our salvation. When we accept our own suffering, we help to spread the grace of God.

VISITING THE SICK

Some of us may find it difficult or depressing to visit those who are sick. We should remind ourselves, though, that caring for the suffering is not an option but a requirement. We may often feel awkward when trying to make conversation, yet we must keep in mind that our presence alone is a sign of support to someone who is ill. The best rule for conversation is to permit the sick person to lead the way. If he wishes to discuss his illness, then be willing to follow that lead. Many sick persons find it makes things easier if they are able to discuss their problem and their feelings during this time. Sometimes, the sick person may wish to say nothing, in which case we have to accept that our presence is all the support that is wanted.

MESSAGE OF A CARDINAL

Joseph Cardinal Bernardin served as the Archbishop of Chicago from 1982 until his death from pancreatic cancer in 1996. In the last weeks of his life, he wrote a book, *The Gift of Peace*, discussing the trials he faced in the last years of his life. He finished the book just thirteen days before he died. In the following passage, Cardinal Bernardin discusses an event that took place immediately after he disclosed that his cancer was terminal:

"On August 31, 1996, the day after I announced that the cancer had spread to my liver and was inoperable, I presided at a communal Anointing of the Sick at Saint Barbara Church in Brookfield, Illinois. I told my fellow sick that, when we are faced with serious illness (or any serious difficulty), we should do several things—things that have given me peace of mind personally.

"The first is to put ourselves *completely* in the hands of the Lord. We must believe that the Lord loves us, embraces us, never abandons us (especially in our most difficult moments). This is what gives us hope in the midst of life's suffering and chaos. It is the same Lord who invites us: 'Come to me all you who are weary and find life burdensome, and I will refresh you. Take my yoke upon your shoulders and learn from me, for I am gentle and humble of heart. Your souls will find rest, for my yoke is easy and my burden light' (Mt 11:12-30)."

Caring for the suffering is not an option but a requirement.

"We must believe that the Lord loves us, embraces us, never abandons us…"

Joseph Cardinal Bernardin
from *The Gift of Peace*

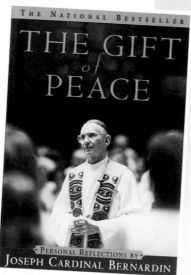

> *Anointing of the Sick has been given to us by Jesus to enable us to embrace the Spirit, to see us safely through the doorway into the next life, and to enter the presence of the Father for all eternity.*

CONCLUSION

From time to time, we should meditate on the love that Jesus has for us. Christ loves us so deeply that he has given us the sacraments, which enable us to share in his life and to remain close to him throughout our lives.

For many people, the most feared moment in life is the moment of death. As a sacrament, Anointing of the Sick has been given to us by Jesus to enable us to embrace the Spirit, to see us safely through the doorway into the next life, and to enter the presence of the Father for all eternity. Those in danger of death should be administered this sacrament without delay to make the passage between this life and the next as simple as possible. Every time we embrace suffering out of love for God, it prepares us for the final reception of Anointing and enables us to reduce our purgatorial suffering.

EXAMINATION FOR ANOINTING OF THE SICK

✝ Do I remember I could die at any moment?

✝ Do I maintain myself in the state of grace?

✝ Do I carry a card that indicates I am a Catholic?

✝ Do I pray to have a happy death?

SUPPLEMENTARY READING

A Saint who Killed?

On February 25, 1954, Alexandre Silberstein was changing two million francs into gold bars. While his son was downstairs, the customer drew a revolver and demanded money from the register. Silberstein tried to reason with the man, but he was whacked in the head and about 300,000 francs were taken. Outside the villain tried to melt into the crowd, but Silberstein recovered and began shouting that he'd been robbed. When a 35-year-old policeman, a widower with a 4-year-old daughter, ordered him to put his hands up, the suspect shot him through the heart.

Jacques was a lost soul, the son of wealthy parents who never took an interest in him. The boy failed to take an interest in his schoolwork or his job at the bank when he'd graduated. His anti-Semitic parents were horrified when he married Pierrette, a Catholic girl who had a Jewish father. They had a daughter together but Jacques continued to see other women. He had an illegitimate son with one of these and his marriage soon broke up.

After this Jacques decided to purchase a boat and sail around the South Pacific. Unfortunately, his parents refused him the money so he decided to rob Mr. Silberstein. In court he defiantly declared that his only regret was not carrying a submachine gun. In prison, he told a chaplain, *"I've got no faith. No need to trouble yourself about me."* Many people made efforts at his conversion—his attorney, a Dominican chaplain Pere Devoyod, Brother Thomas (a Benedictine and friend of Pierrette), and his mother-in-law Madame Polack—but none were successful.

It was only on February 28, 1955, when as he writes: *"I was in bed, eyes open, really suffering for the first time in my life...It was then that a cry burst from my breast, an appeal for help – My God – and instantly, like*

Jacques Fesch
(1930-1957) France
Murderer, Convert, Mystic

a violent wind which passes over without anyone knowing where it comes from, the spirit of the Lord seized me by the throat. I had an impression of infinite power and kindness and, from that moment onward, I believed with an unshakeable conviction that has never left me." Later he wrote:

A powerful hand has seized me. Where is it? What has it done to me? I do not know, for his action is not like the action of men. It is unknowable and effective. It constrains me, and I am free. It transforms my being, yet I do not cease to be what I am.

Then comes the struggle — silent, tragic — between what I was and what I have become. For the new creature who has been planted within me calls for a response which I am free to refuse.

My viewpoint has changed, but my habits of thought and action have not. God has left them as they were. I have to fight, adapt,

Continued

reconstruct my inner being; I cannot be at peace unless I accept to fight.

While in prison, he began to live a very sober life, giving up chocolates and cigarettes, praying often, and going to bed at 7:00 each evening. More than three years after his crime, Fesch was sentenced to death despite his acts being unpremeditated. In overcoming his temptation to hate those who sentenced him, he wrote, *"May each drop of my blood wipe out a mortal sin."*

On the last night of his life, Jacques wrote, *"I wait in the night; I wait in peace. I wait*

for Love! Within 5 hours…I will see Jesus!" The prison chaplain arrived at 5:30 and gave him the last rites (the Sacraments of Confession, the Anointing of the Sick, and the Eucharist). As he was led up the scaffold, he said to the chaplain, *"The crucifix, Father, the crucifix,"* and kissed it fervently. Fesch is often likened to the good thief who died with Jesus on Calvary.

Recently Jacques' writings have been published as *Light Over the Scaffold and Cell 18* by Augustin-Michel Lemmonier.

VOCABULARY

ANOINTING OF THE SICK
One of the seven sacraments, also known as the sacrament of the dying, administered by a priest to a baptized person who is in danger of death because of illness or old age, through prayer and the anointing of the body with the oil of the sick.

COMPASSION
The loving kindness, mercy, or forbearance shown to your neighbor, especially to the needy.

CONVERSION
A radical reorientation of the whole life away from sin and evil, and toward God; a central element of Christ's preaching, of the Church's ministry of evangelization, and of the Sacrament of Penance and Reconciliation.

DROPSY
A morbid condition characterized by the accumulation of watery fluid in the connective tissue of the body.

PASSION
The suffering and death of Jesus.

SALVIFIC
Pertaining to the salvation of souls: freedom from attachment, enjoying the vision of God, consummating our happiness; union with God and our own flourishing; all of this is joined to Christ's saving Passion.

VIATICUM
The Eucharist received by a dying person.

STUDY QUESTIONS

1. What does Anointing of the Sick give?

2. For the Jewish people of the Old Testament, what was the relationship between illness and healing?

3. What is the cause of human suffering?

4. How can illness harm a person's soul? How can it help?

5. What are two reasons Christ healed people?

6. Who instituted Anointing of the Sick?

7. Who administers Anointing of the Sick?

8. What are the principal elements of Anointing of the Sick?

9. What two sacraments are usually done with Anointing of the Sick? Why these two?

10. Should this sacrament be administered only in the moments before death?

11. What are the graces of Anointing of the Sick?

12. Are sickness and suffering evils?

13. How can we make our suffering fruitful?

14. What happens when we imitate the crucified Christ and accept suffering for the good of others?

PRACTICAL EXERCISES

1. If someone receives Anointing of the Sick and then dies, does that mean that the sacrament didn't work? What does it mean? What good does the sacrament do if it doesn't heal a person?

2. Suppose someone were very ill and had only a few weeks left to live. Should this person be told of his condition? Why or why not? How could Anointing of the Sick help this person?

3. Suppose a friend has a parent who is sick and probably going to die. Your friend says he doesn't believe in God anymore because his parent is suffering for no reason. What could you say to your friend? What is the source of suffering? Can suffering help a person in any way?

4. Go with a friend or group of friends to visit someone you know who is sick or visit the gravesite of someone who died — grandparents, etc.

FROM THE CATECHISM

1526 "Is any among you sick? Let him call for the presbyters of the Church, and let them pray over him, anointing him with oil in the name of the Lord; and the prayer of faith will save the sick man, and the Lord will raise him up; and if he has committed sins, he will be forgiven" (Jas 5:14-15).

1527 The sacrament of Anointing of the Sick has as its purpose the conferral of a special grace on the Christian experiencing the difficulties inherent in the condition of grave illness or old age.

1528 The proper time for receiving this holy anointing has certainly arrived when the believer begins to be in danger of death because of illness or old age.

1529 Each time a Christian falls seriously ill, he may receive the Anointing of the Sick, and also when, after he has received it, the illness worsens.

1530 Only priests (presbyters and bishops) can give the sacrament of the Anointing of the Sick, using oil blessed by the bishop, or if necessary by the celebrating presbyter himself.

1531 The celebration of the Anointing of the Sick consists essentially in the anointing of the forehead and hands of the sick person (in the Roman rite) or of other parts of the body (in the Eastern rite), the anointing being accompanied by the liturgical prayer of the celebrant asking for the special grace of this sacrament.

1532 The special grace of the sacrament of the Anointing of the Sick has as its effects:

† the uniting of the sick person to the passion of Christ, for his own good and that of the whole Church;

† the strengthening, peace, and courage to endure in a Christian manner the sufferings of illness or old age;

† the forgiveness of sins, if the sick person was not able to obtain it through the sacrament of Penance;

† the restoration of health, if it is conducive to the salvation of his soul;

† the preparation for passing over to eternal life.

Endnotes

1. *LG,* 11; cf. Jas 5:14-16; Rom 8:17; Col 1:24; 2 Tm 2:11-12; 1 Pt 4:13.
2. Cf. Mk 5:34, 36; 9:23.
3. Cf. Mk 7:32-36; 8:22-25.
4. Cf. Jn 9:6-7.
5. Lk 6:19; cf. Mk 1:41; 3:10; 6:56.
6. Lk 7:16; cf. Mt 4:24.
7. Cf. Mk 2:5-12.
8. Cf. Mk 2:17.
9. Cf. Mt 10:38.
10. Mk 6:12-13.
11. Council of Trent, 1551, DS 1695.
12. Cf. *SC,* 27.

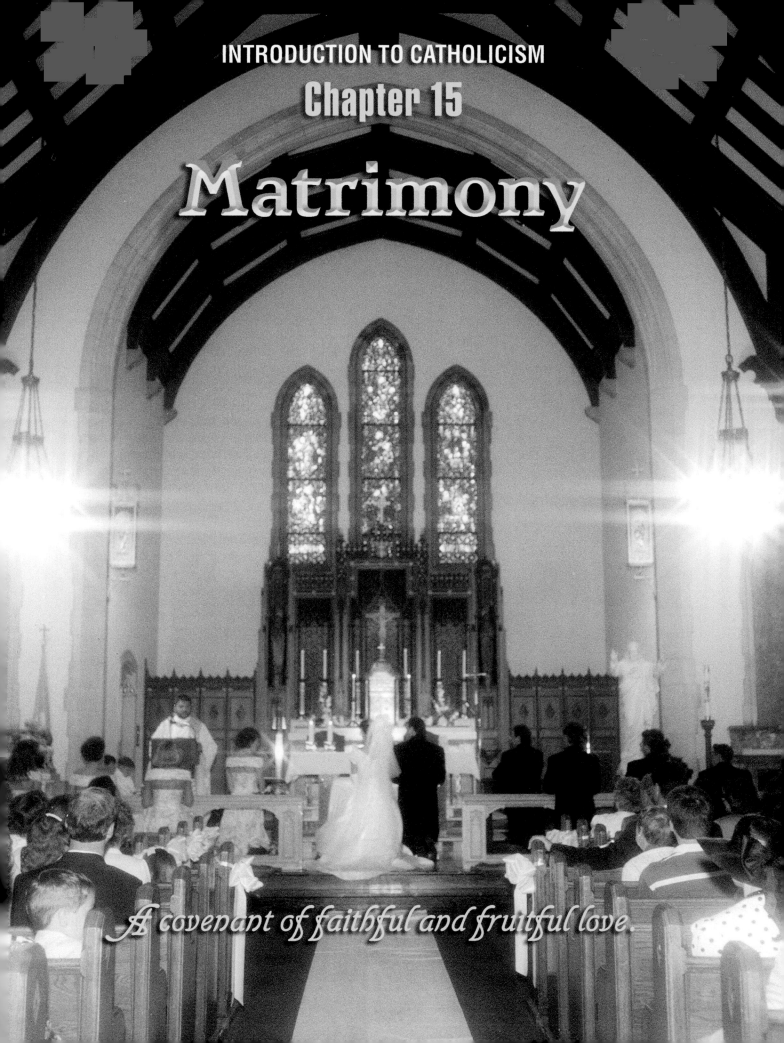

Matrimony

A covenant of faithful and fruitful love.

Chapter 15

Matrimony

This is a story that shows how marriage should be — both people in the marriage should silently and happily give up their own desires for the happiness of the other person.

There was a married couple, and the husband loved going to football games. Almost every weekend for years, the couple went to a football game, and both seemed to have a wonderful time. Eventually the couple grew old together. One night, the husband turned to his wife and said, "I hope you won't be upset, but I don't think I can go to the game this weekend. In fact, I don't think I'll be able to go much at all any more. My eyes have gone bad, so I can't see much, and all the yelling and commotion just make me tired."

"That's fine," said the wife.

"You're not upset. But I thought you loved going to the games," the husband said.

"Not really," said the wife. "All these years, I just saw how happy you were going to the games, and that made me happy. I really didn't enjoy the games themselves; I just enjoyed knowing that what I did made you happy."

MATRIMONY

Matrimony is a Sacrament at the Service of Communion that joins a man and woman in a covenant for life, for the good of the spouses and the procreation and education of children.

> ...[F]rom the beginning of creation, God made them male and female. 'For this reason a man shall leave his father and mother and be joined to his wife, and the two shall become one.' So they are no longer two but one. What therefore God has joined together let not man put asunder. (Mk 10: 6-9)

These words of Jesus indicate to us the importance of marriage in a person's life. The decision to marry a specific individual is probably the most significant choice a person can make. This is because marriage, when approached as God wants us to approach it, is not a simple contract, as some people see it, but a holy union that has very specific purposes: marriage was created for the mutual help of the spouses and the procreation of children.

> The marriage covenant, by which a man and a woman form with each other an intimate communion of life and love, has been founded and endowed with its own special laws by the Creator. By its very nature it is ordered to the good of the couple, as well as to the generation and education of children. Christ the Lord raised marriage between the baptized to the dignity of a sacrament.[1] (CCC 1660)

People marry, then, to help each other get to heaven and to raise Christian children who will join them in Heaven. It is truly amazing that a commitment between two people takes on such a serious role. But remember that marriage, as Scripture says, is a great mystery. So much about it surpasses our understanding: its institution, its purposes, the difficulties married people face because of sin, and the many forms marriage has taken throughout history.

By divine design, Matrimony signifies the union of Christ and his Church. Since it is a creation of God, it is endowed with special graces to enable the couple to love each other with the same self-sacrificing love with which Christ loved his bride the Church. This grace enables them to perfect and sanctify their love and maintain it indissoluble.

The details of a particular marriage are also mysterious. Why are two people drawn to marry each other at a particular time in their own lives and in history? Likewise, why does God grant children to a couple at one time and not at another? Why does it appear that some families suffer more than others? How does God's plan for marriage help a couple reach heaven? What does God wish for a couple to accomplish at their particular time and place in history?

Though all these questions cannot be answered in this life, they will be answered in the next. There, we will meet the members of our family tree and see how our family history unfolded as God knew it would, even before we were born. It may seem strange to think that God plans all this, but the Lord created marriage, and therefore he is active in each one.

> "The intimate community of life and love which constitutes the married state has been established by the Creator and endowed by him with its own proper laws.... God himself is the author of marriage" (GS, 48 § 1).

The decision to marry a specific individual is probably the most significant choice a person can make.

Why are two people drawn to marry each other at a particular time in their own lives and in history?

Matrimony

Genesis tells us that the union of man and woman in marriage is the image and likeness of God.

The vocation to marriage is written in the very nature of man and woman as they came from the hand of the Creator. Marriage is not a purely human institution despite the many variations it may have undergone through the centuries in different cultures, social structures, and spiritual attitudes. These differences should not cause us to forget its common and permanent characteristics. Although the dignity of this institution is not transparent everywhere with the same clarity,[2] some sense of the greatness of the matrimonial union exists in all cultures. "The well-being of the individual person and of both human and Christian society is closely bound up with the healthy state of conjugal and family life."[3] (CCC 1603)

Marriage has been important from the very beginning of creation. Genesis tells us that man and woman were created in the state of marriage, for God saw that it was "not good that the man should be alone" (Gn 2:18). Therefore, a husband is "joined to his wife" (Mk 10:7), as Christ tells us, indicating the permanence of the union. Why, then, did Jesus ~~ve to explain what marriage is, if it had always been so clear?

~~swer can be traced to original sin. Genesis tells us that the union ~~ and woman in marriage is the image and likeness of God: for ~~le says that God is love, and marriage is a union of love (cf. Gn ~~). This, as we have seen, is the original plan for marriage; however, ~~e first sin of Adam and Eve, the natural unity of husband and wife ~~rupted. When Adam and Eve ate the forbidden fruit, they became ~~d of their nakedness in front of each other and in front of God. ~~hame shows that the complete union and openness between husband and wife had been ruptured by original sin. This rupture has had serious consequences for marriage.

In spite of man's sin, though, God has not forsaken him. He has graced marriage with his gifts to make it fruitful both physically and spiritually.

This was done when Jesus reestablished the permanence of marriage by making it a sacrament. Simply stating that marriage should be a lifelong commitment would not have enabled people to live their union in a Christian way—original sin would prevent this. By making Matrimony a sacrament, though, Jesus made special graces available to married couples so that they can live as Christ wants them to live:

> To heal the wounds of sin, man and woman need the help of the grace that God in his infinite mercy never refuses them.[4] Without his help man and woman cannot achieve the union of their lives for which God created them "in the beginning." (CCC 1608)

Marriages in which the grace of God is not present can easily go wrong.

This grace is needed not only to overcome the sin that all people inherit from Adam (original sin) but to overcome the sinfulness that is active in the world. Man experiences the evil caused by sin both around him and within himself. This experience affects both partners in a marriage. A married person's rejection of God can cause his or her marriage to degenerate into discord and jealousy, leading to disunion. Marriages in which the grace of God is not present can easily go wrong, possibly focusing on the potential for evil rather than the good that is possible in marriage, or focusing on self-interest instead of self-sacrifice.

For marriage to overcome these human failings, the couple must cooperate with God's gifts and follow the teachings of Christ and his Church.

Marriage is about salvation, so the more heaven is made the goal, the more fruitful the marriage.

CELEBRATION OF MATRIMONY

A couple should receive the Sacrament of Reconciliation prior to marriage. When starting something that will affect the rest of your life, it only makes sense to be in God's grace.

The celebration of marriage normally takes place at Mass. This is fitting because the Sacrament of Matrimony is, in a supernatural way, bound up with the union of Christ and his Church, and it is in the sacrifice of the Mass that Christ's love for his Church is most manifest. Through the power of the sacrament, married couples are empowered to attain for each other this love that Christ has for his Church, using sacramental graces that perfect their human love, strengthen the indissoluble bond, and enable the couple to become holy.

> It is therefore fitting that the spouses should seal their consent to give themselves to each other through the offering of their own lives by uniting it to the offering of Christ for his Church made present in the Eucharistic sacrifice, and by receiving the Eucharist so that, communicating in the same Body and the same Blood of Christ, they may form but "one body" in Christ.[5] (CCC 1621)

The Sacrament of Matrimony is, in a supernatural way, bound up with the union of Christ and his Church.

Among all the sacraments, the celebration of Matrimony is unique. Under normal circumstances, all other sacraments are conferred by an ordained minister. In the Latin Church, however, the Sacrament of Matrimony is understood to be conferred by the couple *upon each other*, with the minister acting as the Church's witness.

A marriage is formed when the couple exchanges promises to give themselves mutually and freely to each other in a definitive way, vowing to live a covenant of faithful and fruitful love. This exchange of consent between the spouses is the indispensable element of the Sacrament of Matrimony. To form a valid bond, both the man and woman must consent to a permanent, indissoluble union and the openness to having children. If either person does not accept either one of these elements, there is no sacramental marriage.

> The consent consists in a "human act by which the partners mutually give themselves to each other": "I take you to be my wife" – "I take you to be my husband."[6] This consent that binds the spouses to each other finds its fulfillment in the two "becoming one flesh."[7] (CCC 1627)

To form a valid bond, both the man and woman must consent to a permanent, indissoluble union.

WHO CAN RECEIVE THE SACRAMENT

The parties to a marriage covenant are a baptized man and woman, free to contract marriage, who freely express their consent; "to be free" means:

† not being under constraint;

† not impeded by any natural or ecclesiastical law. (CCC 1625)

Since marriage is a public state of life, the Church requires that the couple enter it publicly in a liturgical celebration before an assembly of the

Christ gives a state of grace to married couples that helps them keep their marital promises.

When someone is unfaithful, a marriage lacks stability and suffers great harm.

faithful. The celebrant receives the consent of the spouses in the name of the Church and gives the Church's blessing. The presence of the celebrant and the witnesses demonstrates the reality of sacramental marriage within the Church.

EFFECTS OF MATRIMONY

The first effect of this Sacrament at the Service of Communion is the formation of a permanent bond between the spouses. The marriage covenant unites the couple in God's covenant with man, forming a bond between two baptized persons which, once consummated, is established and guaranteed by God and can never be dissolved. Put simply, in every marriage there are three parties: the two people getting married and God, who never consents that a valid sacramental marriage be dissolved.

To live out this permanent bond, then, Christ gives a state of grace to married couples that helps them keep their marital promises. Essentially, all of these promises point to the same goal: a total gift of self to the other person. The graces that come with the Sacrament of Matrimony, then, make this gift of self possible. They enable the couple to perfect their love, strengthen the indissolubility of the marriage, welcome children, and attain holiness. This supernatural assistance from Christ also helps a couple to take up their crosses and follow him, forgive one another, rise after falling into sin, bear each other's burdens, be subject to each other out of reverence for each other, and love each other with a supernatural, tender, and fruitful love.

Love practiced within marriage, of course, involves sexual relations between husband and wife. When done between husband and wife, this is a good and noble act that strengthens the marriage bond as long as the act is understood properly:

> "Conjugal love involves a totality, in which all the elements of the person enter—appeal of the body and instinct, power of feeling and affectivity, aspiration of the spirit and of will. It aims at a deeply personal unity, a unity that, beyond union in one flesh, leads to forming one heart and soul; it demands *indissolubility* and *faithfulness* in definitive mutual giving; and it is open to *fertility*. In a word it is a question of the normal characteristics of all natural conjugal love, but with a new significance which not only purifies and strengthens them, but raises them to the extent of making them the expression of specifically Christian values."[8] (CCC 1643)

Because it involves so many aspects of a person, conjugal love can add strength to a marriage—strength that will benefit both the couple and any children they may have. And because it involves the total person, conjugal love may be practiced *only* between husband and wife. For when someone is unfaithful, a marriage lacks stability and suffers great harm. On the other hand, a couple's fidelity shares in and witnesses to the totality of God's love for men.

THE DOMESTIC CHURCH

The family is the first school of life for all people. This statement applies especially to Christian homes, where children will receive their first instruction in the life of children of God. For this reason, the Christian home is called the domestic church—a community of grace and prayer, a school of human virtues and Christian charity.

Practically speaking, most of the knowledge children receive in the domestic church will not be directly taught, but will be learned as they see the love with which parents live out their commitment to each other and to God. Marital love, then, should be aimed toward caring for God's creation of the family. If the family is oriented toward Christ and his Church, the children will learn how to love from a Christian perspective, personal priorities will be in order, and life will be viewed as a struggle to get to heaven through complete involvement in Christ's redeeming love. The mutual self-sacrificing love of the spouses will educate the children in the true self-sacrificing love that was demonstrated by Christ. And children will see themselves as a gift to the marriage rather than as burdens of questionable value.

The domestic church will also teach children how to approach the troubles of life. A family that is centered around Christ will bear life's sufferings more easily. Every family has its good and bad times, but if a family endures its trials with a Christian attitude, the times of suffering become redemptive while drawing the family closer together.

On the other hand, even in good times, those marriages in which Christ is not the head are afflicted with discord, infidelity, jealousy, and conflicts, which can rupture the marriage. Most often, this problem arises when one or both partners do not attend the sacraments, for if someone refuses the grace that comes from the sacraments, how can he expect to live a grace-filled life?

A Christian home, then, must be a place where love of God and obedience to his will are at the center of a marriage, where Christ is the head, and where selfless love can provide happy citizens for the kingdom of heaven.

SINS AGAINST MARRIAGE

God created marriage as an indissoluble union of two people that must be open to children, who are God's gifts to the marriage. All actions contrary to this union are seriously sinful:

- ◆ Contraception – Deliberate interference with marital intercourse to prevent conception;

- ◆ Adultery – Acts of marriage between a married person and a party other than his or her spouse;

- ◆ Divorce – an action that claims to break a valid marital bond;

- ◆ Polygamy – the state or institution of an individual contracting more than one marriage or contracting marriage with an already married individual;

- ◆ Trial marriage – the state of a man and a woman living together in a relationship that involves sexual intimacy outside of marriage in an attempt to evaluate what marriage would be like;

The family is the first school of life for all people.

A family that is centered around Christ will bear life's sufferings more easily.

> *Because God himself is thus its author, marriage is of its very nature a holy institution, requiring of those who enter into it a complete and unreserved giving of self.*

◆ Concubinage – the state of a man and a woman living together in a relationship that involves sexual intimacy outside of marriage. This includes trial marriages, in which a couple claims to be testing what a marriage would be like.

Of course, some people find themselves in marriages that do not appear to be working. Their first move should be to seek the assistance of the Church in counseling to save the marriage.

There are also occasions, such as physical abuse and alcoholism, in which it might be best for a couple to separate, but in no case may the separated husband and wife date third parties or attempt divorce with the purpose of entering into a second marriage.

Since the remarriage of persons who have a valid first marriage is a serious offense against the plan and law of God as taught by Christ, those who enter into a second marriage, though they are still members of the Church, may not receive the Eucharist. Their obligation to educate any children in the faith remains. The Church offers these people her love, prayers, and support in their difficult situation and encourages them to seek full communion with the Church through whatever means necessary.

A DEFINITION OF MARRIAGE

The opening words of the former rite of marriage are one of the most moving passages of Christian writing on marriage. In just a few paragraphs, it explains beautifully what a Christian marriage is:

> Dear friends in Christ: As you know, you are about to enter into a union which is most sacred and most serious, a union which was established by God himself. By it, he gave to man a share in the greatest work of creation, the work of the continuation of the human race. And in this way he sanctified human love and enabled man and woman to help each other live as children of God, by sharing a common life under his fatherly care.

> Because God himself is thus its author, marriage is of its very nature a holy institution, requiring of those who enter into it a complete and unreserved giving of self. But Christ our LORD added to the holiness of marriage an even deeper meaning and a higher beauty. He referred to the love of marriage to describe his own love for his Church, that is, for the people of God whom he redeemed by his own blood. And so he gave to Christians a new vision of what married life ought to be, a life of self-sacrificing love like his own. It is for this reason that his apostle, St. Paul, clearly states that marriage is now and for all time to be considered a great mystery, intimately bound up with the supernatural union of Christ and the Church, which union is also to be its pattern.

> This union then is most serious, because it will bind you together for life in a relationship so close and so intimate that it will profoundly influence your whole future. That future, with its hopes and disappointments, its successes and its failures, its pleasures and its pains, its joys and its sorrows, is hidden from your eyes. You know that these elements are mingled in every life and are to be expected in your own. And so, not knowing what is before you, you take each other for better or for worse, for richer or for poorer, in sickness and in health, until death.

Truly, then, these words are most serious. It is a beautiful tribute to your undoubted faith in each other, that, recognizing their full import, you are nevertheless so willing and ready to pronounce them. And because these words involve such solemn obligations, it is most fitting that you rest the security of your wedded life upon the great principle of self-sacrifice. And so you begin your married life by the voluntary and complete surrender of your individual lives in the interest of that deeper and wider life which you are to have in common. Henceforth you belong entirely to each other; you will be one in mind, one in heart, and one in affections. And whatever sacrifices you may hereafter be required to make to preserve this common life, always make them generously. Sacrifice is usually difficult and irksome. Only love can make it easy; and perfect love can make it a joy. We are willing to give in proportion as we love. And when love is perfect, the sacrifice is complete. God so loved the world that he gave his only begotten Son, and the Son so loved us that he gave himself for our salvation. "Greater love than this no one has, that one lay down his life for his friends."

No greater blessing can come to your married life than pure conjugal love, loyal and true to the end. May, then, this love with which you join your hands and hearts today, never fail, but grow deeper and stronger as the years go on. And if true love and the unselfish spirit of perfect sacrifice guide your every action, you can expect the greatest measure of earthly happiness that may be allotted to man in this vale of tears. The rest is in the hands of God. [Nor will God be wanting to your needs; he will pledge you the lifelong support of his graces in the holy sacrament which you are now going to receive.]

CONCLUSION

One of the greatest mysteries of life is marriage. In this sacrament, two people willingly agree to share a life in which their individual wills are submerged for the benefit of their bond and for the earthly and eternal benefit of themselves and their children.

This is obviously a huge commitment, but it is one that can be fulfilled with the help of sacramental graces. Through these graces, God allows two people to grow in love for each other throughout their lives.

God grants these graces because he is the creator and a party in every marriage. He watches over each married couple with loving care. As the former marriage rite states, "Nor will God be wanting to your needs; he will pledge you the lifelong support of his graces in the holy sacrament you are going to receive."

God watches over each married couple with loving care.

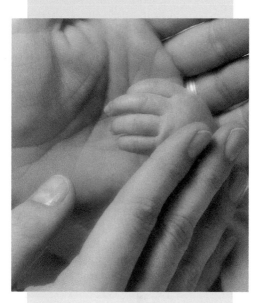

No greater blessing can come to your married life than pure conjugal love, loyal and true to the end.

Chapter 15 Study Guide

SUPPLEMENTARY READING

Georges and Pauline Vanier were one of those couples who were made for each other. He grew up bilingual (French and English) and was a lifelong daily Communicant. After earning his degree, he considered entering the priesthood, but when World War I broke out he flew to the aid of his country and raised the first French Canadian battalion. After being made colonel, he married Pauline Archer.

Pauline had contemplated being a nun, but when the War broke out, she applied to the army as a foot soldier. Unsuccessful, she enrolled in nursing school and took a job in a military hospital. After their marriage, Pauline went with Georges to Geneva where he was a military advisor for the League of Nations disarmament: "I ask you to open your eyes to human suffering, to direct your ears to those who have not the strength to ask for help."

As the Canadian ambassador to France in 1939, Georges' warnings of imminent war soon came true. Pauline was given her chance to show her courage, compassion and complete trust in God in her wartime escape from Paris with her four children. When a German fighter plane crashed in front of her car on the jammed roads out of Paris, Pauline ran to drag the pilot to safety but he had died in the accident.

With the fall of France, Germany set up a puppet regime known as the Vichy government. Georges' warnings about this government's treachery proved remarkably accurate, and he was named Canada's first ambassador to the newly-liberated country. While the French capital was still considered too dangerous for women, Pauline persuaded the Red Cross to allow her to be their representative and made her way to her husband. While Pauline provided food for returning refugees and established an information network to reunite them with their families, Georges worked on international agreements to aid the plight of Jewish survivors, orphans, and the elderly.

Georges and Pauline Vanier
Two lives filled with heroic, loving action.

The Vaniers' inner prayer life was the wellspring of all their efforts. They rarely made any major decision without first considering it in prayer. In 1959, Georges was made the governor-general of Quebec. As he took his oath of office Vanier said, "May almighty God in His infinite wisdom and mercy bless the sacred mission which has been entrusted to me…and help me to fulfill it in all humility. In exchange for His strength, I offer Him my weakness. May He give peace to this beloved land of ours and…the grace of mutual understanding, respect and love.

Their efforts to improve Canadian family life led to the Vanier Institute of the Family, whose research continues today. Their son Jean founded l'Arche community for mentally handicapped adults. After her husband's death, Pauline held weekly prayer meetings here for the next nineteen years because she believed that "Faith, far from being outmoded or old-fashioned, imparts a beauty, a richness, and a radiance that can be found in no other source."

These two Christians give all others an example to follow. Their lives were filled with heroic, loving action that springs from a life of prayer. This husband and wife understood that God is a necessary ingredient in all our worldly undertakings and the rock upon which we should build lives of virtue.

VOCABULARY

ADULTERY
Marital infidelity, or sexual relations between two partners, at least one of whom is married to another party.

CONJUGAL LOVE
A total, faithful, exclusive, willing, unitive love coming not only from the senses, but primarily from the spirit and is such that one desires children and is willing to suffer.

CONSUMMATED MARRIAGE
A marriage in which the spouses have engaged together in the conjugal act that is apt for the generation of offspring.

CONTRACEPTION
The use of mechanical, chemical, or medical procedures to prevent conception from taking place as a result of sexual intercourse; offends against the openness to procreation required of marriage and also the inner truth of conjugal love.

DIVORCE
The claim that the indissoluble marriage bond validly entered into between a man and a woman is broken. Divorce introduces disorder into the family and into society. It brings grave harm to the deserted spouse and to the children traumatized by the separation. In some cases one of the spouses is the innocent victim of a divorce decreed by civil law; this spouse therefore has not contravened the moral law. A civil divorce is sometimes a tragic necessity, but it does not dissolve a marriage bond. Even when civil divorce is allowed by the country's law, marriage, in God's eyes, still exists.

DOMESTIC CHURCH
An ancient expression for the family, recognizing the parents as the first heralds of the faith to their children in both word and example.

FAMILY
A man and a woman united in marriage, together with their children; a domestic church; a community of faith, hope, and charity.

INDISSOLUBLE
Incapable of being erased, destroyed or removed.

MATRIMONIAL CONSENT
An act of the will by which a man and a woman, in an irrevocable covenant, mutually give and accept each other, declaring their willingness to welcome children and to educate them.

MATRIMONY
A covenant or partnership of life between a man and woman, which is ordered to the well-being of the spouses and to the procreation and upbringing of children. When validly contracted between two baptized people, marriage is a sacrament.

POLYGAMY
The practice of having more than one wife at the same time, which is contrary to the unity of marriage between one man and one woman, and which offends against the dignity of woman. In the Old Testament polygamy was permitted in certain circumstances, as, for example, in the case of King Solomon.

PROCREATION
The formation of new life through a married couple's cooperation with God and in response to their vocation.

STUDY QUESTIONS

1. What is the most important decision most persons can make? *Whether or not to marry*

2. When two people marry, should they each give 50% to the marriage?

3. How did original sin hurt the establishment of marriage?

4. Why did Christ make marriage a sacrament?

5. Why should a couple go to Confession before their wedding? *So that the change their lives in a state of purity*

6. When is a marriage between two people formed?

7. What are the two aspects of marriage that must be accepted by both partners to form a valid bond? Can a marriage be valid without these in both parties?

8. Who confers the Sacrament of Marriage? How is this different from all the other sacraments?

9. What is the first effect of the sacrament?

10. What do all the promises of Matrimony point toward? *heaven*

11. What aspects of the human person does sex involve?

12. Why should sex be reserved to marriage?

13. Where should people first learn about life as a Christian?

14. Does the Church ever permit separation of spouses? What about divorce? What's the difference?

15. Who are the three parties in a marriage? *Husband + wife + god*

PRACTICAL EXERCISES

1. Some people argue that if a person is unhappy in a marriage, then that person has the right to end the marriage. List two things that are wrong with this opinion. Consider what the marriage promises say about how long the couple will be together. Think about what a promise is, and who is involved in every union.

2. Explain what self-sacrificing love is. Give three examples. John 3:16 may be of some help.

3. Read the Song of Songs in the Old Testament. What type of love is expressed?

4. The First Letter of John is often called the "Book of Love." Read Chapter 4, Verses 7-21 and see what kind of love is expressed here. Describe what the world would be like if everyone lived with this kind of love.

FROM THE CATECHISM

1659 St. Paul said: "Husbands, love your wives, as Christ loved the Church....This is a great mystery, and I mean in reference to Christ and the Church" (Eph 5: 25, 32).

1660 The marriage covenant, by which a man and a woman form with each other an intimate communion of life and love, has been founded and endowed with its own special laws by the Creator. By its very nature it is ordered to the good of the couple, as well as to the generation and education of children. Christ the Lord raised marriage between the baptized to the dignity of a sacrament (cf. CIC, can. 1055 § 1; cf. GS, 48 § 1).

1661 The sacrament of Matrimony signifies the union of Christ and the Church. It gives spouses the grace to love each other with the love with which Christ has loved his Church; the grace of the sacrament thus perfects the human love of the spouses, strengthens their indissoluble unity, and sanctifies them on the way to eternal life (cf. Council of Trent: DS, 1799).

1662 Marriage is based on the consent of the contracting parties, that is, on their will to give themselves, each to the other, mutually and definitively, in order to live a covenant of faithful and fruitful love.

1663 Since marriage establishes the couple in a public state of life in the Church, it is fitting that its celebration be public, in the framework of a liturgical celebration, before the priest (or a witness authorized by the Church), the witnesses, and the assembly of the faithful.

1664 Unity, indissolubility, and openness to fertility are essential to marriage. Polygamy is incompatible with the unity of marriage; divorce separates what God has joined together; the refusal of fertility turns married life away from its "supreme gift," the child (GS, 50 § 1).

1665 The remarriage of persons divorced from a living, lawful spouse contravenes the plan and law of God as taught by Christ. They are not separated from the Church, but they cannot receive Eucharistic communion. They will lead Christian lives especially by educating their children in the faith.

1666 The Christian home is the place where children receive the first proclamation of the faith. For this reason the family home is rightly called "the domestic church," a community of grace and prayer, a school of human virtues and of Christian charity.

Endnotes

1. Cf. CIC, can. 1055 § 1; cf. GS, 48 § 1
2. Cf. GS, 47 § 2.
3. GS, 47 § 1.
4. Cf. Gn 3: 21.
5. Cf. 1 Cor 10: 17.
6. GS, 48 § 1; OCM, 45; cf. CIC, can. 1057 § 2.
7. Gn 2: 24; cf. Mk 10: 8; Eph 5: 31.
8. FC, 13.

Holy Orders

*Servants of the Word of God
and God's sacraments.*

Chapter 16

Holy Orders

People who are not Catholic could erroneously think of Catholicism as having two levels of power and importance. On the lower level, they see those who are not priests as having no power in the Church, and are there only to serve the demands of priests. On the upper level, they see priests and bishops, who exist to be served by the unimportant lay people.

Despite its prevalence, this understanding of the priesthood is completely contrary to reality. In being ordained to the priesthood, a man renounces the possibility of having a wife and family of his own, and he promises to put aside what he desires in order to live a life in obedience to his bishop. Does this sound like the path to earthly power?

Though priests can perform acts that the laity cannot, such as hearing confessions or consecrating the Eucharist, they do not have these graces so that others may serve them. A priest is given these graces so that he can serve everyone else. As priest, it is his duty to administer the sacraments, thereby offering people the grace they need to get into heaven.

The priesthood, then, is not made up of power-hungry men wanting to rule other people. It is made up of men who, out of great love, have dedicated their lives to service.

HOLY ORDERS

Holy Orders is a Sacrament at the Service of Communion that Jesus gave the Church to pass on the ministries of deacon, priest, and bishop until the end of time.

> Do this in remembrance of me. (Lk 22:19)

With this command from Jesus to celebrate the Eucharist, the Sacrament of Holy Orders was established. Through this sacrament, the mission entrusted by Christ to the apostles has been handed down to our day and will continue until the end of time.

> Christ is himself the source of ministry in the Church. He instituted the Church. He gave her authority and mission, orientation and goal:

> "In order to shepherd the People of God and to increase its numbers without cease, Christ the Lord set up in his Church a variety of offices which aim at the good of the whole body. The holders of office, who are invested with a sacred power, are, in fact, dedicated to promoting the interests of their brethren, so that all who belong to the People of God...may attain to salvation."[1] (CCC 874)

The Sacrament of Holy Orders has been set up by Christ to provide ministers of service to his people, the Church. All people who have received Holy Orders are members of a college (an assembly) dedicated to service. Since the purpose of Holy Orders is so vast, the sacrament is given on three different levels, with differing powers and authorities:

† Bishops are at the highest level of the Holy Orders. They participate in the full priesthood of Christ. The main power they have over priests is the ability to ordain deacons, priests, and other bishops. They are the successors of the apostles and members of the college of bishops, which has the Pope at its head. The normal role of a bishop is to head a local church, which is called a diocese.

† Priests, whose role is to assist and obey the orders of the bishop, often care for communities of the faithful. They have the ability to administer the Sacraments of Reconciliation, the Eucharist, Baptism, Anointing of the Sick, as well as Confirmation when authorized by the proper authority.

† Deacons are ministers of the Gospel but cannot consecrate the Eucharist or hear Confession. They are ordained to perform acts of service and charity.

> Sacramental ministry in the Church, then, is a service exercised in the name of Christ. It has a personal character and a collegial form. This is evidenced by the bonds between the episcopal college and its head, the successor of St. Peter, and in the relationship between the bishop's pastoral responsibility for his particular church and the common solicitude of the episcopal college for the universal Church. (CCC 879)

It is clear from these descriptions that service is the main purpose of Holy Orders. Those who receive this sacrament become servants of the Word of God and God's sacraments. They dedicate themselves to a life of self-denial and sacrifice for the good of other people. St. Paul goes so far as to refer to himself as a slave, showing how serious the obligation to serve Christ becomes when a person receives Holy Orders.

St. Thomas Aquinas

(1225-1274) A Doctor of the Church The greatest of the Catholic theologians and one of the most brilliant minds in the Western world. Church doctrine that he wrote is still heeded today as are his prayers and hymns.

Holy Orders

St. Charles (Carlo) Borromeo

b.1538; d.1584, Father of the Clergy, Apostle to the Council of Trent, Archbishop of Milan at age 24, nephew of Pope Pius IV.

Devoted to the Passion and a true devotee of the Trinity, St. Charles fervently enforced the decrees of the Council of Trent, founded schools for the poor, seminaries for clerics and hospitals for the sick.

This life of service may seem difficult, but in truth, when approached properly, it is a great blessing. Every ordained person has been personally called by Christ, so answering that call brings God's grace to the baptized. Priests are called not only to follow Christ by what they say and do, but also to be Christ to others by the lives they lead.

This sacrament, which leaves a permanent mark on the soul, truly consecrates a person to the Lord. The word "orders" in the Roman Empire referred to a governing body, in which membership was considered sacred. The Church has assumed this term when she speaks of the *ordo episcoporum* (order of bishops), *ordo presbyterorum* (order of priests), and *ordo diaconorum* (order of deacons). "Orders" is now used to indicate that a man who has been ordained has a hierarchical role in the Church and has also been consecrated by a gift of the Holy Spirit into sacred service to God, the Church, and his fellow man.

Every baptized person is also called to service. Baptism makes every member of the Church a sharer in Christ's role of priest, prophet, and king. But there is an essential difference between the common priesthood of the faithful, of which non-ordained people are members, and the ministerial priesthood, comprising those who have received the Sacrament of Holy Orders. The priestly function of the lay members of the Church is different from that of those who have been ordained. It is exercised in their particular state in life, which is a call to bring others to the Church by prayer and example in their work, friendships, and family.

Those who are members of the ministerial priesthood are distinguished by a more radical gift of themselves. They dedicate themselves wholly and directly to the building up of the Church. By their ordination, they have the power to act *in persona Christi*, in the person of Christ, to celebrate the sacrifice of Christ in the Mass:

> The redemptive sacrifice of Christ is unique, accomplished once for all; yet it is made present in the Eucharistic sacrifice of the Church. The same is true of the one priesthood of Christ; it is made present through the ministerial priesthood without diminishing the uniqueness of Christ's priesthood: "Only Christ is the true priest, the others being only his ministers."[2] (CCC 1545)

Christ is always present in his Church, acting through the priest as his minister. Each priest acts in the person of Christ, yet Christ is the effective cause of every priest's sacramental action.

> "It is the same priest, Christ Jesus, whose sacred person his minister truly represents. Now the minister, by reason of the sacerdotal consecration which he has received, is truly made like to the high priest and possesses authority to act in the power and place of the person of Christ himself *(virtute ac persona ipsius Christi).*"[3]

> "Christ is the source of all priesthood: the priest of the old law was a figure of Christ, and the priest of the new law acts in the person of Christ."[4] (CCC 1548)

Though the priest acts in the person of Christ, he is not guaranteed to be free from sin and error. A priest remains damaged by original sin and vulnerable to temptation. Even if a priest sins, though, he still is an ordained minister of the Church. The Holy Spirit guarantees his faults do not impede the grace of God. As an example, if a priest were to be in mortal sin while hearing Confessions, he would still be able to forgive the sins of others. Once you realize that priests are capable of sin, you should pray for priests to be truly Christ-like.

MINISTER OF HOLY ORDERS

The minister of Holy Orders is a validly ordained bishop. Every bishop can trace his ordination and his ability to transmit the sacrament of Holy Orders directly back to the apostles in an unbroken line of succession. All bishops, then, have the power to pass on the three ministries of bishop, priest, and deacon.

> The Second Vatican Council "teaches…that *the fullness of the sacrament of Holy Orders* is conferred by episcopal consecration, that fullness namely which, both in the liturgical tradition of the Church and the language of the Fathers of the Church, is called the high priesthood, the acme *(summa)* of the sacred ministry."[5] (CCC 1557)

A bishop can be lawfully ordained only with the special intervention of the pope, who chooses him for this role. At the moment a priest is consecrated as a bishop, through the imposition of hands and the words of consecration, he is given the power to sanctify, teach, and rule. A sacred character is then given to the bishop to perform his roles of teaching, sanctifying and leading in an eminent and visible manner. He takes the place of Christ as visible teacher, shepherd, and priest, and acts as Christ's representative. In virtue of the grace received from the Holy Spirit, a bishop is constituted as a true and authentic teacher of the faith and a bridge-builder between the Church and her members.

Upon ordination, a bishop becomes a member of the college of bishops, a fact symbolized by the participation of several bishops in the consecration of a new bishop. Although a bishop governs directly only a small part of the Church, he is responsible for the good of the Church as a whole in his role as member of this college. The term archbishop usually refers to a bishop who is assigned to head a province of bishops, who are the ordinaries of a regional group of dioceses.

PRIESTS, CO-WORKERS WITH BISHOPS

The power of the bishops is handed over in a lesser way to priests so that they become co-workers with the bishop in sanctifying the Church. The sacrament of Holy Orders assigns a special character or mark upon the soul of the priest to enable him to act in the person of Christ. Priests are consecrated in order to preach the Gospel and shepherd the faithful as well as to celebrate divine worship as priests of the New Testament.

While all priests share in the worldwide dimensions of the mission of the Church, they are normally ordained for service in a particular diocese or religious order. Diocesan priests can exercise their ministry only in union with and dependence on the local bishop, to whom they pledge obedience from the moment of ordination. Every diocesan priest is united to his bishop and to all other priests in the diocese in he serves in a collegial way. Religious priests, through the bishop who ordains them,

The sacrament of Holy Orders assigns a special character or mark upon the soul of the priest to enable him to act in the person of Christ.

The highest act of the office of priest is saying Mass.

pledge obedience not to the bishop, but to their religious superiors, and they are united to others in their religious community.

The highest act of the office of priest is saying Mass. By consecrating the Eucharist during this service, the priest acts in the place of Christ, proclaims Christ's mystery, and unites the offerings of the faithful to the sacrifice of Christ. Priests and bishops can both perform the Anointing of the Sick.

At the lower level of the hierarchy are found deacons, who are united directly to the bishop in service. A special character is conferred on them that configures them to Christ as servants. They assist the bishop and the priests in the celebration of the sacraments, particularly the Eucharist, the distribution of Holy Communion, the blessing of marriages, the proclaiming of the Gospel, presiding over funerals, baptizing, and various ministries of charity in the diocese. They differ from the priest mainly in that they cannot hear Confession or consecrate the Eucharist. The deaconate itself is divided into two categories: transitional deacons are those going on to the priesthood, while those who are not are referred to as permanent deacons.

CELEBRATION OF HOLY ORDERS

The Sacrament of Holy Orders is an apostolic ministry. Only validly ordained bishops in the line of succession to the apostles have the power to ordain.

For the celebration of this Sacrament at the Service of Communion, the Church welcomes the presence of as many lay people as possible. This sacrament is normally celebrated on a Sunday at Mass, preferably at a cathedral, and with great solemnity. The essential rite of the sacrament is the laying of hands on the head of the ordinand (man about to be ordained) and the specific consecratory prayer asking God for the outpouring of the Spirit to give the gifts proper to the ministry of the person being ordained. As in all sacraments, there are additional rites. In ordination, these include instruction by the bishop, examination of the candidate, anointing with chrism, and bestowal of the Book of the Gospels and the chalice and paten.

To receive the sacrament of Holy Orders, a person must:

† Be a baptized male of excellent character. This follows the decision of Jesus, who chose only men as apostles;

† Have an interior and exterior call;

† Have necessary knowledge of the nature of Holy Orders;

† Be the proper age, currently set at 24 years;

† Have a commitment to lifelong celibacy, except for permanent deacons, who can marry before, but not after, being ordained;

† Study theology and be otherwise trained in his profession, in respect to his proper office.

The commitment to a life of celibacy is the most obvious difference between a priest and a layman. At first glance this may seem like a burden, but it is actually a great gift. By remaining celibate, the priest can dedicate his mind, his heart, and his time entirely and directly to the service of God and his fellow man.

The effects of the sacrament are:

✝ The conferral of the office of bishop, priest, or deacon;

✝ An indelible mark upon the soul;

✝ A particular grace proper to the exercise of the recipient's ministry. Deacons are given the grace to serve; priests the grace to hear Confession and say Mass; bishops the ability to ordain.

The grace given by this sacrament also enables the ordained to be strong in his life as another Christ in ministering to all, with a preferential love for the poor and needy.

CONCLUSION

The whole Church is a priestly people. Through Baptism, all share in the priesthood of Christ, which is called the common priesthood. At the same time, the Sacrament of Holy Orders confers a special participation in the priesthood of Christ, a sacred power for the service of the faithful. There are three degrees of Holy Orders: bishop, priest, and deacon. The bishop receives the fullness of orders, which places him in line of succession to the apostles and makes him part of the episcopal college. Priests are co-workers with the bishop, while deacons are ministers of tasks of service. Both are bound to obey the bishop.

When Christ established this sacrament, he chose men alone as its recipients. Therefore, only males may receive Orders. The bishop confers the sacrament by the laying of hands and saying the consecratory prayer.

It has been said that from the East comes our light and from the priest comes our faith. Christ has given the ordained a great dignity and a great obligation to present Christ. We should remember priests in our daily prayer.

Through Baptism, all share in the priesthood of Christ, which is called the common priesthood.

It has been said that from the East comes our light and from the priest comes our faith.

SUPPLEMENTARY READING

Pope John Paul II has offered many insights into the vocation of the priesthood from his own experience found in *Gift and Mystery*. Here he begins to explain how the priesthood is not a decision that man makes and God accepts, but rather a decision that God makes so that man may accept:

A vocation is a mystery of divine election: "You did not choose me, but I chose you and appointed you that you should go and bear fruit and that your fruit should abide" (Jn 15:16). "And one does not take the honor upon himself, but he is called by God, just as Aaron was" (Heb 5:4). "Before I formed you in the womb I knew you, and before you were born I consecrated you; I appointed you a prophet to the nation" (Jer 1:5). These inspired words cannot fail to move deeply the heart of every priest...that God "has called us with a holy calling, not in virtue of our works but in virtue of his own purpose and the grace which he gave us" (2 Tm 1:9).[6]

Later in the book the pope tries to explain the mystery of the priesthood, knowing that human words cannot do it justice. He makes it clear that this vocation is where some young men "will find complete personal fulfillment."

The priestly vocation is a mystery. It is the mystery of a "wondrous exchange"—admirable commercium—between God and man. A man offers his humanity to Christ, so that Christ may use him as an instrument of salvation, making him as it were into another Christ. Unless we grasp the mystery of this "exchange," we will not understand how it can be that a young man, hearing the words "Follow me!" can give up everything for Christ, in the certainty that if he follows this path he will find complete personal fulfillment.[7]

Pope John Paul II entered the seminary when Poland was occupied by Nazi Germany. He and all the other seminarians had to keep their

Pope John Paul II

studies secret or face arrest by the Nazis. Here he is discussing his realization of his vocation during World War II.

The outbreak of the war took me away from my studies and from the University. In that period I also lost my father, the last remaining member of my immediate family. All this brought with it, objectively, a process of detachment from earlier plans; in a way it was like being uprooted from the soil in which, up till that moment, my humanity had grown.

But the process [of detachment] was not merely negative. At the same time a light was beginning to shine ever more brightly in the back of my mind: the Lord wants me to become a priest. One day I saw this with great clarity: it was like an interior illumination bringing with it the joy and certainty of a new vocation.

And this awareness filled me with a great inner peace.[8]

VOCABULARY

BISHOP

One who has received the fullness of the Sacrament of Holy Orders, which makes him a member of the episcopal college and a successor of the Apostles. He is the shepherd of a particular church entrusted to him.

CARDINAL

A bishop that the Pope appoints as a consultant. Cardinals less than eighty years old are responsible for electing the Pope.

CELIBACY

The state or condition of those who have chosen to remain unmarried for the sake of the kingdom of heaven in order to give themselves entirely to God and to the service of his people.

CHASTITY

The moral virtue which, under the cardinal virtue of temperance, provides for the successful integration of sexuality within the person leading to the inner unity of the bodily and spiritual being.

DEACON

A third degree of the hierarchy of the Sacrament of Holy Orders, ordained not to priesthood but for ministry and service.

DIOCESE

A particular church, a community of the faithful in communion of faith and sacraments whose bishop has been ordained in apostolic succession.

EPISCOPAL COLLEGE

All bishops in communion with the Pope.

HOLY ORDERS

The Sacrament of Apostolic Ministry by which the mission entrusted by Christ to his Apostles continues to be exercised in the Church through the laying on of hands, which leaves a sacramental character on the soul.

OBEDIENCE

The submission to the authority of God which requires everyone to obey the divine law. A priest has to obey his bishop or religious superior as representatives of God, and all must obey the ecclesiastical law.

ORDINATION

The rite of the Sacrament of Holy Orders by which the bishop, through the imposition of hands and the prayer of consecration, confers the order of bishop, priest, or deacon to exercise a sacred power which comes from Christ on behalf of the Church.

POVERTY

The condition of want experienced by those who are poor, whom Christ called blessed, and for whom he had a special love. Poverty of spirit signifies detachment from worldly things and voluntary humility.

PRESBYTERATE

The presbyterate (priesthood) is one of the three degrees of the Sacrament of Holy Orders. The other two degrees are the diaconate (deacons) and the episcopate (bishops).

PRIEST

A member of the order of priesthood; co-workers with their bishops that form a unique sacerdotal college or presbyterium dedicated to assist their bishops in priestly service to the People of God.

STUDY QUESTIONS

1. With what words did Christ institute the sacrament of Holy Orders? What was he telling the apostles to do?

2. Who is the source of the ministry of the Church?

3. What are the three different levels of Holy Orders in the Church? What are the powers of each?

4. Why is the life of service a blessing for a priest? Why is celibacy a gift for priests?

5. Are ordained men the only members of the Church who are called to serve? Who else in the Church is called to serve?

6. What are the two kinds of priesthood in the Church? What distinguishes them?

7. Who is the minister of Holy Orders?

8. Upon ordination, of what assembly does the bishop become a member?

9. To whom do priests pledge obedience?

10. What are the essential elements of an ordination?

11. Once someone is made a priest can he ever be unmade a priest? Why or why not?
No

PRACTICAL EXERCISES

1. Invite a priest to class (or to dinner with your family). Ask him to discuss how he serves the Church and why he loves the celibate life.

2. Imagine you have a non-Catholic friend who thinks that Catholic priests are superior to lay people and try to control them. Explain to him why priests may be called "servants of the servants of God."

3. Priests can trace the roots of their ordination all the way back to the apostles. Ask your parents, search on the internet, and/or visit your courthouse to see how far back you can trace your family tree.

FROM THE CATECHISM

1590 St. Paul said to his disciple Timothy: "I remind you to rekindle the gift of God that is within you through the laying on of my hands" (2 Tm 1:6), and "If any one aspires to the office of bishop, he desires a noble task." (1 Tm 3:1) To Titus he said: "This is why I left you in Crete, that you amend what was defective, and appoint presbyters in every town, as I directed you" (Ti 1:5).

1591 The whole Church is a priestly people. Through Baptism all the faithful share in the priesthood of Christ. This participation is called the "common priesthood of the faithful." Based on this common priesthood and ordered to its service, there exists another participation in the mission of Christ: the ministry conferred by the sacrament of Holy Orders, where the task is to serve in the name and in the person of Christ the Head in the midst of the community.

1592 The ministerial priesthood differs in essence from the common priesthood of the faithful because it confers a sacred power for the service of the faithful. The ordained ministers exercise their service for the People of God by teaching *(munus docendi)*, divine worship *(munus liturgicum)* and pastoral governance *(munus regendi)*.

1593 Since the beginning, the ordained ministry has been conferred and exercised in three degrees: that of bishops, that of presbyters, and that of deacons. The ministries conferred by ordination are irreplaceable for the organic structure of the Church: without the bishop, presbyters, and deacons, one cannot speak of the Church (cf. St. Ignatius of Antioch, *Ad Trall.* 3, 1).

1594 The bishop receives the fullness of the sacrament of Holy Orders, which integrates him into the episcopal college and makes him the visible head of the particular Church entrusted to him. As successors of the apostles and members of the college, the bishops share in the apostolic responsibility and mission of the whole Church under the authority of the Pope, successor of St. Peter.

1595 Priests are united with the bishops in sacerdotal dignity and at the same time depend on them in the exercise of their pastoral functions; they are called to be the bishops' prudent co-workers. They form around their bishop the presbyterium, which bears responsibility with him for the particular Church. They receive from the bishop the charge of a parish community or a determinate ecclesial office.

1596 Deacons are ministers ordained for tasks of service of the Church; they do not receive the ministerial priesthood, but ordination confers on them important functions in the ministry of the word, divine worship, pastoral governance, and the service of charity, tasks which they must carry out under the pastoral authority of their bishop.

1597 The sacrament of Holy Orders is conferred by the laying on of hands followed by a solemn prayer of consecration asking God to grant the ordinand the graces of the Holy Spirit required for his ministry. Ordination imprints an indelible sacramental character.

1598 The Church confers the sacrament of Holy Orders only on baptized men *(viri)*, whose suitability for the exercise of the ministry has been duly recognized. Church authority alone has the responsibility and right to call someone to receive the sacrament of Holy Orders.

1599 In the Latin Church the sacrament of Holy Orders for the presbyterate is normally conferred only on candidates who are ready to embrace celibacy freely and who publicly manifest their intention of staying celibate for the love of God's kingdom and the service of men.

1600 It is bishops who confer the sacrament of Holy Orders in the three degrees.

Endnotes

1. *LG,* 18.

2. St. Thomas Aquinas, *Hebr.* 8, 4.

3. Pius XII, encyclical, *Mediator Dei* : AAS, 39 (1947) 548.

4. St. Thomas Aquinas, *STh* III, 22, 4c.

5. *LG,* 21 § 2.

6. John Paul II, *Gift and Mystery: On the Fiftieth Anniversary of My Priestly Ordination,* (Doubleday, 1997), pp. 3-4.

7. Ibid., pp. 72-73.

8. Ibid., pp. 34-35.

Freedom

The power to choose between good and evil.

Chapter 17

Freedom

*H*ave you ever noticed that there are no dog or cat civilizations? Archeologists do not seek to discover lost ape cities. This is because God created only man with the ability to think, choose, and create.

God created man a rational being, conferring on him the dignity of a person who can initiate and control his own actions. "God willed that man should be 'left in the hand of his own counsel,' so that he might of his own accord seek his Creator and freely attain his full and blessed perfection by cleaving to him."[1]

"Man is rational and therefore like God; he is created with free will and is master over his acts."[2] (CCC 1730)

FREEDOM

True freedom is directly connected to doing God's will. Those who strive to do God's will in every instance are forming habits that will make it easier to avoid being a slave to sin.

> Freedom is the power, rooted in reason and will, to act or not to act, to do this or that, and so to perform deliberate actions on one's own responsibility. By free will one shapes one's own life. Human freedom is a force for growth and maturity in truth and goodness; it attains its perfection when directed toward God, our beatitude. (CCC 1731)

Often you hear people say they have the freedom to do whatever they want. Others say they have the freedom to do as they please as long as they do not hurt another person. Some say the government has the final say in how much freedom a person has. All these arguments are incorrect because they overlook the author of our freedom: God. He gave us freedom so we could choose to love and be loved by him, not so we could do whatever we want. Does it make sense to argue that the God who wishes us good would approve our doing evil? Of course not.

Man stands above all created things besides angels in his God-given ability to make choices. The more we make correct moral choices the more Christ-like we become and the greater our inner and outer beauty becomes. The choice to do as God intends is the choice to manifest Christ to others through self sacrifice. This is the secret of Mother Teresa of Calcutta. Her life was dedicated to serving Christ and following his will as she discovered that will in prayer.

> The more one does what is good, the freer one becomes. There is no true freedom except in the service of what is good and just. The choice to disobey and do evil is an abuse of freedom and leads to "the slavery of sin."[3] (CCC 1733)

In simple terms, the choice to do good or evil is a choice to form a habit. The more evil we do, the more difficult it becomes to stop, for we are forming a habit of being evil. Is it easier to stop watching television when we watch it regularly? Of course not. Well, it is the same with doing evil. Evil breeds evil.

In the same way, being good is a habit. Jesus told his followers to "be perfect, as your heavenly Father is perfect" (Mt 5: 48). It is obvious that if we are to imitate God, the imitation lies in forming habits of doing good rather than evil.

Since freedom is exercised in relationship with other human beings, we are obliged to recognize the freedom of others and respect their right to make choices as God intended. The right to freedom in choices of religion and moral matters is inalienable. It must be respected within the limits of law and the common good.

There are some who argue that they are not bound by moral laws that they have avoided learning or refuse to accept. This argument is similar to arguing that you don't have to write the correct answers on a test because you refused to learn them or refuse to accept them as true. Freedom is given to us to seek the truth so we can do as truth indicates.

God gave us freedom so we could choose to love and be loved by him, not so we could do whatever we want.

If we are to imitate God, the imitation lies in forming habits of doing good rather than evil.

Freedom

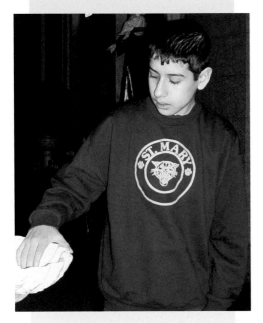

When we choose to sin, we violate freedom, rebel against God and his truth, harm our relationships with others, and imprison ourselves within our selfish desires.

Our responsibility for our actions can be reduced by fear, force, ignorance, habit, inattention, inordinate attachments, and psychological or social factors. However reduced the guilt, though, as long as we are aware of the choice we have made, we always bear some culpability for our actions.

FREEDOM AND SIN

We are all sinners and shall continue to be tempted to sin as long as we live. It is possible to reduce our tendencies to sin only by cooperating with God's grace and following the advice of our spiritual director. Sin does not make us bad persons. It reminds us that we must rely on God if we are to overcome our evil inclinations. Much like football players watching film of their most recent game to find their mistakes, we are led by the Church in Confession to see our flaws and are given direction to overcome them.

Correct political, social, economic, and cultural conditions also play a part in the reduction of sin.

At the present time, it appears that the greatest threat to the avoidance of sin is the culture. A limited examination of the culture in this country indicates that there is an assault on chastity at all levels. From the clothing people wear, to television, radio, and movie productions, the message is that "anything goes." With few exceptions, sexual activity outside marriage is depicted as the norm. The number one cause of death is not disease but abortion. In conditions such as these, a proper exercise of freedom requires that we avoid excessive exposure to cultural influences that could subtly influence us to accept and even act upon these false ideas.

Christ died on the Cross to set us free from the slavery of sin. St. John says that in Christ we have communion with the truth that sets us free (cf. Jn 8: 32).

FREEDOM AND GRACE

In the sacraments, we are freed from sin. We must pray to understand how to cooperate with Jesus to increase this sacramental grace.

In a moment of temptation, grace acts like a device that clears the air. We are tempted; then grace makes it easy to see the correct choice. We make the choice freely, while the grace of God points the way for us. It does not make the choice for us.

> *Freedom and grace.* The grace of Christ is not in the slightest way a rival of our freedom when this freedom accords with the sense of the true and the good that God has put in the human heart. On the contrary, as Christian experience attests especially in prayer, the more docile we are to the promptings of grace, the more we grow in inner freedom and confidence during trials, such as those we face in the pressures and constraints of the outer world. By the working of grace the Holy Spirit

educates us in spiritual freedom in order to make us free collaborators in his work in the Church and in the world:

> "Almighty and merciful God,
> in your goodness take away from us all that is harmful,
> so that, made ready both in mind and body,
> we may freely accomplish your will."[4] (CCC 1742)

CONSCIENCE

Isn't it amazing when we watch a large steel bridge open to permit a boat or barge to pass underneath? Hundreds of tons of steel rise into the air and return to place as if by magic, and it all happens in a matter of moments. The secret of the correct movement of that bridge is counter balances. They work together to keep the bridge from rising too high and becoming locked in place or coming down with a crash and destroying the mechanism.

Conscience operates in much the same way. A correctly formed conscience acts as a counter balance to keep us from becoming stuck in a morality that is too rigid or ignoring God's law and crashing into mortal sin because of wrong positions in our moral judgments.

> Conscience is a judgment of reason by which the human person recognizes the moral quality of a concrete act. (CCC 1796)

Along with the seed of God's eternal love, every human being is formed with a seed of conscience. This seed must be formed correctly so it will flower into a correctly formed conscience that will enable us to make correct moral judgments.

> "Deep within his conscience man discovers a law which he has not laid upon himself but which he must obey. Its voice, ever calling him to love and to do what is good and to avoid evil, sounds in his heart at the right moment....For man has in his heart a law inscribed by God....His conscience is man's most secret core and his sanctuary. There he is alone with God whose voice echoes in his depths."[5] (CCC 1776)

Conscience is a gift from God to enable us to demonstrate our love for him by doing good and avoiding evil. Man uses his reason, informed by the teaching of the Church, to make concrete moral judgments about whether a contemplated action is good or evil. The key to the correct formation of conscience is truth. Just as a building cannot be built safely using incorrect data, likewise, conscience cannot be formed correctly using false data.

Many people struggle with the problem of good and evil because they do not understand that the only way love can be demonstrated is by doing good. There is no love in asking someone to sin with you. How can there be love in an act that requires your neighbor to sin with you and offend God?

FORMATION OF CONSCIENCE

The key to correct moral choices is the correct formation of conscience. For Catholics, this means accepting the teaching of the Church. Christ has

Conscience is a gift from God to enable us to demonstrate our love for him by doing good and avoiding evil.

The key to the correct formation of conscience is truth.

Freedom

When we are having difficulty overcoming a particular sin, a serious self-examination must be made to determine whether it is our choice of friends which has led us into sin.

given us a Church to indicate the correct moral choices for us. The Magisterium guides us by correct interpretation of Sacred Scripture and Sacred Tradition.

A properly formed conscience points the way to correct moral choices in all cases. It is upright and truthful, approves good choices, and denounces those that are evil. God speaks through the conscience. Many people say they hear a "voice" urging them to make the correct moral choice when they are tempted.

> Conscience is a judgment of reason whereby the human person recognizes the moral quality of a concrete act that he is going to perform, is in the process of performing, or has already completed. (CCC 1778)

Since man is led by conscience to do good, he is required to follow the good his conscience urges him to do. It is by following his conscience that man follows divine law, so he must always obey the certain judgment of his conscience. God is the witness to every moral choice we make. He is there at our side assisting us through his grace to make the correct moral choice.

Often we hear some persons referred to as animals. This statement indicates that these persons have lost their ability to make correct moral choices and now respond to stimuli and instinct much as animals respond to stimuli and instinct.

Man, made in God's image, is required to act as God would act in the same situation.

Conscience is formed from:

† Knowing the principles of morality;

† Knowing how to apply the conscience in given circumstances for practical judgments;

† Making concrete judgments about acts considered or performed;

† Regular Confession;

† Praying.

Prudence is required to make correct moral choices. It is acquired by daily examination of the moral choices we make. Those who keep committing the same sins repeatedly are not examining their choices to avoid committing the same sins.

Many people are unable to cease sinning because they refuse to accept the fact that the company they keep is the origin of their sin. When we are having difficulty overcoming a particular sin, a serious self-examination must be made to determine whether it is our choice of friends which has led us into sin.

Every moral choice has the potential to lead us to sin; every moral choice presents the opportunity to bring us closer to Christ. There is no such thing as a sin that causes no harm. If the whole history of the world was changed by the single sin of Adam, it should be evident that sin has serious consequences.

TYPES OF CONSCIENCE

A *true conscience* is a conscience that has been formed correctly, according to the demands of the divine law and the teachings of the Church. It knows which moral choices are correct and which moral choices are wrong.

An *erroneous conscience* does not know in all cases what is the correct moral choice. If the person making the wrong moral choice had no way to know the correct moral choice, he is not guilty of sin, and this is referred to as *invincible* ignorance (ignorance that can't be overcome).

If the person making the wrong moral choice had the opportunity to learn the correct choice and refused or avoided discovering the truth, he is guilty of sin. This is called *vincible* ignorance (ignorance which could have been overcome).

It is always possible to make incorrect moral choices, so there is an obligation to form one's conscience correctly. Those who have blinded themselves by habitual sin or refusal to learn the truth are guilty of sin in their choices that led to sinful habits.

A *doubtful conscience* is one in which the person is not sure of the sinfulness of an act being considered. When one is not sure of the morality of the choice being contemplated, there is a serious moral obligation to discover the truth before making the choice. To act without ascertaining the correct moral choice indicates that you don't care whether the choice is moral or not.

Jesus died to make it possible to know the truth that will set us free.

It is a struggle to return the love of a God who has loved us even unto death.

CONCLUSION

Conscience is the practical judgment of reason which leads a person to make correct moral choices. Correct choices can only be made when the person making them has the truth. We would scoff at those who willingly ran in front of a train or jumped into the deep end of an empty swimming pool. Yet, foolish choices such as these would be far less serious than a choice not to inform one's conscience, which could lead to the loss of one's soul. Man has been given the dignity of being like God, and man is truly like God only to the extent that he acts as God would act in all the moral situations in which he finds himself. Jesus died to make it possible to know the truth that will set us free. It is not simply a struggle to make the correct choice. It is a struggle to return the love of a God who has loved us even unto death. There is no greater or more rewarding struggle.

SUPPLEMENTARY READING

The Freedom of Honesty and Integrity

One statesman of the Middle Ages stands out as a giant of the faith—St. Thomas More. He was Lord Chancellor of England, lawyer, theologian, philosopher, author, diplomat, counselor, teacher, sheriff of London, member of Parliament, and a friend of the great men of his time. His public speaking abilities were unmatched. He was married with one daughter and three sons, though he had considered the priesthood—even living in a monastery for four years. He was an ordinary Christian trying to balance daily Mass and prayer, family life, his work as a lawyer, and his literary and historical studies. While known for his integrity, his splendid court garments often hid a hair shirt and his smile sometimes hid his hunger from regular fasting.

Though he was old friends with King Henry VIII, he decided to resign his post as Chancellor because he opposed the king's divorce. Later, when he refused to sign the Act of Succession stating that the children of Henry VIII and his second wife Anne Boleyn were rightful heirs to the throne, he was imprisoned in the Tower of London. He was thoroughly convinced that no worldly ruler had jurisdiction over the Church of Jesus Christ—so convinced that he was willing to give up his life.

While he was imprisoned before his trial, he continued to keep his good humor. He would dress up on feast days and continued to wear his hair shirt. While in prison, he composed a beautiful prayer in which he exclaimed:

"Grant me, my Lord, a desire to be with you, not so as to avoid the calamities of this world, nor even to avoid the pains of purgatory nor those of hell, not to gain the

St. Thomas More
(1478-1535)
Feast: June 22
Silent Patron of England
Patron of Lawyers and Politicians

joys of Heaven, not out of consideration for my own profit, but simply through true love for Thee."

After a hasty trial, he was sentenced to death by beheading. In a letter to his daughter Margaret (Meg) about his unworthiness to be a martyr, he wrote:

"Although I know well, Margaret, that because of my past wickedness I deserve to be abandoned by God, I cannot but trust in his merciful goodness...I will not mistrust him, Meg, though I shall feel myself weakening and on the verge of being overcome with fear...I trust he shall place his holy hand on me and in the stormy seas hold me up from drowning...Nothing can come but what God wills. And I am very sure that whatever that be, however bad it may seem, it shall indeed be the best." Continued

SUPPLEMENTARY READING CONTINUED

On the scaffold before the executioner's blade fell, Thomas More said to the crowd: *"I die the king's good servant, but God's first."*

Many times today we are faced with the decision to follow God or to follow the crowd—we cannot do both! The devil often uses human respect as a way to tempt us from what God lovingly asks of us. Satan makes us a slave to the ever-changing opinions of others.

Let us pray the words of freedom written by St. Thomas More while he was in the Tower of London,

"Give me thy grace, good Lord,…to have my mind well united to you; to not depend on the changing opinions of others…so that I may think joyfully of God and tenderly implore his help. So that I may lean on God's strength and make an effort to love him…"

VOCABULARY

CULPABILITY
Moral responsibility for one's actions.

DOUBTFUL CONSCIENCE
Somewhat of a contradiction in terms as it is a judgment to hesitate in passing judgment on the moral character of an act.

ERRONEOUS CONSCIENCE
Judgment of the practical intellect that decides from false principles considered as true that something is lawful which in fact is unlawful.

FREE WILL
The ability to shape one's own life.

FREEDOM
The power, rooted in reason and will, to act or not act, to do this or that, and so to perform deliberately on one's own responsibility.

INVINCIBLE IGNORANCE
Lack of knowledge, either of fact or of law, for which a person is not morally responsible due to the difficulty of the object of the knowledge, scarcity of evidence, insufficient time or talent in the person, or some other factor.

REASON
That intellectual power or faculty which is ordinarily employed by man in adapting thought or action to some end; the guiding principle of the human mind in the process of thinking.

TRUE CONSCIENCE
Judgment of the practical intellect that deduces correctly from true principles that some act is lawful.

VINCIBLE IGNORANCE
Lack of knowledge for which a person is morally responsible due to lack of diligence.

STUDY QUESTIONS

1. How does man differ from all other animals? Who decided it should be this way?

2. According to the Catechism of the Catholic Church, where is freedom rooted?

3. Does man have free will so he can do whatever he wants? Why did God give us freedom?

4. How does doing evil in one instance lead to doing evil again? Does the same apply to doing good?

5. Do people have a right to freedom in choices of religious and moral matters?

6. What are the harmful effects of sin?

7. What are some aspects of our culture that encourage sin?

8. Does grace force us to act in a certain way?

9. How does cooperating with grace make us more free?

10. Why does man have a conscience? Is he required to follow it?

11. What are five activities that form the conscience?

12. Is a person who is unaware of moral laws bound by those laws? When is this person guilty of sin?

PRACTICAL EXERCISES

1. Watch the movie *Gandhi.* Who is free and who is enslaved? What tactics are used to achieve freedom?

2. At the beginning of his ministry John Paul II echoed the words of St. Peter at Pentecost by proclaiming, "Do not be afraid!" Contrast positive freedom, "freedom to," and negative freedom, "freedom from." Which of these is most like Christian freedom? Why?

3. Compare and contrast physical laws and moral laws. Why do you think God felt it necessary to reveal one but not the other? How does the truth set us free to: eat, fly, drive cars, SCUBA dive, become friends, or even become saints?

FROM THE CATECHISM

1743 "God willed that man should be left in the hand of his own counsel (cf. Sir 15:14), so that he might of his own accord seek his creator and freely attain his full and blessed perfection by cleaving to him" (*GS*, 17 § 1).

1744 Freedom is the power to act or not to act, and so to perform deliberate acts of one's own. Freedom attains perfection in its acts when directed toward God, the sovereign Good.

1745 Freedom characterizes properly human acts. It makes the human being responsible for acts of which he is the voluntary agent. His deliberate acts properly belong to him.

1746 The imputability or responsibility for an action can be diminished or nullified by ignorance, duress, fear, and other psychological or social factors.

1747 The right to the exercise of freedom, especially in religious and moral matters, is an inalienable requirement of the dignity of man. But the exercise of freedom does not entail the putative right to say or do anything.

1748 "For freedom Christ has set us free" (Gal 5:1).

Endnotes

1. *GS*, 17; Sir 15:14.
2. St. Irenaeus, *Adv. haeres.* 4, 4, 3: PG 7/1, 983.
3. Sf. Rom 6:17.
4. *Roman Missal,* 32nd Sunday, Opening Prayer: *Omnipotens et misericors Deus, universa nobis adversantia propitiatus exclude, ut, mente et corpore pariter expediti, quae tua sunt liberis mentibus exsequamur.*
5. *GS*, 16.

The Moral Virtues

Prudence, Justice, Fortitude, Temperance.

Chapter 18

The Moral Virtues

*O*ur culture has great respect for persons of strength and physical perfection. Marathons are popular events in which thousands of people take part. They are run every year in many of the major cities in the country. All over America, health clubs have sprung up, where people work out daily to increase their strength and perfect their bodies. Weightlifting is a recognized Olympic event.

While physical health is thought by many to be a necessity, moral perfection does not often receive the same respect. Unfortunately, people do not usually apply the principles they learn at health clubs to their moral lives. Human moral perfection requires daily effort too. Just as certain principles make physical perfection possible, so other principles make moral perfection possible. Moral perfection is possible through the application of the moral virtues to one's life.

THE MORAL VIRTUES

God made us to love and be loved. The love of which we are capable is not restricted only to persons, for we are capable of loving many things. A virtuous person can truly be said to be in love with goodness. Virtuous persons understand clearly that God has made them for good and to be good in imitation of his perfection. The completely virtuous person can be said to have transformed all human capacities and mastered true love of God.

Stop for a moment and consider working with someone who never bathed or brushed his or her teeth. It would be difficult, to say the least. We encounter the same difficulty when dealing with someone who is dishonest and is always telling lies. For persons to live in harmony, they need to acquire human virtues. Society cannot function as God intended without virtuous people.

A virtue is a habitual and firm disposition to do the good. Virtues enable a person to act well by shaping the mind to choose good actions. Human virtues are firm attitudes, stable dispositions, and perfections of the will that govern our actions, control the passions, and guide human conduct according to faith and right reason. The virtues do not suppress our urges but order them according to the mind of Christ. They place them under control of the mind.

Perfection in human virtue leads to a sense of peace and joy based on the mastery of oneself. Virtuous persons freely practice the good that God requires and that their neighbor has a right to expect.

Prudence, justice, fortitude, and temperance play a pivotal role in the life of virtue, so they are called the *cardinal virtues* after the Latin word, *cardo,* which means "hinge." All the other virtues hinge or depend on the cardinal virtues for their success.

> Four virtues play a pivotal role and accordingly are called "cardinal"; all the others are grouped around them. They are: prudence, justice, fortitude, and temperance. "If anyone loves righteousness, [Wisdom's] labors are virtues; for she teaches temperance, and prudence, justice, and courage."[1] These virtues are praised under other names in many passages of Scripture. (CCC 1805)

These virtues grow through instruction, perseverance in struggle, and regular choices to act morally, and they are elevated and perfected by God's grace.

The Bible does not present these virtues in an organized manner, for it is not a manual of theology. In both the Old and New Testaments, there are moral rules and prohibitions, but they are not presented in an organized fashion. The wisdom books present ideas regarding morality to appeal to the moral judgment of the reflective reader.

The cardinal virtues demand human effort and are acquired through prayer, docility, and the repetition of virtuous actions joined to the life of grace acquired through the sacraments. Sanctifying grace raises the cardinal virtues to a higher level.

Correct moral choices should be based on loving the God who loved us first. When we act out of love for God, we find ourselves coming face-to-face with him.

Society cannot function as God intended without virtuous people.

The virtues do not suppress our urges but order them according to the mind of Christ.

The prudent person acquires the habit of examining every action in light of its capacity to bring him closer to God.

Conscience is its guide.

THE VIRTUE OF PRUDENCE

Prudence is the virtue that disposes practical reason to discern our true good in every circumstance and to choose the right means of achieving it; "the prudent man looks where he is going."[2] "Keep sane and sober for your prayers."[3] Prudence is "right reason in action," writes St. Thomas Aquinas, following Aristotle.[4] It is not to be confused with timidity or fear, nor with duplicity or dissimulation. It is called *auriga virtutum* (the charioteer of the virtues); it guides the other virtues by setting rule and measure. It is prudence that immediately guides the judgment of conscience. The prudent man determines and directs his conduct in accordance with this judgment. With the help of this virtue we apply moral principles to particular cases without error and overcome doubts about the good to achieve and the evil to avoid. (CCC 1806)

Prudence establishes a right norm or standard for human conduct. It applies moral principles to particular moral choices here and now. Its aim is to develop the intellectual capacity so that it will habitually make correct moral choices.

Prudence in action is practical reasoning. Prudence requires foresight to operate successfully. The prudent person acquires the habit of examining every action in light of its capacity to bring him closer to God. Conscience is its guide. Conscience applies principles and sound moral judgment to every decision that has a moral component. Both the means to achieve a moral action and the correct action are the subject of prudence.

Prudence signifies the wisdom called for in the Old Testament. The prudent person has put on the mind of God, which can transform all his choices. Prudence has its origin in the Holy Spirit and is directed toward him. The prudent man is saved from decisions based on an erroneous conscience by his possession of moral truth.

The operation of all the infused virtues is made possible by the existence of the theological virtues (faith, hope, and love) in a person. A prudent person has joined knowledge of morality to love of God in the quest for perfection, and this leads directly to a sense of joy and tranquility.

Like any virtue, prudence is acquired over time, and its success is tied directly to a regular examination of moral choices both before and after a particular act is willed. For this reason, the Church recommends daily examination of conscience as a stepping stone to acquiring prudence. A person is not prudent until he is able to make correct moral judgments by himself and act on them in light of his own experience. Prudence can be perfected through spiritual direction.

A prudent choice includes three moments: counsel, judgment, and command. Counsel involves rational deliberation regarding the means to an end and presupposes the knowledge of the required truth and control of the emotions to ensure they do not hinder a correct choice.

Judgment confirms the means selected as morally best in this particular situation.

Command is an act of the intellect upon judgment to make the choice, and the choice to do or to avoid an action. Upon completion of these three components, the will chooses.

It must be kept in mind that there are situations in which prudence could also preclude choosing what is moral. For example, consider a situation in which a thief steals a bike. After searching, the person who has lost the bike locates it in the thief's yard, where there are two vicious dogs. Although the victim of the theft has a right to enter the yard and reclaim his property, prudence would dictate he refrain from doing so under this circumstance.

THE VIRTUE OF JUSTICE

> *Justice* is the moral virtue that consists in the constant and firm will to give their due to God and neighbor. Justice toward God is called the "virtue of religion." Justice toward men disposes one to respect the rights of each and to establish in human relationships the harmony that promotes equity with regard to persons and to the common good. The just man, often mentioned in the Sacred Scriptures, is distinguished by habitual right thinking and the uprightness of his conduct toward his neighbor. "You shall not be partial to the poor or defer to the great, but in righteousness shall you judge your neighbor."[5] "Masters, treat your slaves justly and fairly, knowing that you also have a Master in heaven."[6] (CCC 1807)

Justice is the moral virtue that enables a person steadfastly to will what is right with regard to what is due to God and neighbor. It is an impersonal measure regulated by nature, law, or prior agreement and is done free from the intrusion of human feeling. Just persons are guided by even-handedness in relation to others. It is true love of neighbor in action. A just person is able more happily, easily, and readily to control his dealings with others, whether God or man.

As an example, consider the offer by John to purchase a house from Harry. In justice, Harry owes John a statement of any serious defects in the house, and provision should be made for Harry to compensate John for the expense of repairing the defects. John has a right to be treated with justice by Harry.

Giving your neighbor his just due is required because your neighbor has individual, personal rights. A right is the moral quality or capability of doing, omitting, or demanding some action. Some rights based on natural law arise out of the personal dignity of a child of God; such rights include the right to life, the right to marriage and children, and the right to employment. Other rights are determined in laws made by the consent of the people or legitimate public authority. In applying justice to society, the Christian seeks to strike a balance between individual rights and the common good.

General justice regulates the obligations that members of society have toward the common good, the well-being of society. It is the act of each member of society rendering what is due to the common good.

Public authority has the right and obligation to determine by just legislation what general justice requires. Some examples are the right to collect taxes, set up courts, and raise an army for the defense of the country. Societies in which there is a respect for justice based on the eternal law offer the best opportunity for the individual to save his soul.

Justice is the moral virtue that enables a person to will what is right with regard to what is due to God and neighbor.

In applying justice to society, the Christian seeks to strike a balance between individual rights and the common good.

> *The Christian who lives justly is directed toward perfecting the city of man so that it more closely approximates the city of God.*

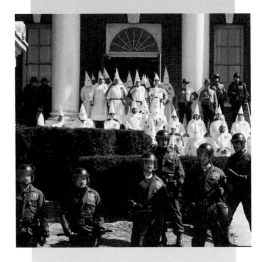

> *Injustice is a sin that damages the perpetrator, the recipient, and in many instances the community at large.*

True Christian social justice is always based on attaining the common good. Since true freedom is directed toward the good, the Christian who lives justly is directed toward perfecting the city of man so that it more closely approximates the city of God. This is part and parcel of every Christian's vocation.

Particular justice is divided into *distributive* and *commutative* justice.

Commutative justice protects rights and strives to attain equal justice between two persons. Commutative justice is not based on the equality between two persons but rather is based on what one owes the other as a result of some agreement or transaction. It seeks to establish an objective balance between individual persons or groups of persons. Actions contrary to the good of the person or the community require restitution.

Distributive justice regulates what an individual receives as a just share of the common good. It is aimed at securing a fair proportion of the benefits that society distributes to its members. It regulates how public taxing authorities take money for taxation from the whole of society and return it to parts of the society, with complete respect for the dignity of each person and the well-being of society at large.

As an example, consider taxation to support education. Every family that has children attending school has a right to a proportional share of the taxes levied for education to educate their child or children, although that is not currently the case in the United States. All public authority should distribute goods, honors, and spiritual goods on the basis of proportionate need without favoritism. Racism is a prime example of a failure to operate without favoritism.

The virtue of justice also deals with the individual's requirement to treat his own person as the image of God with dignity. Therefore, willful harm to oneself is forbidden as a matter of justice.

It must be kept in mind that injustice is a sin that damages the perpetrator, the recipient, and in many instances the community at large.

Restitution is required to make amends for unjust acts. Restitution is an act of commutative justice that compensates for unjust injury or restores to a person or group something of which it has been deprived. In the main, it involves restoring whatever external goods have been unjustly taken to restore the balance that existed prior to the unjust act.

THE VIRTUE OF FORTITUDE

> *Fortitude* is the moral virtue that ensures firmness in difficulties and constancy in the pursuit of the good. It strengthens the resolve to resist temptations and to overcome obstacles in the moral life. The virtue of fortitude enables one to conquer fear, even fear of death, and to face trials and persecutions. It disposes one even to renounce and sacrifice his life in defense of a just cause. "The Lord is my strength and my song."[7] "In the world you have tribulation; but be of good cheer, I have overcome the world."[8] (CCC 1808)

Fortitude uses personal discipline to control the irascible appetite, which comes into play when the emotions of fear and daring are energized.

Irascible appetites are aroused when one is faced with special evils that cause great fear, which could lead to weakening or overcoming the will.

Fortitude is the virtue that enables us to control the passion of fear so that we don't abandon a good action out of fear or commit a foolhardy action out of pride. It enables a person to endure the dangers and difficulties of life, even the danger of death, whether death occurs naturally or through martyrdom. The person of fortitude holds on to the good despite every obstacle, whereas the coward refuses to endure the afflictions that fighting for the good necessitates. The grace given by the Spirit in support of virtue enables the recipient to act rightly in the face of what is difficult or evil.

Martyrdom, dying for Christ, is the highest act of fortitude. It is the most prudent act one can choose. To die for Christ or to offer one's life in defense of one's neighbor, who is made in the image of Christ, is the highest act of love. Fortitude is impossible without love. A martyr willingly gives up human life to attain eternal life. Those who die martyrs for Christ emulate Christ, who died for the truth.

The first four letters of the word fortitude, "fort-," are a pattern for this virtue.

A fort is something strong and difficult to overcome, and the virtue of fortitude implies a strength of mind that can overcome all difficulties. It is a form of spiritual bravery.

Brave men endure nobly all the evils of life, including death itself. Among all the saints listed in the Roman martyrology, soldiers are at the top of the list. Nor is fortitude a virtue of the moment, for it often requires great endurance, as the witness of the many martyrs of the twentieth century demonstrates.

Difficulties are a part of life. Standing up for the truth of Christ is one of life's greatest difficulties.

An American bishop referred to the present time as a period of "dry martyrdom." For most of us, it is not death that will have to be faced but the constant ridicule and rejection of our Christian beliefs, both by the media and by those with whom we come in daily contact. Today in America, no one is killed for following Christ, but many Christians must face the constant mockery of their pseudo-Christian friends day after day, like so many shallow cuts of a razor blade. It is often our own brothers and sisters who laugh at us as being out-dated because we defend the pope or the Church.

Fortitude takes two forms, *active* and *passive*.

Active fortitude moves a person to face evil and attack it without being foolhardy. A high school student who refuses to smoke dope when pressured by his friends demonstrates active fortitude.

Passive fortitude strengthens a person to bear up when faced by great evil, even death. The many martyrs who died for Christ in the last century exhibited passive fortitude.

In the former rite of Confirmation, the bishop administered a slight slap on the cheek to remind the confirmed that he was expected to suffer for Christ, a suffering that might include death itself.

To die for Christ or to offer one's life in defense of one's neighbor, who is made in the image of Christ, is the highest act of love.

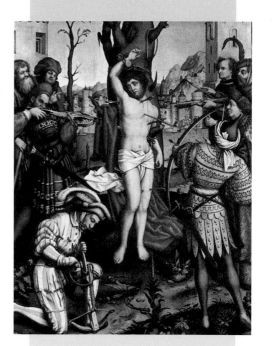

Saint Sebastian

Died a martyr c. 288 – Emperor Diocletian ordered archers to execute Sebastian, a soldier in the Roman army and Christian responsible for many converts. The arrows hit him and he was left for dead, but he didn't die. A Christian woman found him and nursed him back to health. Sebastian continued to denounce the Emperor for his cruelty to Christians. He was again sentenced to die, this time he was beaten to death.

Moderation is the virtuous middle between the extremes of none and all.

The Penance of Mary Magdalene

St. Mary Magdalene is a great example of a sinner whom grace changed into a saint. Her jar of ointment is a sign of love and repentance.

The enemies of fortitude are cowardice, fearlessness, and foolhardiness.

Cowardice is inordinate fear of the evils that must be faced in life, particularly pain and death. Fearlessness is total lack of fear; it demonstrates a lack of balance in dealing with the evils that must be faced in life. Foolhardiness is rushing into every danger or evil in life without considering the consequences beforehand.

Another enemy of fortitude is self-indulgence. Easy living tends to weaken a person's resolve, for where there is little sacrifice, there is little challenge to be a person of strong will.

Without the virtue of fortitude, it is impossible to face life's trials and defeats.

THE VIRTUE OF TEMPERANCE

> *Temperance* is the moral virtue that moderates the attraction of pleasures and provides balance in the use of created goods. It ensures the will's mastery over instincts and keeps desires within the limits of what is honorable. The temperate person directs the sensitive appetites toward what is good and maintains a healthy discretion: "Do not follow your inclination and strength, walking according to the desires of your heart."[9] Temperance is often praised in the Old Testament: "Do not follow your base desires, but restrain your appetites."[10] In the New Testament it is called "moderation" or "sobriety." We ought "to live sober, upright, and godly lives in this world."[11] (CCC 1809)

Temperance is perhaps the virtue most under attack in the present culture. Magazines, movies, media, and music send the message, "Do whatever feels good to you." Sex is used to sell everything from automobiles to housewares. In effect, the culture has made the denial of temperance one of its tenets.

Christ's Church offers the infused virtue of temperance as an antidote to this madness.

Moderation is an excellent synonym for temperance. Moderation is the virtuous middle between the extremes of none and all. Human drives are meant to serve human needs to enable man to live temperately and to moderate the drives of passion. Temperance should be a way of life.

Food, drink, goods, and sexuality are the things God has given to man for the continuance of the human race. The desire for pleasure is morally neutral, but desire must be made subject to reason. Nature draws us to these goods by our need for love and our desire for pleasure. However, in choosing to seek pleasure, a person must choose what is objectively good, that is, the true good. The temperate person seeks pleasure based on the Creator's plan for his moral existence.

It is possible to sin by wanting too much or too little of a good thing, such as food, or by desiring something contrary to the Creator's plan for human nature, such as sex outside of marriage.

Unfortunately, a major effect of original sin is that it is a constant struggle to control our senses with our will. Often, you hear someone called an animal. Animals are instinctive creatures who respond to preprogrammed desires without choice or self-control. When a human being is called an animal, it is an indication that the person has lost self-control and responds instinctively without control. Our desires for food, drink, things, and sexuality must be controlled or else they will control us.

Supernatural temperance promotes the health of both soul and body. It moderates those senses that are motivated by touch. To be temperate, one must admit one's true biological needs but reject one's attractions to many sensual pleasures.

St. Thomas Aquinas pointed out that a sinner does not see a choice between sinning or not sinning as a choice between a good and evil. Rather, the sinner sees the choice as between two goods. Temperate choices are made in conformity with the true good. Choices that are truly temperate enable a person to perfect himself and promote his overall well-being. For example, consider the evidence accumulated by medical professionals that a properly balanced diet enables a person to live a healthier life. Temperate persons would make use of this information to eat balanced diets to protect their well-being; intemperate persons would ignore the recommendations.

Many modern media presentations are directed toward overcoming the public's sense of shame by presenting in public actions that by their nature are private or by promoting gross activity for its own sake. Thus, the natural human desire to know becomes corrupted through the presentation of material that has a stimulating effect. These presentations destroy the sense of shame. They also blur the distinction between what is appropriate pleasure within one's state in life and what is excess. The term applied to this is the "consumerist mentality." Everyone is encouraged to purchase whatever goods they desire without regard to whether they are needed or appropriate to their state in life.

The sins against temperance are insensibility and intemperance.

In the current cultural climate, it may seem out of order to discuss the vice of insensibility. Insensibility is the vice of a man who rejects pleasure to the extent that he omits things necessary to live as prescribed by the divine law and reason. Someone who willfully refuses to eat enough to keep himself healthy or refuses to go to a doctor when suffering from a serious illness would be guilty of insensibility.

Intemperance is another vice opposed to temperance. The intemperate person seeks pleasures contrary to the moral law and right reason. Intemperance opposes itself to reason and gradually destroys a person's will to overcome his desires for sinful pleasures. Those who get drunk are intemperate.

A sense of both honor and shame is necessary for the practice of temperance. Honor promotes a sense of propriety and rejects moral ugliness. A human act is honorable when it possesses a certain degree of perfection that arouses respect and praise. A sense of shame reminds a person that there exist lines, not to be crossed, between what is acceptable and what is unacceptable. Those who are shameless are capable of the worst moral crimes.

A sense of shame reminds a person that there exist lines, not to be crossed, between what is acceptable and what is gross. Those who are shameless are capable of the worst moral crimes.

The Moral Virtues

Four pivotal human virtues: prudence, justice, fortitude, and temperance.

The human virtues are stable dispositions of the intellect and will that govern our acts, order our passions, and guide our conduct in accordance with reason and faith.

Justice

Raphael's personification of Justice holding her symbols, weighing scales and a sword. Justice was said by Plato to play a decisive role among the cardinal virtues.

CONCLUSION

What makes Christian morality distinctive is that its starting point is non-Christian. The moral virtues do not rely on Christian revelation. In fact, they can be found in the writings of non-Christian thinkers like Plato and Aristotle. This fact illustrates the point that one does not need to be a Christian in order to be prudent, just, temperate, or fortitudinous. All human beings, even pagans, are supposed to exercise the cardinal virtues, for they help us lead happy, healthy lives.

As we will see in the next chapter, the cardinal virtues make us more able to practice the theological virtues. Faith, hope, and charity presuppose prudence, justice, temperance, and fortitude and go beyond them. Each of the theological virtues is a step beyond a cardinal virtue; therefore, one cannot exercise the theological virtues without first practicing the cardinal virtues.

SUPPLEMENTARY READING

Racism is one of the great lies in today's culture. This idea completely contradicts the moral virtues. It defies the reasoning of prudence, the will of fortitude, the sensibility of temperance, and most obviously the amiability of justice. In the 21st century, America continues to face this great demonic influence.

Few have helped to destroy the roots of racism to the same degree as Katharine Drexel. Born one of three daughters of a rich banker, she learned from her parents that wealth was to be shared with the less fortunate. When her father died, he left the three daughters an estate worth more than $15 million (in 1885 money!). After hearing of the plight of the Indians, Katharine asked Pope Leo XIII what should be her vocation. He replied with all simplicity, "Why not become a missionary yourself, my child?"

Now, she continued to give charitably, but in the words of John Paul II, "She understood that more was needed. With great courage in God's grace, she chose to give not just her fortune but her whole life, totally, to the Lord." She founded the Congregation of the Sisters of the Most Holy Sacrament for Indians and Colored People. Along with establishing over 60 schools (including Xavier University in New Orleans, the first Catholic university for African-Americans) and doing missionary work, her Order brought the Eucharist to thousands.

She founded the Catholic Indian Bureau in Washington, D.C. In many things, she relied on divine intervention. When she ran into trouble with the Ku Klux Klan in Texas, the head klansman was struck dead by a lightning bolt during one of their meetings.

St. Katharine Drexel
(1858-1955)
Feast on March 3
Founder of the Congregation of Sisters
of the Most Holy Sacrament for
Indians and Colored People

Mother Katharine's speeches were ahead of their time in opposing segregation, demanding educational opportunities for non-Caucasians, and exposing biased press reports.

According to John Paul II, Katharine Drexel taught her sisters a "spirituality based on a praying union with the Lord in the Eucharist and in the service of the poor and victims of racial discrimination." In addition, "Her apostolate served to highlight the growing concern over the need to combat all forms of racism through education and social service." It is estimated that Katharine Drexel gave away over $14 million by the time of her death in 1955, most of it to works she had established for American Indians and African-Americans.

VOCABULARY

CARDINAL VIRTUES
Four pivotal human virtues: prudence, justice, fortitude, and temperance. The human virtues are stable dispositions of the intellect and will that govern our acts, order our passions, and guide our conduct in accordance with reason and faith.

COMMUTATIVE JUSTICE
Regulates exchanges between persons and between institutions in accordance with a strict respect for their rights, i.e. fulfilling contracts.

DISTRIBUTIVE JUSTICE
Regulates what the community owes its citizens in proportion to their contributions and needs.

FORTITUDE
One of the four cardinal moral virtues which ensures firmness in difficulties and constancy in doing the good.

GENERAL JUSTICE
Steadfastly willing what is right with regards to society or the common good.

INSENSIBILITY
Purposeful deprivation of physical feeling or sensation.

INTEMPERANCE
Lack of moderation or restraint; excess in any kind of action; excessive indulgence of any passion or appetite.

JUSTICE
The cardinal moral virtue which consists in the constant and firm will to give their due to God and to neighbor.

MODERATION
See temperance.

MORALITY
The goodness or evil of human acts. The morality of human acts depends on the object (or nature) of the action, the intention or end foreseen, and the circumstances in which it takes place.

PRUDENCE
The virtue which disposes a person to discern the good and choose the correct means to accomplish it. One of the cardinal moral virtues that dispose the Christian to live according to the law of Christ.

RESTITUTION
The return of what has been unjustly taken from another.

TEMPERANCE
The cardinal moral virtue that moderates the attraction of pleasure and provides balance in the use of created goods. It ensures the mastery of the will over instinct, and keeps natural desires within proper limits.

VIRTUE
A habitual and firm disposition to do the good.

STUDY QUESTIONS

1. A virtuous person directs his or her love toward what human act?

2. How do virtues enable a person to act well?

3. What are the qualities of human virtues?

4. To where does perfection in human virtue lead?

5. How do virtues grow?

6. What does prudence establish?

7. What guides prudence?

8. How is prudence acquired?

9. What does a prudent choice include?

10. What are the fruits of acting justly?

11. What is the highest act of fortitude?

12. What are active and passive fortitude?

13. List and explain the enemies of fortitude.

14. What does temperance promote?

PRACTICAL EXERCISES

1. As we grow in virtue, we must learn to: 1) do the *right* things that we don't want to do and 2) avoid the *wrong* things we want to do. Explain how the virtues of fortitude and temperance are necessary to perform these complementary actions. What vices prevent us from doing these two things?

2. In his autobiography, Ben Franklin presented a system in which he worked on just one virtue every week while not concerning himself with the others. This focused method allowed each virtue to become more of a habit. What virtues do you most need to work on? For ideas see his book or discuss this with your spiritual director, parents, and friends. Try the Franklin method and see if you don't begin to grow in virtue.

3. Virtue comes from the Latin word *virtus*. What other Latin and English words share this root? Have you ever thought of the virtues as "strong"?

4. In 1999, Pope John Paul II said that sports competition can promote "attitudes which give birth to the most noble human virtues… solidarity, loyalty, proper behavior, and respect for others." He also said that athletes should be encouraged to grow in "good will, patience, perseverance, a sense of equilibrium, sobriety, a spirit of sacrifice, and self-control." He noted that this is particularly true of team sports and when opposing teams are viewed as competitors rather than enemies. See if you can be an assistant coach for a team of younger kids (maybe your own siblings) and help instill in them the moral virtues.

FROM THE CATECHISM

1833 Virtue is a habitual and firm disposition to do good.

1834 The human virtues are stable dispositions of the intellect and the will that govern our acts, order our passions, and guide our conduct in accordance with reason and faith. They can be grouped around the four cardinal virtues: prudence, justice, fortitude, and temperance.

1835 Prudence disposes the practical reason to discern, in every circumstance, our true good and to choose the right means for achieving it.

1836 Justice consists in the firm and constant will to give God and neighbor their due.

1837 Fortitude ensures firmness in difficulties and constancy in the pursuit of the good.

1838 Temperance moderates the attraction of the pleasures and the senses and provides balance in the use of created goods.

1839 The moral virtues grow through education, deliberate acts, and perseverance in struggle. Divine grace purifies and elevates them.

Endnotes

1. Wis 8:7.
2. Prv 14:15.
3. 1 Pt 4:7.
4. St. Thomas Aquinas, *STh* II-II, 47, 2.
5. Lv 19:15.
6. Col 4:1.
7. Ps 118:14.
8. Jn 16:33.
9. Sir 5:2; cf. 37:27-31.
10. Sir 18:30.
11. Ti 2:12.

The First Commandment

True worship belongs only to the Lord.

Chapter 19

The First Commandment

*W*hen the people saw that Moses delayed to come down from the mountain, the people gathered themselves together to Aaron, and said to him, "Up, make us gods, who shall go before us; as for this Moses, the man who brought us up out of the land of Egypt, we do not know what has become of him." And Aaron said to them, "Take off the rings of gold which are in the ears of your wives, your sons, and your daughters, and bring them to me." So all the people took off the rings of gold that were in their ears, and brought them to Aaron. And he received the gold at their hand, and fashioned it with a graving tool, and made a molten calf; and they said, "These are your gods, O Israel, who brought you up out of the land of Egypt!" (Ex 32:1-4)

When we read the story of Moses and the golden calf, there's a tendency to laugh and say, "Well, that's a good one. Can you imagine people worshipping something they made with their own hands? How dumb could they have been?"

It's so easy to view the act of worship as nothing more or less then bowing down in front of an object, so we have a picture in our minds of this large group bowing in front of the golden calf. How ridiculous.

Viewing idol worship in this way is missing the point entirely. Worship involves giving the highest form of honor, and it becomes idolatry when what is worshipped is not God. In the current culture, there is a strong tendency to do exactly this. When someone uses drugs, alcohol, or sex improperly, it is a form of idol worship. When a sin is committed, it is a matter of honoring a set of personal moral rules rather than those God has given to us. This is exactly what Adam did when he ate the apple. Remember the promise of the devil, "You will be as gods knowing both good and evil." Another way to say this is, "You will get to play God when you make up your own moral rules."

THE FIRST COMMANDMENT AND THE OLD TESTAMENT

> I am the Lord your God, who brought you out of the land of Egypt, out of the house of bondage. You shall have no other gods before me. You shall not make for yourself a graven image, or any likeness of anything that is in heaven above, or that is in the earth beneath, or that is in the water under the earth; you shall not bow down to them or serve them. (Ex 20: 2-5)

When Moses was given the Ten Commandments, the Jewish people had just been freed from the slavery of the Egyptians. They were freed because God led them and protected them. He inflicted plagues on the Egyptians until the Egyptian pharaoh released the Jews. He sent a pillar of fire and smoke to stand between the Jewish people and the Egyptians who were pursuing them. This prevented the Egyptians from reenslaving the Jews. God parted the Red Sea when Moses and his people needed to cross and closed it again over the army of pharaoh, ending the chase.

Because of all that God has done for them, the Jews owe much to the Lord. First and foremost, they owe him worship. God is owed this worship because of his power and goodness—a power and goodness that can readily be seen by looking at the help God gave Moses and his people.

It is not only the Jews, though, who owe God worship, but all people, throughout all time.

God created everything that exists; he created each and every one of us out of nothing, and if he *ever* stopped thinking about us, even for the shortest moment, we would no longer exist. Because of his power, goodness, and the love he has for all things, God continues to care for us, and we shall not stop living, stop existing. We owe him our existence, so we should worship the one, true God.

In the days of the Old Testament, the first commandment's *literal* interpretation held much greater meaning than it does today. The first commandment prohibits both polytheism, the worship of more than one god, and idolatry, the worship of idols (false gods).

> The first commandment condemns *polytheism*. It requires man neither to believe in, nor to venerate, other divinities than the one true God. Scripture constantly recalls this rejection of "idols, [of] silver and gold, the work of men's hands. They have mouths, but do not speak; eyes, but do not see." These empty idols make their worshippers empty: "Those who make them are like them; so are all who trust in them."[1] God, however, is the "living God"[2] who gives life and intervenes in history. (CCC 2112)

The need to reject the idols of silver and gold was a genuine challenge for the Jewish people in the Old Testament. Men of that era fashioned idols out of precious metals and worshipped these idols as gods. These idols were not thought of as images, pictures of gods; rather, these figures of metal were seen as the *gods themselves*. This fact sheds new light on the term "living God." The God of the Jews is indeed alive, is really God, unlike the "gods" made by men, which are just lifeless pieces of metal or wood.

You shall have no other gods before me.

The God of the Jews is indeed alive, is really God, unlike the "gods" made by men, which are just lifeless pieces of metal or wood.

Christ's teachings show us how to live according to the spirit of the law...

"I have come not to abolish them but to fulfill them." (Mt 5:17)

The commandment not to worship idols was indeed a task for the Jewish people — one they fell short of on several occasions. For instance, the Ten Commandments are first revealed to the people in the twentieth chapter of Exodus. By the thirty-second chapter, the people who had received the Ten Commandments have created a golden calf and are worshiping it as the god who brought them out of slavery in Egypt. In such a short time, they have already abandoned the true God.

Similarly, polytheism (from the Greek words *polys*, "many," and *theos*, "god") was practiced during that time. Except for the Jewish people, all other peoples had religious systems that believed in the existence of many gods. Egypt, for example, the land from which the Jews had just escaped, worshipped a god of death, a god of the sun, and many more.

The first commandment makes it clear that these other gods are not gods at all, and that true worship belongs only to the Lord.

Also forbidden are idolatry, superstition, and divination. Idolatry is the elevation of other realities to the state of gods, thereby making them take the place of the real God. Superstition is any belief or practice that renders false worship to God. Superstition is any belief or practice that renders false worship to God, or attributes supernatural or magical powers to certain objects or ritual actions. Divination is the prediction of the future or the revelation of the unknown through so-called paranormal means.

The first commandment lays out the most basic requirement for the Israelites, as well as for all people: the worship of the one, true, living God. Worship of other gods is a sin because it places the worship of a thing before the true God who brought the Jewish people (our spiritual forefathers, the first to hear God's word) out of Egypt.

THE FIRST COMMANDMENT AND THE NEW TESTAMENT

> And one of them, a lawyer, asked him a question, to test him. "Teacher, which is the great commandment in the law?" And he said to him, "You shall love the Lord your God with all your heart, and with all your soul, and with all your mind. This is the great and first commandment." (Mt 22:35-38)

One of the most memorable facts about Jesus is *that he simply asks* people to follow him. He wishes to be followed out of love, not fear of the law. Jesus wants people to follow the spirit of the law, not the letter of the law. Of course, what is written in the commandments should be followed — it is the minimum asked of a person who desires to save his soul. But, following only what is clearly stated in the law is too limited and can cut off the true meaning of the law. This was the practice of the scribes and Pharisees, who followed only the letter of the law. This led them to mis-understand Jesus and his teachings.

Rather, Christ's teachings show us how to live according to the spirit of the law — what is ultimately motivating the commandments. "Think not that I have come to abolish the law and the prophets," Jesus said. "I have come not to abolish them but to fulfill them" (Mt 5:17). From this, it is clear that Jesus wants us to follow the Ten Commandments, but he also wants us to do more—to live according to love, which is the basis for all the commandments.

In the case of the first commandment, "doing more" means loving God completely and fully. Each and every person is supposed to love God with his whole soul, whole heart, and whole mind. In short, God should be the most important being in the world for us. We should love God more than anything or anyone else.

THE THEOLOGICAL VIRTUES

Faith, hope, and charity are the theological virtues. These three virtues are bound up in the first commandment. Since there is only one God, this commandment, as a matter of justice, calls us to practice the theological virtues by having faith in him, hoping in him, and loving him above all else.

> "The first commandment embraces faith, hope, and charity. When we say 'God,' we confess a constant and unchangeable being, always the same, faithful and just, without any evil. It follows that we must necessarily accept his words and have complete faith in him and acknowledge his authority. He is almighty, merciful, and infinitely beneficent.... Who could not place all hope in him? Who could not love him when contemplating the treasures of goodness and love he has poured out on us? Hence the formula God employs in the Scripture at the beginning and end of his commandments: 'I am the Lord.'"[3] (CCC 2086)

The theological virtues are great and complex gifts. To understand more about them, we need to examine the word theological, which is derived from Greek and pertains to thought or teaching about God. These virtues come directly from God and put us directly in touch with God. They are, in fact, "infused by God into the souls of the faithful to make them capable of acting as his children and of meriting eternal life" (CCC 1813).

We receive the theological virtues from the Lord at Baptism, and because the theological virtues come directly from the Lord, we must cooperate with his grace in order to make good use of them. Through prayer, the sacraments, and virtuous practice, the theological virtues will grow in us.

FAITH

> Faith is the theological virtue by which we believe in God and believe all that he has said and revealed to us, and that the Holy Church proposes for our belief, because he is truth itself. (CCC 1814)

Faith is belief in God and acceptance of those things revealed by God without proof. It enables us to accept the truths God has revealed through his Church.

Faith is a great gift from God that is given to all who ask for it, not only in words, but with their behavior, but it can easily be lost if it is neglected. Many young persons, however, do not put forth much effort to understand Jesus or his teachings. During their teen years, many students begin to have questions about God's existence and religion in general. This time of searching for answers is a grace from God that calls the questioner to seek him out. Religion class offers the opportunity to have

Faith, hope, and charity are the theological virtues.

Faith in him, hoping in him, and loving him above all else.

Faith is a great gift from God that is given to all who ask for it.

Faith can easily be lost if it is neglected.

It is wise to have someone who can advise us when we have questions about books, movies, or activities that might harm the faith.

Allegory of Faith

The inscription on the band of the bouquet reads: *IVSTUS EX FIDE VIVIT* (The just lives with faith).

these questions answered. For faith to survive, it must be considered honestly.

To increase our faith, we must live the faith. Studying the truths that the Church proposes and praying can accomplish this. Another simple yet pivotal way to care for one's faith is through leading a good life. If a person lives according to rules of faith, he will receive the grace to continue living and believing in God and his Church.

The care that we give to faith requires us to reject everything that opposes it. This means that we must avoid books, movies, and activities that would place our faith at risk. Many would argue that they have a right to read and view whatever they wish. But can there be a right to risk losing one's belief in God? Is it sensible to read or watch things that can lead us away from God? In fact, it would be foolish for someone to take that risk.

It is wise to have someone who can advise us when we have questions about books, movies, or activities that might harm the faith. Such an adviser might be one of your parents, a teacher, or a counselor.

Faith requires more from us than just caring for it within ourselves. "The disciple of Christ must not only keep the faith and live in it, but also profess it, confidently bear witness to it, and spread it" (CCC 1816).

We are called not only to believe in Christ but also to spread the faith to others. This calling to evangelize other people is a serious and demanding task. To be able to spread the faith to others, we must first know it ourselves. Secondly, we must pray to understand it. Finally, and most importantly for evangelization, we must bear witness to our beliefs.

Once we understand our faith better, we shall discover that many opportunities present themselves for us to demonstrate what we believe about Jesus. Remember, since we are made in God's "image and likeness," we are to act in his "image and likeness" (cf. Gn 1: 26).

SINS AGAINST FAITH

Since faith is precious, we must treat it with great care. Despite faith's great value, sometimes people directly and willfully commit sins that can damage and even destroy their faith.

Attendance at non-Catholic services is not a sin. However, a Catholic sins against faith when he receives "communion" in non-Catholic worship services (this bread which has not been consecrated by a priest is *NOT* the Body, Blood, Soul, and Divinity of Jesus Christ) or replaces Mass with such services. When a person participates in such a service, it can be a danger to his faith and can give the *false* impression that all beliefs are of equal value. For this reason, Catholics should usually avoid attending non-Catholic worship services.

This prohibition does not include attending ecumenical prayer services, which are just and holy things and which often have the unity of Christians, which is God's will, as an object of prayer. One may participate in these services and formal religious services, as long as there is a serious reason for doing so and participation does not cause scandal. It is only formal religious services of other faiths in which a Catholic may not participate.

Voluntary doubt is also a sin against faith. It is disregard for or refusal to hold as true what God has revealed and the Church proposes for our belief. It is also willful hesitation to overcome difficulties regarding belief. Someone who doubts voluntarily does not *want* to believe or does not believe *by choice*. Obviously, intentionally refusing to believe closes the door to faith.

Incredulity is also a sin against faith. Incredulity is the neglect of or willful refusal to accept truths of the faith. There are three types of incredulity:

- *Heresy*, which is the determined post-baptismal denial or obstinate doubt of some truth that must be believed with divine and Catholic faith. An example of a heresy is the denial by a baptized person of the real presence of Christ in the Eucharist, or the false belief that the Virgin Mary was born with original sin;

- *Apostasy*, which is the total repudiation of the Christian faith by a baptized person. A baptized person who does not accept Christianity as the truth, or who converts to a non-Christian religion, has committed apostasy;

- *Schism*, which is the refusal of submission to the Roman Pontiff or of communion with churches associated with him. When Henry VIII of England stated that he, not the pope, was the head of the Church in England, this was an act of schism.

Prayer for Faith

O, my God, I firmly believe you are one God in three divine persons. I believe your divine Son became man and died for our sins. I believe these and all the truths that the Church teaches because you have revealed them who can neither deceive nor be deceived.

HOPE

> Hope is the theological virtue by which we desire the kingdom of heaven and eternal life as our happiness, placing our trust in Christ's promises and relying not on our own strength, but on the help of the grace of the Holy Spirit. (CCC 1817)

Hope is the confident expectation that God will give us the capacity to return his love.

We cannot respond to God's call through our own power or strength. We are too weak to follow the Lord without his help. We must expect that God, not because of anything we do, but out of his goodness, will give us the necessary knowledge and graces to love him so we can act in conformity with his wishes, thereby attaining eternal life. This confident expectation is called hope. The virtue of hope makes possible the belief that God will give the grace to return his love, to expect his blessing, to joyfully anticipate the beatific vision with him, and to overcome temptations to offend him or reject his love.

Through hope, we can expect that God will supply all graces necessary to save our souls.

Allegory of Hope
The youthful Hope flies upward to receive the crown that awaits her.

Through hope, we can expect that God will supply all graces necessary to save our souls.

One who despairs rejects God's power, mercy, and love.

The very reason we were created is to love and to be loved by God.

"For to this end we toil and strive, because we have our hope set on the living God, who is the Savior of all men, especially of those who believe." (1 Tm, 4:10)

Hope, like the other theological virtues, must be nurtured. We can foster hope in ourselves through prayer, which both increases hope and helps us follow God's will, helping us realize the object of hope: salvation. We can nurture hope in others by reminding them of God's providence and love and by praying to God to give them hope in difficult situations.

SINS AGAINST HOPE

There are two primary sins against hope. One of them is the sin of despair. We are guilty of despair if we deliberately and willfully abandon hope in God and the possibility of salvation. One who despairs rejects God's power, mercy, and love.

Despair is the most serious sin against hope. If someone despairs, he does not think that God will aid him or love him. The most obvious and most common example of despair is a person who commits suicide. When a person kills himself, he does not think God will take care of him and finds a drastic and terrible way to end his suffering in life. It is important to keep this in mind and to help someone who is going through difficult times. This requires that you support your friends, *and* you should inform a responsible adult if a friend or acquaintance mentions that he or she is considering suicide.

It should be noted that some who commit suicide are suffering from a seriously diminished ability to make correct moral choices as a direct result of eroding psychological difficulties, which would reduce or eliminate personal responsibility.

Presumption is the other sin against hope and is basically the opposite of despair. It takes two forms, both of which are offensive to God.

One form is the expectation that you can save your soul without God's assistance. This is offensive to God because it denies the fact that *we need God's help*.

The other form of presumption is the expectation that God will save you without effort on your part. This view is an affront to God because it implies that you think you deserve grace and salvation, instead of recognizing your own unworthiness.

Presumption is a sin against hope because there is a serious lack of humility in the presumptive person. In some way, he considers himself worthy of or even equal to God.

Prayer for Hope

O, my God, relying on your infinite promises, I hope to obtain pardon for my sins, life everlasting through the merits of Jesus Christ, my Lord and Redeemer.

CHARITY

> Charity is the theological virtue by which we love God above all things for his own sake, and our neighbor as ourselves for the love of God. (CCC 1822)

God loves us freely, without any conditions or requirements. It is only just and right, then, that we love God, who is all goodness in return. The love of God requires that we return his love. Charity is a virtue that enables us to love God above all things.

As a consequence of original sin, the call to love God as he deserves is difficult. Often, we do what we know is wrong; we ignore what we know we should do. These sins cause us to drift away from the Lord. As we have already seen, humans are too weak and sinful to do this alone, but with God's help it is possible for us to love him. Charity is the virtue that makes this possible. With the grace of charity, we are able to return God's love and love our neighbor. However, God's love for us is so great that he does not ask us to love him without the assistance of his grace, which adds a supernatural power to our love. God makes his grace available to us in the virtue of charity.

To love God, it is helpful to recall his goodness. God has called us into existence, has given us life. Even more, he freely loves us and calls us to love him in return. The very reason we were created, in fact, was to love and to be loved by God. "See what love the Father has given us, that we should be called children of God; and so we are" (1 Jn 3:1).

Charity also allows us to love our fellow men for God's sake. In other words, it allows us to love others because we recognize that God loves them.

This call to active love of neighbor should not be confused with feelings of love. Love of neighbor is not a feeling. Rather, it is a sincere resolution to render goodness to others. This desire will motivate us to give of ourselves freely to others—a gift that betters both the giver and the recipient.

For someone to love God properly, he must, in fact, love his neighbor; it is ridiculous to try and separate the two. God is love, and in choosing not to love another person, we are in effect choosing to deny God. The beauty of the virtue of charity is that it enables us to want the best for those we find unlovable, for when we love our neighbor we are basing our love on God's wishes rather than our own. The key, then, to every relationship—both human and divine—is charity.

SINS AGAINST CHARITY

St. Paul, in his First Letter to the Corinthians, writes one of the most well-known and beautifully written passages of the Bible. This treatise on charity concludes with the words, "So faith, hope, and love abide, these three; but the greatest of these is love."

Even though love is the greatest virtue, some people reject it through sins against charity:

◆ *Indifference* is refusing to reflect on the existence of divine goodness and the power of God's love.

With the grace of charity, we are able to return God's love and love our neighbor.

The beauty of the virtue of charity is that it enables us to want the best for those we find unlovable.

The four purposes of prayer—adoration, atonement, petition, and thanksgiving—are, in fact, the specific acts of the virtue of religion.

◆ *Acedia* is refusing to accept the joy that comes from God or being repelled by God's goodness. Basically, the person guilty of spiritual sloth is too lazy to return God's love.

◆ *Lukewarmness* is hesitation or neglect to respond to God's love. "So, because you are lukewarm, and neither cold nor hot, I will spew you out of my mouth" (Rv 3:16).

◆ *Hatred of God* is another sin against charity. It is denying God's love out of pride and cursing God for forbidding sin and inflicting punishment. This is obviously a sin against charity, and one that will damn a person who fails to repent.

◆ *Ingratitude* is the failure to acknowledge God's love and return it. When you receive a gift from someone, there is an obligation to thank the person who gave it. The sin of ingratitude is greater when it involves the person of God. The person guilty of ingratitude receives the gift of God's love, but acts as though he has received nothing.

Prayer for Charity

O, my God, I love you above all else, for you are all good and worthy of all my love. I love my neighbor as myself to secure your love. I forgive all who have injured me and ask pardon of all whom I have injured.

THE VIRTUE OF RELIGION

The virtue of religion requires us to give to God the worship, honor, devotion, and service he deserves. We fulfill this virtue when we do those things formally directed to worshipping God.

Worship of God must be fulfilled in both an interior and exterior manner, for both our bodies and our souls belong to God. Interior worship is accomplished when we adore God inwardly, with acts of the heart and mind such as contemplating God's goodness or meditating on all he has done for us. Worship is exterior when we accompany interior worship with outward acts, such as making the sign of the cross or praying vocally.

The four purposes of prayer—adoration, atonement, petition, and thanksgiving—are, in fact, the specific acts of the virtue of religion. All of these are accomplished most perfectly in the sacrifice of the Mass. This sacrifice is explained in detail in the chapter on the Eucharist, but know without a doubt that participating in the Mass is most pleasing to God.

The virtue of religion also includes rendering honor to Mary and the saints, as well as venerating sacred images. This latter practice is based on the mystery of Jesus' Incarnation. Because Jesus had a true body, a physical presence in the world as real as that of any other person, it is acceptable to venerate sacred images that are physical representations of the one being venerated. Such veneration leads one to a greater love for the one being represented; it is not an act of worshipping the image itself. When we pray in front of a statue of Jesus, we are praying not to the statue but to the one the statue represents. This image simply helps us to focus our thoughts on Christ.

SINS AGAINST THE VIRTUE OF RELIGION

Sinning against the virtue of religion is a blatant act against the Lord. It is directly acting against the honor and love we know God deserves. These sins are a departure from the worship owed to God.

These sins against religion are:

- *Idolatry* – putting a thing or person in the place of God. Idolatry includes honoring Satan, pleasure, power, money, the state, or drugs in place of God;

- *Superstition* – attributing magical power to certain created things or practices. It includes belief in and use of so-called "good luck charms," such as rabbits' feet, chain letter prayers that claim to bind God to an answer, and similar practices;

- *Divination* – the attempt to predict the future based on the assistance of Satan or the dead. It also includes belief in the power of horoscopes, fortunetellers, astrology, ouija boards, and omens. These are false attempts to control one's future and deny the power of God to care for us directly;

- *Magic* – the desire to know and control demonic powers in order to place them at one's service. Attempting to make a deal with the devil or asking his help in order to place a curse on someone are examples. Though sometimes called magic, slight-of-hand tricks do not apply here;

- *Irreligion* – direct disrespect for God or sacred things. Examples are:

  - Testing God in word or deed, for example, asking God to damn a person;

  - Sacrilege, which is disrespect for sacred persons, places, or things. This includes disrespect for Mary, the saints, sacred images, and places of worship;

- *Simony* – the buying or selling of spiritual powers or offices. The very first person to be cast out of the church was Simon the magician, who tried to buy from Peter the power to call upon the Holy Spirit;

- *Atheism* – the denial or rejection of the existence of God.

A person involved in these irreligious practices is engaged in false forms of worship. He has lost a true sense of the nature of the relationship between God and man. Man should love and honor God above all else. Someone guilty of these sins is openly doing the opposite of this.

RELIGIOUS FREEDOM

There is an incorrect modern idea that man has an absolute right to believe whatever he wishes about God's existence. The right to believe whatever one wishes is a false concept—for it allows us to believe anything instead of seeking the truth regarding important questions. Human beings do not have this right to believe whatever they wish, but rather are required to seek what is true. This search may lead people down different paths to the truth, but truth must always be the goal.

Human beings do not have this right to believe whatever they wish, but rather are required to seek what is true.

This search may lead people down different paths to the truth, but truth must always be the goal.

The First Commandment

Man does not have freedom to risk his soul.

He has given us the theological virtues of faith, hope, and charity in Baptism to empower us to serve him.

Jesus' statement, "You will know the truth, and the truth will make you free," points to one simple fact: answers to all the questions that arise in one's life require knowledge of the truth, and the greatest question that concerns all of us is what is the true way to find God and serve him.

No one should be coerced into belief in God or profession of a certain religion. The Church indicated during the recent Vatican Council that the right of all to seek God must not be coerced or restricted.

> The Vatican Council declares that the human person has a right to religious freedom. Freedom of this kind means that all men should be immune from coercion on the part of individuals, social groups and every human power so that, within due limits, nobody is forced to act against his convictions nor is anyone to be restrained from acting in accordance with his convictions in religious matters in private or in public, alone or in associations with others.[4]

Respect for all men's freedom to seek the truth does not mean everyone is free to believe whatever he wishes without regard for the truth. Those who reject the idea that God does exist and refuse to seek him place themselves in direct danger of losing their souls. Man does not have freedom to risk his soul.

CONCLUSION

It is easy to say that we don't worship false idols as people in the Old Testament did. Idolatry, however, is simply placing some thing or person in God's place. The sin of Adam and Eve, the "original sin," was the desire to make themselves equal to God. Those who skip Mass on Sunday, involve themselves in drugs and alcohol, seek sex outside of marriage or break other commandments are involved in the very sin of Adam and Eve, the false worship of self. They have set themselves up as arbiters of right and wrong rather than accepting what God requires.

In Baptism, man promises to worship God, and when we practice the virtue of religion by adoring him and praying to him, we fulfill these promises.

God has loved us from all eternity. The God who calls us to do great things for him has planned our arrival at this point in the history of the world to accomplish a part of his plan. To ensure that we can accomplish all he has planned for us, he has given us the theological virtues of faith, hope, and charity in Baptism to empower us to serve him.

How insulting it would be if we turn from fulfilling his plan to place our trust in the false gods of these times. The worst personal experience we can have is to be refused love by someone who ought to love us. How much worse will it be if we refuse to accept or return the love so freely given to us by God?

SUPPLEMENTARY READING

It occurs to all of us from time to time that there is a day known only to God when we will die. Few of us are called upon to consider whether we will be killed in the cause of Jesus Christ. Those who die for Christ have their faith tested to the limit.

The following testament was written by Fr. Christian De Chergé, a Catholic monk who lived in a monastery in Algeria. He was not planning to die, but he wrote in the eventuality that he might be killed by Algerian Muslim guerillas, who had earlier threatened the monastery. This message is a supreme example of the three theological virtues of faith, hope, and love being lived out in a very real way.

I go to God.

If it should happen one day—and it could be today—that I become the victim of an act of terrorism which now appears ready to engulf all foreigners living in Algeria, I would like my community, my Church, my family to remember that my life was given to God and to this country.

I ask them to accept that the sole master of all life was not a stranger to this brutal departure. I ask them to pray for me, for how could I be found worthy of such an offering? I ask them to be able to link this death with so many other deaths which were just as violent but forgotten through indifference and anonymity.

My life has no more value than any other, nor any less value. In any case it has not the innocence of childhood. I have lived long enough to know that I am an accomplice in the evil which seems, alas, to prevail in the world today, even in that which would strike me blindly.

I should like, when the time comes, to have a moment of lucidity which would allow me to beg forgiveness of God and of all of my fellow human beings, and at the same time to forgive with all my heart the one who would strike me down. I could not desire such a death. It seems to me important to state this. I do not see in fact how I could rejoice if this people I love were to be accused indiscriminately of my murder.

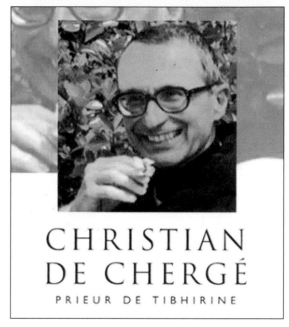

Fr. Christian De Chergé
(1937-1996)

To owe it to an Algerian, whoever he may be, would be too high a price to pay for what will, perhaps, be called the "grace of martyrdom," especially if he says he is acting in fidelity to what he believes is Islam. I am aware of the scorn which can be heaped on Algerians, indiscriminately. I am also aware of the caricature of Islam which a certain islamicism encourages. It is too easy to salve one's conscience by identifying this religious way with the fundamentalist ideologies of its extremists.

For me Algeria and Islam are something different; they are a body and a soul. I have proclaimed this often enough; I believe in the sure knowledge of what I have received from it, finding there so often that true strand of the gospel I learned at my mother's knee, my very first Church, in Algeria, itself, and already inspired with respect for Muslim believers.

My death will appear to justify those who hastily judged me naïve or idealistic: "Let him tell us now what he thinks of it." But these people must realize that my most avid curiosity will then be satisfied. This is what I will be able to do, if God wills, immerse my gaze in that of the Father, and contemplate him with his children of Islam just

Continued

SUPPLEMENTARY READING CONTINUED

as he sees them, all shining with the glory of Christ, the fruit of his Passion, and filled with the gift of the Spirit, whose secret joy will always be to establish communion and to refashion the likeness, playing delightfully with the differences.

For this life lost, totally mine, and totally theirs, I thank God who seems to have willed it entirely for the sake of that joy in everything and in spite of everything.

In this thank you, which sums up the whole of my life from now on, I certainly include you, friends of yesterday and today, and you my friends of this place, along with my mother and father, my sisters and brothers and their families, the hundredfold granted as was promised.

And also, you, the friend of my final moment, who would not be aware of what you are doing.

Yes, I also say this "thank you" and this A-Dieu to you in whom I see the face of God. And may we see each other, happy good thieves in the Paradise if it pleases God, the Father of us both. Amen, Insha Allah.

The guerillas returned two years later and cut the throats of Fr. De Chergé and six other monks.

VOCABULARY

ACEDIA
A less common synonym for sloth, one of the seven capital sins.

CHARITY
The theological virtue by which we love God above all things for his own sake, and our neighbor as ourselves for the love of God.

DIVINATION
Sin against the virtue of religion in which one attempts to tell of future events by means of occult forces—Satan, demons, spirits, astrology, etc.

FAITH
Both a gift of God and a human act by which the believer gives personal adherence to God who invites his response, and freely assents to the whole truth that God has revealed; a theological virtue given by God.

HOPE
The theological virtue by which we desire and expect from God both eternal life and the grace we need to attain it.

INCREDULITY
The willful refusal to assent to revealed truth, or even the neglect of this truth.

RELIGION
A set of beliefs and practices followed by those committed to the service and worship of God.

SIMONY
The buying or selling of spiritual things, which have God alone as their owner and master.

SUPERSTITION
Sin against the virtue of religion involving the attribution of a kind of magical power to certain practices or objects, like charms or omens.

THEOLOGICAL VIRTUES
Gifts infused by God into the souls of the faithful to make them capable of acting as his children and of meriting eternal life. The theological virtues are faith, hope, and charity.

VENERATION
Showing devotion and respect to Mary, the apostles, and the martyrs, who were viewed as faithful witnesses to faith in Jesus Christ; must be clearly distinguished from adoration and worship, which are due to God alone.

WORSHIP
Adoration and honor given to God, which is the first act of the virtue of religion.

STUDY QUESTIONS

1. Why do the Jewish people owe so much to God?

2. Why do we owe our total allegiance to God as a matter of justice?

3. What are the theological virtues?

4. When were the theological virtues received?

5. What is our first obligation to God?

6. What does the virtue of faith oblige us to do?

7. Explain voluntary doubt.

8. Explain the three forms of incredulity.

9. List and explain the sins against hope.

10. What is the key to all relationships?

11. What difficult act of love does charity enable us to accomplish?

PRACTICAL EXERCISES

1. Read the parable of the "pearl of great price" (Mt 13: 45-46). Why did the man sell everything he had to obtain the pearl? How is the gift of faith similar?

2. Catholics have always held the Virgin Mary and other saints up for veneration. Often people address these saints in prayer. How do these acts differ from practices such as divination or polytheism?

3. Some people believe that once they accept Christ as their personal savior, they will go to heaven no matter what else happens in their lives. How does this contradict the virtue of hope?

4. In his testament, Fr. Christian De Chergé says he wishes to be able to forgive the person who would kill him, and he also wishes to beg God for forgiveness. How would God's forgiveness of Fr. De Chergé be grounded in love? How is Fr. De Chergé's desire to forgive his killer related to God's love?

FROM THE CATECHISM

162 Faith is an entirely free gift that God makes to man. We can lose this priceless gift, as St. Paul indicated to St. Timothy: "Wage the good warfare, holding faith and a good conscience. By rejecting conscience, certain persons have made shipwreck of their faith" (1 Tm 1:18-19). To live, grow and persevere in the faith until the end we must nourish it with the word of God; we must beg the Lord to increase our faith; it must be "working through charity," abounding in hope, and rooted in the faith of the Church (cf Mk 9:24, Lk 17:5; 22:32, Gal 5:6, Rom 15:13, Jas 2:14-26).

1840 The theological virtues dispose Christians to live in a relationship with the Holy Trinity. They have God for their origin, their motive, and their object—God known by faith, God hoped in and loved for his own sake.

1841 There are three theological virtues: faith, hope, and charity. They inform all the moral virtues and give life to them.

1842 By faith, we believe in God and believe all that he has revealed to us and that Holy Church proposes for our belief.

1843 By hope we desire, and with steadfast trust await from God, eternal life and the graces to merit it.

1844 By charity, we love God above all things and our neighbor as ourselves for love of God. Charity, the form of all the virtues, "binds everything together in perfect harmony" (Col 3:14).

1845 The seven gifts of the Holy Spirit bestowed upon Christians are wisdom, understanding, counsel, fortitude, knowledge, piety, and fear of the Lord.

2133 "You shall love the Lord your God with all your heart, and with all your soul and with all your strength" (Dt 6:5).

2134 The first commandment summons man to believe in God, to hope in him, and to love him above all else.

2135 "You shall worship the Lord your God" (Mt 4:10). Adoring God, praying to him, offering him the worship that belongs to him, fulfilling the promises and vows made to him are acts of the virtue of religion which fall under obedience to the first commandment.

2136 The duty to offer God authentic worship concerns man both as an individual and as a social being.

2137 "Men of the present day want to profess their religion freely in private and in public" (*DH*, 15).

2138 Superstition is a departure from the worship that we give to the true God. It is manifested in idolatry, as well as in various forms of divination and magic.

2139 Tempting God in word or deeds, sacrilege, and simony are sins of irreligion forbidden by the first commandment.

2140 Since it rejects or denies the existence of God, atheism is a sin against the first commandment.

2141 The veneration of sacred images is based on the mystery of the Incarnation of the Word of God. It is not contrary to the first commandment.

Endnotes

1. Ps 115: 4-5, 8; cf. Is 44: 9-20; Jer 10: 1-16; Dn 14: 1-30; Bar 6; Wis 13: 1-15; 19.
2. Jos 3: 10; Ps 42: 3; etc.
3. *Roman Catechism*, 3, 2, 4.
4. *DH*, 2

The Second Commandment

God's name is hallowed.

Chapter 20

The Second Commandment

*N*o one likes to be treated with disrespect. When someone talks down to us, we get angry. We feel insulted when someone acts as if we're not worth his time. People know instinctively that they have a certain dignity that means they should be treated with respect. When people treat us poorly, we feel that that our natural dignity is not being recognized.

God too has a dignity that should be respected, but his dignity is much greater than ours. For we are weak, fallen creatures who ignore what we know is right and do what we know is wrong. This is part of our nature. God, though, is perfect. His very nature is love itself. How much greater is the dignity of God, who is all goodness, than the dignity of human beings?

God should be treated with more respect and dignity than any of his creatures. Everything he does, everything about him should be held in the highest reverence – including his name. As Jesus tells us in the "Our Father," God's name is hallowed. We should remember to treat it this way.

THE SECOND COMMANDMENT AND THE OLD TESTAMENT

You shall not take the name of the Lord your God in vain. (Ex 20:7)

The Second Commandment prohibits taking God's name in vain, forbidding its use for irreverent purposes—such as calling upon God to damn a person—while at the same time requiring us to speak with reverence of God, the saints, and holy things. Like the first commandment, the second belongs to the virtue of religion and governs our speech in matters of religion.

To understand why we should respect God's name, we need to understand what a name is. A person's name contains his very identity, and therefore, the meaning of his life. This means that if someone reveals his name to you he is partly revealing who he really is to you. Each person's name has been carefully chosen and is special.

You can see this is true by looking at other cultures. In some Native American tribes, for instance, a person had two names: one that family and close friends alone knew and used, and one for everyone else. It might be the same way with you today. If you have a nickname, does everyone know and use it, or just the people close to you? These examples show how a name is special to a person.

Not only does a name reveal something personal about someone, but if you know and use someone's name, that shows you have some power over that person. This may sound strange at first, but actually it makes sense. Think about it. There is a reason you call your teacher "Mr. Smith" or "Mrs. Jones." These titles show respect and acknowledge authority. If you called your teachers by their first names, the relationship would be changed. You would have the power that comes with familiarity over them, and you might fail to recognize their authority.

For the people of Moses' time, the use of a person's name indicated a certain power as well, and many believed they could have power over even a spirit, if they knew the spirit's name. This was a temptation for people because they were aware of the presence of active evil spirits, which many people believed could be controlled if their names were known. We are familiar with the story of the golden calf and know that the worship of false idols was a serious problem in the time of Moses.

God called on Moses to establish the worship of the one true God to overcome the idolatries practiced by the human race.

> Among all the words of Revelation, there is one which is unique: the revealed name of God. God confides his name to those who believe in him; he reveals himself to them in his personal mystery. The gift of a name belongs to the order of trust and intimacy. "The Lord's name is holy." For this reason man must not abuse it. He must keep it in mind in silent, loving adoration. He will not introduce it into his own speech except to bless, praise, and glorify it.[1] (CCC 2143)

God gave Moses the right to call upon him. He chose to reveal himself to the Jewish people through Moses, to whom he said, "I AM WHO I AM" (Ex 3:14). The power to use God's name gave Moses the power to call upon God himself. In fact, in the Hebrew scriptures so much reverence was shown to the sacred name revealed to Moses, Yahweh, that it

The Second Commandment

You shall not take the name of the Lord your God in vain.

God chose to reveal himself to the Jewish people through Moses, to whom he said, "I AM WHO I AM." (Ex 3:14)

Blasphemy is disrespect for the names of Jesus, Mary, and the saints.

If we were to speak badly of the saints or Mary, we would be criticizing God's choices and actions.

was never pronounced in later Judaism. The term Adonai (Lord) was substituted.

If his name is such a powerful thing, then why did God reveal his name to us?

God told us his name because he loves us infinitely. We have seen how one's identity is bound up in one's name. In revealing his name to us, God shows us he desires that we should know him and draw close to him, and in return, he will be close to us. With the knowledge of the name of the Lord, God becomes not just a powerful being set completely apart, but a being with whom we can have a personal relationship. This is a very intimate revelation, and one that we would be highly insensitive to ignore, for the Lord desires personal communion with us. God revealed who he was to his people so that he and his people might love each other more fully.

THE SECOND COMMANDMENT AND THE NEW TESTAMENT

> Again you have heard that it was said to the men of old "you shall not swear falsely..." but I say to you, Do not swear at all, either by heaven, for it is the throne of God, or by the earth, for it is his footstool. (Mt 5:33-35)

Jesus, as the one who fulfills the law, spoke of the practice of swearing, of calling upon higher things as witnesses to the truth of a statement. When Jesus spoke of not swearing at all, his intent was not to forbid the use of God's name in any circumstance. Rather, he meant to purify the practice of calling upon God.

Following the practice of St. Paul, God's "chosen instrument" (Acts 9:15) of evangelization, the Church accepts that calling upon God is acceptable in serious situations. In his writings, Paul himself at least twice calls upon God to witness to the truth of his words. Jesus' declaration on swearing is an attempt to bring reverence to a practice that had become tainted, telling us to be more selective in the use of God's name.

Blasphemy is disrespect for the names of Jesus, Mary, and the saints. God's name is not the only name that the second commandment orders us to respect. Through the life and death of Jesus and the covenant he made, we also must show respect for the Blessed Virgin Mary and the saints. If we were to speak badly of the saints or Mary, we would be criticizing God's choices and actions, which is clearly sinful.

So far we have only discussed what the second commandment prohibits us from doing or saying. This commandment, however, requires more than just avoiding some things (negative precepts). It also requires us to do certain things (positive precepts).

The idea of respecting God is at the heart of the second commandment. We act with respect toward God when we:

✝ Give due praise to God our Creator and Redeemer. Calling upon God in prayer is a just and righteous act. In doing this, we must use God's name as he expected we would when he revealed it to us. Drawing closer to God through our prayer, we love God more;

† Acknowledge him before others in word and conduct. When we confess our faith in God, we pay him the respect that lies at the center of the second commandment. When we act as he has told us to act, we demonstrate that respect;

† Use his name with reverence. There are times when we *should* use God's name, when we should refer to the Lord (e.g., when discussing morality or religion with people);

† Pray, learn, use, and study God's word.

There are other special situations that allow us to call upon God. These include oaths and vows.

OATHS

An oath is the act of calling upon God as a witness to the truth of a statement one is making. Both the Old and New Testaments permit the swearing of oaths, but there must be a serious reason for doing so.

> The holiness of the divine name demands that we neither use it for trivial matters, nor take an oath which on the basis of the circumstances could be interpreted as an approval of an authority unjustly requiring it. When an oath is required by illegitimate civil authorities, it may be refused. It must be refused when it is required for purposes contrary to the dignity of persons or to ecclesial communion. (CCC 2155)

This commandment permits the taking of oaths when there is a legitimate reason to do so. An oath may not be taken except in truth, necessity, and justice, for a morally good reason—for example, when one is called upon to be a witness in court.

A valid oath requires:

† Calling God as witness to the truth;

† That it be spoken aloud;

† Knowledge and intention to swear an oath.

People often make statements such as "honest to God" and "so help me God." Usually, they are not intending to swear an oath or to offend God. However, the use of such language, since it is not intended as an oath, is improper and an offense to God's name. A serious effort must be made to break this habit.

Some examples of circumstances when oaths may be sworn are in court or when joining the armed services or police department. Swearing an oath to harm something or someone is wrong. Swearing a false oath is perjury, calling upon God to witness to a lie, which is gravely sinful.

Additional conditions regulate the swearing of oaths:

† Oaths may not be taken to support a lie. You must be morally certain the statement you make is true. Swearing a false oath is a grave sin.

† Oaths should be taken only out of necessity and with discretion. Normally, your word should be enough.

† Oaths should be taken, as a matter of justice, only for morally good purposes.

An oath is the act of calling upon God as a witness to the truth of a statement one is making.

St. John the Evangelist

One of three apostles closest to Jesus, John was the only apostle at the Crucifixion. It was there that Jesus placed his mother, Mary, into John's care. He wrote the Fourth Gospel, three epistles and the Book of Revelation. John was the only apostle who was not martyred.

The eagle is John's emblem.

Examples of private vows are commitments to say certain prayers, do almsgiving, go on a pilgrimage, or perform specific acts of fasting.

"How majestic is thy name in all the earth!" (Ps 8:1)

VOWS

"A *vow* is a deliberate and free promise made to God concerning a possible and better good which must be fulfilled by reason of the virtue of religion."[2] A vow is an act of *devotion* in which the Christian dedicates himself to God or promises him some good work. (CCC 2102)

Since a vow is a promise *made to God*, it is the most solemn promise that can be made, and because vows are voluntary, they are most pleasing to the Lord.

Vows are made which establish one's state in life. These vows include the promises made upon marriage as well as the vows of poverty, chastity, and obedience taken by members of religious orders (called "religious"). In most cases, such vows bind the person for life, although certain people may be released from these vows under very specific circumstances. Married persons and religious who break their vows are guilty of grave sin.

Since a vow is such a serious commitment, certain requirements must be met for it to be legitimate. For a vow to be binding:

☩ It must be a firm promise;

☩ It must be done in public;

☩ It must be deliberately done after serious thought, and freely done with no exterior pressure. No one can be forced to make a vow;

☩ It must be made to God;

☩ It must promise a good action;

☩ It must be possible;

☩ It must be better than the situation that would result if the vow were not fulfilled.

As an act of personal devotion to God, a person may make a private vow. Examples of private vows are commitments to say certain prayers, do almsgiving, go on a pilgrimage, or perform specific acts of fasting. A confessor must be consulted before making this type of commitment.

RESPECT FOR GOD'S HOLY NAME

On a very literal level, God's name must be respected and used only in certain circumstances. Unfortunately, many have acquired the habit of using his name without giving much thought to what they are saying, as is manifest in such common exclamations as "Oh God" or "Christ."

We can make up for the disrespect shown for God's name by saying some aspirations such as "My Jesus Mercy" or "Sweet Heart of Jesus" when we hear others use his name inappropriately.

Even worse than these absent-minded abuses is the sin of blasphemy. Blasphemy is uttering against God, internally or externally, words of hatred, reproach, or defiance, or speaking ill of God. Clearly, such an act of hatred towards the Lord is intrinsically evil and gravely sinful. This prohibition against speaking directly against the Lord extends to language against his Church, the saints, and sacred things.

Asking God to damn a person to hell is called cursing. It is gravely sinful when the speaker desires the eternal damnation of the person named. It is an act that goes against the love we owe each person because of his uniqueness as a person created and loved by God.

CONCLUSION

A person's name is very special to him. It is how he is knowable and, in a way, contains his identity.

God's name is no less special. The Lord revealed his name to man to show us his nature so that we may know him. This is an act of tremendous love, that an infinite being would reveal himself to us — a sign of the communion the Lord desires with us. We should recognize this gesture as truly profound, and respect the name of the Lord, saying with the psalmist, "How majestic is thy name in all the earth!" (Ps 8:1).

Often, people use the Lord's name in casual conversation. Although they do not intend to offend God, this shows a lack of respect for a very personal revelation made by the Lord.

There do exist times when it is acceptable to use the Lord's name, such as when we pray, take vows, or make oaths. Remember, though, that whenever we use God's name it must be done out of a true desire to demonstrate and increase our love for the Lord.

Whenever we use God's name it must be done out of a true desire to demonstrate and increase our love for the Lord.

SUPPLEMENTARY READING

St. Polycarp was born sometime in the first century A.D. Although not many details are known about him, it is believed that he was converted to Christianity by St. John the Apostle when John was the bishop of Smyrna. In about A.D. 80, John was exiled to Patmos, the island where he saw the vision recorded in the Book of Revelation. Before John's exile, he consecrated Polycarp, who was only in his late teens or early twenties, as bishop of Smyrna.

For decades, Polycarp loyally served as bishop during a very demanding time for Christianity. In this era, the Church was suffering great persecutions, her members being fed to wild animals or burned alive for their faith. As bishop, it was Polycarp's duty to care for the faith of his flock throughout these persecutions, as well as to root out heresies that were springing up in the young religion. He was renowned for his piety.

When Polycarp was eighty-six, the persecution of Christians in his region became even more severe. Eventually Polycarp himself was singled out. Taken prisoner and brought in front of a vengeful crowd, Polycarp was told to renounce Christ or suffer greatly. He then gave the response that would lead to his martyrdom: "I have served him these eighty-six years, and he never did me any harm, but much good, and how can I blaspheme my King and my Savior?....Hear my free confession—I am a Christian."

Because he was unwilling to blaspheme Christ, Polycarp was killed and his body burned down to the bones. His example, though, lives on even now. Centuries later he is still providing an example of respect and love for God.

St. Polycarp
(died c. 155)
Feast on February 23

VOCABULARY

BLASPHEMY
Speech, thought, or action involving contempt for God or the Church, or persons or things dedicated to God.

DIGNITY
The quality of being worthy, or honorable; worthiness, worth, nobleness, excellence.

DISCRETION
Power to decide. See true conscience (Chapter 17).

NAME
Not only the title by which a person is called, but the term by which the person is identified.

OATH
Invocation of God's name to bear witness to the truth.

PERJURY
Giving ones word under oath falsely, or making a promise under oath without intending to keep it.

PRAISE
The form of prayer which focuses on giving recognition to God for his own sake, giving glory to him for who he is.

REVERENCE
Deep respect felt or shown towards a person on account of his or her position or relationship.

VOW
A deliberate and free promise made to God concerning a possible and better good which must be fulfilled by reason of the virtue of religion.

STUDY QUESTIONS

1. Why is a name special to a person?

2. Why did God reveal his name to us?

3. Besides God, whom does the second commandment require us to respect? Why?

4. What is at the heart of the second commandment?

5. Why is abusing God's name a sin?

6. What are some things we can do to show respect for God?

7. Why should you not take an oath over a small matter?

8. What are the conditions for an oath to be valid?

9. How is disrespect for God's name seen in everyday life?

10. Why would someone make a vow to God?

PRACTICAL EXERCISES

1. In the following cases, to what degree do the oaths or vows taken oblige, and why?

a. Laura and her sister Theresa have not spoken to each other for seven years as a result of a fight over some antiques that their grandmother left behind when she died. Because he was angry with Laura at the time of her argument with Theresa, Laura's father supported Theresa and gave all the property to her, an action he later deeply regretted. Although he apologized to Laura and asked Theresa to share the property with her sister, she refused to do so, resulting in the rift between the sisters. Laura's father recently decided to rewrite his will, and Laura demanded that he swear to name her as his sole heir, leaving her sister out of his will. Because he still feels guilty about what occurred before, her father has done so, but his conscience is bothering him. Must he do what he swore to do?

b. Peter promised to give his friend Sara a ring that he won in a contest and that she liked very much. Although he believed the ring to be of little value, he later discovered that it is actually worth quite a lot of money. Now he doesn't want to give Sara the ring. Must he?

c. Because he had been only an average student for the first three years of high school, David found it difficult to be accepted to the extremely competitive premedical program at the college he had chosen at the beginning of his senior year. His family was poor and could not afford to send him to the school, and it wasn't very likely that he was going to get a scholarship because of his past academic performance.

But David thought and prayed a lot about it, and he wanted to be a doctor. He worked hard during his senior year and succeeded in earning straight A's both semesters. In addition, he went to a local community college for one year, where he also earned straight A's. All the time he worked on his lately-developed dream of attending medical school, he prayed to God to help him and to grant him the favor of becoming a doctor. At one point, after careful consideration, he even vowed that if God would help him gain admittance to medical school, he would devote his first two years as a doctor to serving as a missionary doctor with a lay volunteer program in a poor country in Asia or Africa. Now that he has graduated at the top of his class from medical school, David has been offered a position at one of the most prestigious research hospitals in the U.S. He remembers the vow that he made, but this is a chance that he may not get again for a long time. What should he do?

2. It is easy to think of popular words, phrases, and expressions that are blasphemous or sacrilegious in nature. List instead common expressions, popular, and solemn practices that indicate respect for God and his name.

3. Read the following Scripture passages about the punishment that befalls blasphemers: 1 Kings 21:13-16; 2 Kings 19:4-7. Why do you think that God punished so severely those who blasphemed his name among the people of Israel?

FROM THE CATECHISM

2160 "O Lord, our Lord, how majestic is your name in all the earth." (Ps 8:1)

2161 The second commandment enjoins respect for the Lord's name. The name of the Lord is holy.

2162 The second commandment forbids every improper use of God's name. Blasphemy is the use of the name of God, of Jesus Christ, of the Virgin Mary, and of the saints in an offensive way.

2163 False oaths call on God to be witness to a lie. Perjury is a grave offense against the Lord, who is always faithful to his promises.

2164 "Do not swear whether by the Creator, or any creature, except truthfully, of necessity, and with reverence" (St. Ignatius of Loyola, *Spiritual Exercises*, 38).

2165 In Baptism, the Christian receives his name in the Church. Parents, godparents, and the pastor are to see that he be given a Christian name. The patron saint provides a model of charity and the assurance of his prayer.

2166 The Christian begins his prayers and activities with the sign of the cross: "in the name of the Father and of the Son and of the Holy Spirit. Amen."

2167 God calls each one by name (cf. Is 43:1).

Endnotes

1. Cf. Zec 2:13; Ps 29:2; 96:2; 113:1-2.
2. CIC, can. 1191 § 1.

The Third Commandment

Honor the Sabbath as God intends.

Chapter 21

The Third Commandment

*T*ry this math problem. Take seven times twenty-four times fifty-two. That comes to 8,736. Now take seven times fifty-two times eight, which comes to 2,912, and subtract that from 8,736. That leaves you with 5,824. From this, subtract fifty-two, which leaves you with 5,772. As a fraction of 5,772, fifty-two is almost one one-hundredth, or 1/100.

Let's state the problem another way: Take seven days in a week times twenty-four hours in a day times fifty-two weeks in a year, which comes to 8,736 hours. From that, subtract eight hours in a day times seven days in a week times fifty-two weeks in a year, which comes to 2,912, the number of hours we sleep. Now, subtract this from the 8,736 hours in a year, which leaves us with 5,772 hours when we are not sleeping. Jesus asks us to attend church for fifty-seven hours per year, or less than 1/100 of the whole year.

Is Jesus asking too much?

Remember the Sabbath day, to keep it holy.

THE THIRD COMMANDMENT AND THE OLD TESTAMENT

> Remember the sabbath day, to keep it holy. Six days you shall labor, and do all your work; but the seventh day is a sabbath day to the Lord your God; in it you shall not do any work, you, or your son, or your daughter, your manservant, or your maidservant, or your cattle, or the sojourner who is within your gates; for in six days the Lord made heaven and earth, the sea, and all that is in them, and rested the seventh day; therefore the Lord blessed the Sabbath day and hallowed it. (Ex 20: 8-11)

With the third commandment, God tells us to keep his day holy, for it has been set aside for the Lord.

God reserved a day for rest for many reasons, all of which are still in force. First, it served as a sign of the Lord's covenant with the Jewish people, reminding everyone that time must be set aside to worship and praise God in his work of creation. We must also thank the Lord for his saving actions on behalf of Israel, a praise which we extend toward Jesus' salvation of all mankind from sin and death.

The Sabbath day is also an instruction to copy the actions of the Lord. Since God rested on the Sabbath, man must follow God's lead by resting and relaxing. Man's need for rest is obvious. In fact, human life by its nature has a rhythm of work and rest. The Sabbath day ('Sabbath" is based on a Hebrew word meaning "rest") is God's way of sanctioning rest and leisure, which enable man to cultivate familial, social, cultural, and religious ties. As a day of rest, the Sabbath serves as a protest against the servitude of work and the worship of money. Moses, the prophet who received the Ten Commandments from God, said that this day was to be "a day of solemn rest, a holy Sabbath to the Lord."

Clearly, then, the Sabbath day is a time to rest and consider the things of God. The Jewish people dedicated this time to the Lord through public, group worship, which is what we, as Christians, do as well.

THE THIRD COMMANDMENT AND THE NEW TESTAMENT

> The Sabbath was made for man, not man for the Sabbath; so the Son of Man is lord even of the Sabbath. (Mk 2: 27-28)

Centuries passed between the time Moses was given the Commandments and the time Jesus began his ministry. In Jesus' time, abuses of the Sabbath had entered into Jewish worship, which caused God to be displeased.

We have already seen how the invocation of God's name had lost its value through misuse. In a similar way, the meaning of the Sabbath had also lost its original purpose. The Sabbath day was no longer a time made for man, a time to rest and grow closer to God. It became a strict prohibition against all labor, even if it was completely justified—a prohibition that often worked against man.

We see this clearly in the Gospel. At one point, the Pharisees accused Jesus' disciples of breaking the Sabbath by picking grains of wheat and eating them, even though there was no specific prohibition against this act in Jewish law. The Pharisees considered gathering food in this manner

The Sabbath day is God's way of sanctioning rest and leisure, which enable man to cultivate familial, social, cultural, and religious ties.

From Jesus' words, it is evident that God intended the Sabbath for good acts, for saving life.

Sunday worship celebrates the completion of the first creation, the new creation in Christ.

work, and work was strictly forbidden on the Sabbath. This accusation caused Jesus to reply that "the Sabbath was made for man, not man for the Sabbath," i.e., the day dedicated to the Lord was not meant to place unnecessary or burdensome rules on people (Mk 2: 27-28). It was made for people to worship God, to rest, and to enjoy time with their families.

When Jesus healed a person on the Sabbath, the Pharisees accused him of working when it was forbidden. Jesus' response summed up the real purpose of the Lord's day. "Is it lawful on the Sabbath to do good or to do harm, to save life or to kill?" (Mk 3: 4) From Jesus' words, it is evident that God intended the Sabbath for good acts, for saving life.

THE DAY OF REST IS CHANGED TO SUNDAY

> Jesus rose from the dead "on the first day of the week."[1] Because it is the "first day," the day of Christ's Resurrection recalls the first creation. Because it is the "eighth day" following the sabbath,[2] it symbolizes the new creation ushered in by Christ's Resurrection. For Christians it has become the first of all days, the first of all feasts, the Lord's Day *(he kuriake hemera, dies dominica)* — Sunday:
>
> > "We all gather on the day of the sun, for it is the first day [after the Jewish sabbath, but also the first day] when God, separating matter from darkness, made the world; and on this same day Jesus Christ our Savior rose from the dead."[3] (CCC 2174)

Almost from the beginning of the Church, the apostles changed the day of public worship from Saturday to Sunday (cf. Acts 20: 7). Sunday worship celebrates the completion of the first creation, the new creation in Christ. We commemorate the Resurrection of Jesus, which occurred on a Sunday. In making this change, the feasts of the old law were replaced by the feasts of the new law. That is not to say, however, that the old law no longer has any place in the new covenant. Saturday, the day of the Jewish Sabbath, still holds a special place in the week of the Church—it is the day chosen to honor Mary, the mother of Christ.

The Sunday celebration of the Eucharist, however, is at the heart of the Church's life. It is an invitation to relive the experience of the two disciples whom Jesus met on the road to Emmaus, when Jesus explained the Scriptures to them. Christian activity is nourished, and moral life is strengthened, by participation in the Sunday liturgy. Sunday is the foremost holy day of obligation, on which all the faithful are obliged to attend Mass. Also to be observed are the holy days that do not fall on Sunday. In the United States, these days are the following solemnities:

† Nativity of Our Lord Jesus Christ (Christmas), December 25;

† Mary, Mother of God, January 1;

† Assumption of Mary, August 15;

† All Saints, November 1;

† Mary's Immaculate Conception, December 8.

In some dioceses, Ascension Thursday is still celebrated as a holy day on Thursday rather than the following Sunday.

Holy days of obligation usually fall outside the Sundays of the year. The local bishop may excuse us from the obligation to attend Mass when some of these days fall on Saturday or Monday.

The requirement that we attend Mass on Sundays and designated holy days is clear in the precepts and laws of the Church. We fulfill this requirement by attending a Mass celebrated in a Catholic rite on the afternoon or evening preceding the day of obligation or on the day itself. Fulfilling the obligation to attend Mass on the previous day does not eliminate the requirement to honor the Lord's day appropriately.

Work must be avoided if it impedes the worship owed to God or makes attendance at Mass impossible on both Saturday and Sunday. Everyone who has reached the age of seven and has sufficient use of reason must go to Mass unless excused for a serious reason. If we deliberately fail in this obligation, we are guilty of mortal sin.

Attending Mass on Sunday holds special value for us as Catholics because the Mass is a re-presentation (a presentation again) of the sacrifice of Christ on the Cross. The bread and wine are turned into his Body and Blood. We discussed the Eucharist in detail in the section on the sacraments, but for now, consider what the *Catechism of the Catholic Church* says about Mass and the Eucharist:

> The Sunday Eucharist is the foundation and confirmation of all Christian practice. For this reason the faithful are obliged to participate in the Eucharist on days of obligation, unless excused for a serious reason (for example, illness, the care of infants) or dispensed by their own pastor.[4] Those who deliberately fail in this obligation commit a grave sin. (CCC 2181)

> Participation in the communal celebration of the Sunday Eucharist is a testimony of belonging and of being faithful to Christ and to his Church. The faithful give witness by this to their communion in faith and charity. Together they testify to God's holiness and their hope of salvation. They strengthen one another under the guidance of the Holy Spirit. (CCC 2182)

Participation in the Mass goes far beyond simply sitting through the hour, waiting to go home. One must assume a prayerful attitude at Mass, recognizing the Mass for what it is—the sacrifice of the Cross made present again by Jesus himself. If someone attending Mass ignores this fact, he is not fulfilling the obligation to keep the day holy—he is actually ignoring the holiest moment of the day.

Many things can be done to help us reap the benefits that the Mass offers:

† Arrive at church a few minutes before Mass and look over the readings in the missalette. This will enable us to understand better when they are read and a homily is preached about them.

† When the holy sacrifice begins, we should follow along in the missalette, which will enable us to avoid distractions.

† As the homily is preached, we should ask ourselves, "how can I apply today's lesson to my life?"

† Receive the Eucharist. Regular reception of the Eucharist enables us to become more Christ-like.

The requirement that we attend Mass on Sundays and designated holy days is clear in the precepts and laws of the Church.

Attending Mass on Sunday holds special value for us as Catholics because the Mass is a re-presentation of the sacrifice of Christ on the Cross.

The Lord has set aside this day for us to worship him, to rest, and to discover the joy proper to the Lord's day.

Good works done for family and humble service to the sick, the infirm, and the elderly are works of sanctification.

Those who are employed should give a fair amount of their income to the collection box. The parish has many expenses, and your contribution will help support the activities that benefit all parish members.

Those who are going to receive the Eucharist must fast from food and drink (except water) for one hour prior to reception. This prohibition includes chewing gum. After the Eucharist is received, some time should be spent talking to Jesus and giving thanks for his gifts.

ABUSE OF THE SUNDAY OBLIGATION

It is one of the great mysteries of life that so many people who accept the gifts of God's creation do not return his love by participation in Sunday worship. The Lord has set aside this day for us to worship him, to rest, and to discover the joy proper to the Lord's day. It is only right for man to set aside time to ponder how God's gifts relate to his purpose in this life.

One of these gifts is freedom. When young people reach high school, they often have a strong inclination to exercise this freedom inappropriately. Unfortunately, this tendency often leads many to stop attending Sunday Mass. This is an abuse of our freedom, though. God gave us free will to enable us to choose what is good, not to do evil. When we choose what is evil, this choice can easily lead to the formation of bad habits, which can ultimately weaken our ability to choose freely. They prevent us from understanding things clearly and lead us to do that which we know is wrong.

Another abuse of the Lord's day is treating it as if it were just any other day. Sunday should have special meaning for us, not only in the way we think about it as the Sabbath, but also in the way we live on Sundays. Sunday work, therefore, should be avoided if possible. Every Christian is obliged to avoid making demands on others that would hinder them from honoring the Lord's day. Family needs and important social service can legitimately excuse from the Sunday obligation, but legitimate needs should not lead to habits prejudicial to honoring the Sabbath. Those who do have leisure time should be mindful of those who do not because of poverty and misery. Good works done for family and humble service to the sick, the infirm, and the elderly are works of sanctification.

Sunday work is permitted:

✝ When it is required by God's honor;

✝ When it is required for the good of one's neighbor;

✝ When it is required by necessity.

THE SABBATH IN THE HISTORY OF THE CHURCH

The apostles began the custom of celebrating the Sabbath on Sunday. In those early Christian times, it was extremely difficult to worship on the first day of the week, as the Greeks and Romans celebrated their feasts on different days from the Christians. Celebrating feasts other than those celebrated by the local culture increased their awareness of the special life they had acquired in becoming Christians. The evangelical call to live a life different from that of the pagans led to the formation of a Christian culture supporting those who had converted.

Prior to the conversion of Emperor Constantine and the sacralization (the making sacred) of Sunday, the early Christians worshipped in private homes on Sunday. After the Edict of Milan in A.D. 313, great churches were constructed and worship became public. Since that time, the Church has maintained Sunday as the day of worship, even in those countries where Christianity is not formally recognized as a religion. While this has meant real sacrifices for some Christians, the custom has been happily maintained.

The Church's concern for the day of worship has been addressed not only to worship of God but also to consideration for human needs. For much of the world's history, most people have been at the mercy of those who control the rhythms of work and rest through their use of money and power. Even in our time, many still eke out their existence under very difficult conditions.

For this reason too, the Church has fought to keep Sunday as a day of rest. Those who are not able to rest on Sunday are in no condition to worship Christ as he deserves. The exploitation of man, even in these times, is a source of great concern for the Church.

Through Sunday rest, we are enabled to give proper perspective to the events of life. Spiritual values can be rediscovered, and a Christian perspective on life can be fostered.

One part of our call to witness to our faith is a call to ensure, to the extent we are able, that everyone has the opportunity to worship as God desires. The minimum for true human dignity is one day per week to rest and celebrate.

CULTURAL DIFFICULTIES

There has been a cultural shift in recent decades from respect for Sunday as the day of the Lord to excessive desire for recreation, shopping, and making money on the Sabbath. Until recently, many states had legal requirements that kept Sunday's commercial activity to a minimum. Sunday was accepted as a day of rest from the work schedule.

However, with the rise of the middle class in America after World War II and the reduction to a forty hour work week, many found themselves with a larger share of their income left over for recreation, in addition to increased free time. Modern production methods reduced the costs of manufacturing cheap sporting goods. New freedom and increased wealth led to an increased desire to find and experience forms of recreation that had previously been impossible.

Out of this desire, a new cultural concept was born, *the weekend of recreation.* Many people began to plan weekends away from home since they were now able to go places they could not afford previously. Airline rates were reduced to encourage weekend trips to cities both at home and in Europe. Weekend trips to Europe were advertised at minimum rates including both lodging and airfare.

Mass attendance defines us as practicing believers.

Another special way to honor Sunday is to go on a pilgrimage to a local shrine.

This has led to a serious cultural shift from the observance of Sunday as the Lord's day to a time of concerted activity directed to enjoying the "good things" of life. Sunday, the celebration of the Easter Resurrection, has been replaced by the weekend as the celebration of self. There has been a shift in focus from God to man. The day of rest and worship has been replaced with the "getaway weekend" dedicated to fun.

While the benefits that come with increased leisure time cannot be denied, we must use that leisure to consider what God expects of us in relation to his plan for the salvation of our fellow man. When man focuses on himself almost exclusively, God begins to fade out of the picture.

> In order that rest may not degenerate into emptiness or boredom, it must offer spiritual enrichment, greater freedom, opportunities for contemplation, and fraternal communion. Therefore among the forms of culture and entertainment which society offers, the faithful should choose those which are most in keeping with a life lived in obedience to the precepts of the Gospel. Sunday rest then becomes "prophetic," affirming not only the absolute primacy of God, but also the primacy and dignity of the person with respect to the demands of social and economic life, and anticipating in a certain sense the "new heavens and new earth," in which liberation from slavery to needs will be final and complete. In short the Lord's Day thus becomes in the truest sense the day of man as well.[5]

RECLAIMING SUNDAY FOR CHRIST

As Christians we have an obligation to reclaim Sunday for Christ.

> Given its many meanings and aspects and its link to the very foundations of faith, the celebration of the Christian Sunday remains, on the threshold of the Third Millennium, an indispensable element of our Christian identity.[6]

We should plan to attend Mass on each and every weekend and holy day—for Mass attendance defines us as practicing believers. It might be better to attend Mass on Sunday rather than Saturday to emphasize the sacredness of the day. We should also pray for our family members and friends who have lost their sense of the sacredness of Sunday while at the same time encouraging them to return to regular attendance at the Eucharist.

The Sabbath day presents us with other opportunities to worship God and do what is pleasing to him. As Christians, we are called to revisit old ways and to formulate new ways to honor God and serve our neighbor in keeping with the requirements of the day of rest. People who are confined to nursing homes, for example, would welcome a visit to help them pass the time.

Another special way to honor Sunday is to go on a pilgrimage to a local shrine, either on foot or by train or automobile. Pilgrimages are a custom dating back to the beginning of the Church. The earliest pilgrimages were made to the graves of St. Peter and St. Paul in Rome and to Jerusalem, where Christ gave his life for us.

The day also presents us with an opportunity to devote ourselves to works of charity and mercy. One of these is giving to the collections in which our parish asks us to participate. These support the local parish as well as diocesan and worldwide needs of the Church.

> Ever since Apostolic times, the Sunday gathering has in fact been for Christians a moment of fraternal sharing with the very poor. "On the first day of the week each of you is to put aside and save whatever extra you earn" (1 Cor 16: 2), says St. Paul, referring to the collection organized for the poor churches of Judaea. In the Sunday Liturgy, the believing heart opens wide to embrace all aspects of the Church.[7]

In addition to attending Mass, we should set aside time for prayer to thank Jesus for the great gift of the Eucharist and to grow closer to him. Time set aside for prayer reminds us that not only is this day holy, but that Jesus calls us to become holier.

When we pray, we should give special thought to the Creed that we say at Mass. It is good to meditate on these truths to acquire a deeper understanding of their place in our lives.

Lived in this way, not only the Sunday Eucharist but the whole of Sunday becomes a school of charity, justice, and peace. The presence of the risen Lord in the midst of his people becomes an undertaking of solidarity, a compelling force for inner renewal, an inspiration to change the structures of sin in which individuals, communities and, at times, entire peoples are entangled. Far from being an escape, the Christian Sunday is a "prophecy" inscribed on time itself, a prophecy obliging the faithful to follow in the footsteps of the one who died to save us from our sins.

Lived in this way, not only the Sunday Eucharist but the whole of Sunday becomes a school of charity, justice, and peace.

CONCLUSION

How great is the Lord who made the gifts of creation that all of us enjoy. Sunday worship enables us to indicate the importance of the Lord in our lives by attending Mass. Worshipping God on Sunday is a sign of our love for him as well as an example to others, for the world needs the witness of believers.

Sanctifying Sundays and holy days requires a common effort. By encouraging others to attend Mass on Sunday, we witness to our belief in God. The re-sanctification of Sunday will only be accomplished when all Catholics return to the practice of honoring the Sabbath as God intends.

Every Christian should avoid making unnecessary purchases or demands on others that would hinder them from observing the Lord's Day. This obligation extends especially to those who are employers. Foresight must be shown in arranging one's business operations to oblige as few persons as possible to work on Sunday.

SUPPLEMENTARY READING

Ars was a small country village in France. When Father John Vianney was assigned there as the parish priest in 1818, he knew he had a difficult task, with high expectations placed upon him. "There is not much love of God in that parish," he was told by his bishop. "You will put some there." When Vianney arrived, he discovered that very few people went to Sunday Mass. They instead preferred to work in their farms. Very few people went to Confession, nor did they visit Jesus in the Blessed Sacrament. They were too busy.

Father Vianney took his calling at Ars seriously. He preached. He visited families. But he found that his words did no good. People still did not care to go to Sunday Mass.

Father Vianney therefore began to punish his body, doing penance for the sins of others, particularly those who did not go to Mass on Sunday.

He fasted, eating only one potato a day. He did not sleep at night but spent the time praying.

Little by little the penance he imposed upon himself for the sake of his parish began to have an effect. His people began to change. On Sundays, the church was filled. Sunday rest was unbroken because the people learned to stay home with their families instead of going to the fields. Rather then seeing a drop in productivity on their farms, however, their work was blessed.

Within a few years after John Vianney arrived in Ars, the people learned to keep Sundays

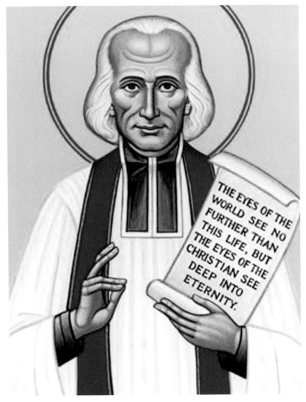

St. John Vianney
(1786-1859)
Feast on August 4

and days of obligation holy. Through his exceptional dedication to the Mass, he helped reconcile many people with God. He was declared a saint in 1925, and made patron of parish priests.

VOCABULARY

HOLY DAY OF OBLIGATION
Feast day to be observed by attendance at Mass and rest from unnecessary servile work. In the U.S.: Solemnity of Mary Mother of God, Ascension of Our Lord, Assumption, All Saints' Day, Immaculate Conception, and Christmas.

LEISURE
Time to cultivate one's familial, cultural, social, and religious life.

MASS
Eucharistic or principal sacramental celebration of the Church, established by Jesus at the Last Supper, in which the mystery of our salvation through participation in the sacrificial death and glorious resurrection of Christ is renewed and accomplished.

PAGAN
Heathen; one who practices idolatry; a person abandoning all religious belief; an irreligious person.

RESURRECTION
Of the dead: The raising of the righteous, who will live forever with the risen Christ, on the last day. *Of Christ:* The bodily rising of Jesus from the dead on the third day after his death on the cross and burial in the tomb.

SABBATH
The Sabbath or seventh day, on which God rested after the work of the six days of creation was completed, as recounted in the opening narrative of the Bible.

SACRALIZATION
Making sacred.

STUDY QUESTIONS

1. List God's purposes in setting aside the Sabbath.

2. How did the Jewish people celebrate the Sabbath?

3. What was Jesus' objection to the Pharisees' rules for the Sabbath?

4. Who changed the worship day to Sunday?

5. What were the reasons for this change?

6. Who is honored on Saturday?

7. What are the benefits of Sunday Mass attendance?

8. What are the six holy days of obligation in the United States?

9. Who is required to attend the celebration of the Eucharist?

10. List the points from the *Catechism of the Catholic Church* regarding Eucharistic attendance.

11. When is Sunday work permitted?

12. Whose decree led to worship in public?

13. What cultural trends are interfering with Sunday worship?

14. What can we do to encourage our friends to attend the Eucharistic celebration?

15. What ways are available to us to honor the Sunday observance?

16. How is every Mass a celebration?

PRACTICAL EXERCISES

1. Plan to arrive at church five minutes early each Sunday. Before the celebration of Mass begins, read the Sunday readings. When they are read during Mass, ask the Holy Spirit to help you understand how Jesus wants you to apply them in your life this week.

2. Read Jesus' words about the correct spirit in which the observance of the Sabbath is to be kept (Mt 12: 9-14; Mk 3: 1-6; Lk 6: 1-11). In the following cases, determine whether or not, in your opinion, these individuals have failed to keep the third commandment. Be sure to offer specific reasons for your conclusions.

a. Miguel and Francisco are brothers who always go to Mass together on Sundays. Last Sunday, they went on spring break, and they decided to attend a Mass celebrated in a parish at nine o'clock at night. It's the last Mass in that city. That day, an unusual traffic jam caused by crowds of other college students made them arrive late and miss the entire Mass. When they returned home, they talked about what happened that day. Miguel said that he didn't feel guilty about anything, since he had the intention of going to Mass as always and the traffic jam was unforeseeable. Francisco, on the other hand, felt guilty. They both go to Confession regularly. In his next Confession, Miguel doesn't plan to mention that he missed Mass last Sunday. Francisco plans to confess that he missed Mass. Who is right, Miguel or Francisco?

b. Jennie is scheduled to take a trip with a group of friends. Their flight leaves early Sunday morning, so Jennie planned to go to the anticipated Mass on Saturday evening. On Saturday morning, Jennie's employer calls her and asks her to work the 1-9 p.m. shift at the restaurant, because another waitress called in to say that she couldn't come to work. Jennie prides herself in being flexible and willing to help people out when they are in a tight spot, but if she agrees, she won't have another opportunity to attend Sunday Mass. Jennie recently had a disagreement with her employer and is also afraid that if she doesn't agree, her employer might view her as uncooperative and give her a lower rating in her next job evaluation. What do you think she should do?

c. Every Sunday Perry sits in the back of church and talks about the weekend with his friends. When challenged by his parents, he justifies what he is doing by stating, "The Church says I have to attend Mass on Sunday; that doesn't mean I have to pay attention." Is Perry fulfilling the obligation of attendance at Mass? Why or why not?

d. Brandy and her father, a doctor in a nursing home, live in a small town where the local Catholic church has only one Mass on Sunday morning. On this particular Sunday morning, her father is working the morning shift. On her way out the door to go to Mass, the telephone rings. It is her elderly grandfather. He is not feeling well and has run out of the medication that his doctor has prescribed for him. He asks if she can come over, pick up his prescription, have it refilled, and stay with him until her father comes home from work. Brandy agrees, but feels guilty about having missed Mass. Do you think she should? How would you explain your answer to her?

FROM THE CATECHISM

2189 "Observe the sabbath day, to keep it holy" (Dt 5:12). "The seventh day is a sabbath of solemn rest, holy to the Lord." (Ex 31:15)

2190 The sabbath, which represented the completion of the first creation, has been replaced by Sunday which recalls the new creation inaugurated by the Resurrection of Christ.

2191 The Church celebrates the day of Christ's Resurrection on the "eighth day," Sunday, which is rightly called the Lord's Day (cf. *SC*, 106).

2192 "Sunday...is to be observed as the foremost holy day of obligation in the universal Church" (CIC, can. 1246 § 1). "On Sundays and other holy days of obligation the faithful are bound to participate in the Mass" (CIC, can. 1247).

2193 "On Sundays and other holy days of obligation the faithful are bound...to abstain from those labors and business concerns which impede the worship to be rendered to God, the joy which is proper to the Lord's Day, or the proper relaxation of mind and body" (CIC, can. 1247).

2194 The institution of Sunday helps all "to be allowed sufficient rest and leisure to cultivate their familial, cultural, social, and religious lives" (*GS*, 67 § 3).

2195 Every Christian should avoid making unnecessary demands on others that would hinder them from observing the Lord's Day.

Endnotes

1. Cf. Mt 28:1; Mk 16:2; Lk 24:1; Jn 20:1.
2. Cf. Mk 16:1; Mt 28:1.
3. St. Justin, I *Apol.* 67: PG 6, 429 and 432.
4. Cf. CIC, can. 1245.
5. *DD*, 68.
6. Ibid., 30.
7. Ibid., 69.

The Fourth Commandment

Love, Honor and Respect.

The Fourth Commandment

*M*ark and his wife and children had just finished dinner when the doorbell rang. He opened the door and found his two younger brothers standing with open cans of beer in their hands.

"Hey, Mark, How's it going? There was nothing else to do, so we decided to bring our dates to meet you."

"Your dates? Give me a break; you're living with those girls. Besides, I don't want my children to see the type of lives you guys are leading."

"The type of lives *we're* leading," they laughed. "Okay, Mr. High and Mighty, you're the one who taught us this lifestyle." They turned and walked away laughing.

An ashamed Mark walked back into the house and said, "I wish I had been a better example to my brothers when I was younger."

THE FOURTH COMMANDMENT AND THE OLD TESTAMENT

> Honor your father and your mother, that your days may be long in the land which the Lord your God gives you. (Ex 20:12)

God has willed that after himself, we are required to honor our parents and all those who have been given authority for our own good.

The command to honor your father and your mother begins the second section of the Ten Commandments, the section that deals with man's relations with his family and fellow humans beings. A person who honors his parents is promised that "your days may be long in the land which the Lord your God gives you" (Ex 20:12). This is the only commandment with a promise and informs us that the Lord gives peace and prosperity to those who keep this command.

Parents have the right to be obeyed and respected. Parents give their lives to rear, protect, and care for their children, making sure family life is stable and safe. The least children can give in return is honor, obedience, love, just assistance, and respect. If love and respect are given in a home, then that family will have the peace and the great prosperity assured by the Lord.

Children should obey their parents for their own welfare. Parents have a better understanding of the world gained from a lifetime of experience. Parents can and will pass on this knowledge to their offspring. If children accept this parental wisdom, they will reap rewards gained from the experience of their parents and lead better, happier lives.

A well-ordered home helps not only the individual family but the entire community as well. The family is the basic unit of society. A healthy family adds to the health of society. Failure to keep the fourth commandment brings great harm to families and ultimately to the community.

> The fourth commandment is addressed expressly to children in their relationship to their father and mother, because this relationship is the most universal. It likewise concerns the ties of kinship between members of the extended family. It requires honor, affection, and gratitude toward elders and ancestors. Finally, it extends to the duties of pupils to teachers, employees to employers, subordinates to leaders, citizens to their country, and to those who administer or govern it.
>
> This commandment includes and presupposes the duties of parents, instructors, teachers, leaders, magistrates, those who govern, all who exercise authority over others or over a community of persons. (CCC 2199)

This statement from the *Catechism of the Catholic Church* clearly indicates that we have obligations to love, honor, and respect all members of society, in varying degrees, and these obligations must be honored.

THE FIRST FAMILY

Adam and Eve, the original man and woman, were created in a state of marriage. They were the parents of the first family, which existed before any other social or political group. Since the family came before the community in God's wise plan, the family has rights that the community may not deny. Society is not superior to families, nor is it superior to the

Honor your father and your mother.

If love and respect are given in a home, then that family will have the peace and the great prosperity assured by the Lord.

The Fourth Commandment

When families are corrupt, their actions lead eventually to corruption of community.

The Holy Family has always been regarded as the model for all Catholic families.

individual. The human person is and should be the principal, subject, and object of every social organization. In other words, social organizations exist for the good of human beings, not human beings for the good of social organizations.

This is not to say that we are commanded to be loyal to our family to the detriment of society. Society benefits from the many rights, duties, and responsibilities of the family. The family owes proper respect and obedience to social and political orders, as implied in the fourth commandment. Fully understood, the fourth commandment tells us to honor God, and after him, our parents and all lawful authority.

Obedience to God's commands is necessary for a just society, and the Book of Genesis is instructive regarding the spread of disobedience in a family leading to corruption in society.

The devil tempted Adam and Eve with the promise that they would be like God if they ate the forbidden fruit. They did the devil's bidding. After they sinned, they rushed to cover their nakedness, for they both realized that they were now capable of taking advantage of each other repeatedly through sin.

They had two sons who bore the mark of original sin: Cain and Abel. When God accepted the offerings of Abel, his brother Cain became jealous. Although God warned Cain that the devil was waiting to tempt him, Cain was overwhelmed by jealousy and killed his brother.

The Bible then relates how men spread over the earth, with each new generation becoming ever more sinful.

In the time of Noah, God decided he had had enough of the sins of mankind. Since Noah was a righteous man, God told Noah to build an ark and take his family into it, for God was planning the destruction of all sinners. Everyone was killed except Noah and his family.

The experiences of these original peoples is a warning to us regarding the spread of sin. When families are corrupt, their actions lead eventually to corruption of community.

JESUS AND THE FOURTH COMMANDMENT

He...was obedient to them. (Lk 2:51)

The most important lesson we can learn from Jesus concerning the fourth commandment is not something he said. It is the way he lived. We know that we are to learn not only from Jesus' words, but his actions also. This is exactly the case with the fourth commandment.

Jesus chose to live his life on earth as part of a family. In the Holy Family was a mother, the Virgin Mary, whom Jesus loved and who loved Jesus as a true mother. There was St. Joseph, the protector and provider for the family, a loving foster father for the Christ child and chaste spouse of the Virgin Mary. And finally there was Jesus himself, who, though he was God, obeyed and loved his parents, knowing that this was proper.

[T]he Holy Family has always been regarded as the exemplar and model for all Catholic families and, by extension, as the exemplar of all persons living in community, whether active or contemplative: the loving faith, obedience and providence of the hard-working Joseph; the faith, love, obedience and strength of the Blessed Mother; the perfection of the Son of God made Man, Who submitted Himself in obedience to a human mother and foster father. Thus in the earthly trinity of Jesus, Mary, and Joseph can be found a perfect model of all the virtues, both personal and social. But not only were they holy, saintly and virtuous, they also lived a human life like ours which makes it possible for us to seek to imitate them and their virtues.[1]

It is easier for us to learn from the Holy Family once we realize that they lived very normally for most of Jesus' first thirty years. Joseph worked as a carpenter to support his family. When Jesus was a child, he probably had friends that he spent time with when he wasn't called on for help by Mary. Later, Jesus himself learned the trade of carpentry from his foster father Joseph. What makes this family an example for all families, though, is the dedication with which they filled their roles. They realized that God had a special plan for them as a family that required the individual members to fill certain roles. We must realize that God has a plan for us and our families and that each of us must play our own role in that plan.

WHAT RELATIONSHIPS DOES THE FOURTH COMMANDMENT ADDRESS?

Since God instituted the human family and directed how it should operate, his wishes must be followed in all matters that relate to the family. While all have equal dignity and by right are to be treated as children of God, different members of the family have different functions.

As the originators of our life and the caretakers of our youth, parents have a most demanding role to play. Though the same original sin that afflicts us afflicts them, parents are called upon to do their best to lead us in pursuit of our goal in life: heaven. Parenting is a humbling experience, for it calls upon both mother and father to sacrifice themselves to a large extent for the good of the children, over and above their own desires and plans.

It is indeed fitting that the fourth commandment be spoken of in terms of the parents first—for it is in the home that most of us begin life and first experience our obligation to others. It is the first school of self-sacrifice. For parents, this sacrifice entails their primary responsibility for the children's education in faith, prayer, and the virtues, as well as for care of their children's physical and spiritual needs. Those who do not learn respect, love, and honor for their parents, who are of their own blood, will hardly be willing to show respect and obedience to others outside their family.

We are, in fact, required to respect other people besides our parents. The fourth commandment relates not only to parents and children but also to others within the same family. All family members are called to render a debt of kinship, respect, honor, gratitude, and affection for one another, elders, and ancestors.

Beyond fulfilling one's obligations to family, obeying the fourth commandment prepares one to enter society. The obedience and respect required

It is easier for us to learn from the Holy Family once we realize that they lived very normally for most of Jesus' first thirty years.

by the fourth commandment is owed to teachers, leaders, lawgivers, those who govern, and those who administer the law, as well as to all just laws of themselves. Simply stated, the fourth commandment binds us to accept all the just commands of lawful authority and the laws of the community of persons in which we reside, both local and national. A lawful authority is any person who by relation or circumstance has the right to tell us what to do.

OBLIGATIONS OF THE FOURTH COMMANDMENT

> The well-being of the individual person and of both human and Christian society is closely bound up with the healthy state of conjugal and family life.[2]

God instituted the family for the good of the spouses—two people dedicated to the salvation of each other—and the procreation and education of children to populate heaven. Obviously, the familial relationship joins members in deeply personal relationships with moral obligations set by God. The fourth commandment is meant to protect those relationships.

Since the family is by its nature hierarchical, its members have certain roles to fill.

The father, as head of the domestic church, has a most serious obligation to demonstrate a concerned love for his spouse and his children. He must respect the rights and see to the obligations of his wife and children, particularly in matters of religious belief and practice.

The father, as head of the domestic church, has a most serious obligation to demonstrate a concerned love for his spouse and his children.

As the heart of the family, the mother has an obligation to counsel and support her husband in his worship of God and in his decisions. She too must be an example of love, and, when necessary, a mediator between the father and the children to avoid misunderstandings.

Together, parents have the primary right to educate their children in the faith—a right that must not be taken from them. This right includes the power to determine the choice of schools best suited to the spiritual and mental needs of the children. Since this is such an important job, parents are not asked to do this alone, but are given the grace of the Sacrament of Matrimony, which empowers them to evangelize their children.

Educating children in the faith should be begun as soon as the children are old enough to say prayers—for the family is the first place in which prayer should be taught. Young children should be taken to church at an early age on appropriate occasions as part of their evangelization. Evangelization begins with prayer and simple stories of Jesus, Mary, and the lives of the saints. Parents are obliged to respect and encourage their children's vocations in life and teach that each child is called personally to follow Jesus.

It is obvious that parenting is a job that requires a couple to give not just a few hours a day but their entire lives. Because of the personal sacrifices parents make for their children, God requires that children show love, respect, gratitude, and just obedience, and that they render assistance to those who gave them life. A child who treats his parents well will make his own life and his parents' lives easier.

There are many concrete things children should do to live out these obligations: obey the lawful commands of parents when they are given, help with the family chores or clean one's room, avoid friends the parents don't approve of, and keep the curfew set by parents.

In families with more than one child, these obligations become even more pressing. Older children must keep in mind that their younger siblings are an impressionable audience who are carefully observing their conduct. When older children sin, they endanger not only their own souls but also the souls of their younger brothers and sisters. If older children disobey their parents or brag about sinful actions, they become occasions of sin to their younger brothers and sisters. Many young children, in fact, are introduced to serious sin by the words and actions of older siblings. We must remember that, since the family is the first school of self-sacrifice, family members must care for each other in both physical and spiritual needs.

Some young people, however, do not wish to talk to an adult when a sibling or a friend is committing serious sin. This is avoided out of a warped sense of loyalty and a desire not to get someone in trouble. Inaction, however, often allows serious sins such as theft, drug abuse, use of pornography, or sexual activity outside of marriage to become habits, which are difficult to break [see *concupiscence* in the vocabulary section of Chapter 9].

When we become aware of such actions by our siblings or friends, we are seriously obligated to seek the assistance of a parent, priest, or other responsible adult before permanent harm is done. The details of the individual's problem should be told honestly; we should not attempt to sugarcoat the truth. One of the reasons that the Church recommends frequent Reconciliation is that it presents an opportunity to discuss difficult moral problems.

In addition to caring for the spiritual health of our siblings, we can contribute to the personal sanctity of our parents through prayer and through making family life easier by quickly forgiving those in our family who offend us. Simply put, a peace-filled home is a happy home.

Children eventually leave their parents' home and begin a life apart from the day-to-day care and structure provided by their mother and father. But leaving home does not free children from the obligation to listen to and seriously consider the advice of parents or to care for their parents when they are in need. Family members should willingly assume the obligation to care for each other, the old and the sick, as well as those who are poor and handicapped.

Finally, one must remember that the family is not restricted to the relationships between parents, brothers, and sisters. The family comprises other members as well, including cousins, aunts and uncles, and in-laws. We must also recognize members of the Church as family, and even the whole of the human race. All must be esteemed before God, for we are all his children. The care we provide to our immediate family, then, is owed to all others in need, including the old, the sick, the poor, and the handicapped.

We can contribute to the personal sanctity of our parents through prayer and through making family life easier by quickly forgiving those in our family who offend us.

If we do not encourage our friends to be good people, it will be difficult to find good friends with whom to associate.

We should be able to look back on our lives and see what our good example accomplished.

SANCTIFICATION OF SOCIAL LIFE

We are all called to live our day-to-day lives in a holy manner. This can be difficult in the modern world. More than one person has compared the current state of the culture to the Roman Empire when paganism ruled. It is no secret that many people in these times, as in Rome at its lowest point, plan their parties around sex, alcohol, and drugs.

Many of us might feel it is not our obligation to speak up when others plan parties organized around sinful actions. This do-nothing attitude is shortsighted for many reasons. First of all, such events are planned occasions of sin that can lead people into immoral conduct and should therefore be avoided. The person who ignores that fact is not being straightforward with himself or with God. Secondly, friendships that develop out of these activities are likely based on these sins, and again could only be damaging to the soul. Thirdly, if we fail to discourage our friends from attending events that could harm their souls and endanger their salvation, we are not acting with the care that true friends should demonstrate. (It is true that some young people feel they will live forever and will try anything, but we all know, deep down, that none of us will live forever.) Finally, if we do not encourage our friends to be good people, it will be difficult to find good friends with whom to associate.

We should not live as Mark did in the story that opened this chapter. Instead, we should be able to look back on our lives and see what our good example accomplished.

OBLIGATIONS OF CIVIL AUTHORITIES

The first true community, as we have seen, is the family, the basis of all other social structures. These social structures are good because they provide man with the opportunity to have the stability and comforts that a community can provide.

As part of his plan, God decided that there should be political communities and public authorities, both of which he has based on human nature—for man needs a system through which he can accomplish his goals.

Because God wanted these institutions, the people who hold positions of power in them will answer to God for their actions on the day of judgment. They have a most grave obligation to respect the fundamental rights of the human person and to care for the common good by promoting and strengthening marriage, safeguarding public morality, and advancing public virtue and prosperity. In short, civil leaders are obliged to see that their society treats the things that are most sacred properly. This foundation is, after all, for the good of the community. Those societies that are not based on the Gospel easily become tyrannical and substitute the whims of man for the law of God.

One of the primary obligations of the political community is to respect the fundamental rights of each person, to honor the family, and to give the family any needed assistance. These obligations require that political authority ensure:

† The freedom to establish a family, have children, and bring them up in keeping with the family's own moral and religious convictions;

† The protection and stability of the marriage bond and the institution of the family;

† The freedom to profess one's faith, to hand it on, and to rear one's children in it, with the necessary means and institutions;

† The rights to private property, free enterprise, work, housing, and emigration;

† In keeping with the country's institutions, the right to medical care, assistance for the aged, and family benefits;

† The protection of security and health, particularly with respect to dangers like drugs, pornography, alcoholism, etc.;

† The freedom to form associations with other families and so to have representation before civil authority.

OBLIGATIONS OF CITIZENS

Just as a government has responsibilities it must fulfill for the good of its citizens, citizens have responsibilities toward their government. Citizens are required to love their country and contribute to the good of society in a spirit of truth, justice, solidarity, and freedom.

Our country is part of the heritage God has given us, so we should love and serve it in gratitude, recognizing this love and service as an obligation. Service to our country is manifested in building up society in a spirit of truth, justice, solidarity, and freedom.

The dignity of the human person requires that all members of society should pursue the common good, that is, the sum total of social conditions that allow people either as individuals or groups to reach their potential more fully and easily. Submission to legitimate authority and service for the common good in matters of taxation, voting, and military duties is required.

Although laws are ideally expressions of morality, this is not always the case. Sometimes societies establish laws that are contrary to the common good. We must be careful not to accept such laws. Citizens cannot follow directions from authority that are immoral, contrary to the rights of persons and the teachings of the Gospel. In the words of St. Peter, "we must obey God rather than men" (Acts 5:29). Examples of such laws are those permitting abortion, the sale of contraceptives, and pornography, and laws promoting divorce. It is the responsibility of citizens to work within legal structures to change immoral laws.

CONCLUSION

The first social group God created was the family, which, like all groups, needs a structure. God deemed that parents, who are responsible for caring for and educating their children, should have the love, respect, and obedience of these same children. When children give their parents this

Those societies that are not based on the Gospel easily become tyrannical.

It is the responsibility of citizens to work within legal structures to change immoral laws.

The Fourth Commandment

People need to discover this demanding love, for it is truly the foundation of the family, a foundation able to "endure all things."

At work within it is the power and strength of God himself.

respect, the entire family benefits from a happy and stable home life. In addition to owing their parents respect and obedience, children are responsible for the example they give to one another, especially to their younger siblings.

The fourth commandment speaks explicitly of the honor owed by children to parents and implies the obedience owed to authority figures in larger social and political structures. The existence of political authority has its origin in God; hence political structures should be designed with God's laws in mind. Societies serve man best when they assist him to save his soul. Such societies can exist only where there is a vision of man based on the Gospels and respect for the rights of all members of society. Societies not based on the Gospels easily turn into ruthless totalitarian structures.

Love is true when it creates the good of persons and of communities; it creates the good and gives it to others. Only one who is able to be demanding with himself in the name of love can give love to others. Love is demanding. It makes demands in all human situations. It is even more demanding to those who are open to the Gospel. Is this not what Christ proclaims in his commandment?

Nowadays, people need to discover this demanding love, for it is truly the foundation of the family, a foundation able to "endure all things." At work within it is the power and strength of God himself, who "is love" at work; also, within it is the power and strength of Christ, the Redeemer of man and the "Savior of the world."[3]

SUPPLEMENTARY READING

Beginning with the Holy Family of Jesus, Mary, and Joseph, Christianity has made the family its center. While the father is often said to be the head, the mother is most definitely the *heart.* It is the mother of the family who possesses what John Paul II calls the "feminine genius," the natural ability to show great warmth and love for others.

Consider for a moment what it must be like then for the parents of a good Christian woman to give her in marriage to a violent unfaithful pagan. Not only this, but also to have her live with his mother who, with the help of gossipy, disobedient servants, continually tried to undermine her authority and spread lies about her. On top of this, imagine if the first of her three children were to follow his father into lying, cheating, robbery, and sex outside of marriage. So far, there does not appear to be much hope for this family.

Yet St. Monica knew that all things were possible with the love of Jesus Christ. First, by persevering through all the unfounded gossip of her servants with meekness and patience, she was able to convert her mother-in-law. With even more time, her husband began to profess Christianity and died a fervent baptized Christian. Her son however, was much tougher to reach.

While away at school, he applied himself to his studies with zeal. Yet he had also taken on a mistress and had a son with her. He even fell so far as to renounce Christianity for Manicheism—a heresy that denied all religious authority and individual responsibility for sins. Monica was heartbroken and went crying to her spiritual director the bishop. He consoled her saying, "Take comfort; the child of such tears can never perish."

After studying philosophy in Rome, her son Augustine finally gave up his Manichean beliefs and entered into a great depression. Aware of her son's distress, Monica sold all she had and went to Rome. There, she finally convinced his mistress of seventeen years to release him and the young man began to study the Scriptures.

St. Monica
(332-387)
Feast on August 27
Patroness of Wives and Mothers

He became convinced that Jesus is the Way, the Truth, and the Life, but hesitated to accept the disciplined life of a Christian. Finally, while reading the epistles of St. Paul one day, Augustine was moved to grief for his sins and threw himself into the outstretched arms of his mother. Soon after, he and his son began to prepare for Baptism with the help of Monica.

St. Monica is a wonderful example of the principle of spiritual multiplication. She poured herself out completely to those around her, but most of all to her eldest son. Besides converting her mother-in-law and husband and raising her two younger children to be good Christians, her daily tears and prayers led to the conversion of St. Augustine, Bishop of Hippo and Doctor of the Church. Augustine is believed to be responsible for thousands of conversions throughout the course of his life and many more from his writings (most notably, *Confessions,* his story from darkness to light). The Church owes a great debt to St. Monica for her motherly care of one of the most brilliant Christian philosophers the world has ever known.

VOCABULARY

CIVIL AUTHORITY
Person or group who governs or controls a certain group of private citizens or a nation.

COMMUNITY
A group of persons who share the same beliefs, live together under authority, and cooperate in pursuing common interests for the good of other people besides their own members.

HERITAGE
That which comes from the circumstances of birth; an inherited lot or portion.

LOYALTY
Faithful adherence to one's promise, oath, word of honor, etc.

OBLIGATION
The moral power of a law commanding obedience; moral necessity imposed on free will.

RESPECT
To esteem, prize, or value a person (or thing).

SELF-SACRIFICE
The giving up of one's own interests, happiness, and desires for the sake of duty or the welfare of others.

SOCIALIZATION
Creation of voluntary associations and institutions which relate to economic and social goals, to cultural and recreational activities, to sport, to various professions, and to political affairs.

SOLIDARITY
Also the principle of "friendship" or "social charity"; manifested first in the distribution of goods and the remuneration of work.

WELFARE
Well-being of the members of a group or community usually provided by legislation or social effort.

STUDY QUESTIONS

1. What is the message behind the story that opens the chapter?

2. Who benefits when the fourth commandment is kept?

3. What is the effect on society when the commandments are obeyed?

4. What effect did the first sin have on Adam and Eve? How does this apply to us?

5. Why is the Holy Family the model for all families?

6. Why is the home called the "first school of self-sacrifice"?

7. Who has the primary responsibility for the education of children in a family?

8. What are the two purposes of matrimony?

9. What are the roles of the father of a family? The mother?

10. What obligations do parents have toward children in relation to religious practice?

11. What obligations do children have toward parents?

12. What obligations do older children have in regard to younger siblings?

13. What obligations are owed to extended family members?

14. List four reasons to sanctify the social life.

15. Who is the principal subject and object of every social organization?

16. What obligations are owed to the government by its citizens?

PRACTICAL EXERCISES

1. Explain the meaning of this text from Vatican II: "The well-being of the individual person and of both human and Christian society is intimately linked with the healthy condition of that community produced by marriage and family." (*GS*, 47).

2. Discuss some of the material benefits possessed by families in this country and the positive and negative effects that they may have on family life. Do you think family life in countries that do not enjoy as many material benefits as ours is generally better, or do you think that things are generally the same everywhere? Support your answer with specific examples.

3. Comment on the following situation, evaluating Pat's attitude, actions, or decisions in light of the fourth commandment: Pat was told by his dad that it's all right if he drinks beer at home once in a while. Pat told his buddies, "I am going to get a fake I.D. since my dad says it's all right to drink."

4. Make a list of actions that children can do to make their parents' lives easier.

5. What can be done to sanctify social life during the school day?

    a. During the lunch period

    b. During passing periods

    c. Outside after school

FROM THE CATECHISM

2247 "Honor your father and your mother" (Dt 5:16; Mk 7:10).

2248 According to the fourth commandment, God has willed that, after him, we should honor our parents and those whom he has vested with authority for our good.

2249 The conjugal community is established upon the covenant and consent of the spouses. Marriage and family are ordered to the good of the spouses, to the procreation and the education of children.

2250 "The well-being of the individual person and of both human and Christian society is closely bound up with the healthy state of conjugal and family life" (GS, 47 § 1).

2251 Children owe their parents respect, gratitude, just obedience, and assistance. Filial respect fosters harmony in all of family life.

2252 Parents have the first responsibility for the education of their children in the faith, prayer, and all the virtues. They have the duty to provide as far as possible for the physical and spiritual needs of their children.

2253 Parents should respect and encourage their children's vocations. They should remember and teach that the first calling of the Christian is to follow Jesus.

2254 Public authority is obliged to respect the fundamental rights of the human person and the conditions for the exercise of his freedom.

2255 It is the duty of citizens to work with civil authority for building up society in a spirit of truth, justice, solidarity, and freedom.

2256 Citizens are obliged in conscience not to follow the directives of civil authorities when they are contrary to the demands of the moral order. "We must obey God rather than men" (Acts 5:29).

2257 Every society's judgments and conduct reflect a vision of man and his destiny. Without the light the Gospel sheds on God and man, societies easily become totalitarian.

Endnotes

1. *Our Sunday Visitor's Catholic Encyclopedia*, pp. 497-498.
2. *GS*, 47 § 1.
3. *FC*, 14.

The Fifth Commandment

Human life is sacred.

Chapter 23

The Fifth Commandment

*I*n the summer of 1914, Gavrilo Princip killed the Archduke of Austria, Franz Ferdinand, and his wife Sophie. The murderer, a Serbian, committed the crime because he had a political grievance against the government of Austria.

This single act led to the First World War, in which two million people were killed, including over 800,000 Serbians, fellow citizens of the man who fired the first shot.

Not all murders have such catastrophic effects, but all murders are personal catastrophes affecting not just the two persons immediately concerned – the murderer and his victim – but also the lives of many others.

When a person is murdered, his place in the future history of the world is eliminated. Those left behind find themselves without the companionship, love, and support of the person killed. The loss cannot be recovered.

THE FIFTH COMMANDMENT AND THE OLD TESTAMENT

You shall not kill. (Ex 20:13)

Men find themselves enemies to each other as a direct result of original sin.

The Old Testament, in fact, records many murders, all of which result directly from man's sinful inclinations. One of the earliest sins recorded in the Bible is the murder of Abel by his brother Cain.

Cain said to Abel his brother, "Let us go out into the field." And when they were in the field, Cain rose up against his brother and killed him. Then the Lord said to Cain, "Where is Abel your brother?" He said, "I do not know; am I my brother's keeper?" And the Lord said, "What have you done? The voice of your brother's blood is crying to me from the ground. And now you are cursed from the ground, which has opened its mouth to receive your brother's blood." (Gn 4: 8-11)

In fact, both the Old and New Testaments forbid the killing of the innocent, which is murder. In Exodus, God says that one should not "kill the innocent and the righteous, for I will not acquit the wicked" (Ex 23:7).

The law against murder is the most basic rule for peace and order in society. If killing were not forbidden, individuals could never trust one another, nor could a group of people ever feel secure.

The fifth commandment is based on more than just practical necessity, though. It recognizes the dignity of every human person. Each individual is sacred to God, for God has made man "in his own image." Since we are made in God's image, killing a human being is destroying one of God's greatest creations.

God has fashioned each of us in our mothers' wombs fearfully, wonderfully, down to the last detail. There is *nothing* about *anyone* of which God is unaware. Out of love and respect for the dignity of every human being, God created no two people alike. As a result, each of us has our own mixture of talents and gifts (as well as faults and shortcomings). These talents are given to enable us to accomplish on earth that for which God has created us.

When a person is killed, his murderer interrupts God's plan for his victim. He takes away what belongs to God—the life of a human being.

THE FIFTH COMMANDMENT AND THE NEW TESTAMENT

You have heard that it was said to the men of old, "You shall not kill; and whoever kills shall be liable to judgment." But I say to you that everyone who is angry with his brother shall be liable to judgment. (Mt 5: 21-22)

In the Sermon on the Mount, Jesus recalls the fifth commandment. He goes beyond the prohibition against murder to forbid anger, hatred, and vengeance. These actions go against the dignity of a person made in the image of God. When we choose to be angry with someone, hate someone, or seek vengeance against someone, we act contrary to God's commands. We are refusing to follow God's commands and choosing to do as we ourselves please. When we do this, we deny the special dignity

One of the earliest sins recorded in the Bible is the murder of Abel by his brother Cain.

And the Lord said, "What have you done? The voice of your brother's blood is crying to me from the ground." (Gn 4:10)

The Fifth Commandment

The Gospels not only forbid hatred and revenge, they call us to go further, to love supernaturally.

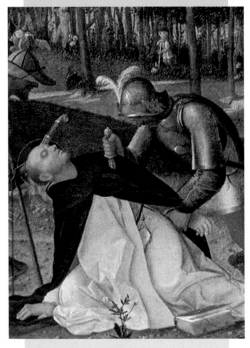

The murder of St. Peter the Martyr

Here silent is Christ's Herald;
Here quenched, the People's Light;
Here lies the martyred Champion
Who fought Faith's holy fight.

Excerpt from the eulogy by St. Thomas of Aquinas for Peter of Verona who was murdered by heretics in 1252 on the road to Milan from Como.

God has given to us as well as the dignity of others.

> "*Human life is sacred* because from the beginning it involves the creative action of God and it remains forever in a special relationship with the Creator, who is its sole end. God alone is the Lord of life from its beginning until its end; no one can under any circumstance claim for himself the right directly to destroy an innocent human being."[1] (CCC 2258)

God has willed each person for his own sake and made each person in his own image and likeness. As a result, the Gospels not only forbid hatred and revenge, they call us to go further, to love supernaturally. Jesus tells his disciples "to turn the other cheek, to love their enemies" (CCC 2262). The requirement to love one's enemy is unique to the Christian religion.

Christ models a life of forgiveness and love. He refused to defend himself when he was falsely accused and arrested. While nailed to the cross, he asked the Father to forgive those who were crucifying him.

To the prohibition against murder is added the requirement to avoid all physical and moral harm to one's neighbor, including the sin of scandal, by which a person is led into sin.

The key to following this commandment is to recognize the dignity of each person and his right to be treated as a child of God. Every one of us is dignified by the fact that we are made by God in the image and likeness of God.

INTENTIONAL MURDER

> The fifth commandment forbids *direct and intentional killing* as gravely sinful. The murderer and those who cooperate voluntarily in murder commit a sin that cries out to heaven for vengeance.[2] (CCC 2268)

Murder of a human being is gravely contrary to the dignity of that person and is a denial of the holiness of the God who created him. Every murder is gravely sinful.

Particularly serious is the murder of a person by a member of the same family. Such an act destroys a life belonging to God and can do further serious harm to the natural ties that bind family members together.

Even more offensive to God is the sin of so-called "ethnic cleansing," in which entire groups of people are murdered because of their ethnic background or religious belief.

The prohibition against intentional murder extends to willing the death of an innocent person indirectly. If we put someone's life at risk without grave reason or refuse to offer help to someone in danger, we have violated the fifth commandment.

An example of refusing to render required assistance is societal acceptance of famines without taking action to relieve the suffering.

Also, those who take advantage of famines by raising the price of food to those in need commit indirect homicide, for which they will have to answer.

LEGITIMATE SELF-DEFENSE

The prohibition against murder does not conflict with the right to self-defense. When a person's life is threatened, he has a right to defend himself.

The right of a person to self-defense permits him to use only the force necessary to protect himself against an unjust attacker. Obviously, this right does not free a person from the obligations related to the fifth commandment. The use of force in self-defense must match the threat. Put simply, if someone knows that all he has to do to defend himself adequately is strike the attacker, intentionally doing more than that is wrong. In a case of self-defense, one is obliged not to seek the death of the attacker directly.

> The legitimate defense of persons and societies is not an exception to the prohibition against the murder of the innocent that constitutes intentional killing. "The act of self-defense can have a double effect: the preservation of one's own life; and the killing of the aggressor...The one is intended; the other is not."[3] (CCC 2263)

Legitimate defense is not only a right for all people, but for some it is also a grave obligation.

Legitimate defense can be a grave duty for someone responsible for another's life, in defense of the common good of the family, or in defense of the state against forces that would seek to destroy it from within or without.

Those who are required to defend themselves, then, are people who are depended upon by others to the extent that their death would cause great harm to their dependents, such as parents with young children or political leaders.

Since this concept of preserving the common good of society is part of the principle of self-defense, the Church has always defended the right of properly constituted authority to punish evildoers with penalties that match the gravity of the offense against the common good.

The state's right to punish the guilty is not a matter of "getting even." The purpose is to require the law-breaker to make restitution, as a matter of justice, for a particular offense. This power of the state also helps to preserve public order and safety. A bloodless means of punishment is always preferred to its opposite when it is possible. This is because even those who have committed grave evils are still made in God's image and likeness and have the dignity that God gives to all people, and should be afforded the opportunity for repentance.

Use of the death penalty is appropriate only when a person is a continuing threat to the lives of others. Today, especially in developed countries, situations requiring the death penalty are *very* rare or even *nonexistent.*

Legitimate defense can be a grave duty for someone responsible for another's life.

From the moment of conception, God is at work in the creation of a new human being whom he loves infinitely.

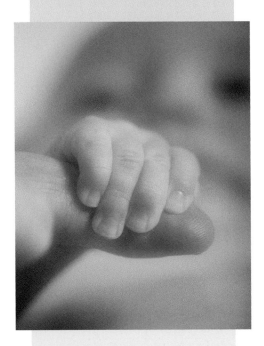

ABORTION

> Human life must be respected and protected absolutely from the moment of conception. From the first moment of his existence, a human being must be recognized as having the rights of a person—among which is the inviolable right of every innocent being to life.[4] (CCC 2270)

Since the first century, the Church has condemned abortion as intrinsically evil. This teaching is unchangeable. Abortion directly willed as a means or an end is a criminal act gravely contrary to moral law. Anyone who formally cooperates in an abortion is automatically excommunicated.

From the moment of conception, God is at work in the creation of a new human being whom he loves infinitely. Hence, an embryo has infinite dignity from the moment of its conception, and its right to health services and care, along with all other human rights, must be honored.

> The inalienable rights of the person must be recognized and respected by civil society and political authority. These human rights depend neither on single individuals nor on parents; nor do they represent a concession made by society to the state; they belong to human nature and are inherent in the person by virtue of the creative act from which the person took its origin. Among such fundamental rights one should mention in this regard every human being's right to life and physical integrity from the moment of conception until death.
>
> The moment a positive law deprives a category of human beings of the protection which civil legislation ought to accord them, the state is denying the equality of all before the law. When the state does not place its power at the service of the rights of each citizen, and in particular of the more vulnerable, the very foundations of a state based on law are undermined.... As a consequence of the respect and protection which must be ensured for the unborn child from the moment of conception, the law must provide appropriate penal sanctions for every deliberate violation of the child's rights.[5]

With advancements in medical technology in recent years, many facts are known about a person prior to birth.

Only medical procedures that respect its life and integrity may be carried out on the embryo or fetus. Such procedures are moral to the extent that they do not involve a risk greater than the good to be accomplished. These procedures must be directed to healing, improving the health, or promoting the survival of the unborn child.

Prenatal diagnosis is morally acceptable "if it respects the life and integrity of the embryo and the human fetus and is directed towards its safeguarding or healing as an individual...It is gravely opposed to the moral law when this is done with the thought of possibly inducing an abortion, depending upon the results; a diagnosis must not be the equivalent of a death sentence."[6]

It is never morally acceptable to produce human embryos outside the act of marriage. Those who produce embryos in an immoral manner are treating the embryo as a product to be manufactured rather than as a human being with personal dignity.

Likewise, it is immoral to test or to change an unborn person's genes simply in order to produce children of a specific sex or other pre-determined qualities. Such procedures violate the dignity, integrity, and identity of the unborn person whose genetic structure is unique and unrepeatable.

EUTHANASIA

Euthanasia means "good death" and is a term used to promote killing the chronically sick or aged.

The principle that life is sacred applies equally to those who are sick, handicapped, or aged. Direct euthanasia, the act of directly ending the lives of sick, handicapped, aged, or dying persons, is murder.

> Thus an act or omission which, of itself, or by intention, causes death in order to eliminate suffering constitutes a murder gravely contrary to the dignity of the human person and to the respect due to the living God, his Creator. The error of judgment into which one can fall in good faith does not change the nature of the murderous act, which must always be forbidden and excluded.[7]

The term "ordinary care" refers to medical care required under all circumstances. It includes feeding, respiration, drugs, and care of the body, e.g., bathing and preventing bedsores.

Ordinary care could also include the use of painkillers to alleviate suffering of the dying, even if this treatment might have the secondary effect of shortening their days. It is morally correct as long as death is not willed as a means or end.

The requirement to give ordinary care applies also to those in the so-called "persistent vegetative state," as Pope John Paul II indicated in a statement on health care in 1998. All sick persons have an unconditional right to ordinary care.

Extraordinary care for the sick is not required. The term extraordinary care is applied to procedures that are burdensome, inordinately expensive, dangerous, or disproportionate to the expected outcome.

Refusing extraordinary care is not an act of killing. It is simply accepting what is medically unavoidable.

When there is a question regarding what constitutes ordinary or extraordinary care, the decision is to be made by the patient after consultation with the physician or by those legally entitled to act for the patient, whose legitimate interests and reasonable will must be respected. It is wise to consult a priest to determine if the correct moral choice has been made.

There are four conclusions to be drawn regarding appropriate care in serious medical cases:

† It is always wrong to directly take the life of a sick person;

† Ordinary means to sustain life are required in all cases;

† Extraordinary means are never required;

† It is permissible to allow the imminent death of a person.

The principle that life is sacred applies equally to those who are sick, handicapped, or aged.

Refusing extraordinary care is not an act of killing. It is simply accepting what is medically unavoidable.

> *Suicide results in endless pain and suffering for family and friends, who are left with the burden of a loss that is both unexplained and unexplainable.*

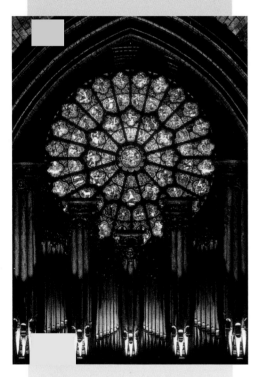

> *The Church includes in her prayers those who have taken their own lives.*

SUICIDE

> Everyone is responsible for his life before God who has given it to him. It is God who remains the sovereign Master of life. We are obliged to accept life gratefully and preserve it for his honor and the salvation of souls. We are stewards, not owners, of the life God has entrusted to us. It is not ours to dispose of. (CCC 2280)

Suicide is the intentional taking of one's own life. It is an intrinsically evil act that contradicts the purpose of everyone's existence: to love and serve God in order to save one's soul and to assist others in the salvation of their souls. It is contrary to hope, justice, and charity. It unjustly breaks the ties of solidarity with one's family and one's community.

Suicide results in endless pain and suffering for family and friends, who are left with the burden of a loss that is both unexplained and unexplainable. Voluntary cooperation in or the encouragement of suicide is contrary to moral law and a grave sin. In fact, all of us are bound by a serious obligation of love to seek assistance for those who talk about ending their own lives.

Though suicide is unquestionably a grave evil, personal responsibility for suicide may be diminished by suffering, torture, grave fear of hardship or anguish, and grave psychological disturbances. The eternal salvation of those who take their own lives should not be despaired of—God can provide by ways known only to him the opportunity for remedial penitence. The Church includes in her prayers those who have taken their own lives.

SCANDAL

> Scandal is an attitude or behavior which leads another to do evil. The person who gives scandal becomes his neighbor's tempter. He damages virtue and integrity; he may even draw his brother into spiritual death. Scandal is a grave offense if by deed or omission another is deliberately led into a grave sin. (CCC 2284)

Anyone who uses the power at his disposal in such a way that it leads others to do wrong becomes guilty of scandal and responsible for the evil that he has directly or indirectly encouraged. "Temptations to sin are sure to come; but woe to him by whom they come!"[8] (CCC 2287)

Scandal can be provoked by persons, laws, or institutions and takes many forms: pressure by friends, our classmates' example, television programs, immodest fashions, public opinion, and the movies.

We all have a tendency, born of original sin, to partake of the sinful actions of others. Often, this leads individuals to ignore the evil of following others into sin without caring about the effect this sin will have on their lives.

During the teen years, this is complicated by the almost overwhelming tendency to act as one's peers act. Young people are often introduced to sins involving drug abuse, sexuality, alcohol, gambling, and pornography through the actions of their peers as well as the culture at large.

Young people tend to absorb their morals from the culture without regard to moral law. For instance, currently, popular culture promotes some immoral music, provocative dress, and warped attitudes about sex. Christians have an obligation to live counter-culturally and resist these pressures as an example for others.

> Therefore, they are guilty of scandal who establish laws or social structures leading to the decline of morals and the corruption of religious practice, or to "social conditions that, intentionally or not, make Christian conduct and obedience to the Commandments difficult and practically impossible."[9] This is also true of business leaders who make rules encouraging fraud, teachers who provoke their children to anger,[10] or manipulators of public opinion who turn it away from moral values. (CCC 2286)

RESPECT FOR HEALTH

The precious gifts of life and health given to us by a loving God require that reasonable care be taken of them, taking into account the needs of others and the common good. All members of society have an obligation to promote decent living conditions that permit everyone to reach maturity with the necessities—food, clothing, housing, health care, basic education, employment, and social assistance—available to them.

On the other hand, the neo-pagan cult of the body, which is prevalent today, is to be avoided. Too much stress has been laid upon the perfection of the body while ignoring the perfection of the soul. The perfection of a person includes both spirit and body; neither should be stressed to the detriment of the other. Therefore, the all-too-common idolization of sports and the use of illicit drugs to enhance performance must be avoided.

In reaction to this over-emphasis on the body, some people tend to go in the complete opposite direction. They view the body as a prison for the soul and a source of sinfulness. This is simply not true. Human beings are not simply souls trapped in bodies for a time on earth. Rather, a person is both soul and body; one without the other is incomplete. After the coming of Christ, all those who have died will be reunited with their bodies, which will be glorified. Then those in heaven will be completely human, with purified souls in incorruptible bodies.

In the meantime, we should strive to achieve true virtue for ourselves and others by finding a happy medium, where we neither seek holiness of soul by devaluing the body nor struggle for physical perfection without caring for spiritual health.

Because the body has a dignity granted to it by God, care must be taken to respect and protect it. No exterior reason or end justifies the mutilation of the body. The following conclusions may be drawn:

- Kidnapping, torture, and hostage-taking are serious violations of the rights and persons of others.

- Selling or promoting use of harmful drugs is likewise mortally sinful.

- Amputation, mutilation, and sterilization are permitted in cases of medical necessity only. The fad of having oneself tattooed could be a mutilation with no necessary or just reason.

The perfection of a person includes both spirit and body; neither should be stressed to the detriment of the other.

Because the body has a dignity granted to it by God, care must be taken to respect and protect it.

The best way to deal with anger is to forgive and pray for the person who made us angry.

Peace can only be achieved by men following Jesus' example of love for all.

◆ Experimentation on human beings that is contrary to the dignity of the human person and the moral law, even with the consent of the person, is not morally legitimate.

◆ Organ transplants are morally permissible if the donor has given permission and if the psychological and physical dangers to the donor are proportionate to the good sought for the recipient. It is never permissible to cause death or disabling mutilation of a human being to secure an organ, even to save the life of another person.

KEEPING THE PEACE

> Earthly peace is the image and fruit of the peace of Christ, the messianic "Prince of Peace."[11] By the blood of his Cross, "in his own person he killed the hostility,"[12] he reconciled men with God and made his Church the sacrament of the unity of the human race and of its union with God. "He is our peace."[13] He has declared: "Blessed are the peacemakers."[14] (CCC 2305)

Christ came to end hostility between people, nations, and cultures. God did not want to force peace upon men. Peace can only be achieved by men following Jesus' example of love for all.

Human beings, then, are to be the ones who work to bring about the peace of Christ. Anger, hatred, revenge, and grudge-bearing are sins against the fifth commandment. Often these sins occur because the actions of another cause hurt feelings. It is normal to react with strong feelings when another harms us, but feelings must be controlled, for they can easily lead one to sinful actions.

Anger is a sin contrary to peace. It leads to evil thoughts and revenge. The best way to deal with anger is to forgive and pray for the person who made us angry. Jesus said, "Everyone who is angry with his brother shall be liable to punishment" (Mt 5:22).

Deliberate hatred is also a sin against peace. It is contrary to the call to love our neighbor. Christ calls us to a higher standard. "Love your enemies and pray for those who persecute you" (Mt 5:44).

Revenge is the desire to "get even" with another for the real or perceived harm he has done. This is, of course, sinful. It is not right to want another person to suffer. Ultimately, God gives to each man his due. "Vengeance is mine," says the Lord (Dt 32:35). As we do not wish evil upon ourselves, we are required to wish good for others.

Forming cliques with the intention of excluding others is to be avoided. It's natural for us to spend time with those with whom we share common interests. However, it is wrong for a group to exclude other persons intentionally for frivolous reasons.

Holding grudges is refusing to forgive those who have offended us. How can we act this way when Christ forgives our sins so willingly in Confession? Difficulties with anger, hatred, revenge, and grudge-bearing should be discussed with a confessor.

WAR

The common good of the whole human family requires that society be organized on an international level. Neither the intent nor the result of this is to eliminate nations, but the first fruit would be an end to all wars.

Everything that is reasonably possible must be done to avoid war, which causes evils and injustices. In fact, all citizens and all governments are required to work to prevent war.

The Church recognizes the right of nations to legitimate self-defense by military force, but strict conditions are placed on those who would wage war. The moral law must be maintained always, even during armed conflicts. Practices contrary to accepted international practices and principles must not be allowed. Those who have responsibility for the common good must make the decision to go to war, and they may impose on citizens the obligation to bear arms. Men, women, and children who are non-combatants, the wounded, and prisoners must all be treated humanely.

As the Church has a fundamental bias against war, strict conditions are laid on those who wish to conduct one:

◆ War may be declared by proper authority for only a grave and legitimate cause;

◆ Military action must be a last resort;

◆ The good accomplished must outweigh the evil permitted;

◆ Non-combatants may not be targeted.

The Church requires the moral law to be observed even during war. War often leads to serious crimes against man and God. The practice of so-called ethnic cleansing is a great evil, as is indiscriminate destruction of cities and populated regions.

Nuclear weapons capable of mass destruction have been stockpiled over the past 50 years. Such weapons present a grave danger to all humanity.

> "The arms race is one of the greatest curses on the human race, and the harm it inflicts on the poor is more than can be endured."[15] (CCC 2329)

The so-called arms race leads to the use of money and goods for the never-ending production of weapons of ever-greater destructive power. The monies wasted in this endeavor would be better used to aid the poor to live a better standard of life.

HUMAN SOLIDARITY

In light of Christ's teachings, the fifth commandment, which is based on respect for the human person, requires us to love every individual just as we love ourselves (cf. Mt 19:19). Jesus' call to solidarity is a call to see your neighbor as another self. If the world were based on the bond of love, the deep connection among all people would be realized. A world based on solidarity would have the following benefits:

† Sharing of spiritual goods would be easier;

† Social and economic inequalities would be reduced;

The Church recognizes the right of nations to legitimate self-defense by military force, but strict conditions are placed on those who would wage war.

If the world were based on the bond of love, the deep connection among all people would be realized.

Since life is the primary right of every person, it should be obvious that any action that directly violates the freedom or bodily integrity of innocent persons is wrong.

† Human rights would be respected;

† Money currently spent on weapons could be turned to social goods.

The call for solidarity is not about ignoring our individuality but is rather about making the Gospel a reality in the lives of everyone. Jesus commands us to love all people. If this love were realized, there would be true peace on earth.

CONCLUSION

The Father has given us both spirit and body to make our way through this life. Since life is the primary right of every person, it should be obvious that any action that directly violates the freedom or bodily integrity of innocent persons is wrong. There can be no double standard that allows us to claim personal integrity for ourselves while violating the personal integrity of others.

On the other hand, those guilty of crimes may forfeit their right to freedom as a result of their actions. The civil courts exist to make that determination.

The fifth commandment, understood in light of Christianity, not only prohibits us from harming others but requires that we have concern for the well-being of others. We must not hate or desire harm to fall upon any person. We also have a serious obligation to avoid leading others into sin by scandalous conduct. Remember that our call is to imitate Jesus in all our actions.

SUPPLEMENTARY READING

During the 1994 International Year of the Family, the Holy See clashed with the Clinton administration and the United Nations bureaucracy at the Cairo population conference. The core issue was the promotion of abortion as a means of family planning.

On one hand, the Cairo conference proposed a view of women as autonomous agents, for whom sexual expression was but one aspect of self-development, which required liberation from the burdens of child-bearing and child-rearing in order to achieve equality with men. On the other hand, the Church insisted that authentic human development comes from using one's freedom to give oneself to others. For women in particular, that personal development cannot be separated from what Pope John Paul II has called the 'feminine genius,' namely, the woman's ability to care for the other.

On April 24, 1994, just four months before the Cairo conference was to begin, John Paul beatified the woman who could be thought of as an incarnation of the 'feminine genius' in the world and in the home, Gianna Beretta Molla.

Gianna was born as the tenth of 13 children to Alberto and Maria Beretta. Gianna learned a deep spirit of prayer and care for the poor from her parents and saw in her own mother a model of strength and humility. After making her First Communion in 1928, Gianna attended daily Mass for the rest of her life.

The Molla family moved several times during Gianna's youth, and Gianna struggled to pass some high school courses and even failed her courses in Italian and Latin. Her final year of school though marked a turnaround, and she went on to study medicine at the University of Milan in 1942, the same year that both her parents died.

In 1950 Gianna graduated with a diploma in medicine and surgery and opened a practice

St. Gianna Beretta Molla
(1922-1962)

with her brother, Ferdinando, who was also a doctor. She often served the poor for free and traveled — sometimes by bicycle, sometimes on her motorcycle — long distances to treat shut-ins.

Gianna discerned after much prayer that her vocation was to marriage and family life. Having devoted herself to her professional work, Gianna was already 33 when she married Pietro Molla, who was ten years her senior. Gianna wrote to Pietro:

With the help and blessing of God, we shall do all in our power that our family may be a little room where Jesus may reign over all affections, desires and actions. We become cooperators with God in the work of creation. Thus we can give Him children who love Him and serve Him. Pietro, will I be able to be the wife you always wished to have? I want to be!

The Mollas were blessed with three children in four years. After several miscarriages, Gianna

Continued

SUPPLEMENTARY READING CONTINUED

was pregnant with her fourth child when a tumor was discovered in her ovary. Faced with several options, Gianna chose the surgery that would save the baby but was riskier for herself.

On April 21, 1962, she gave birth to a daughter. "If you must decide between me and the child, do not hesitate: choose the child," Gianna told her husband a few days before the child was to be delivered by caesarean section. "I insist on it—save the baby." While the baby was healthy, the mother was not. Gianna suffered for a week from agonizing pain. She was not able to speak in her final days, though she clearly maintained an intense dialogue with God during her death agony. She was returned home on the morning of April 28, 1962, and she died that same day.

Three decades later that child was present in St. Peter's Square to see her mother beatified. For millions of young women around the world trying to balance work and family, professional life and spiritual life, femininity and equality, Dr. Gianna Beretta Molla may just be the ideal model. If the Church needs a patron saint of the modern woman, Gianna Molla, the happy pediatrician, devout Catholic, and caring mother, would be a good choice, demonstrating with her passion for life that the Gospel is still good news for the women of our time.

VOCABULARY

ABORTION
Deliberate termination of pregnancy by killing the unborn child. Such a serious offense results in immediate excommunication.

CLIQUE
A small exclusive party or set, a narrow coterie or circle.

ETHNIC CLEANSING
Genocide; the destruction of a group of people based on ancestry or ancestral traditions i.e., religion, customs, etc.

EUTHANASIA
An action or an omission which, of itself or by intention, causes the death of handicapped, sick, or dying persons—sometimes with an attempt to justify the act as a means of eliminating suffering.

EXCOMMUNICATED
Penal exclusion from the faith community intending to bring about reform and resulting in being forbidden to have any share in the Eucharist and all other acts of public worship and sacraments.

EXTRAORDINARY CARE
Life-sustaining forms of medical care that are either 1) radically painful, 2) excessively expensive, 3) doubtfully able to accomplish their designated objective, or 4) radically burdensome.

JUST WAR
Legitimate defense by military force as noted in CCC 2309.

MURDER
Intentional killing of a person.

VOCABULARY CONTINUED

NON-COMBATANT
One not involved in a conflict (especially war), such as a civilian in time of war; one whose duties do not include fighting, such as a surgeon or chaplain.

ORDINARY CARE
Forms of medical treatment given under the authority of a physician which are 1) not radically painful for the patient, 2) not extremely expensive, 3) readily available, and 4) expected to achieve their designated clinical objective.

PRENATAL DIAGNOSIS
Medical examination of the womb and child of a pregnant woman before she gives birth.

SCANDAL
An attitude or behavior which leads another to do evil.

SELF-DEFENSE
Necessary protections of persons and societies that may result in the taking of life.

SUICIDE
The willful taking of ones own life; a grievous sin against the fifth commandment.

STUDY QUESTIONS

1. What has made people enemies of each other?

2. Why is God offended by the taking of life?

3. What does it mean to treat someone with dignity?

4. How does one manifest true love of neighbor?

5. What is the basis of ethnic cleansing?

6. Why is self-defense permissible?

7. When is self-defense an obligation?

8. For how long has the Church condemned abortion?

9. What is the penalty for those directly involved in abortion?

10. Is it moral to carry out medical procedures on the unborn? Explain your answer.

11. What four factors must be considered when contemplating the cessation of extraordinary care?

12. Is assisted suicide permitted? Explain your answer.

13. List and explain four causes of scandal.

14. Why should both the soul and body be perfected?

15. May a government require military service in a just war?

16. What is the rule for treating non-combatants?

17. What benefits accrue to those who practice human solidarity?

PRACTICAL EXERCISES

1. Susan's younger sister Jane visited Susan at college. While there, Susan took Jane to a party and let her get drunk. How are Susan's actions a scandal to her younger sister?

2. The editor of your local newspaper has written an editorial condemning the Catholic Church's teaching that euthanasia is immoral. In the editorial, he says that the Church's position is "outdated" and "insensitive to the suffering endured by the terminally ill and their families." He argues that it is cruel to allow someone to suffer needlessly and that people have a right to control their own lives, including when their lives are to end. Ask yourself to whom a person's life belongs and what makes a life valuable. Then write a letter to the editor defending the Church's teaching and explaining the reasons for the Church's position against euthanasia. Be sure to address his specific points in your response.

3. During an argument on the basketball court about two months ago, Tom insulted Bill. Tom eventually felt bad about it, but now he refuses to apologize because Bill wouldn't speak to him for weeks, and he is still giving Tom the cold shoulder. What is Tom doing wrong? What is Bill doing wrong? How do their mistakes transgress the fifth commandment?

4. Joe is so obsessed with fitness that he wants to skip Mass on Sunday morning so he can start off early on a day of bike riding to get in better shape. When his parents tell him he should go to Mass, Joe argues that the Bible says the body is a temple of the Holy Spirit, so he strives for perfection of the body. What is wrong with Joe's argument?

FROM THE CATECHISM

2318 "In [God's] hands is the life of every living thing and the breath of all mankind" (Jb 12:10).

2319 Every human life, from the moment of conception until death, is sacred because the human person has been willed for its own sake in the image and likeness of the living and holy God.

2320 The murder of a human being is gravely contrary to the dignity of the person and the holiness of the Creator.

2321 The prohibition of murder does not abrogate the right to render an unjust aggressor unable to inflict harm. Legitimate defense is a grave duty for whoever is responsible for the lives of others or the common good.

2322 From its conception, the child has the right to life. Direct abortion, that is, abortion willed as an end or as a means, is a "criminal" practice (*GS*, 27 § 3), gravely contrary to the moral law. The Church imposes the canonical penalty of excommunication for this crime against human life.

2323 Because it should be treated as a person from conception, the embryo must be defended in its integrity, cared for, and healed like every other human being.

2324 Intentional euthanasia, whatever its forms or motives, is murder. It is gravely contrary to the dignity of the human person and to the respect due to the living God, his Creator.

2325 Suicide is seriously contrary to justice, hope, and charity. It is forbidden by the fifth commandment.

2326 Scandal is a grave offense when by deed or omission it deliberately leads others to sin gravely.

2327 Because of the evils and injustices that all war brings with it, we must do everything reasonably possible to avoid it. The Church prays: "From famine, pestilence, and war, O Lord, deliver us."

2328 The church and human reason assert the permanent validity of the moral law during armed conflicts. Practices deliberately contrary to the law of nations and to its universal principles are crimes.

2329 "The arms race is one of the greatest curses on the human race and the harm it inflicts on the poor is more than can be endured" (*GS*, 81 § 3).

2330 "Blessed are the peacemakers, for they shall be called sons of God" (Mt 5:9).

Endnotes

1. CDF, instruction, *Donum vitae,* intro. 5.
2. Cf. Gn 4:10.
3. St. Thomas Aquinas, *STh* II-II, 64, 7, *corp. art.*
4. Cf. CDF, *Donum Vitae,* I, 1.
5. CDF, *Donum Vitae,* III.
6. CDF, *Donum Vitae,* I, 2.
7. CDF, *Donum Vitae,* I, 3.
8. Lk 17:1.
9. Pius XII, *Discourse,* June 1, 1941.
10. Cf. Eph 6:4; Col 3:21.
11. Is 9:5.
12. Eph 2:16 J.B.; Cf. Col 1:20-22.
13. Eph 2:14.
14. Mt 5:9.
15. *GS*, 81 § 3.

The Sixth & Ninth Commandments

Commandments to strengthen and protect marital love.

Chapter 24

The Sixth & Ninth Commandments

Society places the highest value on those things that are most rare.

Platinum and gold bring the highest prices, for they are the rarest of metals. The Star of India, a twenty-carat diamond, is the most valuable diamond in the world because of its rare size.

In a similar manner, the work of a great artist immediately becomes more valuable when he dies, for the creator is no longer present to produce more of his work. Paintings that once sold for just a few dollars bring millions after the artist's death.

Each of us is born with a priceless gift. This gift cannot be bought or sold and can be given only once. Once it is given, it cannot be reclaimed. In his wisdom, God has set this gift aside to be shared between a husband and wife. It should be preserved so it can be given as a gift on the day of marriage.

It is the gift of one's virginity.

THE SIXTH AND NINTH COMMANDMENTS

You shall not commit adultery. (Ex 20:14)

One afternoon King David was watching from the roof of his palace and saw a woman bathing. He sent for her and slept with her even though he knew the woman was married to Uriah, one of his soldiers. Then he arranged for Uriah to be placed in the front line of battle, so he would be killed. God saw the evil David had committed and sent Nathan, a prophet, to inform David of the punishment for his sins. God told Nathan to say,

Why have you despised the word of the Lord, to do what is evil in his sight? You have smitten Uriah the Hittite with the sword, and have taken his wife to be your wife, and have slain him with the sword of the Ammonites....Thus says the Lord, "Behold, I will raise up evil against you out of your own house; and I will take your wives before your eyes, and give them to your neighbor, and he shall lie with your wives in the sight of this sun. For you did it secretly; but I will do this thing before all Israel, and before the sun." (2 Sm 12: 9, 11-12)

The story of David's evil deed indicates how seriously God views violations of the powers reserved for marriage.

God made marriage so that man could be happy. This is clear from the story of Adam and Eve. God himself said: "It is not good that the man should be alone; I will make him a helper fit for him" (Gn 2:18). After seeing Eve, Adam was overjoyed, saying, "this at last is bone of my bones and flesh of my flesh" (Gn 2: 23).

Much of the happiness of marriage is founded on the proper use of the marriage act, which is a stabilizing force for individual marriages as well as for the whole of society. Through these acts, God chose to share his creative power with mankind.

The logic here is simple: since God created out of his unlimited love, he determined that the human person should procreate through love for another person, and that this love should be sanctified and strengthened by the Sacrament of Matrimony. In each marriage, the partners share life-giving power, a gift from God to be used as he dictates.

Since the act of creating a child in marriage is sharing in God's power, the couple reaches out of themselves toward God in a truly transcendent experience. When this act is done sinfully, the experience of transcendence is directed toward evil and is turned toward the devil.

The Jewish people in the Old Testament were hard-hearted, so Moses permitted them to issue decrees of divorce. Then, the power to divorce became a tool that men used against women. This led to loss of respect for women, concubinage, and the relegation of women to a lesser place in marriage.

JESUS AND THE SIXTH COMMANDMENT

Jesus came to perfect the law of the Old Testament. His teaching on sexuality was a shock to the scribes and Pharisees—for it forbade not only sinful actions but also sinful desires.

You shall not commit adultery.

Bathsheba goes to King David

"David sent messengers, and took her; and she came to him, and he lay with her." (2 Sm 11: 4)

Man's capacity to love is a great mystery. It is a gift from God, who is love.

Men and women are called by their natures to identify with the roles God has given them.

Pharisees came up to him and tested him by asking, "Is it lawful to divorce one's wife for any cause?" He answered, "Have you not read that he who made them from the beginning made them male and female, and said, 'For this reason a man shall leave his father and mother and be joined to his wife, and the two shall become one flesh'? So they are no longer two but one flesh. What therefore God has joined together, let not man put asunder." (Mt 19: 3-6).

This commandment to fidelity in marriage is meant both to strengthen and to protect marital love. As a sacrament, this is exactly what marriage should do. It "signifies and communicates grace," which strengthens the marital bond (CCC 1617). When we cooperate with God's grace, we imitate him in the most direct way we can and live according to his intentions.

> "God is love and in himself he lives a mystery of personal loving communion. Creating the human race in his own image....God inscribed in the humanity of man and woman the *vocation*, and thus the capacity and responsibility, *of love* and communion."[1]

> "God created man in his own image...male and female he created them"[2]; He blessed them and said, "Be fruitful and multiply"[3]; "When God created man, he made him in the likeness of God. Male and female he created them, and he blessed them and named them Man when they were created."[4] (CCC 2331)

Man's capacity to love is a great mystery. It is a gift from God, who *is* love. This reality calls every person, both male and female, to imitate the highest form of love, which is the love of God for man.

How great is the beauty of nature, which surrounds everyone. Yet, despite its beauty, no plant or animal can love. How much more blessed is man, who has been called into existence to love and to be loved.

We can know a person's love is real when he sacrifices himself for his beloved. Love is a call to sacrifice, as clearly seen in Christ, who sacrificed himself for love of all. This totally self-sacrificing love, which God has revealed, calls man to act the same—for the basis of the sixth and ninth commandments is true love of neighbor.

Man's capacity to love is a great opportunity. This gift of God presents everyone with the opportunity to imitate God's love, which is totally self-sacrificing. So, in the correct context, sexuality is directed toward the good of the other. It is a gift that must first be given to be received.

First of all, sexuality affects the capacity to love and procreate, and also, more generally, to form relationships with others. Men and women are called by their natures to identify with the roles God has given them. There are physical, psychological, moral, and spiritual differences between man and woman, but these are not opposed to each other. Rather, the distinctions are complementary and are willed by God for the harmony and right ordering of society. By creating human beings as both man and woman, God called everyone to accept his or her natural sexual identity and gave equal dignity to each.

> Each of the two sexes is an image of the power and tenderness of God, with equal dignity though in a different way. The *union of man and woman* in marriage is a way of imitating in the flesh the Creator's

generosity and fecundity: "Therefore a man leaves his father and his mother and cleaves to his wife, and they become one flesh."[5] All human generations proceed from this union.[6] (CCC 2335)

Jesus came as the model of chastity to restore creation to the purity of its origins: the unity of one man and one woman in the sacred bond of marriage for the whole of their lives. Every baptized person is called to be chaste in keeping with his or her individual state of life. God gives us the grace to do this at Baptism and renews it in the *all* the Sacraments and in prayer.

CHASTITY

Chastity is a moral virtue that regulates the powers of procreation according to faith and one's state in life.

> Chastity means the successful integration of sexuality within the person and thus the inner unity of man in his bodily and spiritual being. Sexuality, in which man's belonging to the bodily and biological world is expressed, becomes personal and truly human when it is integrated into the relationship of one person to another, in the complete and lifelong mutual gift of a man and woman. The virtue of chastity therefore involves the integrity of the person and the integrality of the gift. (CCC 2337)

Chastity means the integration of sexuality within the person and requires development of self-mastery, the ability to control one's thoughts and actions with regard to the passions. Self-mastery can only be acquired by serious effort to overcome the passions so that one can act out of conscious and free choice. It is the choice to form good moral habits. If a person is chaste, he has made his sexuality a part of who he is, but only a part—no more. The chaste person is not controlled by his sexuality. It is a part of him and is lived according to the type of life he is called to live: married or celibate.

Feelings must be mastered if one is to remain chaste. Young people who date on a regular basis begin to have strong feelings for each other. These feelings of joy are a foretaste of the joy of the marital relationship, but they can lead to serious sin if passions are not recognized and controlled. All occasions of sin that threaten chastity must be avoided. Occasions of sin are places, persons, and things that can lead a person to sin. God will give us the grace not only to overcome these occasions, but also to avoid them if we ask for such grace in prayer.

The chief dangers to the virtue of chastity are too much free time, sinful curiosity, bad companions, immodest dress, and books and entertainment that arouse the passions.

Self-mastery requires much time and is demanding work. The virtue of chastity comes under the cardinal virtue of temperance, which seeks to control the passions and the appetites through the use of reason.

Success in the virtue of chastity is possible through the following means:

† Regular reception of Reconciliation and the Eucharist;

† Complete honesty with your spiritual director;

† A prayer life with Jesus and Mary;

> *The chaste person is not controlled by his sexuality.*
>
> *It is a part of him and is lived according to the type of life he is called to live: married or celibate.*

St. Agnes

Martyred c. 305; the patron saint of virgins, betrothed couples and bodily purity; at the age of 13, Agnes consecrated her virginity to God; Diocletian was enraged at her firmness of purpose and ordered her executed. Her emblem is a lamb.

The chief dangers to the virtue of chastity are too much free time, sinful curiosity, bad companions, immodest dress, and books and entertainment that arouse the passions.

✝ Friends who share your desire to be chaste, who think and act purely;

✝ Keeping eyes, mind, moods, and feelings under control.

Chastity is a task that each person can and must accomplish using the means listed above. It is a virtue acquired by repeated effort, much as strength is built by exercise. One can only be chaste if one cooperates with God's grace to be chaste. In the case of chastity it is necessary to "pray as if it all depends on God and work as if it all depends on you."

> Chastity is a moral virtue. It is also a gift from God, a *grace*, a fruit of spiritual effort.[7] The Holy Spirit enables one whom the waters of Baptism has regenerated to imitate the purity of Christ.[8] (CCC 2345)

CHASTITY IN MARRIAGE

> "The acts in marriage by which the intimate and chaste union of the spouses takes place are noble and honorable; the truly human performance of these acts fosters the self-giving they signify and enriches the spouses in joy and gratitude." Sexuality is a source of joy and pleasure.[9] (CCC 2362)

The marital covenant is a great blessing that God has given to marriage and ordered to the conjugal love of man and woman. This marital covenant, which the spouses enter into freely, requires faithful love until death. It is an act that touches man at the deepest part of his being. When you give yourself wholly to another in marriage, you are pledging yourself completely to the marriage. Any action that willfully acts counter to this pledge attacks the promise of lifelong commitment and injures the bond of marriage at its root. Separating yourself from the beloved, whether God or man, destroys the love that you have pledged to the beloved alone.

CHILDREN

Children are a gift of God to marriage. Every conjugal act must be open to this gift and to God's plan for each particular marriage. Married couples must strive through prayer to understand God's plan for their family. From the beginning, God has called upon married couples "to be fruitful and multiply." Large families have always been considered a sign of God's blessings and a couple's generosity. When love is fruitful, it is expansive and naturally shares itself.

> In relation to physical, economic, psychological, and social conditions, responsible parenthood is exercised either by the deliberate and generous decision to raise a numerous family, or by the decision, made for grave motives and with due respect for the moral law, to avoid for the time being, or even an indeterminate period, a new birth.[10]

One aspect of responsible parenthood is the determination of when and how often to have children. This is a decision that the couple makes without recourse to morally unacceptable means such as contraception or sterilization.

Difficulties may arise in determining what conditions are grave enough to purposefully limit the size of a family. The Church approves the wish to postpone pregnancies for grave reasons within moral means. It is appropriate for couples to seek advice regarding this decision with their confessor, but the ultimate decision is theirs. It is well to keep in mind, however, that at all times in life we are in God's hands, and he will see us through in all our needs. Natural Family Planning (abstinence during periods of fertility) has been developed as a help when grave reasons are present.

Those who are apparently unable to have children may seek medical assistance, within moral means, to overcome the problem. There are no circumstances that allow them morally to seek conception outside the act of marriage. Should a couple prove unable to have children, they should consider adoption as a way to overcome their suffering. God meant for all children to have a family, and adoption presents an opportunity to share love and life with those without families.

SINS AGAINST CHASTITY

Every action knowingly willed against the prohibitions of the sixth and ninth commandments is mortally sinful. Grave sins against chastity are:

- Lust – the disordered desire for or inordinate enjoyment of sexual pleasure;
- Adultery – sexual relations between two people when at least one is married to a third person;
- Masturbation – deliberate stimulation of the genital organs to derive sexual pleasure;
- Contraception – the use of devices or drugs to prevent conception;
- Fornication – sexual union of an unmarried man and an unmarried woman;
- Pornography – the removal of sexual acts, real or simulated, from the intimacy of the partners in order to display them deliberately to third parties;
- Prostitution – the selling of one's body for sexual relations for either money or goods;
- Incest – sexual relations between relations or in-laws within a prohibited degree;
- Direct sterilization – medical procedures used to prevent conception;
- Rape – violation by force of the sexual intimacy of a person;
- Homosexual acts – sexual acts between two people of the same sex;
- Divorce – the attempt to break up a valid marriage through civil procedures;
- Polygamy – the state or practice of one individual attempting marriage with more than one person;
- In vivo or in vitro fertilization – conceiving a child through medical means outside the act of marriage;
- Trial marriage – living together prior to marriage with the intention to get married "if things work out";
- Child molestation – involving children in intimate acts.

God has called upon married couples "to be fruitful and multiply."

Large families have always been considered a sign of God's blessings and a couple's generosity.

You shall not covet your neighbor's wife.

Everyone experiences this tension in the daily struggle to be holy.

JESUS AND THE NINTH COMMANDMENT

"You shall not covet your neighbor's wife." (Ex 20:17)

St. John distinguishes three kinds of covetousness or concupiscence: lust of the flesh, lust of the eyes, and pride of life.[11] In the Catholic tradition, the ninth commandment forbids carnal concupiscence. (CCC 2514)

To covet a person or to lust is sinfully to desire another person. Concupiscence is a movement of the sensible appetite contrary to the operation of human reason. In other words, concupiscence can lead us to desire what we should not want or have. It is the most obvious effect of original sin. St. Paul refers to it as a rebellion of the flesh against the soul of man, which inclines us to sin.

The ninth commandment prohibits coveting another person. Some may object that thoughts cannot harm another person. That argument ignores the fact that every sin harms first of all the sinner.

Jesus said, "You have heard that it was said, 'You shall not commit adultery.' But I say to you that everyone who looks at a woman lustfully has already committed adultery with her in his heart" (Mt 5:27).

> Because man is a *composite being, spirit and body,* there already exists a certain tension in him; a certain struggle of tendencies between "spirit" and "flesh" develops. But in fact this struggle belongs to the heritage of sin. It is a consequence of sin and at the same time a confirmation of it. (CCC 2516)

Coveting primarily hurts the individual who is committing the sin. It leads one to view persons as things to be exploited, denies the dignity of the other, and places sinful satisfaction ahead of both God and neighbor. It is a practice that clouds the mind and easily leads to sinful actions.

Everyone experiences this tension in the daily struggle to be holy. It is not a battle between a good soul and a bad body. Rather, it is a struggle to use an immortal soul to control a finite body. Before a sin can be committed, it is a thought in a person's intellect. In the Gospel of St. Matthew, Jesus says, "Out of the heart come evil thoughts, murder, adultery, fornication" (Mt 15:19). With this in mind, it can be said that the ninth commandment protects the sixth—for it forbids thoughts that lead to immoral actions.

The virtue that protects against sins of covetousness is purity. Purity moderates the desire for sexual activity according to one's state in life. The unmarried have no right to thoughts or acts that can lead to acts of marriage. Those who are married must direct their thoughts and actions toward their spouse.

The sixth beatitude, "Blessed are the pure in heart, for they shall see God," calls us to accept the commands of God to be pure, loving, and chaste. There is a connection between purity of heart, of body, and of faith.

> The "pure in heart" are promised that they will see God face to face and be like him.[12] Purity of heart is the precondition of the vision of God. Even now it enables us to see *according to* God, to accept others as "neighbors;" it lets us perceive the human body—ours and our

neighbor's—as a temple of the Holy Spirit, a manifestation of divine beauty. (CCC 2519)

Although Baptism purifies the recipient from all sins, it does not eliminate the temptation to sin, which is part of every human life. God has given us his actual graces to help us prevail over concupiscence in life and the unruly desires of the body. To win the battle, it is necessary to have purity of intention, which guides us to seek God's will in everything. Purity of intention leads us diligently to avoid occasions of sin. Occasions of sin can only be avoided if we honestly acknowledge and try to avoid those persons, places, and things that can lead us into temptation.

> [T]he baptized must continue to struggle against concupiscence of the flesh and disordered desires. With God's grace he will prevail... by *purity of vision*, external and internal; by discipline of feelings and imagination; by refusing all complicity in impure thoughts that incline us to turn aside from the path of God's commandments: "Appearance arouses yearning in fools."[13] (CCC 2520)

To be pure, we must be modest. Modesty is the virtue that guides how one looks at others and behaves toward them in conformity with the solidarity and dignity of persons. Everyone has an obligation toward others as members of God's universal community. Modesty refuses to unveil what must be covered.

> Modesty protects the mystery of persons and their love. It encourages patience and moderation in loving relationships; it requires that the conditions for the definitive giving and commitment of man and woman to one another be fulfilled. Modesty is decency. It inspires one's choice of clothing. It keeps silence or reserve where there is evident risk of unhealthy curiosity. It is discreet. (CCC 2522)

Modesty stands against the allure of the present culture, which admits few limits in dress, conduct, and language. It is counter-cultural. Intimate things are for married persons, who have a right to them by virtue of their union. That some things are deemed fashionable does not mean they are moral. The easy acceptance of suggestive dress and conversation can lead only to thoughts and actions counter to purity and modesty. Many advertisements and media presentations present sexuality in a manner that leads to seeing others as objects of pleasure rather than as fellow creatures of God, to whom we have serious moral obligations. Sexuality must not be taken out of marriage, where God ordained it to remain.

CONCLUSION

God's call to share in his creative power is a great gift. It contains elements of mystery which man can never understand. The capability to procreate a child must never be taken outside of marriage. God has established this sacrament not only for the good of the couple but for the care and protection of the child. While every act of marriage within marriage is a great good for the couple, there is an attendant rule of harm for a couple who acts outside of marriage.

Success is possible only for those who use the means to remain chaste. The reward for chastity is an undivided heart and interior peace.

Purity of intention leads us diligently to avoid occasions of sin.

Modesty stands against the allure of the present culture, which admits few limits in dress, conduct, and language.

SUPPLEMENTARY READING

Maria Goretti was born on October 16, 1890, in Corinaldo at the Marches of Ancona, Italy. Her parents were peasants who raised their children with piety and love. Maria was noted as an exceptionally holy young girl, referred to as the "little Madonna."

During her youth, Maria, her parents, sister, and two brothers moved to a seaside town where her father could get work as a laborer. To save money, the Gorettis took a house with another laborer, Giovanni Serenelli, and his son Alessandro. The Serenellis had a poor reputation throughout their town. Giovanni was given to drunkenness, and Alessandro had acquired a reputation as a lout.

In 1900, Maria's father passed away. Though young, she took it upon herself to help her mother, who now was faced with great burdens.

With the father gone, the Gorettis faced life without their chief provider and protector.

In 1902, when Maria was twelve, Alessandro began to make unwanted advances towards her. She refused, angering the young man. Incensed by her rejection, Alessandro one day attempted to assault her purity. Though young, she was able to resist his advances. He was so enraged that he threatened to kill her if she reported the attack.

Ten days later, on July 5, he lured her into a room under the pretense of mending some of his garments. There, Alessandro again attacked her, and again she was able to fight him off. Alessandro then grabbed a knife and stabbed her several times. Though mortally wounded, Maria had enough strength to call out, and Alessandro was caught.

Maria lingered for hours before her death. Her last words were those of forgiveness to the man who killed her.

St. Maria Goretti
(1890-1902)
Feast on July 6

Alessandro was tried for the crime and sentenced to thirty years of hard labor. For years, he refused to show sorrow for his crime. Then, one night in a dream, he saw himself in a garden of flowers. There, Maria Goretti appeared and offered him a bouquet of flowers. "With this gift," said Alessandro, "came the new life of peace with God." After his release, he sought pardon from the Goretti family, who immediately forgave him.

Maria is a sterling example of holy purity. Her intercession is credited for over forty miracles. In 1950, in the presence of her elderly mother, her siblings, and the man who killed her, Maria was officially declared a saint.

VOCABULARY

CHASTITY

The moral virtue that, under the cardinal virtue of temperance, provides for the successful integration of sexuality within the person leading to the inner unity of the bodily and spiritual being.

COMPLEMENTARY

That which completes or makes perfect; the completion, perfection, consummation.

COVET

Unjust desire to possess in a way that exceeds the limits of reason what is not ours and belongs to another or is owed to him.

FECUNDITY

Literally "fruitfulness;" an end of marriage and flowering of conjugal love by which children are produced.

FORNICATION

Sexual intercourse between an unmarried man and an unmarried woman.

INCEST

Intimate relations between relatives or in-laws within a degree that prohibits marriage between them.

LUST

Disordered desire for or inordinate enjoyment of sexual pleasure.

MASTURBATION

The deliberate stimulation of the genital organs in order to derive sexual pleasure.

MODESTY

Refusing to unveil what should remain hidden; a part of chastity.

PASSIONS

The emotions or dispositions which incline us to good or evil actions, such as love and hate, hope and fear, joy and sadness, and anger.

PURITY

Attuning the intellect and will to the demands of God's holiness, chiefly in 3 areas: 1) charity, 2) chastity or sexual rectitude, and 3) love of truth and orthodoxy of faith.

RAPE

The forcible violation of the sexual intimacy of another person; deeply wounds the respect, freedom, and physical and moral integrity to which every person has a right.

SELF-MASTERY

Mastery of oneself; essential virtue for charity and therefore holiness.

STUDY QUESTIONS

1. Why did God make a helper for Adam?

2. Why does God have the right to determine rules for marriage?

3. What were the effects of divorce in the Old Testament?

4. What does Jesus command in regard to divorce?

5. What two roles has God given human beings?

6. Why do we say men and women are complementary?

7. How do you treat another with dignity?

8. How does chastity relate to the integration of sexuality?

9. What are the means for remaining chaste?

10. How is the virtue of chastity acquired?

11. What are the most obvious gifts of God to a marriage?

12. Explain: "Every act of marriage must be open to life."

13. Who determines family size?

14. When and why may a couple postpone pregnancy?

PRACTICAL EXERCISES

1. Suppose a friend is dressing and acting in a way that is intentionally provocative. When told not to do so, your friend says, "It's not my fault what others think. Don't blame me if they can't control themselves." What could you say to that person against the argument presented?

2. Some people think that troubles with purity are caused because the body itself is bad and leads a good soul to want bad things. They think that the body, then, is the enemy to be defeated. Is this correct? How does this idea contradict the idea of chastity? What is the real cause of impurity?

3. What could you say to someone who said he was going to do whatever he wanted now, and then, in a few years, would start obeying the rules of purity and chastity that Jesus laid out for us? What does chastity free us to do? What does it free us from?

4. People who have large families are often treated as though they are simply adding to a population problem. What does a large family really demonstrate about a married couple?

5. "Sow a thought, reap an action. Sow an action, reap a habit. Sow a habit, reap a virtue. Sow a virtue, reap a character. Sow a character, reap a *destiny.*" As in Chapter 13, imagine you are the great tempter Uncle Screwtape from C. S. Lewis's *Screwtape Letters.* How would you tell your nephew Wormwood to go about tempting a dating couple?

FROM THE CATECHISM

2392 "Love is the fundamental and innate vocation of every human being" (*FC*, 11).

2393 By creating the human being man and woman, God gives personal dignity equally to the one and the other. Each of them, man and woman, should acknowledge and accept his sexual identity.

2394 Christ is the model of chastity. Every baptized person is called to lead a chaste life, each according to his particular state of life.

2395 Chastity means the integration of sexuality within the person. It includes an apprenticeship in self-mastery.

2396 Among the sins gravely contrary to chastity are masturbation, fornication, pornography, and homosexual practices.

2397 The covenant which spouses have freely entered into entails faithful love. It imposes on them the obligation to keep their marriage indissoluble.

2398 Fecundity is a good, a gift, and an end of marriage. By giving life, spouses participate in God's fatherhood.

2399 The regulation of births represents one of the aspects of responsible fatherhood and motherhood. Legitimate intentions on the part of the spouses do not justify recourse to morally unacceptable means (for example, direct sterilization or contraception).

2400 Adultery, divorce, polygamy, and free union are grave offenses against the dignity of marriage.

2528 "Everyone who looks at a woman lustfully has already committed adultery with her in his heart." (Mt 5:28)

2529 The ninth commandment warns against lust or carnal concupiscence.

2530 The struggle against carnal lust involves purifying the heart and practicing temperance.

2531 Purity of heart will enable us to see God: it enables us even now to see things according to God.

2532 Purification of the heart demands prayer, the practice of chastity, purity of intention and of vision.

2533 Purity of heart requires modesty which is patience, decency, and discretion. Modesty protects the intimate center of the person.

Endnotes

1. *FC*, 11.	7. Cf. Gal 5:22.	13. Wis 15:5.
2. Gn 1:27.	8. Cf. 1 Jn 3:3.	
3. Gn 1:28.	9. *GS*, 49 § 2.	
4. Gn 5:1-2.	10. *GS*, 49 § 2.	
5. Gn 2:24.	11. Cf. 1 Jn 2:16.	
6. Cf. Gn 4:1-2, 25-26; 5:1.	12. Cf. 1 Cor 13:12; 1 Jn 2:16.	

The Seventh & Tenth Commandments

Justice and Charity

Chapter 25

The Seventh & Tenth Commandments

$\mathcal{T}$om and John were late for the high school basketball game, so they took a short cut through the team locker room. New uniforms were laid out on the bench.

"Hey, Tom, look at those. Let's take a couple — no one will know."
"C'mon, John, I don't want to be a thief."
"Tom, it's not stealing; the school has lots of money."

They each took one uniform.

Later on, Tom's conscience bothered him, and he asked John to give him the uniforms so he could return them. John agreed, and Tom returned the uniforms. When Tom and John met on their first break from college, John brought up the uniform incident.

"You know, I've asked myself a hundred times, why did we do that? I am glad you talked me into returning them."

"Well, John, I never told you, but when I returned the uniforms, I found out the kids who were given the uniforms were told they had to pay for them. From the looks on their faces I learned that I can never realize how much theft could hurt someone. I promised myself I would never steal anything again."

THE SEVENTH AND TENTH COMMANDMENTS IN THE OLD TESTAMENT

You shall not steal. (Ex 20:15)

You shall not covet...anything that is your neighbor's. (Ex 20:17)

> The seventh commandment forbids unjustly taking or keeping the goods of one's neighbor and wronging him in any way with respect to his goods. It commands justice and charity in the care of earthly goods and the fruits of men's labor. For the sake of the common good, it requires respect for the universal destination of goods and the respect for the right to private property. Christian life strives to order this world's goods to God and to fraternal charity. (CCC 2401)

The Pentateuch records that after the creation, God entrusted the earth and its resources to the first man, Adam, and to his heirs. In subsequent chapters of the Old Testament, God lists specific rules governing property. In addition to forbidding theft, he sets out laws regulating the tithing of produce, the keeping of slaves, and the treatment of those who borrow money, as well as warning that prosperity can be dangerous to the Jewish people's relationship with God.

Through our inheritance from Adam, the earth and all it produces is meant for all people. This ultimate purpose of the fruits of the earth is known as the *universal destination of goods*.

The fact that the products of the earth should benefit all people, however, does not cancel out the use of private property. Man does in fact have a right to own and make use of private property—because ownership can benefit both individuals and societies. For individuals, this right is united with man's dignity because private property allows him to secure basic needs for himself and those for whom he is responsible. For societies, private property can contribute to proper order within a community because respect for ownership leads to natural unity among men.

There may seem to be some tension between the right to private property and the universal destination of goods. Some may ask, "how can the earth belong to all people, while at the same time individuals have a right to own part of the earth and its products?" This problem is solved when you realize that ownership is not absolute.

> The *right to private property*, acquired or received in a just way, does not do away with the original gift of the earth to the whole of mankind. The *universal destination of goods* remains primordial, even if the promotion of the common good requires respect for the right to private property and its exercise. (CCC 2403)

Property is held from God in stewardship: everything that exists belongs to the Lord, who has placed us in charge to manage it for him. Therefore, we must use things responsibly in ways that glorify him, not in any way we please. Stewardship, then, requires that a person take care of his family's needs first and use the excess of need for the good of others, who in fraternal charity have a right to what is left over. People are required to use their belongings to help those in need as much as is possible and reasonable. A portion of what a person has in excess of his own needs should go to the poor.

You shall not steal.

You shall not covet... anything that is your neighbors.

Property is held from God in stewardship: everything that exists belongs to the Lord, who has placed us in charge to manage it for him.

Every human person needs the products of this life, but goods and the desire for them must not take priority over one's relationship with God.

Goods of production—material or immaterial—such as land, factories, practical or artistic skills, oblige their possessors to employ them in ways that will benefit the greatest number. Those who hold goods for use and consumption should use them with moderation, reserving the better part for guests, for the sick, and the poor. (CCC 2405)

In spite of God's plan for the universal destination of goods, many people live in poverty. When someone is facing the hardships of poverty, he is perfectly just to want the basic goods—food, shelter, clothing, etc.—that he sees others possessing. This desire is not sinful—a person has a right to these goods if he cannot justly earn them. If basic goods cannot be acquired through charity from others, then the state has an obligation to offer assistance.

THE SEVENTH AND TENTH COMMANDMENTS AND THE NEW TESTAMENT

And he said to them, "Take heed, and beware of all covetousness; for a man's life does not consist in the abundance of his possessions." And he told them a parable, saying, "The land of a rich man brought forth plentifully; and he thought to himself, 'What shall I do, for I have nowhere to store my crops?' And he said, 'I will do this: I will pull down my barns, and build larger ones; and there I will store all my grain and my goods. And I will say to my soul, Soul, you have ample goods laid up for many years; take your ease, eat, drink, be merry.' But God said to him, 'Fool! This night your soul is required of you; and the things you have prepared, whose will they be?' So is he who lays up treasure for himself, and is not rich toward God." (Lk 12:15-21)

In this parable, Jesus makes clear two sins against the seventh and tenth commandments. First, he warns against desiring more goods than one needs, and second, he warns against securing goods without regard for salvation. Every human person needs the products of this life, but goods and the desire for them must not take priority over one's relationship with God. This tendency is a problem of particular importance in our time.

The second half of the twentieth century enabled ordinary men in many places to acquire goods and property on a scale formerly reserved to the rich. This accumulation of wealth has led to the false idea that people can use their property as they wish, without regard for the needs of others. This attitude is clearly demonstrated by the rich man in the parable, who was concerned only for his own personal happiness.

The example of many people in sports and entertainment has led to easy acceptance of the so-called "good life" mentality, which sees in wealth the opportunity to sit back and enjoy life however one's desires dictate. Christians are obliged in charity to assist their neighbors with the excess of their property. Each person is required to use his goods in moderation so there will be a portion left for the sick and the poor.

On coming into the world, man is not equipped with everything he needs for developing his bodily and spiritual life. He needs others. Differences appear tied to age, physical abilities, intellectual or moral aptitudes, the benefits derived from social commerce, and the distribution of wealth.[1] The "talents" are not distributed equally.[2]

These differences belong to God's plan, who wills that each receive what he needs from others, and that those endowed with particular "talents" share the benefits with those who need them. These differences encourage and often oblige persons to practice generosity, kindness, and sharing of goods; they foster the mutual enrichment of cultures. (CCC 1936-1937)

Since we are interdependent, we ought to practice social charity. Social charity, or solidarity, is a virtue which is manifested by setting up programs to insure the fair distribution of goods and equitable compensation for work. A commitment to solidarity will overcome the tendency within communities for men to seek unfair advantage over their neighbors. The net result will be a reduction of tensions and conflicts between different social classes and economic groups. Social charity requires the good will of all men and becomes more dispersed to the extent that it is practiced. One of the best witnesses to social charity is the giving of alms to the poor.

For human dignity to be respected, not only must social charity be practiced, but also the virtues of temperance and justice:

† Temperance moderates the attraction of pleasures and provides balance in the use of created goods;

† Justice makes it possible to have a constant and firm will to give both God and neighbor their dues.

Those who prefer Jesus to the goods of this world will have a correct balance between goods and love of God. This is set forth in the first beatitude, which states, "Blessed are the poor in spirit, for they shall see God" (Mt 5: 3-10). The vision of God is a greater blessing than all the earth's treasures, and life with and in God is preferable to any other happiness. Those who want to achieve life with God must strive to live as if they had no goods; then their goods will not possess them.

We are not required, however, to give all money that is not spent on food, shelter, and clothing to charity. Since leisure is necessary to restore energy, it is moral to set aside a portion of one's income for entertainment. This would include games of chance, which are not immoral but can become so when they deprive someone of what is necessary to supply his own needs or his dependents' needs.

> All Christ's faithful are to "direct their affections rightly, lest they be hindered in their pursuit of perfect charity by the use of worldly things and by an adherence to riches which is contrary to the spirit of evangelical poverty."[3] (CCC 2545)

SINS AGAINST THE SEVENTH COMMANDMENT

The most obvious sin against the seventh commandment is theft, the taking of another's property against his reasonable will. This sin deprives someone of what is rightly his.

Every use of another person's property without permission, however, does not constitute theft. For example, if you know the owner would have no objection to the use, or if his refusal would be contrary to justice, right reason, and the universal destination of goods, no theft is committed. Nor would it be theft in cases of obvious and urgent necessity. Two examples:

For human dignity to be respected, not only must social charity be practiced, but also the virtues of temperance and justice.

Christ has given the Church the authority to make judgments about economic and social matters to defend the fundamental rights of all persons.

◆ A friend has a heart attack, and no ambulance is available. You have no automobile but are aware that a neighbor who is not home leaves his keys in the car. It would be moral to use his car to get your friend to a hospital;

◆ Skiers are lost in the mountains, and a snowstorm is raging. If their lives are in danger, it would be moral for them to take shelter in the cabin of a person who is not present.

Listed below are some common sins against the seventh commandment:

◆ Robbery, the taking of another's goods through force;

◆ Keeping borrowed property;

◆ Work purposefully done poorly;

◆ Use of stolen credit cards;

◆ Paying politicians bribes to secure unfair advantage;

◆ Willfully damaging property;

◆ Breaking promises that are morally upright;

◆ Destroying your own property when it could be sold to assist the poor;

◆ Cheating on tests and at games;

◆ Stealing from an employer;

◆ Buying or selling stolen goods;

◆ Charging unfair interest rates;

◆ Committing fraud in business;

◆ Charging higher prices to those in dire need;

◆ Cheating employees out of commissions;

◆ Refusing to do work for agreed wages;

◆ Breaking contracts;

◆ Evading taxes.

In cases of fraud, damage to property, theft, and robbery, the guilty person is required to make restitution: to return or replace the goods stolen or their value to the person or persons harmed. Restitution may be made secretly.

THE SEVENTH COMMANDMENT AND COMMERCE

Christ has given the Church the authority to make judgments about economic and social matters to defend the fundamental rights of all persons, for a minimum of wealth is necessary to enable one to save one's soul. The Church's instructions on relations between individuals in society are called *social justice* or *solidarity.* The purpose of this teaching is to explain how secular life among members of society should be lived in light of Christ's teachings. It is a collection of papal teachings that began with Pope Leo XIII in the nineteenth century. It lists the principles that should direct the public life of society. It is a collection of truths based on natural law, the Gospels, moral principles, and magisterial teachings. Its purpose is to order men to act justly toward their neighbors in all financial dealings.

Man has been made by God to be the author, center, and goal of all economic life. Business is not to have profit as its highest goal. Though profit must be a consideration if the business is to survive, the main goals of economic activity should be the support and development of individuals through work and service of human beings:

† By his work, man participates in the work of creation, and in a sense, participates in the redemptive work of Jesus of Nazareth, the carpenter who was crucified for the sins of all men. Every occupation, however high or low, offers an opportunity for man to find perfection and save his soul. Work also entitles man to a just wage determined by both his contributions and his needs and the needs of his dependents;

† The earth is abundantly supplied with resources, and individuals are abundantly supplied with unique skills and talents, all of which come from God. The goods and services brought about by economic life ought to reach everyone if the virtues of justice and charity are practiced.

> Everyone has the *right of economic initiative;* everyone should make legitimate use of his talents to contribute to the abundance that will benefit all and to harvest the just fruits of his labor. He should seek to observe regulations issued by legitimate authority for the sake of the common good.[4] (CCC 2429)

> The seventh commandment forbids acts or enterprises that for any reason — selfish or ideological, commercial, or totalitarian — lead to the *enslavement of human beings,* to their being bought, sold and exchanged like merchandise, in disregard for their personal dignity. It is a sin against the dignity of persons and their fundamental rights to reduce them by violence to their productive value or to a source of profit. [As a call to solidarity] St. Paul directed a Christian master to treat his Christian slave "no longer as a slave but more than a slave, as a beloved brother,…both in the flesh and in the Lord.[5] (CCC 2414)

This obligation to solidarity includes giving assistance to the extent it is possible to those who suffer inequalities in their standard of living, as occurs in many parts of the world.

The earth is made for all people, so its fruits must be treated in a responsible manner. Natural resources are destined for the common good not only of those living now but also of people who will live in the future. The use of vegetable, mineral, and animal resources, then, cannot be separated from the obligation to use them responsibly, as God intended.

Medical and scientific experimentation upon animals, for example, is legitimate when it is kept within reasonable limits since it contributes to caring for or saving human lives. But intentionally harming animals without cause is an abuse of the earth and its resources.

> It is contrary to human dignity to cause animals to suffer or die needlessly. It is likewise unworthy to spend money on them that should as a priority go to the relief of human misery. One can love animals; one should not direct to them the affection due only to persons. (CCC 2418)

The earth is made for all people, so its fruits must be treated in a responsible manner.

Natural resources are destined for the common good not only of those living now but also of people who will live in the future.

Envy is one of the capital sins, and it is good to remind ourselves that the sin of envy entered the world with the devil's envy of God.

St Francis Giving his Mantle to a Poor Man

The poor need special care and consideration as a matter of justice and charity.

YOU SHALL NOT COVET YOUR NEIGHBOR'S GOODS

The tenth commandment forbids *greed* and the desire to amass earthly goods without limit. It forbids *avarice* arising from a passion for riches and their attendant power. It also forbids the desire to commit injustice by harming our neighbor in his temporal goods:

When the Law says, "You shall not covet," these words mean that we should banish our desires for whatever does not belong to us. Our thirst for another's goods is immense, infinite, never quenched. Thus it is written: "He who loves money never has money enough."[6] (CCC 2536)

A person who covets has a sinful desire for the goods of another. Covetousness takes many forms:

◆ Desiring goods to which you have no right;

◆ Wishing your neighbor would lose his goods out of envy;

◆ Reducing the quantity of goods to create artificial scarcity.

Envy is one of the capital sins, and it is good to remind ourselves that the sin of envy entered the world with the devil's envy of God (Wis 2: 24). It is wrong to be sad at the good fortune of another. Those who wish their neighbor grave harm out of envy are guilty of mortal sin. Envy is a form of sadness that results from lack of charity toward one's neighbor. It must be banished from the human heart. Envy can only be conquered by abandonment to God's providence as an act of humility.

CONCLUSION

According to the wise plan of God, man seeks his salvation in society. As a member of society, he has a right to own and use property. The right ordering of society requires that all use their property in keeping with the norms of justice and charity. This means that no one has a right to deprive a person of property unjustly, nor does ownership allow someone to use his belongings however he wants, without regard to the needs of others. Detachment from riches is necessary for entrance into God's kingdom.

The poor need special care and consideration as a matter of justice and charity. One way to accomplish this is through alms-giving.

True development of society concerns not just a more efficient economic system but the whole person. Societies should strive to increase each person's ability to respond to the call of God to save his soul. If a person is reduced to nothing but his "productivity," this call is being ignored.

It should be obvious that man can live in peace only to the extent that he is willing to deal with his neighbor in charity and justice. These two virtues enable human solidarity to flourish even among people of different races and cultures. Where there is a willingness to love one's neighbor, there will be a strong inclination to work out any problems that arise by negotiation rather than by conflict.

Chapter 25 Study Guide

SUPPLEMENTARY READING

John Bernadone was born in Assisi, a small town in the Umbrian region of Italy, in 1182. The son of Peter Bernadone, a prosperous cloth merchant who traded heavily with the French, John was quickly nicknamed Francis, a name people have used now for centuries.

In his youth, Francis had a genuine passion for living. He was outgoing and charismatic, traits that made him popular with the other young people of the town. This zeal would lead him to revel a bit too much in material pleasures. Because his father enjoyed seeing Francis so popular among the other wealthy youths of the area, Peter Bernadone gladly supported these expensive tastes. Francis, however, never became a wanton sinner, having too much good sense to fall into such traps.

As part of his love for life, Francis relished the ideal of knighthood, painting a picture for himself of chivalry and high adventure. When his hometown went to war with the nearby town of Perugi, Francis quickly volunteered to fight. He was soon captured by the Perugians, and spent one year in captivity. His father eventually paid ransom to release Francis, but Francis fell seriously ill for a year.

After his recovery, still in love with the idea of knighthood, Francis joined the company of a knight who was off to fight for the pope. Well dressed, as usual, and also wearing fine armor, Francis' company came across a knight who had fallen on hard times. Taking pity on this man, and probably realizing that the knight was more in need than he himself was, Francis traded clothes with the knight.

That evening, Francis had a powerful dream. He saw his father's house transformed into a castle and covered with shields, all marked with the sign of the Cross. When Francis awoke, he felt the dream predicted success for himself as a knight, but this was not to be. Again, Francis fell ill. While lying helpless, he

St. Francis of Assisi
(1181-1226)
Feast on October 4

heard a voice telling him to return home and "serve the Master rather than the man." Francis returned to Assisi, confused about what God wanted him to do. He knew he was tired of trivial pleasures and gains, but he did not know to what he should dedicate his life.

While walking one day in a field, thinking about what was being asked of him, Francis came upon a leper. Although the sores of the leper initially filled Francis with disgust, he quickly recovered and kissed the hand of the sick man. At the same time, Francis gave all of his money to the leper.

This act gave Francis such peace and happiness that he then began visiting the sick and giving all that he had to the poor—for he realized that when he served the suffering he

Continued

was serving Christ. While all this was occurring, many people in Assisi, including Francis' father, noticed the changes in the young man. Some even thought he had gone mad.

The next turning point in Francis' life came during a pilgrimage to Rome. While he was leaving St. Peter's Basilica, Francis was approached by a group of beggars. He pulled aside the one who looked most in need and traded clothes with the man. Francis then spent the rest of the day begging with the poorest of Rome. This was the future saint's first serious pursuit of the love of his life, poverty. Francis' desire for poverty was so intense that artists have portrayed poverty as a beautiful woman, Lady Poverty, whom Francis was courting.

After his pilgrimage to Rome, Francis went to his father's warehouse, and, out of pure generosity and love, took a horse-load of cloth to the market and sold both the cloth and the horse.

He took the money to a poor local priest, offering it as support for the parish while asking for a place to stay and reflect. The priest accepted Francis' company but refused the money. Francis placed the money on a windowsill.

When Francis' father, Peter, realized his horse and cloth were missing, he tracked down his son. Peter was calmed a bit when the priest gave him the money, but he still demanded to see Francis.

The young man, however, hid himself and spent the next few days in solitary prayer. He then went to see his father, who was again angered, this time by his son's shabby appearance — a result of Francis' generosity to the poor. Peter beat his son, chained him to a wall, and locked him away. But Francis remained determined to live a life of poverty and service to the poor.

Eventually his mother set him free. One final confrontation with his father followed, in which Peter demanded that Francis obey or lose his inheritance. Francis gladly chose a life of poverty, and they went before the local bishop to formalize the disinheritance. While before the bishop, Francis so wanted to stress his love of poverty and disregard for belongings that he even gave the clothes he was wearing back to his father, saying, "Hitherto, I have called Peter Bernadone father....From now on I say only, 'Our Father who art in heaven.'" The bishop was deeply moved by this act. He covered Francis with his own garments until someone could get some clothes for the young saint. Given a simple robe, Francis marked the sign of the Cross on the shoulder with a piece of chalk.

Francis went on to found a religious order that renounces ownership of trivial belongings on earth, stressing poverty, love, and service to all, especially the poor. This order now bears his name. During the thirteenth century, the Franciscans helped revive the spiritual life of a struggling Church, making people realize that it was not treasure on earth that matters, but treasure in heaven.

St. Francis of Assisi Receiving the Stigmata

VOCABULARY

ARTIFICIAL SCARCITY
Hoarding of goods, especially in times of disaster.

BRIBERY
Knowingly offering money or other valuable objects so as to corrupt a person.

ENVY
Resentment or sadness at another's good fortune, and the desire to have it for oneself.

FRAUD
Sin of deception related to cheating.

GREED
The desire to amass earthly goods without limit.

PRIVATE PROPERTY
Individual ownership of a part of creation.

ROBBERY
Stealing by force or threatening of force.

SOCIAL CHARITY
The principle of friendship or solidarity manifested first in the distribution of goods and the remuneration of work.

STEWARDSHIP
God's entrusting of the resources of the world to mankind to care for it, master it by labor, and enjoy its fruits.

THEFT
Unjustly taking and keeping the property of another, against the reasonable will of the owner.

UNIVERSAL DESTINATION OF GOODS
Term used to describe the idea that the earth was originally given for the good of all mankind and that all resources should be used accordingly.

STUDY QUESTIONS

1. Does man have a right to own property? If so, is this right absolute?

2. What should the extra goods that a person has be used for?

3. What are some of the overlooked sins against the Seventh Commandment?

4. What is the purpose of economic activity?

5. Why does the Church have a right to give teachings on social and economic matters?

6. Is every case of taking or using a person's belongings a sin against the Seventh Commandment?

7. Are we required to give all money that is not spent on essentials to the poor?

8. What is the purpose of private property?

9. The biggest problem in economics is scarcity—the principle that each person has "unlimited wants but limited resources." How does the Tenth Commandment free us from this problem?

10. What do you think is the minimum amount of wealth that a person requires for salvation?

PRACTICAL EXERCISES

1. Jim is employed at a small grocery store. The owner pays him less than he pays the full-time employees who do the same work. The reason he gives is that part-time employees have less value than full-time. Would it be all right for Jim to take money from the register to make up for the difference in pay?

2. Bart and Jim plan to "T-P" the rival football captain's house for homecoming. Is there a moral problem with a "harmless" act of vandalism like this? Why or why not?

3. While Teresa was at college, she purchased a new wardrobe on a time payment plan. She used the information she learned in law school to file bankruptcy and kept the clothes. What she did was perfectly legal, but what is the moral nature of her actions? Can something be immoral if it is legal?

4. Put together a clothing/canned food drive at your school and/or parish. Ask your classmates, teacher, principal, pastor, family, and friends to help support the needy in your area.

FROM THE CATECHISM

2450 "You shall not steal" (Ex 20:15; Dt 5:19). "Neither thieves, nor the greedy..., nor robbers will inherit the kingdom of God" (1 Cor 6:10).

2451 The seventh commandment enjoins the practice of justice and charity in the administration of earthly goods and the fruits of men's labor.

2452 The goods of creation are destined for the entire human race. The right to private property does not abolish the universal destination of goods.

2453 The seventh commandment forbids theft. Theft is the usurpation of another's goods against the reasonable will of the owner.

2454 Every manner of taking and using another's property unjustly is contrary to the seventh commandment. The injustice committed requires reparation. Commutative justice requires the restitution of stolen goods.

2455 The moral law forbids acts which, for commercial or totalitarian purposes, lead to the enslavement of human beings, or to their being bought, sold or exchanged like merchandise.

2456 The dominion granted by the Creator over the mineral, vegetable, and animal resources of the universe cannot be separated from respect for moral obligations, including those toward generations to come.

2457 Animals are entrusted to man's stewardship; he must show them kindness. They may be used to serve the just satisfaction of man's needs.

2458 The Church makes a judgment about economic and social matters when the fundamental rights of the person or the salvation of souls requires it. She is concerned with the temporal common good of men because they are ordered to the sovereign Good, their ultimate end.

2459 Man is himself the author, center, and goal of all economic and social life. The decisive point of the social question is that goods created by God for everyone should in fact reach everyone in accordance with justice and with the help of charity.

2460 The primordial value of labor stems from man himself, its author and beneficiary. By means of his labor man participates in the work of creation. Work united to Christ can be redemptive.

2461 True development concerns the whole man. It is concerned with increasing each person's ability to respond to his vocation and hence to God's call. (cf. *CA*, 29)

2462 Giving alms to the poor is a witness to fraternal charity: it is also a work of justice pleasing to God.

2463 How can we not recognize Lazarus, the hungry beggar in the parable (cf. Lk 17:19-31), in the multitude of human beings without bread, a roof or a place to stay? How can we fail to hear Jesus: "As you did it not to one of the least of these, you did it not to me" (Mt 25:45)?

2551 "Where your treasure is, there will your heart be also" (Mt 6:21).

2552 The tenth commandment forbids avarice arising from a passion for riches and their attendant power.

FROM THE CATECHISM CONTINUED

2553 Envy is sadness at the sight of another's goods and the immoderate desire to have them for oneself. It is a capital sin.

2554 The baptized person combats envy through good-will, humility, and abandonment to the providence of God.

2555 Christ's faithful "have crucified the flesh with its passions and desires" (Gal 5: 24); they are led by the spirit and follow his desires.

2556 Detachment from riches is necessary for entering the Kingdom of heaven. "Blessed are the poor in spirit."

2557 "I want to see God" expresses the true desire of man. Thirst for God is quenched by the water of eternal life (Cf. Jn 4: 14).

Endnotes

1. Cf. *GS*, 29 § 2.
2. Cf. Mt 25: 14-30; Lk 19: 27.
3. *LG*, 42 § 3.
4. Cf. *CA*, 32; 34.
5. *Phlm* 16.
6. *Roman Catechism*, III, 37; cf. Sir 5: 8.

The Eighth Commandment

*God is the source of all truth
and wills the truth in our relationships.*

Chapter 26

The Eighth Commandment

*J*eremy went to confession on Saturday afternoon. He told the priest that he had to confess the sin of lying. The priest inquired what lie had he told. He responded that he had become angry because his friend, Jim, was dating a girl who had turned him down for a date. In order to get even, he told several of his schoolmates that Jim was selling drugs.

The priest thought for a moment and said, "Would you consider doing the following penance? After you leave confession, will you tell the first ten friends you meet you are a poor loser and a liar?"

Jeremy objected strongly, "I can't do that. Are you trying to ruin my reputation? If I did that, no one would trust me."

"What about what you did to Jim's reputation?" responded the priest.

Jeremy was silent.

"I am not surprised you don't wish to harm your reputation, but you should have considered Jim's reputation before you lied. For your penance, I want you to tell all the people to whom you told this story that you lied and that you are sorry for what you said."

Jeremy agreed to do the penance and left the confessional resolved to make up for what he had done.

THE EIGHTH COMMANDMENT AND THE OLD TESTAMENT

You shall not bear false witness against your neighbor. (Ex 20:16)

The eighth commandment forbids misrepresenting the truth in our relations with others. This moral prescription flows from the vocation of the holy people to bear witness to their God who is the truth and wills the truth. Offenses against the truth express by word or deed a refusal to commit oneself to moral uprightness: they are fundamental infidelities to God and, in this sense, they undermine the foundations of the covenant. (CCC 2464)

The eighth commandment requires that we speak the truth, particularly in what concerns others. We are obliged to speak with them honestly and to honor their good names because of the human dignity that belongs to all people. Being truthful links us to the Lord in a very fundamental way: for God himself is the origin of truth.

The Old Testament attests that *God is the source of all truth.* His Word is truth. His Law is truth. His "faithfulness endures to all generations."[1] Since God is "true," the members of his people are called to live in the truth.[2] (CCC 2465)

Indeed, respecting the truth not only links man to God but allows people to live in communities. Trust and truth have a close relationship: where there is no truth, there is no trust, for trust is based on the belief that one can rely on the words of another. "Man tends by nature towards the truth. He is obliged to honor and bear witness to it...." (CCC 2467). This tendency toward truth allows men to trust each other enough to form communities. When the truth is not adhered to, human relations are damaged. "Men could not live with one another if there were not mutual confidence that they were being truthful to one another."[3]

THE EIGHTH COMMANDMENT AND THE NEW TESTAMENT

Jesus then said to the Jews who had believed in him, "If you continue in my word, you are truly my disciples, and you will know the truth, and the truth will make you free." (Jn 8:31-32)

Jesus clearly says that those who wish to be his followers must accept his teachings, live his word, and his truth will set them free—free from the bondage of sin and death.

Indeed, being truthful in all things gives us true freedom, whereas telling lies binds us to the evil of sin. We can see this in the old saying that a liar must remember every lie he tells to keep from getting caught.

This means that one lie can force us to lie over and over again. When one chooses to become a liar, it is similar to the experience of falling into quicksand. Just as the person in quicksand is drawn in deeper by the struggle to become free, the liar is drawn deeper into the sinful habit by his attempt to avoid being caught.

In our culture, it has become customary to accept so-called "white lies" told to avoid hurting another's feelings. Though not serious enough by themselves to endanger a person's soul, white lies are still sins. In addition, these small lies can lead to bigger ones. It is, in fact, a short step from

The Eighth Commandment

You shall not bear false witness against your neighbor.

This tendency toward truth allows men to trust each other enough to form communities.

The Eighth Commandment

The person who gives his life for his beliefs is called a martyr.

St. Lawrence

A Christian martyr of Spanish birth who died in Rome in 258, one of the most venerated saints since the 4th century. He was ordained deacon by Pope Sixtus II and met his death shortly after the pope's own martyrdom. Lawrence was ordered by the Roman prefect to surrender the Church's treasures to him, whereupon Lawrence indicated the poor and sick around him, saying, "Here are the treasures of the Church." For this he was condemned to be roasted alive, a torture he underwent with calm and courage.

telling these "white lies" to lying in order to cover up almost anything. This is because lying, no matter what it is about, leads to lying as a habit, a vice.

> Truth or truthfulness is the virtue which consists in showing oneself true in deeds and truthful in words, and guarding against duplicity, dissimulation, and hypocrisy. (CCC 2505)

It must be borne in mind, however, that we are not obliged to tell the truth to those who have no right to hear it. There are some people who are always trying to find out what's going on in other people's lives. If someone tries to gossip with you, simply refuse to answer.

There are also those who lie in their daily lives, sometimes just for fun. In doing this they ignore the damage that their words cause—when they lie they hurt the mutual trust upon which societies are built. It is easy to see the chaos that would be created by distorting numbers: if you build with a yardstick three inches short, you have a flawed building. However, if you lie, you can sometimes ignore the damage, the destruction of trust among men that you are inflicting on all people.

Jesus' words at the beginning of this section speak of continuing in Christ's word. This means that we should bear witness to the truth of the Gospels not only by our words, but also by our actions. Doing so is an act of love toward God and our neighbors, who will be spiritually uplifted by this witness to the truths given by God.

A disciple of Christ lives the truth, and his conduct clearly indicates this truth. Christians are called upon to witness to the Gospel first. Witnessing to the truth of the Gospel can sometimes place a person in difficult situations, even forcing the choice between saving one's life or denying one's faith. The person who gives his life for his beliefs is called a martyr. The word martyr, which the Romans applied to the first century Christians, in fact means "witness."

> *Martyrdom* is the supreme witness given to the truth of the faith: it means bearing witness even unto death. The martyr bears witness to Christ who died and rose, to whom he is united by charity. He bears witness to the truth of the faith and of Christian doctrine. (CCC 2473)

Though Christians in our society are rarely called to die for their faith, young Christians are called to be witnesses to Christ for those who disobey their parents, use drugs, cheat on tests, and become sexually active outside of marriage. Though you won't be killed by those with whom you disagree, you may have to suffer the martyrdom of being rejected by those whom you would call your friends.

SINS AGAINST THE EIGHTH COMMANDMENT

Every offense against justice and truth obliges the perpetrator in conscience to make reparation, whether the damage has been caused through lying or detraction. It is best to discuss proper reparation with your confessor to determine the best solution.

Of course we should always struggle to avoid sinning against the truth. These sins take many forms:

- ◆ Detraction – disclosing the faults or sins of another to a person who does not need to know them;

- ◆ Calumny – telling lies that will harm another person's reputation;

- ◆ Duplicity – the act or practice of exhibiting different or contrary conduct or sentiment at different times in relation to the same thing; using trickery with others;

- ◆ Dissimulation – using false pretense with others;

- ◆ Perjury – deliberately making a statement contrary to the truth or withholding the truth under oath;

- ◆ Rash judgment – assuming as true the fault of a neighbor, even tacitly, without foundation;

- ◆ Flattery – excessive, untrue, or insincere praise;

- ◆ Bragging – making an ostentatious display of one's own conduct or attributes; claiming sole credit for accomplishments that would not be possible without gifts received from God;

- ◆ Mockery – maliciously characterizing a particular aspect of another's behavior;

- ◆ Revealing secrets one is required to keep;

- ◆ Lying – telling a falsehood with the intention of deceiving someone.

Christ specifically says that lying is the work of the devil, for to lead someone into error deliberately by lying is a sin against justice and charity.

To determine whether a lie is a mortal sin, the following criteria must be determined:

- ◆ The intention of the person telling the lie;

- ◆ The nature of the truth it deforms;

- ◆ The circumstances surrounding the lie;

- ◆ The harm suffered by the victim or victims.

Lies are most serious when they hide the truth from someone who has a right to hear it. Parents, for example, have a right to know where their children are and with whom they are associating. They should not be misled. When parents inquire about a child's friends and whereabouts, they should be told the truth. Very often, students complain, "My parents don't trust me anymore." This problem usually arises when children associate with those whom the parents believe are not good companions or when parents find out that their child has lied. Since parents have the responsibility of caring for their children, they also have the responsibility, and the right, to make decisions that they believe are best for their children.

THE TRUTH IN PRACTICE

Truthfulness and trust are the basis for good relations in society, so we should act honestly whenever we deal with others. This does not mean, though, that people do have a right to communicate or to hear the truth in every circumstance. If they did, gossiping would become an obligation instead of a petty habit. People have a right to the truth only when they

Lies are most serious when they hide the truth from someone who has a right to hear it.

Parents have a right to know where their children are and with whom they are associating.

Honoring the secrecy of the confessional is one of the most sacred aspects of the priesthood.

are involved in the situation in question. In other cases, we either do not have to or are even required not to reveal specific information.

Love of neighbor requires everyone to determine in concrete situations whether it is just to reveal the truth to someone who asks for it. The common good, respect for privacy, the possibility of scandal, and the safety of others must be considered before answering a question. There is no requirement to reveal the truth to someone who has no right to know it.

Professional secrets shared by physicians, office holders, lawyers, and servicemen or confidential information given under the seal of secrecy must not be revealed unless the secret is bound to cause great harm to the one who confided it, the one who heard it, or to a third party, and where grave harm can be avoided only by telling the truth.

We are obliged to keep a secret:

† When our office requires it;

† When the good name of another requires it;

† When we have promised to do so.

We may reveal a secret:

† When it is for the good of a guilty person;

† When it will save ourselves or others from evil;

† When it is contrary to justice or the general welfare to keep it;

† When the person to whom we reveal it has a right to know.

In the public realm, people have a right to information based on truth, freedom, and justice; however, the media must not violate individual rights. Interference in the private lives of persons engaged in political or public activity is condemned whenever it infringes upon their privacy and freedom.

Reparation must be made for all sins committed against the eighth commandment.

THE SEAL OF CONFESSION

Under no circumstances may a priest ever reveal the sins he has been told under the seal of Confession. If a priest were to do so deliberately, he would sin gravely, and he would be automatically excommunicated under canon law and suspended from his priestly office, unless the pope himself decided to revoke the sanction.

> The *secret of the sacrament of reconciliation* is sacred and cannot be violated under any pretext. "The sacramental seal is inviolable; therefore, it is a crime for any confessor in any way to betray a penitent by word or in any other manner or for any reason."[4] (CCC 2490)

Even in extreme cases, a priest is bound to the secrecy of the confessional. If a person were to confess a murder, the priest would not be able to tell the authorities. Honoring the secrecy of the confessional is one of the most sacred aspects of the priesthood. A confessor who violates the seal automatically incurs excommunication.

In addition, any lay person who overhears the sins of another during the Sacrament of Confession is bound by the seal of Confession. They may not reveal the sins of another overheard during Confession under just penalty not excluding excommunication.

CONCLUSION

It should be obvious at this point that truth is sacred. Human relationships must be built upon trust, and where there is no truth, there is no trust. Christ, who is all truth, expects Christians to testify to him by the truthfulness of their lives, actions, and words.

The obligation to tell the truth is binding not only on a person-to-person basis but also at every level of society. Businesses, social organizations, and governments are required to have policies that make clear the obligation to tell the truth where the truth of necessity must be told.

Society has a right to information based on truth, freedom, and justice, so the media have an obligation to make correct moral judgments prior to presenting news to the public.

The obligation to tell the truth is binding not only on a person-to-person basis but also at every level of society.

SUPPLEMENTARY READING

St. Catherine of Siena had a vivid imagination. Unfortunately, this led to many people not believing in her dazzling visions of Jesus and Mary. Catherine tried many different ways to bring silence into her life so that she could better hear the truths God was speaking to her. She even went so far as to run away to a small cave outside the city walls to be a hermit—of course, she returned the same day.

However, God asked her to grow in love of him, by loving her neighbor. So Catherine began to minister to prisoners on their way to execution. She even followed Niccolo di Toldo, an inmate condemned to death, all the way to the chopping block and prayed for him until she caught his severed head in her hands.

Catherine understood very few things, but she did understand the need for obedience to Jesus Christ. She understood it so well that one might find her yelling, cajoling, exhorting, crying all in the name of Jesus. Catherine knew that the Pope's place was in Rome, not in Avignon where he had lived in exile for the past 70-plus years. Not very literate herself, Catherine dictated hundreds of letters to the Pope as well as various cardinals and bishops in an effort to get the Holy Father back to his rightful place in Rome. While fearless, she was somewhat uncomfortable in this role as she is quoted as asking God, "How can I, a poor and miserable woman, be able to do any good in Your Church? How shall I instruct wise and learned men, or how will it be even seemly for me to live and converse with them?"

St. Catherine of Siena
(1347-1380)
Feast on April 29

Catherine always wrote and spoke very bluntly and always took her message to the person who could enact the needed reforms. Despite her lack of education and the fact that she was a woman during the Middle Ages, she fought for the truth. Eventually this led to her going to Avignon to plead with the Pope and several cardinals personally. After much prayer and struggle, the truth finally won out. Catherine's tireless proclamation of the truth concerning the successor of Peter had set the Pope free.

VOCABULARY

CALUMNY
A false statement that harms the reputation of others and gives occasion for false judgments concerning them.

DETRACTION
Disclosure of another's faults and sins, without an objectively valid reason, to persons who did not know about them, thus causing unjust injury to that person's reputation.

DISSIMULATION
To act deceitfully.

DUPLICITY
The quality of being "double" in action or conduct; the practice of acting two different ways at different times, openly or secretly; deceitfulness.

GOSSIP
Spreading idle rumors of a personal or intimate nature; tale bearing.

LIBEL
Wrongful, untrue defamation of a person in writing or printing.

PREJUDICE
Preconceived opinion formulated without consideration of known facts and usually based on erroneous knowledge leading to wrong judgments and rendering a person blind to reason and closed to argument.

PRIVACY
Right of a person to keep part of their life not open to the public.

SEAL OF CONFESSION
The confessor's obligation to keep absolutely secret what a penitent has told to him in the Sacrament of Penance; also known as the sacramental seal.

SLANDER
A false statement which harms the reputation of others and gives occasion for false judgments concerning them; same as calumny.

TRUTHFULNESS
Uprightness, sincerity, or candor in human action and speech.

STUDY QUESTIONS

1. What does the Eighth Commandment require?

2. What is the meaning of the statement, "Where there is no truth, there is no trust"?

3. How does "telling the truth give us true freedom"?

4. What is the seriousness of "white lies"?

5. Does everyone have a right to be told the truth? Explain.

6. To which truths are Christians called upon primarily to give witness?

7. How does one witness to the truth in the highest way?

8. List the sins against truth, and indicate why they are wrong.

9. Deliberate lies sin against what two virtues?

10. What four questions are used to determine if a lie is a mortal sin?

11. When are we obliged to keep a secret?

12. In what situations may we reveal a secret?

13. May a priest tell what he has heard in confession?

PRACTICAL EXERCISES

1. Anne is aware that her brother Jerry has been getting drunk on the weekend and is concerned about him. She promised Jerry that she wouldn't tell their parents. Is this promise binding?

2. Look up St. Thomas More in a book on saints. Write a paragraph explaining the oath King Henry VIII wanted him to take, why he would not take it, and what happened because of his refusal.

3. Ed arrived home after 3 a.m. Although he hadn't been drinking, he knows that his mother would disapprove of the hour at which he arrived home because he is only 16 years old. The next morning, his mother asked him what time he came in. Does he have to tell the truth?

4. Suppose a friend tells you about something gravely sinful that he did. He wants to go to confession, but he is afraid that his parents might find out from the priest. Write a paragraph explaining why your friend's fears are groundless.

FROM THE CATECHISM

2504 "You shall not bear false witness against your neighbor" (Ex 20:16). Christ's disciples have "put on the new man, created after the likeness of God in true righteousness and holiness" (Eph 4:24).

2505 Truth or truthfulness is the virtue which consists in showing oneself true in deeds and truthful in words, and guarding against duplicity, dissimulation, and hypocrisy.

2506 The Christian is not to "be ashamed of testifying to our Lord" (2 Tm 1:8) in deed and word. Martyrdom is the supreme witness given to the truth of the faith.

2507 Respect for the reputation and honor of persons forbids all detraction and calumny in word or attitude.

2508 Lying consists in saying what is false with the intention of deceiving one's neighbor.

2509 An offense committed against the truth requires reparation.

2510 The golden rule helps one discern, in concrete situations, whether or not it would be appropriate to reveal the truth to someone who asks for it.

2511 "The sacramental seal is inviolable" (CIC, can. 983 § 1). Professional secrets must be kept. Confidences prejudicial to another are not to be divulged.

2512 Society has a right to information based on truth, freedom, and justice. One should practice moderation and discipline in the use of the social communications media.

2513 The fine arts, but above all sacred art, "of their nature are directed toward expressing in some way the infinite beauty of God in works made by human hands. Their dedication to the increase of God's praise and of his glory is more complete, the more exclusively they are devoted to turning men's minds devoutly toward God" (*SC*, 122).

Endnotes

1. Ps 119:90; cf. Prv 8:7; 2 Sm 7:28; Ps 119:142; Lk 1:50.
2. Rom 3:4; cf. Ps 119:30.
3. St. Thomas Aquinas, *STh* II-II, 109, 3, *corp. art.*
4. CIC, can. 983 § 1.

The Beatitudes

Living a moral life at the highest level.

Chapter 27

The Beatitudes

*W*hen asked, "What do you want most out of life?" most people would probably say, "I want to be happy." The problem with this answer is that few people agree on how to define happiness, probably because most people seek happiness in the here-and-now. The problem is that here-and-now happiness is just that: here today and gone tomorrow.

True happiness is permanent, and there is only one place where permanent happiness can be found: in the presence of Jesus in Heaven.

Jesus began the Sermon on the Mount with the Beatitudes to indicate that those who follow them are living moral life at the highest level. Those who seek the highest levels of sanctity are truly blessed. As a result of seeking personal sanctity, they reach the highest levels of happiness and personal sanctity in this life. The closer we come to union with God in this life, the happier we will be. It is a foretaste of the permanent happiness which is Heaven.

THE BEATITUDES

The word beatitude comes from the Latin word meaning "blessed." Those who keep the Beatitudes will be blessed with the love of God both here and in the heavenly home. Jesus' preaching takes up the promises made to Abraham and his descendants that they would possess the earth. Jesus leads us to see that this promise refers to heavenly territory.

> The Beatitudes take up and fulfill God's promises from Abraham on by ordering them to the Kingdom of heaven. They respond to the desire for happiness that God has placed in the human heart. (CCC 1725)

When we study the Beatitudes, we notice first that they do not reflect the manner in which many people live their lives. Second, we see that they require self-sacrifice.

In the first chapter, we found that we are called to imitate Jesus to the point of identifying totally with him. Total identification with Jesus means accepting a life of sacrifice for the salvation of others, just as he did. To accomplish this, we must learn to live the Beatitudes, which take us beyond the commandments and lead us to perfection. They lead us to heaven, the vision of God, permanent participation in his divine nature, and rest in God as his children.

In the Gospel of Matthew, eight Beatitudes are listed:

† Blessed are the poor in spirit, for theirs is the kingdom of heaven.

† Blessed are those who mourn, for they shall be comforted.

† Blessed are the meek, for they shall inherit the earth.

† Blessed are those who hunger and thirst for righteousness, for they shall be satisfied.

† Blessed are the merciful, for they shall obtain mercy.

† Blessed are the pure in heart, for they shall see God.

† Blessed are the peacemakers, for they shall be called sons of God.

† Blessed are those who are persecuted for righteousness' sake, for theirs is the kingdom of heaven. (Mt 5: 3-10)

The Beatitudes reflect the love of Christ and call the baptized to live them as a way of demonstrating that they share in the love and mission of Christ, a mission of self-sacrificing love.

> The Beatitudes depict the countenance of Jesus Christ and portray his charity. They express the vocation of the faithful associated with the glory of his Passion and Resurrection; they shed light on the actions and attitudes characteristic of the Christian life; they are the paradoxical promises that sustain hope in the midst of tribulations; they proclaim the blessings and rewards already secured, however dimly, for Christ's disciples; they have begun in the lives of the Virgin Mary and all the saints. (CCC 1717)

The search for happiness is the longest unbroken quest in every human life. For many, the search is for individual pleasure over every other consideration, a love of self over everything else. Ultimately, such pleasures leave humans empty, for happiness cannot be found in self-seeking. Through the Beatitudes, we can attain the highest measure of

Total identification with Jesus means accepting a life of sacrifice for the salvation of others, just as he did.

Through the Beatitudes, we can attain the highest measure of true happiness in this life by denying self, seeking Christ, and assisting others to their salvation.

The Beatitudes

We were created to attain perfect happiness, which is found only in loving and in being loved by the Lord.

Mother Teresa of Calcutta

To see her was to experience a strong measure of the total love which is found in Jesus.

true happiness in this life by denying self, seeking Christ, and assisting others to their salvation. Jesus has placed this desire to serve other people in man's heart to draw all men to himself.

> The Beatitudes reveal the goal of human existence, the ultimate end of human acts: God calls us to his own beatitude. This vocation is addressed to each individual personally, but also to the Church as a whole, the new people made up of those who have accepted the promise and live from it in faith. (CCC 1719)

The New Testament describes the Beatitudes in such terms as the vision of God, the joy of the Lord, and the coming of God's kingdom. This is because by denying ourselves and following the Beatitudes, we are joined to the divine life of the Trinity, a life of complete love, true knowledge, and service of God.

In a culture that stresses wealth and success, the idea of completely denying oneself may not seem like the path to happiness. Christ, however, offers true peace to those who seek personal sanctity through self-sacrifice. This is a peace that seems to go against our understanding. The life of sacrifice must be practiced for one truly to understand its value. Such a life is an invitation to purify all earthly desires from our hearts and to seek the love of God above all else.

It is only right for people to seek God's love and to love him in return. This is God's call to all people. We were created to attain perfect happiness, which is found only in loving and in being loved by the Lord. When we act with love toward God and other people, we can be sure of the mutual love between ourselves and God.

Indeed, we should try to show this love throughout our lives. The benefits of science, human fame, wealth, power, or any other human achievement, as great as they may seem, are left behind at the hour of death. The only riches to be taken into the next life are the fruits of our relationship with Jesus, who came so that man may participate in his divine life. Those who seek sanctity demonstrate true and real participation in the life of Jesus. Mother Teresa may be the best-known example of this identification with Christ's sufferings. To see her was to experience a strong measure of the total love which is found in Jesus.

Conforming ourselves to Christ is the work of a lifetime. But our goal should be to say with St. Paul, "It is no longer I who live, but Christ who lives in me" (Gal 2: 20).

> The Decalogue, the Sermon on the Mount, and the apostolic catechesis describe for us the paths that lead to the Kingdom of heaven. Sustained by the grace of the Holy Spirit, we tread them, step by step, by everyday acts. By the working of the Word of Christ, we slowly bear fruit in the Church to the glory of God.[1] (CCC 1724)

BLESSED ARE THE POOR IN SPIRIT, FOR THEIRS IS THE KINGDOM OF GOD.

The first beatitude is the key to the others. To state it another way, "Blessed are those who realize that even with all their talents and possessions they are poor in God's sight. As a result, they have no attachment to goods, fame, power, name, opinion, control over others, or their own life." In a word, those who have no attachment to this life or its pleasures will find it much easier to become saints.

Who is poor in spirit? You could think of someone who has no attachment to God or God's grace as poor in spirit. Obviously, he would be the poorest of spirits, for he is not blessed in the manner of the Beatitudes. On the other hand, someone who is poor in spirit could be a person who does not have an undue attachment to this world and its attractions. As with people who are materially poor, possessions do not get in between the person who follows this beatitude and God. This is what the first beatitude is about.

Does this mean a person has no need of material goods? Of course not. All of us, depending on our state in life, have need of some goods on a regular basis. The best way to express what this beatitude encourages is to say that while we may own goods, they do not own us. We do not seek after more than we need, and the excess of our goods is given away for the good of the poor.

The first beatitude warns us that those who are more attached to goods than to God will wind up with neither God nor goods. It is possible to have too many clothes, CDs, or other possessions. Many people find this statement foolish, since the culture in which we live encourages us to own more and more things, whether we need them or not. The large number of public storage warehouses, though, indicates that many people own more than they could ever use. Though there are some people who genuinely need this extra space, for many others it is a matter of holding onto possessions they could just as easily do without.

Those who are poor in spirit desire only the goods necessary to ensure a healthy standard of living in accordance with their particular state of life. Those who live this beatitude will love their neighbors enough to share the excess of their personal goods with them. The problem arises for most of us when a determination must be made: what exactly are "excess goods"? The answer lies in the phrase "state of life." For those who are poor, it is an easy answer: there is no excess. For the rest of us, the phrase indicates that there are different levels of need for goods. For example, those whose professions require that they present themselves as successful, such as a lawyers or stockbrokers, have a greater need to show off personal wealth than those whose job doesn't have such an emphasis.

The real goods each of us has, though, are acts compiled at the end of a lifetime of struggle. In the matter of goods, we must keep in mind the promise of Jesus, who said, "Seek you first the kingdom of God, then all the rest will be added unto you."

Examination for being poor in spirit:

† Do I take good care of the goods I own?

† Do I contribute to my church?

† Do I always purchase whatever I want, whether I need it or not?

† Do I have more clothes than I need?

† Do I share with those in need?

The first beatitude warns us that those who are more attached to goods than to God will wind up with neither God nor goods.

Those who live this beatitude will love their neighbors enough to share the excess of their personal goods with them.

Since loss is a part of everyone's life, the suffering that comes from any loss, whether from death or other causes, should be accepted as a means to strengthen oneself to accept future suffering as Christ did.

BLESSED ARE THEY WHO MOURN, FOR THEY SHALL BE COMFORTED.

Possibly the most difficult mystery to understand is death. It's easy to accept that the sin of Adam and Eve is the cause of death, yet it is another thing when death becomes a personal reality. In an instant, you lose all contact with someone you love. Although we know otherwise, the separation feels permanent. We can no longer see or converse with the person who died.

In this situation, our faith may be tested as never before. It is then that we must recall the words, "Blessed are they who mourn, for they shall be comforted." How? Our faith tells us that the union of our suffering with the suffering of Christ is of benefit to those for whom we offer it. Christ turns our suffering into an act of salvation for others. It is also of benefit to us when we accept the suffering of loss as a mortification for our personal sins. The greater the suffering, the closer Christ is to us, and he will see us through. Remember that Jesus mourned the death of Lazarus with Mary and Martha; he understands human suffering (cf. Jn 11:1-44).

It must also be born in mind that Christ blesses those who comfort people in mourning for their act of Christian love. Jesus said, "what you have done to the least of my brothers, you have done unto me."

This beatitude applies to other mourners in addition to those who sorrow over death. It is also a promise to those who are genuinely sorry for their offenses to God. If someone mourns over his sins, either his own or another's, God will recognize his prayer and give graces accordingly. In this way too, those who mourn will be comforted.

Also, many people mourn over the loss of opportunities or earthly goods. Their mourning might be better converted to praying for God's assistance in accepting the loss and in understanding whether personal failings caused this loss. Since loss is a part of everyone's life, the suffering that comes from any loss, whether from death or other causes, should be accepted as a means to strengthen oneself to accept future suffering as Christ did, to give it real and permanent meaning. This is the work of a lifetime.

Examination for comforting those who mourn:

† Do I pray for those who are suffering?

† Do I attend wakes and funeral services even if they make me feel uncomfortable?

† Do I comfort those obviously in pain?

† Do I accept suffering willingly?

† Do I offer my suffering so as to make up for sin?

BLESSED ARE THE MEEK, FOR THEY SHALL POSSESS THE EARTH.

It has been said that the Christian should be counter-cultural, that is, counter to any trends in the culture that go against Christianity. If there is any virtue that is truly counter-cultural in these times, it is meekness.

Every year it seems that some new award or honor is set up so that people can come together to glory in their achievements. A true understanding of one's talents, however, should enable us to see that all our gifts come from God. God is "Number One," not us. The desire to use one's talents well is to be commended, but care must be taken to be certain that success does not turn into self-glorification. Jesus said, "Without me you can do nothing."

Meekness allows us to endure suffering, recognizing it as being part of God's plan for our lives. It also leads directly to humility. Since humility is a virtue acquired by accepting situations in which we are humbled, humility cannot be acquired through one's own actions. The humble person has a true sense of his worth and recognizes that all talents are on loan from God rather than selected by personal choice.

A humble person is not so filled with pride that any disagreement, slight, or insult angers him. It is good to examine oneself each evening regarding any offenses we believe we suffered during the day and how we responded in each circumstance. Holding one's tongue when someone says something with which we may disagree presents an excellent opportunity to mortify oneself. An honest examination of perceived offenses should lead to the realization that there is no need to respond to them unless it is a case of an injustice that must be rectified.

Examination for meekness:

† Do I accept correction with a smile?

† Do I brag about my accomplishments?

† Do I correct others with gentleness?

† Do I accept compliments graciously?

† Do I seek the best place for myself?

† When things go wrong do I get angry or violent?

The humble person has a true sense of his worth and recognizes that all talents are on loan from God rather than selected by personal choice.

BLESSED ARE THEY WHO HUNGER AND THIRST FOR RIGHTEOUSNESS, FOR THEY SHALL BE SATISFIED.

If you desire a rule to live your life by, make it, "Go for greatness in the Lord," or simply, "Be the very best you can be for Jesus." For that is the meaning of this beatitude. How does one achieve this greatness? By working toward becoming a saint. In the Old Testament, the "just man" is one who is busy giving to his neighbor what is due to him, recognizing this as a work owed to God. In the New Testament, we have the model of Jesus himself, who went beyond justice, doing good to those who did not deserve it, making up for the sins he had not even committed, the sins of us all.

When Jesus tells us, "Love your enemies and pray for those who persecute you," he is calling us to be more than just; he is calling us to give people more than we think they deserve (Mt 5:44). It is a call to identify totally with Jesus, the Holy One, who himself prayed for those who persecuted him while he was on the cross. Those who hunger and thirst for righteousness seek to imitate the holiness of Jesus.

Holiness is possible if we are willing to conform our will to God's.

As Christians called to imitate Christ, we must be merciful as Christ is merciful.

The only way for some to find Christ, in fact, is to see his love reflected in our actions.

At first, it may seem impossible to achieve this holiness, yet Jesus told us, "You, therefore, must be perfect, as your heavenly Father is perfect" (Mt 5:48). Holiness is possible if we are willing to conform our will to God's. We will accomplish this if we have a spiritual director and a regular prayer life with Jesus. Regular prayer helps us establish a strong relationship with Jesus, and a spiritual director will guide us to see what the Holy Spirit is asking of us.

The use of the phrase "hunger and thirst" is key to understanding this beatitude. Think of the times we have been extremely hungry or thirsty. Real hunger and thirst cause a constant ache in mind and body that will not leave us till we are satisfied. In the same way, there is no true search for holiness unless there is an ache in the mind that will only be satisfied in the continuing search for Christ. If we have this kind of desire, we will place God's will above our own throughout our lives.

Examination for holiness:

† Do I strive to do God's will?

† Do I look for spiritual direction when I need it?

† Do I read Sacred Scripture to learn how to imitate Jesus?

† Do I go to confession and receive communion regularly?

† Do I seek to identify with Jesus' life and actions?

† Do I devote specific time to prayer and learning my faith better?

BLESSED ARE THE MERCIFUL, FOR THEY SHALL OBTAIN MERCY.

Who does not need mercy in their life at one time or another? What would be the effect on society and human relations if justice were always meted out on a strict basis? Whereas the Old Testament calls for an "eye for an eye," Christ told people to "love your enemies and pray for those who persecute you" (Mt 5:44).

Following this beatitude offers a singular opportunity for us to show the love of Christ to others. The only way for some to find Christ, in fact, is to see his love reflected in our actions. When we do this, we build the kingdom of God on earth: for love begets love, and mercy begets mercy, whereas turning away from these virtues can only destroy people. Christ demonstrates in the parable of the unjust steward, who was forgiven his large debt and then refused to forgive a small debt, that he will be merciful to those who show mercy, and that he will judge harshly those who have judged harshly (cf. Mt 18:23-35).

Humanly speaking, it is too easy to overlook the seriousness of sin as a great offense to God that deserves penance, yet the great love God has for us is manifested in his willingness to forgive sin as often as we are sorry. There is no human mercy to match this mercy, but his actions indicate to us that as Christians called to imitate Christ, we must be merciful as Christ is merciful.

When we are offended, it is well to remember that we, too, offend others, regret it later, and desire to be forgiven. To be merciful is a sign of strength, not weakness.

Examination for mercy:

† Do I ask for the grace to forgive others easily?

† Do I have compassion for those who suffer?

† Do I keep in mind the many times Christ has shown mercy to me?

† Do I try to avoid grudges against those who offend me?

† Do I try to forget the offenses of others as quickly as I wish my offenses to be forgotten?

BLESSED ARE THE PURE IN HEART, FOR THEY SHALL SEE GOD.

> The sixth beatitude proclaims, "Blessed are the pure in heart, for they shall see God."[2] "Pure in heart" refers to those who have attuned their intellects and wills to the demands of God's holiness, chiefly in three areas: charity;[3] chastity or sexual rectitude;[4] love of truth, and orthodoxy of faith.[5] There is a connection between purity of heart, of body, and of faith:
>
> > The faithful must believe the articles of the Creed "so that by believing they may obey God, by obeying may live well, by living well may purify their hearts, and with pure hearts may understand what they believe."[6] (CCC 2518)

A pure heart is a heart that has a special place reserved for Jesus. Because of this, it is a heart that guards itself against temptations against the sixth and ninth commandments. The practice of this beatitude leads us to see the person of others as God sees while avoiding seeing them solely in their sexual dimension, which reduces the neighbor to an object of personal pleasure. Sexual rectitude obliges us to approach every person and every occasion as an opportunity to demonstrate the total love Jesus demands of us for our neighbor. Lack of sexual rectitude, on the other hand, commits us to seeking only a particular personal pleasure in others and denying their dignity and worth as children of God. Since practice leads to morality, those who violate chastity soon find themselves in opposition to the Church's teaching on sexual morality.

Being pure of heart also requires that we love the truth. We have been given the truth by Christ and through his Church. Many people who are Catholic do not have a real love for Christ and his Church. We can see this in the poor turnout at Mass on Sunday. Only about 25% of Catholics go to weekly Mass. Love of the truth should inspire us to worship as the Church instructs us.

Examination for purity of heart:

† Do I strive to live according to the teachings of the Church? Do I do so with love or grudgingly?

† Do I turn to Jesus and Mary in prayer when I am tempted?

† Do I seek advice in Confession regarding the virtue of purity?

† Do I ask the assistance of my guardian angel when I am tempted?

† Do I avoid the influence of those who do not think and act in purity?

† Do I avoid places where I may be tempted against purity?

A pure heart is a heart that has a special place reserved for Jesus.

Lack of sexual rectitude commits us to seeking only a particular personal pleasure in others and denying their dignity and worth as children of God.

Peacemakers must first of all be people of peace.

Peacemakers do not have a passion for argument but are passionate for the truth.

† Do I know the truths of the Church?

† Do I strive to understand these truths and believe them completely?

BLESSED ARE THE PEACEMAKERS, FOR THEY SHALL BE CALLED SONS OF GOD.

In a world of strife and multiple disagreements, there is need for many peacemakers. Peacemakers must first of all be people of peace. Peaceable people are unwilling to force their views on others. They are aware that they have the truth and are willing to defend the truth, but they are completely opposed to forcing others to see life as they see life. They adhere to the advice of St. Paul, "Keep peace with all men, where it is possible, for your part (Rom 12:18). They are aware that the truth they offer will often be a source of division for those who should accept it, particularly when the recipient is not acting morally.

Peacemakers are not willing to compromise their beliefs to avoid a disagreement. They are not fearful people, for they are allied with Jesus in attempting to spread the truth. They therefore have the power to free from sin those with whom they come into contact. They do not have a passion for argument but are passionate for the truth. They discuss; they do not argue. They grant the other his opinion, but are not willing to accept opinion as fact. They can disagree without being disagreeable. They do not label others or call names.

Examination for being a peacemaker:

† Do I accept that others can have opinions contrary to mine?

† Do I seek to win in every discussion?

† Do I see others as adversaries?

† Do I disagree without being disagreeable?

† Do I ask the Holy Spirit for assistance in seeking the truth?

BLESSED ARE THEY WHO ARE PERSECUTED FOR RIGHTEOUSNESS' SAKE, FOR THEIRS IS THE KINGDOM OF HEAVEN.

More Christians died for Christ in the twentieth century than in any other. As we read this chapter, Christians are being persecuted in China, where they are imprisoned and killed, and in the Sudan, where they are kidnapped and sold as slaves.

The word traditionally applied to Christians who die for Christ is martyr, which comes from a word meaning "witness." Martyrs who die for Christ are rewarded with his presence in heaven.

A famous American bishop, Fulton Sheen, coined the phrase "dry martyr" to describe those who are made to suffer for Christ without being killed for their witness. There are times when Jesus expects us to be dry martyrs for him. This occurs when our friends tempt us to break the commandments and ridicule us for refusing to turn our backs on God.

Many Americans find it difficult to go against the culture when it promotes evil ideas and actions, yet we must remember that even though it is not easy, we are called to be virtuous. Virtue is acquired by repeatedly choosing good actions over evil ones.

To build this habit of virtue, young people need witnesses to Christ, and the best witnesses are often those from their own peer group who refuse to go along with the crowd. When we are pressured by our friends to commit sin, we must call upon the Holy Spirit, who gave us special graces in Confirmation, to enable us to do what Jesus expects of us.

Jesus consoled all Christians, "In the world you have tribulation; but be of good cheer, I have overcome the world" (Jn 16:33).

Examination for suffering persecution:

† Do I pray daily for those Christians suffering persecution?

† Do I encourage others to stand up for what is right?

† Do I support my friends who do stand up for what is right?

† Do I offer my suffering for acting virtuously for those who persecute me?

† Do I turn to Jesus when tempted to go along with the crowd?

CONCLUSION

Everyone who strives to keep the commandments will reach heaven. Yet, Jesus has called everyone to a higher life. It is the life of sanctity as lived by his mother and all the saints.

Sanctity is accomplished by learning Jesus' teachings, especially the Beatitudes. By living them, we are able to live a life that imitates Jesus and joins us to the divine nature of the Trinity. This type of life will gain us greater rewards in heaven.

When we are pressured by our friends to commit sin, we must call upon the Holy Spirit, who gave us special graces in Confirmation, to enable us to do what Jesus expects of us.

St. Lucy

Martyred c. 304 – A Sicilian, Lucy was the daughter of wealthy and noble parents. She was a dedicated virgin who gave away her goods to feed the poor.

Under the reign of the anti-Christian Emperor Diocletian, Lucy refused a marriage proposal. The rejected suitor denounced Lucy to the Emperor as a Christian. Lucy was sentenced to a brothel, but when the guards came to to take her away, she became as stone and could not be moved. She was then ordered burned to death, but the flames would not touch her. Lucy was finally stabbed in the throat.

Lucy is patron of eye diseases because her name comes from the latin "lux" meaning "light."

Chapter 27 Study Guide

SUPPLEMENTARY READING

Agnes was born in Albania. While in school, Agnes sang in the choir, played the mandolin, and volunteered at the Legion of Mary. At the age of twelve she began to feel called to life as a missionary. Yet she was *very* uncertain. How could she be sure?

She began to pray a lot about her vocation. She also talked with her mother, her sister Aga, and her confessor. When she asked the confessor, "How can I be sure?" He replied, "Through your JOY. If you feel really happy by the idea that God might call you to serve him, him and your neighbor, then this is the evidence that you have a call. The deep inner joy that you feel is the compass that indicates your direction in life." Finally at age 18, the decision was made. Agnes was going to India after assisting in several religious retreats for the past two years.

In Darjeeling, she finished her training and made her first vows as Sister Teresa. After helping at a little hospital in Bengali, she was sent to Calcutta to be a teacher. As she went deeper into the Indian culture, she became more enamored with the poor. Sister Teresa was finally inspired to live among the poor, assisting them in all their needs.

The climate was a scorching 115°F with 95% humidity. The trash, open sewers, insects, rats, and cockroaches must have left her dreaming for a return to her clean classroom complete with fan and mosquito netting. One day as an American journalist commented on Mother Teresa's tending to a gangrenous patient: "I wouldn't do that for a million dollars!" The Mother replied, "Neither would I, but I do it for Christ."

Mother Teresa of Calcutta
(1910-1997)

The Missionaries of Charity, Mother Teresa's order, are first and foremost a contemplative order, devoting several hours a day to prayer. Mother Teresa rhetorically asks, "If we were not in constant union with God, how could we endure the sacrifices we must make by living in the most miserable conditions?" Besides the vows of poverty, chastity, and obedience, these sisters take a fourth vow: service to the poorest of the poor. Throughout the world, the Missionaries have started houses for the terminally ill, for abandoned children, for lepers, and for AIDS patients.

Many choose to undertake difficult and unpleasant tasks in pursuit of some greater good. Mother Teresa and her sisters enjoyed sacrifice and service for its own sake.

Continued

SUPPLEMENTARY READING CONTINUED

Consumerism says, "If I have this; if I don't have to do that; if I could only be entertained in such a way, *then* I would be happy." Eventually the drive for pleasure leads to addictions, perversions, and depression. Western society suffers not so much from material poverty, as spiritual poverty, *a poverty of love.* As a cure, Mother Teresa offers this prayer:

The fruit of silence is prayer.
The fruit of prayer is faith.
The fruit of faith is love.
The fruit of love is service.
The fruit of service is peace.

Mother Teresa's message is that by service that flows from a deep prayer life, one can be at peace…fulfilled…happy…*holy.*

VOCABULARY

ATTACHMENT
Unwillingness to abandon worldly riches for the Kingdom of Heaven.

BEATITUDE
Happiness or blessedness, especially the eternal happiness of heaven, which is described as the vision of God, or entering into God's rest by those whom he makes partakers of the divine nature.

COUNTERCULTURE
A mode of life opposed to the conventional or dominant, that rejects established social values and practices, esp. among the young.

DETACHMENT
Willingness to abandon worldly riches for the Kingdom of Heaven.

GUARDIAN ANGEL
Angels assigned to protect and intercede for each person.

HUMILITY
The virtue by which a Christian acknowledges that God is the author of all good; avoids inordinate ambition or pride, and provides the foundation for turning to God in prayer; poverty of spirit.

MEEKNESS
Quality of relying on God's mysterious plan; kindness or indulgence as opposed to anger; see hope, humility.

MERCY
The loving kindness, compassion, or forbearance shown to one who offends (e.g., the mercy of God to us sinners).

MORTIFY
To overcome sin and one's sinful tendencies by various exercises.

RIGHTEOUSNESS
Justice, uprightness; conformity of life to the requirements of the divine or moral law; virtue, integrity.

SERMON ON THE MOUNT
One of Jesus' first and most famous proclamations of the Gospel. The Beatitudes were given in the Sermon on the Mount.

SEXUAL RECTITUDE
See Chastity, Chapter 16.

STUDY QUESTIONS

1. List some things that make you happy. What do you think would make you eternally happy? Is this thing possible to possess forever? Is it internal or external?

2. Why is happiness on this earth not true happiness?

3. Do you truly believe God is Infinite Goodness and that the goodness seen in created things is just a reflection?

4. Are Jesus' promises what you really want? Why or why not?

5. Explain all eight Beatitudes.

6. Do you believe Jesus will fulfill the promises made in the Beatitudes? Why or Why not? Has God ever *not* kept a Biblical promise?

7. Which group mentioned in the Beatitudes do you most identify with? Are you content with your reward?

8. Which of the promises made in the Beatitudes do you most desire?

9. Where does man find true happiness?

PRACTICAL EXERCISES

1. Write down a specific action to be followed for each beatitude. Set aside an action to be applied for each beatitude for the next eight days. After eight days, write an essay describing your experiences.

2. What are you most attached to: possessions, money, human respect, power, reputation, friends, athletic/artistic/scholastic ability? How can *detachment* bring you freedom? (Remember there is both "freedom from" and "freedom to.")

3. How do you think denying yourself leads to happiness? Think about the value of the temptations that people face in day-to-day life compared to the love of God. Write a paragraph answering this question.

4. Which beatitude should you apply to the following situations and how?

a. Albert's parents are going out of town for the weekend. He knows they would not want him to throw a party, but they did not say so specifically. When his friends find out there were no direct rules about not having a party, they insist that he throw one. Should Albert throw the party?

b. Lucia's history class just covered Martin Luther's split from the Catholic Church in 1517, which led to the founding of Protestant churches. Since the class is almost 50-50 Catholic to Protestant, there has been much discussion. Now, it seems that people are getting angry with each other. What beatitude should Lucia apply and how?

c. Pete's father is a surgeon and has done very well financially. Consequently, Pete has a lot of things, many of which his friends cannot afford. In Mass one Sunday, he hears in the Gospel reading that it is "easier for a camel to go through the eye of a needle than for a rich man to enter into the kingdom of God." Pete gets a bit worried when he hears this. What beatitude should he follow and how?

FROM THE CATECHISM

1725 The Beatitudes take up and fulfill God's promises from Abraham on by ordering them to the Kingdom of heaven. They respond to the desire for happiness that God has placed in the human heart.

1726 The Beatitudes teach us the final end to which God calls us: the Kingdom, the vision of God, participation in the divine nature, eternal life, filiation, rest in God.

1727 The beatitude of eternal life is a gratuitous gift of God. It is supernatural, as is the grace that leads us there.

1728 The Beatitudes confront us with decisive choices concerning earthly goods; they purify our hearts in order to teach us to love God above all things.

1729 The beatitude of heaven sets the standards for discernment in the use of earthly goods in keeping with the law of God.

Endnotes

1. Cf. the parable of the sower: Mt 13: 3-23.
2. Mt 5: 8.
3. Cf. 1 Tm 4: 3-9; 2 Tm 2: 22.
4. Cf. 1 Thes 4: 7; Col 3: 5; Eph 4: 19.
5. Cf. Ti 1: 15; 1 Tm 1: 3-4; 2 Tm 2: 23-26.
6. St. Augustine, *De fide et symbolo* 10, 25: PL 40, 196.

Art and Photo Credits

Cover
Dome of St. Peter's Basilica; Corbis Royalty Free Image

Introduction

Chapter 1

Chapter 2

Chapter 3

Chapter 4

Art and Photo Credits

Chapter 9 Continued

120 Northridge Preparatory School, Niles, Illinois; Julie Koenig, photographer
121 *The Penance of St. Jerome*, Piero della Francesca; Staatliche Museen, Berlin; Web Gallery of Art
122 Photo courtesy of Greg Huster
123 Mother Teresa, Shishu Bavan 1970; Missionaries of Charity
124 Blessed Otto Neururer; Chronik Fliess, Germany

Chapter 10

129 Pope John Paul II Baptizing; Photo courtesy of Grzegorz Galazka
130 Comstock Royalty Free Image
131 *Baptism*; Urbine Collection of the Vatican Library; Folio 215 verso in Latin manuscript 2
132 *Baptism of Christ*, Guido Reni; Kunsthistorisches Museum, Vienna; Web Gallery of Art
133 St. Thomas the Apostle Church, Naperville, Illinois; Photo courtesy of Debbie Snyder
134 *Baptism of Christ*, Bellini; Santa Corona, Vicenza; Web Gallery of Art
135 Baptismal Font; St. Thomas the Apostle Church, Naperville, Illinois; Photo courtesy of Debbie Snyder
136 *Baptism of Christ* (detail), Pietro Perugino; Cappella Sistina, Vatican; Web Gallery of Art
137 *The Miracle of St. Francis Xavier* (detail), Nicolas Poussin; Louvre, Paris; Olga's Web

Chapter 11

141 Sts. Peter and Paul Church, Naperville, Illinois; Julie Koenig, photographer
142 *Confirmation*, Giuseppe Crespi; Gemäldegalerie, Dresden
143 Stockbyte Royalty Free Image
144 Northridge Preparatory School, Niles, Illinois; Julie Koenig, photographer
145 Photo courtesy of Greg Huster
146 *St. Helena* (detail), Cima da Conegliano; National Gallery of Art, Washington; Web Gallery of Art
147 Left: *Pope Pius XII*, Midwest Theological Forum Archives; Right: *The Holy Trinity*, Master of Flémalle; Städelsches Kunstinstitut, Frankfurt; Web Gallery of Art
148 *St. Thérèse et Lisieux*; Genevieve of the Holy Face; Descouvement and Loose; Helmuth Loose, photographer
152 *Missale Romanum*, Ratisbonae; Neo Eboraci et Cincinnatii, Typ. Fr. Pustet, MDCCCLXXXII, Segrestia Pontificia, Citta del Vaticano

Chapter 12

153 *The Last Supper* (detail), Titian; Galleria Nazionale delle Marche, Urbino; Scala/Art Resource, New York
154 Northridge Preparatory School, Niles, Illinois; Julie Koenig, photographer
155 Willows Academy, Des Plaines, Illinois; Julie Koenig, photographer
156 *Friend of the Humble* (Supper at Emmaus) (detail), León Augustin Lhermitte, 1892; Museum of Fine Arts, Boston
157 Carmel High School, Mundelein, Illinois
158 *The Institution of the Eucharist* (detail), Joos van Wassenhove; Galleria Nazionale delle Marche, Urbino; Web Gallery of Art
159 Northridge Preparatory School, Niles, Illinois; Julie Koenig, photographer
160 Carmel High School, Mundelein, Illinois
161 St. Mary of the Angels Church, Chicago, Illinois; Julie Koenig, photographer
162 Sts. Peter and Paul Church, Naperville, Illinois; Julie Koenig, photographer
163 *The Institution of the Eucharist* (detail), Nicolas Poussin; Musée du Louvre, Paris
164 *Disputa* (Dispute Over the Sacrament), Raphael; Stanza della Signatura, Vatican Palace, Rome; The Artchive
165 *St. Pius X*, Rafael Casal, artist, Manila, Philippines; Midwest Theological Forum Archives
170 Comstock Royalty Free Image

Chapter 13

171 Sts. Peter and Paul Church, Naperville, Illinois; Julie Koenig, photographer
172 Pope John Paul II; Catholic News Service
173 Northridge Preparatory School, Niles, Illinois; Julie Koenig, photographer
174 *The Prodigal Son* (detail), Salvator Rosa; The Hermitage, St. Petersburg; Web Gallery of Art
175 *The Return of the Prodigal Son* (detail), Rembrandt; The Hermitage, St. Petersburg; The Artchive
176 Comstock Royalty Free Image
177 Willows Academy, Des Plaines, Illinois; Julie Koenig, photographer
178 *Crucifixion and Saints*, Andrea Del Castagno; Ospedale Santa Maria Nuova; Web Gallery of Art
179 Willows Academy, Des Plaines, Illinois; Julie Koenig, photographer
180 *The Expulsion from the Garden of Eden* (detail), Masaccio; Cappella Brancacci, Santa Maria del Carmine, Florence; Web Gallery of Art
181 St. John Nepomucene; www.ainglkiss.com

Art and Photo Credits

Chapter 14

185 Comstock Royalty Free Image
186 Photo courtesy of Fr. Peter Clark, Lansing, Michigan Diocese
187 *Jesus Healing the Blind of Jericho,* Nicolas Poussin; Louvre, Paris; Olga's Web
188 *St. Paul Healing the Cripple at Lystra,* Karel Dujardin; Rijksmuseum, Amsterdam; Web Gallery of Art
189 PhotoSpin Royalty Free Image
190 *The Annunciation and Expulsion from Paradise* (detail), Giovanni di Paolo; Metropolitan Museum, New York; Web Gallery of Art
191 *The Gift of Peace* Book Jacket; Joseph Cardinal Bernardin, author; Loyola Press, publisher
192 *The Little Children Being Brought to Jesus* ("The 100 Guilder Print"), Rembrandt; Rijksmuseum, Amsterdam; The Artchive
193 Jacques Fesch; www.annball.com

Chapter 15

197 St. Peter's Church, Antioch, Illinois; Photo courtesy of the Aschbacher-Burrell Family
198 Comstock Royalty Free Image
199 Comstock Royalty Free Image
200 St. Peter's Church, Antioch, Illinois; Photo courtesy of the Aschbacher-Burrell Family
201 Midwest Theological Forum; Wojtek Dubis, photographer
202 Comstock Royalty Free Image
203 Comstock Royalty Free Image
204 Rubberball Royalty Free Image
205 Comstock Royalty Free Image
206 Georges and Pauline Vanier; National Archives of Canada
210 PhotoSpin Royalty Free Image

Chapter 16

211 Midwest Theological Forum; Blaine Davis, photographer
212 Midwest Theological Forum; Wojtek Dubis, photographer
213 *Triumph of St. Thomas Aquinas,* Benozzo Gozzoli; Musée du Louvre, Paris; Web Gallery of Art
214 *St. Carlo Borromeo,* Orazio Borgianni; Chiesa di San Carlo alle Quattro Fontane, Rome; Web Gallery of Art
215 Ordination; Photo courtesy of Fr. Marty Miller
216 Northridge Preparatory School, Niles, Illinois; Julie Koenig, photographer
217 Ordination; Photo courtesy of Fr. Marty Miller
218 Pope John Paul II; Catholic Extension
222 PhotoSpin Royalty Free Image

Chapter 17

223 Comstock Royalty Free Image
224 *The Hands of God and Adam,* (detail from *The Creation of Adam*), Michelangelo; The Sistine Chapel, Vatican; Web Gallery of Art
225 Photo courtesy of Mt. St. Joseph, Lake Zurich, Illinois
226 St. Mary of the Angels Church, Chicago, Illinois; Julie Koenig, photographer
227 Julie Koenig, photographer
228 Midwest Theological Forum; Luke Mata, photographer
229 *Descent from the Cross,* Rembrandt; The Hermitage, St. Petersburg; The Artchive
230 *Sir Thomas More,* Hans Holbein; Frick Collection, New York; Web Gallery of Art
234 PhotoSpin Royalty Free Image

Chapter 18

235 Corbis Royalty Free Image
236 *St. Francis of Assisi at Prayer,* Bartolomé Esteban Murillo; O.-L. Vrouwekathedraal, Antwerp; Web Gallery of Art
237 Northridge Preparatory School, Niles, Illinois; Julie Koenig, photographer
238 Northridge Preparatory School, Niles, Illinois; Julie Koenig, photographer
239 Stockbyte Royalty Free Image
240 Corbis Royalty Free Image
241 *The Martyrdom of St. Sebastian,* Hans Holbein the Elder; St. Sebastian Alter (Center Panel), Alte Pinak Othek, Munich
242 *Magdalene,* Carlo Dolci; Galleria Palatina (Palazzo Pitti), Florence; Web Gallery of Art
243 Stockbyte Royalty Free Image
244 *Justice* (ceiling tondo), Raphael; Stanza della Segnatura, Palazzi Pontifici, Vatican; Web Gallery of Art
245 St. Katherine Drexel; www.catholic-forum.com

Art and Photo Credits

Chapter 19

Chapter 20

Chapter 21

Chapter 22

Chapter 23

Chapter 23 Continued

313 Midwest Theological Forum; Luke Mata, photographer
314 Midwest Theological Forum Archives
315 MediaRights Royalty Free Image
316 *Madonna and Child Enthroned with Saints,* Ghirlandaio; Galleria degli Uffizi, Florence; Web Gallery of Art
317 Blessed Gianna Beretta Molla; Gesuiti Italia
322 Midwest Theological Forum Archives

Chapter 24

323 Comstock Royalty Free Image
324 Comstock Royalty Free Image
325 *Bathsheba Goes to King David,* Francesco Salviati; Palazzo Sacchetti, Rome; Web Gallery of Art
326 Rubberball Royalty Free Image
327 *St. Agnes,* Cesare Dandini; Web Gallery of Art
328 Rubberball Royalty Free Image
329 *Becoming Family,* Fall 2001: 39; Jim Summaria, photographer
330 Rubberball Royalty Free Image
331 Northridge Preparatory School, Niles, Illinois; Julie Koenig, photographer
332 *St. Maria Goretti;* www.catholic.org
336 *Madonna del Gran'Duca,* Raphael; Firenze-Galleria Pitti, Roma

Chapter 25

337 *Apostles Peter and Paul,* El Greco; The Hermitage, St. Petersburg; Web Gallery of Art
338 Midwest Theological Forum; Luke Mata, photographer
339 Corbis Royalty Free Image
340 Rubberball Royalty Free Image
341 Midwest Theological Forum; Luke Mata, photographer
342 Midwest Theological Forum; Luke Mata, photographer
343 Corbis Royalty Free Image
344 *St. Francis Giving His Mantle to a Poor Man,* Giotto; Upper Church, San Francesco, Assisi; Web Gallery of Art
345 *St. Francis of Assisi,* Pedro de Mena; Sacristy of the Cathedral, Toledo, Spain
346 *St. Francis of Assisi Receiving the Stigmata* (detail), Rubens; Museum voor Schone Kunsten, Ghent, Belgium; Web Gallery of Art

Chapter 26

351 Corbis Royalty Free Image
352 St. Mary of the Angels Church, Chicago, Illinois; Julie Koenig, photographer
353 Northridge Preparatory School, Niles, Illinois; Julie Koenig, photographer
354 *Martyrdom of St. Lawrence,* Valentin de Boulogne; Museo del Prado, Madrid; Web Gallery of Art
355 Stockbyte Royalty Free Image
356 St. Mary of the Angels Church, Chicago, Illinois; Julie Koenig, photographer
357 *Blessing Christ and Praying Virgin* (detail), Master of Flémalle; Philadelphia Museum of Art, Philadelphia; Web Gallery of Art
358 *The Ecstasy of St. Catherine of Siena,* Pompeo Batoni; Museo di Villa Guinigi, Lucca; Web Gallery of Art
362 St. Mary of the Angels Church, Chicago, Illinois; Julie Koenig, photographer

Chapter 27

363 *Christ the Redeemer;* Rio de Janeiro Brazil; PhotoDisc Royalty Free Image
364 Indian Boy at Mother Teresa's Funeral, 1997, Calcutta; John Moore, photographer; AP/Wide World Photos
365 *Sermon on the Mount* (detail); Midwest Theological Forum Archives
366 Mother Teresa; motherteresa.com
367 Midwest Theological Forum; Luke Mata, photographer
368 Sts. Peter and Paul Cemetery, Naperville, Illinois; Julie Koenig, photographer
369 Willows Academy, Des Plaines, Illinois; Julie Koenig, photographer
370 Cappella Graziolo; Immagine de Salvatore (Perugino); Basilica di S. Maria Minerva, Roma
371 *The Virgin in Prayer,* Sassoferrato; National Gallery, London; Web Gallery of Art
372 Midwest Theological Forum; Luke Mata, photographer
373 *Martyrdom of St. Lucy* (predella 5), Domenico Veneziano; Staatliches Lindenau Museen, Berlin; Web Gallery of Art
374 Mother Teresa and Pope John Paul II; motherteresa.com

Illuminated Alphabet, Theodore Menten, artist; Dover Publications

Index

A

Abortion, 143, 226, 310, 318

Acedia, 258, 262

Act of Contrition, 175

Acts of the Apostles, 109

Adoration, 23, 27, 166, 258
Eucharistic, 163

Angel(s), 5, 18, 22, 39, 60, 72
archangel Gabriel, 69, 70, 107
guardian, 183, 371, 375

Annunciation, 69, 75

Anointing of the Sick, 128, 185-196
celebration of, 188
effects of, 189
examination (preparation) for, 192
recipients of, 190

Apostle(s), 4, 33, 39, 53, 56-58, 82-84, 105, 106,
113, 131, 134, 143, 213, 216

Apostolate, 5, 56, 146, 149. *See* evangelization

Ascension of Christ, 42, 113

Assumption. *See* Mary

B

Baptism, 129-140
celebration of, 133
effects of, 5, 132
examination regarding, 136
of Christ, 39
recipients of, 134
types of, 135

Beatitudes, 106, 364, 377

Benediction of the Eucharist, 163, 166

Bible. *See* Scripture

Bishop(s), 43, 53, 57, 58, 144-147, 213-219

Blasphemy, 268, 270, 275

Body of Christ. *See* Eucharist, Church

Bribery, 347

C

Calumny, 355

Canon, 83, 88. *See* Scripture

Cardinal(s), 219

Catechesis, 47

Catechumenate, 134, 138

Celebrant(s), 125

Celibacy, 75, 216, 220, 221

Charism(s), 47

Charity, 252, 253, 256
prayer for, 258
sins against, 257

Chastity, 219, 327, 328, 333

Chrism, 125, 133, 144, 151, 216

Christian initiation, 127, 140, 145, 151

Church, 3, 22, 51-66
marks of the, 57
precepts of the, 55
roles within the, 55
the Mystical Body of Christ, 4, 56
the People of God, 54

Church Fathers, 33, 47, 88, 126

Civil authority, 299, 304

Communion. *See* Eucharist

Compassion, 68, 97, 98, 188, 206, 371, 375

Concupiscence, 125, 159

Confession. *See* Penance

Confirmation, 141-151
celebration of, 144
effects of, 146
minister of, 146
recipients of, 145
requirements for reception, 145

Conscience, 176, 177, 182, 227, 228
examination of, 175, 182
formation of, 177, 227
types of, 229

Consecration, 161, 166
episcopal, 215
of bread and wine, 157
priestly, 214
words of, 157, 161

Contemplation, 22, 23, 27

Contraception, 143, 328, 335

Contrition, 23, 24, 27

Conversion, 21, 30, 58, 128, 134, 138, 173, 182, 184,
187, 193, 283, 301

Council(s), 4, 35, 57, 62, 109

Courage, 142, 144, 189, 196, 206, 237, 245

Cross, 36, 40, 41, 58, 109, 156, 226
and the Eucharist, 36, 155, 156, 281
of Christ, 29, 36
sharing in the, 7, 41, 188, 190

D

Deacon(s), 125, 133, 135, 160, 163, 213-219

Death, 58-60, 131, 132, 168, 186-192, 241, 242, 310,
311, 366, 368
a consequence of sin, 132
of Christ, 40, 58, 109, 131
spiritual, 59, 174, 312